Class, ethnicity and religion in the Bengali East End

MANCHESTER
1824

Manchester University Press

Class, ethnicity and religion in the Bengali East End

A political history

Sarah Glynn

Manchester University Press

Published by Manchester University Press
Altrincham Street, Manchester M1 7JA, UK
www.manchesteruniversitypress.co.uk

British Library Cataloguing-in-Publication Data is available

ISBN 978 1 5261 0746 6 *paperback*

First published by Manchester University Press in hardback 2014

This edition first published 2017

The publisher has no responsibility for the persistence or accuracy of URLs for any external or third-party internet websites referred to in this book, and does not guarantee that any content on such websites is, or will remain, accurate or appropriate.

Printed by Lightning Source

Contents

List of figures

(Every effort has been made to contact copyright holders of the photographs.)

Preface and acknowledgements

My relationship with the East End could be said to have begun in the 1890s, when my infant grandparents arrived at London Docks to exchange the uncertainties and worries of life in the Russian Empire for the uncertainties and possibilities of life in London's Jewish ghetto. But I did not get to know the place until 1998, when I embarked on a PhD that compared the political mobilisation of the Jewish immigrants with that of the Bengalis who now live in this same area of London. After fifteen years' researching in Tower Hamlets, I have a wide network of Bengali contacts (and some dear friends) but I have never lived there. I am an experienced political activist outwith Tower Hamlets - and this has given me invaluable insights into the workings of political mobilisation and organisation – however, my political involvement in the borough has only been as an observer. So, for example, at the time of the 2005 general election, I went out with canvassers from both Labour and Respect, after first explaining that I would not take any active role. When, as sometimes happened, interviewees asked about my own ethnic background, I explained my family connection to the area, which maintained my distance from current events (though it could obviously have affected people's willingness to make comments that might be perceived as anti-Semitic). However, I have found that, for this type of research, good background knowledge and an ability to get on with all sorts of people and to portray their views honestly are more important than the personal 'identity' of the researcher. I hope my interviewees feel that I have succeeded in this protrayal, even if they do not agree with all the conclusions that I have drawn.

This book was made possible by all those who gave me their time and their memories – the many people quoted in the text (and all interviews not otherwise attributed were carried out by me), and also others who do not appear directly but whose thoughts and recollections helped me develop a fuller and more nuanced understanding of the events they lived through. My first thanks, then, must go to all those I interviewed – both in long recorded oral histories and in more informal discussion. It is a sadness of oral history work that some of those who have taken part may be no longer alive at the end of the project, but I am particularly glad to have had the opportunity to meet and to listen to Shiekh Abdul Mannan, Shah Lutfur Rahman, Mala Sen, Jack Shapiro, Peter Shore, Lew Cherley and Jack Cigman. I would also like to thank (for interviews and in many cases further information and advice as well): Helal Uddin Abbas, Zoinul Abidin, Hena Ahmed, Junaid Ahmed, Maniruddin Ahmed, Massud Ahmed, Nahin Ahmed, Abu Sayad Ali, Afsar Ali, Farhad Ali, Rushanara Ali, Sunahwar Ali, Bodrul Alom, M. Hamid Hossain Azad, Rahim Baksh, Alima Begum, Amina Begum, Runa Bibi, Aziz Choudhury, Shofiqur Rahman Chowdhury, Abdul Gaffar Chowdhury, G.M. Chowdhury Najim, Jill Cove, Syed Nurul Islam Dulu, Uma Ezra, Shahagir Bakth Faruk, Terry Fitzpatrick, George Galloway, Ali Syed Goyas, Abdul Hannan, Emdad Haque, Anamul Hoque, Mohammad Hussain, Azmul Hussein, Abul Ishaque, Nurul Islam, Shirazul Islam, Hussain Ismail, Rajonuddin Jalal, Rahman Jilani, Dan Jones, Shirajul Alam Khan, Rohima Khanom, Shiria Khatun, Tahura Khatun, Max Levitas, Fatima Matin, Abdul Miah, Abjol Miah, Aisha Miah, Fanu Miah, Hanufa Miah, Harun Miah, Jusna Begum Miah, Sajjad Miah, Shazid Miah, Sundor Miah, Kumar Murshid, Ghulam Murtaza, Golam Mustafa, Michael Myers, Noore Nazneen, Nehar Begum Quddus, Masud Rahman, Oliur Rahman, Ruksana Rahman, Shanaz Rashid, Abdul Razzak, Muhammad Abdus Salique, Jack Shapiro, Abdus Shukur, Barney Shuster, Bertha Sokoloff, Azam Tamimi, Pola Uddin, Alhaj Shams Uddin, Jannathara Uddin, Ansar Ahmed Ullah and others who asked not to be named.

I am grateful to all those who helped me to get my bearings in a place I have now learnt to love, and especially the late Caroline Adams, who is justly remembered with affection throughout Tower Hamlets for her pioneering community work with young Bengalis and also for her unique account of the early Bengali immigrants. She assisted me in piecing together events in the early stages of this research, and was generous with ideas of people to contact. I wish she could know how valuable I have found her tapes and papers, which she left to the local history library.

My first regular contact with the area was through St Hilda's East Community Centre, where I did some voluntary work with Bengali women and children in 1999, and also organised and edited an oral history project. My thanks to all the staff and users for making me welcome. Thanks too, to all those we interviewed for the oral history project, and to Jasmine Begum-Miah and Subo Basu who conducted the Bengali interviews.

In recent years, my East End base has been the offices of the local Bengali radio station, and I would like to thank Najim Chowdhury, Shahina Moni and all my other friends at Betar Bangla for making me feel part of their community. And thanks too to Ansar Ahmed Ullah and Jamil Iqbal for sustaining me over the years with information and friendship.

I am grateful to Abdul Hannan and Harun Miah for introducing me to their work with young people on the area's streets, to Tower Hamlets College for enabling me to meet sixth-form students, and to Ali Mohammad Azhar for showing me the manuscript autobiography by his brother Ali Abbas. I also want to express my thanks for help and for discussions on my work (and other subjects) to Anis Ahmed, Farukh Ahmed, Abul Kalam Azad, Farid Bakht, Stephen Beckett, Simon Blumenfeld, Sue Carlyle, Michael Glynn, Simon Glynn, Clive Heemskerk, Nazrul Islam, Abdul Jalil, Denise Jones, Kay Jordon, Solly Kaye, Joanna Kernaghan, Kevin Morgan, Dilu Naser, Mimi Romilly, John Twigg, Ahmed Ullah, Andrew Whitehead, Nigel Winfield, the Tarling Tenants and Residents Association, the pupils of Madani Muslim Girls' School, and members of Al Muhajiroun, the Awami League, Brick Lane Mosque management committee, Stepney Jewish Community Centre, the Young Muslim Organisation, Tower Hamlets Labour Party and Tower Hamlets Respect. On the other side of the 'seven seas' I would like to thank Babul and Nipa Asan who – despite a much too rushed visit to Bangladesh – enabled me to get a sense of life in Sylhet.

Parimal Ghosh deserves the credit (or should it be the blame) for encouraging me when I was working as an architect to believe it was possible to move onto a serious academic path; and James Laidlaw and Chris Bailey gave vital help and advice. I am gratefully indebted to University College London – especially my PhD supervisors, Richard Dennis and Claire Dwyer – and to the ESRC for making this work possible, and for having faith in me despite my lack of formal training in social science. I would also like to thank John Eade for his generous assistance and for making his own collection of material on the Bengali community available to other researchers. Others who have given me help or shared their own research findings include Bill Fishman, David Garbin, Katy Gardner, Andrew Godley, Richard Halpern, Anne Kershen, Basil Mustafa, Richard Phillips, Willian Radice, Balihar Sanghera and Sallie Westwood.

My search for archival material has taken me to a variety of different collections. I want to join so many previous chroniclers of this area of London in thanking the endlessly patient and knowledgeable librarians at Tower Hamlets Local History Library – Chris Lloyd, Malcolm Barr-Hamilton and David Rich. My thanks, too, to all those who helped me at Bradford Local Studies Library, Cambridge University Library, Camden Local Studies and Archives Centre, the Jewish Museum in Finchley, LSE Archive, Merseyside Maritime Museum Archives, the Modern Records Centre in Warwick, the National Library of Scotland, the National Museum of Labour History in Manchester, the Marx Memorial Library, and Queen Mary University of London Archive. Thank you to Niki Brown and her helpers for transcribing the many different accents in my recorded interviews, and thank you to Tony Mason at Manchester University Press for your belief in my book.

This work would not have been possible without all those who helped look after my children when I was away in Tower Hamlets, or my sister Judith and her family who provided a home in London – often at very little notice. My parents have given constant support, as well as detailed comments on the final product. Through their rigorous criticism, they have passed on to me a love of the craft of writing – and I hope that they have found that each time they read something I have written they have to make fewer suggestions. (What mistakes are left remain, of course, entirely my responsibility.) And thank you to Rebekah and Hadassah for your patience with an often abstracted mother and for keeping me connected to the world beyond my research.

Finally, I want to thank my partner Tony Cox, not just for his companionship, encouragement and confidence in me, but for enabling me to benefit from his experience of political involvement and of historical research. In so many different ways, without him this book could not have been written.

This book has allowed me, for the first time, to bring together all my research on the Bengali community – to present the whole story and develop fully the theoretical arguments that this generates. However, over the years, much of the material has appeared in different journals and edited volumes, which are all fully listed in the bibliography. In particular, Chapter 3 uses material from my article in the *Socialist History Journal*, Chapter 6 uses material from my article in the *Journal of Historical Geography*, Chapter 7 uses material from my chapter in *New Geographies of Race and Racism* and my article in *Urban Studies*, Chapters 8 and 9 use material from my articles in *Ethnic and Racial Studies* and *Ethnicities* and my chapter in *Muslim Spaces of Hope*, and Chapter 10 uses material from my article in *Human Geography*.

Sarah Glynn
November 2013

Introduction

This is a study of political mobilisation in one of the most physically concentrated immigrant 'communities' in Britain: the Bengali Muslims who live in the London Borough of Tower Hamlets. It shines a light on a unique political history, and it also serves as a lens through which to examine wider changes in progressive left politics and their relationship to ethnic minorities. It charts how the East End Bengalis have responded to the pulls of class, ethnicity and religion, and how these have been differently reinforced by evolving political movements over more than six decades. Drawing on extensive recorded interviews, ethnographic observation of numerous local meetings and other political activities, and long sorties into the local archives (carried out between 1998 and 2013), it recounts the experiences of many of those who took part in this active and varied political history; and it uses these experiences to build a picture of the different forms political mobilisation has taken and the different forces with which the immigrant Bengalis have interacted. Detailed observation is used to capture the complications and contradictions of the lived experience and the messy reality in which political decisions are made and put into practice; while the large quantity of data enables the revelation of underlying patterns that can be generalised to other situations. The empirical account is integrated with political analysis that relates events in the Bengali East End to ethnic minority politics more generally, and contextualises them within wider political developments, allowing this history to serve as a case study of these bigger changes.

Research in this field tends to examine ethnic minority mobilisation through the perspective of the progressive liberal/left paradigm dominant at the time of the events being discussed, which academic research has, itself, often helped to develop or consolidate. Even where this research acknowledges the evolution of these dominant paradigms, it is only rarely critical of their impact. The purpose of this study is to step outside these paradigms so as to examine more critically how the changes in political discourse that generated them also impacted on ethnic minority mobilisation. In doing so, I do not pretend to occupy ideologically neutral space. (No one does – though a passive acceptance of dominant views is often portrayed as though it were non-ideological.) My own perspective is that of a loosely Marxist materialism. I examine these political developments in their wider socio-economic and political context, and I relate what has happened in ethnic minority politics to wider ideological and tactical developments on the political left. This different perspective allows me to develop a critical overview of this political history and of the impacts of post-modern understandings and to put forward a radically different alternative.

This book exposes the fundamental flaws in the culturalist approaches and identity politics that have become shibboleths of 'progressive' thought; and it puts forward a call for a return to materialist understandings that can be used to underpin a new attack on fundamental socio-economic inequalities. The point is not to ignore or belittle racism and discrimination, but to strike at its roots. That 'race' is a social construct is now widely accepted, but not enough attention is given to how the racialisation process worked and continues to work and, importantly, whose interests it serves. The re-emergence of a potent neoliberal capitalism has been facilitated by a weak and divided working-class movement. Central to this division is the tendency to pursue sectional interests in isolation, and often in competition, with each other. This has been actively encouraged by those in power – witness how governments try to set poorly paid 'hardworking families' against people struggling to survive on benefits. Political and business leaders are adept at playing one group off against another and keeping both in 'their place': skilled against unskilled, men against women and, of course, people from one ethnic background against another. When racialisation is used to justify a group of people getting lower wages or worse housing, the majority white working class do not benefit – but they are fed racist myths to win their support for a system that exploits them too, just not as much. In a competitive labour market, low wages for any group will act to reduce wage levels for everyone in the same area of work; and, rather than invest in more and better housing, authorities attempt to divert frustrations onto other ethnicities, whose bad housing is presented as a consequence of their ethnic life-style and as bringing the area down. Racism is used to persuade the majority population to be complicit in their own exploitation, and focus their anger over their own predicament on those even worse off, rather than on a system that exploits workers of all ethnicities. Of course there are anti-racists and racists at every level of society, but we cannot fight against racism without fighting against the structures that promote and thrive on racism and that use it to maintain a profoundly unequal society for people of all backgrounds. We cannot fight against racism without understanding how and why it works, because that understanding is the key to its destruction. It is the realisation of shared interests, not just an appeal to morality, that will stop working-class racism in its tracks. In that old slogan, 'black and white, unite and fight', coined by the Communist Party at the time of the Great Depression, both actions are important and each supports the other. The act of uniting is a direct blow to racism and an indirect blow to a system that relies on racism. And the fight is not just against the latest motley bunch of would-be fascists. It is against racism per se, it is against racism as a tool for wider socioeconomic exploitation, and it is against a system that relies on that exploitation and on the promotion of racism.

If, as argued in this book, racism and other forms of discrimination and prejudice are fundamentally an integral part of our economic and political system, where, then, does culture come in? Clearly, cultural difference is used to fuel prejudice, and a lot of positive work has been done to break down barriers and make many of the traditions brought by immigrants from other countries seem less alien. But this on its own is not enough – and can even be counter-productive if it is overplayed and perceived to be undervaluing 'British' culture. In addition, the active promotion of different cultures through political multi-culturalism can result in the essentialising of cultural practices. This risks both restricting cultural and individual development and hybridity, and – which is crucial to the argument in the preceding paragraph – strengthening the compartmentalisation of society at the expense of cross-cultural unity. British culture has never been a homogenous or static thing, and in a globalised world cultural evolution has speeded up. Our cultural lives have probably been more changed by Hollywood than by our immigrant neighbours, but, one way and another, Britain is and will continue to be increasingly multicultural, in a non-political sense. We can enjoy our multicultural society (as most of us do) or hate it; but we can't stop it. And we should beware of letting it be used to obscure the political and economic structures that shape our lives.

Another way in which this study differs from most research in this field is in its combination of history and sociology. We often talk about learning from history. Bringing past and present together can help us do just that, and deepen our understanding of current developments. The story told in the following chapters is a fascinating narrative on its own account, and I hope that I have done justice to it. At the same time, the central concern that runs through the book is the perennial question of how to propagate an effective radical politics in a multicultural society: the question of how to promote greater equality that benefits both ethnic minorities and the wider population, and the linked question of why so little has been achieved. The different political movements that make up this history all eventually fizzled out into forms of pragmatic politics that posed no threat to structural inequalities. In looking for answers to why this has happened, the book makes detailed acknowledgement of the specificities of the Bengali experience and of the changing historical context, but it also demonstrates the overriding impact of political theories and tactics developed by wider progressive movements. It argues that a crucial key to understanding this history can be found by tracing the development and adoption of the Stalinist concepts of popular frontism and revolutionary stages theory and of the New Social Movements that these ideas made possible. This case study provides a critique of these theories and tactics, showing how, in every campaign in which they were employed, the organisational separateness they encouraged cut across working-class unity and acted as an impediment to addressing socio-economic inequalities.

After a first chapter that sets the scene with a brief history of the Bengali immigration, the structure of the book is thematic – concentrating on salient political influences – but also largely chronological. Theoretical discussion is integrated into the empirical account, with the final chapter culminating in a critique of liberal multiculturalism and the argument for a left alternative.

Before beginning my story, I want to say a few words on that most slippery of subjects, the choice of terms. First, a note on the term 'Bengali' itself, and why I have used it in preference to 'Bangladeshi': Bangladeshi was adopted as the official name for the people of Bangladesh in the Islamicising constitutional amendments introduced by President Ziaur Rahman. Most Bengalis/Bangladeshis are happy to be described with either term, though Bengali is preferred by those who want to stress a secular cultural identity and Bangladeshi by those who want to draw a distinction between Islamic Bangladesh and Hindu West Bengal (and also by those who argue it is more inclusive of Bangladesh's cultural minorities). My reason for using Bengali is simply that the same term can also be used when referring to the time before the creation of Bangladesh.

I have avoided using the term 'race', with its discredited connotations of biologically distinct groups, but have adopted the generally accepted usage of terms such as 'ethnic group' and 'ethnic minorities'. This is not to deny that these can also be problematic, with contested definitions and often with racialising undertones. 'Ethnicity' has become a blanket definition for different types and levels of identity that intersect and fade into fuzzy borders, but it still conveys important generally recognised ideas.

I have also used the common shorthand phrase, 'Bengali community', to cover everyone in the area who is of Bengali descent, even though they do not in reality function as a single community, but rather as a combination of different overlapping communities and individuals. And I have used 'immigrant' to describe all those who have come to live in Britain, rather than try to make impossible distinctions between those who planned long-term immigration and those who, at least initially, thought of themselves as merely migrant workers passing through. I have also, in places for the sake of simplicity, allowed the term to include the descendants of the original immigrants, even if they themselves were born here.

Finally, a few words on that most contested of terms: class. My discussion of the Bengalis' class position and class identification falls within the fourfold analysis of working-class formation outlined by Ira Katznelson.[1] He builds on Marx's understandings of class-in-itself and class-for-itself and describes connected layers, beginning at the macro-economic level with the structural group of 'people who work for wages, using means of production over whose disposition they have little or no control'.[2] This is linked to lived experience and social organisation, both within the workplace and in the wider community; to shared understandings and 'dispositions'; and – though by no means inevitably – to 'class-based collective action'.[3] As Katznelson explains, this approach allows for and explains variations in historical and geographical experience. The Bengalis' particular experiences and understandings are a product of both their background and of their position within a racialised society and labour market. Bengali workers form what Robert Miles and Annie Phizacklea have described as a racialised fraction of the working class – one of the many, often overlapping fractions divided by differences including gender, skill and religion.[4] This recognition that the working class has never been homogenous does not distract from the importance of class as an explanatory, and potentially an organising, force.

Notes

1 Ira Katznelson, 'Working-Class Formation: Constructing Cases and Comparisons', in Ira Katznelson and Aristide R. Zolberg (eds), *Working-Class Formation: Nineteenth-Century Patterns in Western Europe and the United States* (Princeton: Princeton University Press, 1986).
2 Charles Tilly (1984), quoted in *ibid.*, p. 15.
3 Katznelson, 'Working-Class Formation', p. 21.
4 Robert Miles and Annie Phizacklea, *Labour and Racism* (London: Routledge and Kegan Paul, 1980), pp. 1–25; Robert Miles, *Racism and Migrant Labour* (London: Routledge and Kegan Paul, 1982), pp. 151–88.

1 Sailors, students and settlers

This book tells a specifically political history, but this first chapter sets the scene with a very brief general history of the Bengali East End.

The East End of London

The East End of London is a place associated with strong but, in some ways, contradictory images; a place of cockney kinship and immigrant ghettos, at once English and 'alien'. It is famous for battles with organised racism, but it is also portrayed as a 'multicultural-receptor' and symbol of English tolerance.[1] And overriding all this has been the shared poverty of an area outwith the city walls. Before the recent period of surging land values and encroaching redevelopment, this was a place of almost unremittingly low wages and of making ends meet. It was a working-class area, with an admixture of small-scale, immigrant-run entrepreneurism, which was based around workshop trades (especially clothing) and, latterly, the 'Indian' restaurant industry. Poverty does not respect ethnic boundaries, but different groups tended to concentrate in different areas of work. In recent decades, beginning in the 1980s, the expansion of financial services and related businesses in the former dockland area of Canary Wharf and spilling out from the City of London has created pockets of great wealth. Parts of the old centres of immigration and working-class areas more generally are rapidly succumbing to the dual pressures of office expansion and gentrification. However, despite an influx of people on very high salaries, Tower Hamlets – the borough formed in 1965 through the amalgamation of the old boroughs of Stepney, Bethnal Green and Poplar – is still noted for having a high proportion of areas that are amongst the most deprived in England.[2] Although it provides jobs to many people coming from outwith the borough, it still has exceptionally high levels of unemployment (13.4 per cent in the year to March 2013, when the British average was 7.8 per cent[3]). 43 per cent of all households rely on benefits, and this rises to 73 per cent for Bengali households, a figure matched only by the much smaller and more recently established Somali community.[4] The 2011 Census classed 35 per cent of homes as overcrowded, and overcrowding has always been especially severe among large Bengali households. Child poverty has reached 49 per cent, which is considerably worse than in any other UK local authority.[5]

The relative cheapness of the place, as well as the proximity of the City and of the old London Docks, made the East End a magnet for successive waves of immigrants – including internal migration from more rural parts of Britain. French Huguenots set up their silk looms in seventeenth-century Spitalfields; Irish Catholics worked in the docks loading and unloading the products of the British Empire; Jews escaping the poverty and pogroms of Eastern Europe arrived by boat from Hamburg and the Baltic ports to join an already established Jewish community; and Muslim Bengali seamen, or *lascars*, in the Empire's merchant navy jumped ship and began chains of immigration that expanded with the new pressures and possibilities of the post-colonial world. There are groups of Chinese, Maltese, Cypriots and Africans, and more recent arrivals have included refugees from Somalia and migrant workers from the new EU member states of Eastern Europe, as well as the international business elite. Meanwhile, descendents of earlier immigrants have often moved on. By the time of the 2011 Census, only 31 per cent of respondents described themselves as White British[6] – down from 43 per cent in 2001 – and 32 per cent described themselves as Bangladeshi, much the largest minority group.[7] Many households are long-estab-lished, but there has also been a significant amount of movement in and out of the borough. The total population of Tower Hamlets in 2011 was measured as 254,000, up 26 per cent on the 2001 figure – a higher increase than in any other local authority.

Sylhet

The majority of the East End's Bengali families emigrated from the Sylhet region, in the northeast of what is now Bangladesh. It is a distinctive area that speaks its own version of Bengali, which many claim as a separate language.[8] Despite producing so many *lascars*, Sylhet is not on the coast; however there is a long tradition of Sylheti men working on merchant boats on the inland waterways, and once links had been made with British shipping companies in Calcutta (Kolkata), many of these men were prepared to put up with long waits and bribes to middlemen in order to secure a place on a British ship. In addition, the vagaries of the British land settlement system, whereby the Sylhet region contained a large number of small farmers owning their own land, meant that many Sylheti families had that little extra money needed to finance one of their sons to try his fortune at sea.[9] The homes that the Bengalis left behind followed the traditional village pattern of the extended-family *bari*, with household units belonging to different brothers ranged around a street-like courtyard to create a private domestic world that was closed to male visitors.[10] Patriarchal family ties were of overriding importance and continued to exert their influence in Britain. This is still the standard form of Sylheti village homestead, though village life has become less isolated and traditional with the spread of roads and electricity and modern forms of communication.

Many *Londoni* families − those with members living in Britain − have used their new wealth to build more modern houses, though these may be as much for show as for practical use. Most British Bengali families still have close relations in Bangladesh, and often also land and houses or other investments. The regional capital, despite its important shrine to a fourteenth-century Muslim saint, was, until recently, a place with few urban pretensions. It has now grown to around half a million inhabitants, and expatriate money has helped to generate a boom in development, with a mushrooming of shopping malls and western-style apartment buildings.[11] In the streets of Sylhet town, the local Sylheti language is intermingled with the voices of visiting *Londonis* speaking English in a variety of British regional accents.

Bengali immigration

The East End Bengali community traces its origins to the first *lascars. Lascars* from the Indian subcontinent have played an important part in the British merchant navy since the seventeenth century. By 1938 they made up more than a quarter of British maritime labour, often working in the uncomfortable heat of ships' boiler rooms, and an estimated 6,600 lost their lives on British ships in the Second World War.[12] It was always a hard and disadvantaged life. Accounts from the eighteenth and nineteenth centuries record death and disease at sea and destitution in British ports. An Act of Parliament in 1823 laid down different rules for *lascars* and British sailors. Indian sailors on *lascar* articles (or contracts) were paid less, fed less and given less space, and they had to be discharged back in an Indian port. These rules were not completely repealed until 1983.[13] Many *lascars* jumped ship to try their luck in other work in Britain, often planning to sign on to another ship on the much more generous British articles. The British government and shipping companies worked together setting up regulations and controls to discourage this, especially during periods of economic depression. *Lascar* numbers grew during the First World War − and some were deliberately enticed from their ships by British industries − but the post-war recession and severe jobs crisis resulted in 'race riots' in British ports, demands from the seamen's union for priority to be given to white British sailors, and attempts at repatriation. People of Britain's Indian Empire were legally British citizens, entitled to live and work in Britain, but a 1925 Act of Parliament, ostensibly directed at 'coloured alien seamen', was used to force repatriation of some Indian seamen who did not possess officially accepted proof of British citizenship. The proportion of the *lascars* who jumped ship was never large, but a continuous flow did manage to get away, and this was the only method that those without much money could come to Britain and seek their fortune. Once they had got away from the ship, they had to lie low until their articles expired and the shipping company could no longer claim them as a 'deserter', for which they risked punishment by imprisonment. When, in 1947, the Partition of India and Pakistan cut Sylhetis off from access to Calcutta, the leader of the Indian Seamen's Union, Aftab Ali, actually advised Bengali seamen to leave their ships at British ports.[14] Caroline Adams collected oral histories from several of the Bengali immigrant pioneers, many of which read like adventure stories, and the spirit of adventure must have been an important spur to their actions.[15] But they were also leaving tough peasant life in a poorly developed country for a land of opportunity, to try and achieve financial security, status and greater material comfort for themselves and, most importantly, for their families.

Those first Bengali sailors spearheaded a major immigration, but they themselves were relatively few. At the outbreak of the Second World War, it has been estimated that those in the East End numbered between a hundred and fifty and two hundred,[16] and by the time of the 1951 Census 'Pakistanis' in the East End boroughs were still measured in hundreds. In 1948, the year after Pakistani Independence, the British Nationality Act confirmed that all subjects of the British Crown – that is everyone in the colonies and the Commonwealth – had the right to come and live in Britain. However, there were soon restrictions from the Pakistan Government, which refused to allow emigration from the Eastern, Bengali, half of the country. More significant immigration from what was then East Pakistan can be dated from 1956, when the Pakistan government was finally persuaded to grant one thousand passports to ex-seamen and their survivors or dependants. Further negotiations removed the remaining restrictions, and by 1962 some five thousand men had come to live in East London, close to the first Sylheti links in the docks.[17] Many more went to the North and the Midlands, where they took jobs in factories making textiles, steel, heavy engineering and cars. Often the search for work took them from town to town and job histories were interspersed with periods of unemployment. In each place the men went they would make contact with other Bengali immigrants.[18]

The Bengalis in the East End also interacted with a small group of better-educated fellow countrymen who had come to London to continue their education or take up professional employment. This small Bengali elite were able to help the Bengali workers and played a disproportionate role in the early years of this political history. Some of the students lived or worked alongside East-End Bengalis, as the growing number of Bengali-run restaurants provided them with a source of cheap accommodation and supplementary income.[19]

Most of the first generation of post-war immigrants – and this is especially true of the Sylhetis – were younger men who did not intend to stay on in Britain, but planned to return to their families, and to their native land, once they had earned a reasonable sum of money. While many may have found white girlfriends, and on occasion married them, most Bengalis chose to find a wife through an arranged marriage in Sylhet. Their, generally teenage, brides hardly got a chance to get to know their husbands before being left to live alone with their new in-laws, waiting for an occasional visit. The men worked hard and saved hard, and almost everything they saved they sent back to their extended families in Sylhet, where it was used to buy land and improve houses. But they had not earned the fortunes they had dreamed of, and their families had come to rely on their continued work in Britain. Meanwhile, immigration laws were noticeably constricting, pushing many immigrants to decide to bring their wives and children over to Britain before it was too late. Even after they had been joined by their immediate family, many men continued to remit money to the joint family *bari* in Sylhet.[20]

Immigration legislation and the growth of the community

Just as Britain confirmed that its doors were open to the subjects of its former Empire, their closure was already the subject of debate, both inside and outside government. In an echo of debates over Jewish immigration half a century earlier, the 1950s saw a return to the twin concerns of immigration control and immigrant integration; and the long-standing problems of poor areas such as the East End became associated, in the minds of those who opposed immigration, with those new immigrants who were forced to live in them. In 1962, Britain's growing anti-immigration movement was rewarded with the Commonwealth Immigration Act, under which potential immigrants (other than dependents) from the so-called 'New Commonwealth' countries had to be in possession of a voucher showing that they had a job waiting for them. The rules did not apply to the white-majority 'Old Commonwealth' countries of Canada, Australia and New Zealand. Sylhetis already in England organised themselves to procure vouchers for would-be immigrants. Many became, in Caroline Adam's words, 'latter-day *serangs*'[21] – the term used for the middlemen who controlled *lascar* employment – and arranging vouchers was a major function of the Pakistan Caterers' Association. However, vouchers became increasingly hard to get, and by 1964 were being issued only for highly skilled workers. The Act also stipulated that dependent children under the age of eighteen would only be allowed entry if accompanied by their mother, though many families managed to find ways of sending young sons, and also nephews, to find work in Britain. Shah Lutfur Rahman described single youths, some as young as twelve, arriving in the mid-1960s, whom he helped through evening classes and informal community work.[22]

The Labour Party had criticised the 1962 Act when in opposition, but, after they were returned to power in 1964, they tightened it. In 1965, they brought in the first Race Relations Act. By then, both the main political parties were arguing that limiting immigration and legislating for improved race relations were two sides of the same coin. As put by Roy Hattersley, newly elected Labour MP for multiracial Birmingham Sparkbrook: 'without integration limitation is inexcusable, without limitation integration is impossible'.[23] However, the laws against racial discrimination were limited in their reach, while the immigration controls, by explicitly discriminating against citizens of the New Commonwealth, legitimised the view that racist violence could be blamed on the growth of the black and Asian population, so encouraging racism.

The anti-immigrant movement was still not satisfied. Enoch Powell's warnings of 'rivers of blood'[24] hit a popular chord, and immigration policy became a subject of general debate. The political consequence was the Conservatives' 1971 Immigration Act, which replaced work vouchers with permits that had to be renewed annually, and required other non-dependent immigrants to have at least one British grandparent. The immediate effect of the act was, however, contrary to what had been intended. People were so fearful of the doors shutting further that family reunification was speeded up as dependants hurried to join the pioneer settlers in Britain. Dependent children were not admitted after the age of eighteen, and this set a deadline for many families. The pioneering settlers were also getting older and less physically robust and many wanted the physical care that their, generally much younger, wives could bring.[25] As more Bengalis settled in Tower Hamlets, so it was seen as a less hostile environment for the women to come to, while the devastation resulting from Bangladesh's independence war and the ensuing years of political turmoil and corruption provided further important spurs to emigration.

By the mid-1970s, the East End community was growing rapidly, mainly through the arrival of wives and children from Bangladesh, though also, increasingly, through earlier immigrants who had moved on from the recession-hit towns of the Midlands and the North. (The 1986 parliamentary report on *Bangladeshis in Britain* quoted an estimate of 45 per cent unemployment among male Bengalis in the textile town of Oldham.[26]) Family reunion was a slow process and the 1981 Census recorded that in Tower Hamlets there were still 1.9 Bangladeshi origin men to every woman.[27] Even those immigrants legally entitled to come had to negotiate a sometimes impenetrable, and often very distressing, tangle of red tape, which could take years to sort out. Subsequent immigration acts have generally been concerned with tightening controls – including the Primary Purpose Rule, introduced in 1980 but withdrawn in 1997, which insisted that immigrant spouses had to prove that their marriage was genuine and not for the purpose of acquiring citizenship. In recent years, some men have again been able to come on work permits as restaurant owners successfully argued that they needed to import chefs from their native land, but rule changes have now virtually eliminated restaurant employment as a legal immigration route.

Although immigration is restricted, it is still significant. Tower Hamlets doctors registered two to three thousand Bengali immigrants each year for the period 2003/04 to 2008/09.[28] Strong Bengali identity and community ties (in part perpetuated through the community's relative segregation) mean that marriage partners are still often sought in a family's area of origin back in Bangladesh, and many Bangladeshi families welcome the opportunity for their son or daughter to emigrate to Britain. Others have come on work permits, and there are, of course, other, illegal immigrants (who will not be able to register with a doctor), including people who came in good faith but were the victims of various immigration scams.

There is also some movement in the other direction. Many first generation immigrants still hope to end their days back in their homeland. Some return to live on their pensions once their children have grown up, some others divide their time, and sometimes their family, between Sylhet and Britain. Some return after death, to be buried in their native soil.

Growth of the East End Bengali population does not just depend on immigration, and natural increase has been very significant, despite on-migration to other areas. Large families have produced a Bengali age profile that is heavily slanted towards the younger end, and the 2011 Census found that 53 per cent of people who identified as Bangladeshis in Tower Hamlets were under twenty-five (compared with 31 per cent of the population of England and Wales as a whole). The Census counted 447,200 Bangladeshis in England and Wales; up from 275,000 ten years earlier. Of these, 81,400 lived in Tower Hamlets. The census also tells us that 47 per cent of Tower Hamlets' residents who identified as Bangladeshi were born in South Asia,[29] and that 43,500 people in the borough described Bengali (including Sylheti) as their first language. It is generally claimed that up to 95 per cent of Bengalis in Britain originate from the Greater Sylhet region.[30] The age profile already has implications for schools and also means that, despite incoming marriage partners, the community is becoming rapidly dominated by a generation born and educated in Britain.

A Bengali enclave in London

The first pioneers lived together and helped each other, and as more people arrived they settled close by, near others who spoke their language and understood their needs and who would provide protection in numbers from the unfamiliar and hostile world of white Britain. In keeping with the standard immigrant pattern, the Bengalis have generally relied on their own networks for much of the infrastructure of daily life and, as the community became established, Bengalis sought homes near to the mosque, to the shops that sold Bengali foodstuffs and to the garment workshops where other Bengalis could find them work – and away from racist white estates. The beginnings of community infrastructure had already taken root before the end of the Second World War. Pioneering settlers, such as Ayub Ali, who came to London in 1920, provided an informal support network for new (often illiterate) arrivals, helping them with

Figure 1.1 Ayub Ali 'Master' and nephews

board and lodging as they got established, guiding them through British bureaucracy, and assisting with remittances and letter writing. Bengali lodging houses provided safe, if crowded, accommodation, with earlier immigrants subletting bed spaces to new arrivals, who often had to share the same bed, or part of a bed, with others working a different shift.[31] Bengali cafés acted as social centres, besides providing cheap and familiar food. The Hindustani Social Club, established in the mid-1930s, and the Hindustan Community House, opened in 1937, combined social and welfare functions; the first Bengali grocer, Taj Stores, started up in 1936; and, thanks to funding from prominent Muslims across the world, the East London Mosque opened in three converted houses in Commercial Road in 1941. In 1943 Ayub Ali formalised his voluntary work, combining with Shah Abdul Majid Qureshi to set up the non-political Indian Seamen's Welfare League.[32]

Before the Second World War, the main hub of Bengali settlement was in Canning Town, close to the Docks. But this area was devastated in the Blitz, and many of the post-war settlers established themselves in privately rented rooms in Spitalfields, where Dickensian living conditions meant they met with little competition for tenancies and fewer signs specifying 'no coloureds'.[33] Defensive reactions to racism and discriminatory housing policies have both contributed to continued patterns of ethnic segregation, and segregation has been further encouraged by many of the political developments discussed in this book. As with the earlier Jewish immigration, the area of Bengali settlement has spread eastward from its original nucleus, and many longer established white residents have moved out. At the time of writing, schools are often even more Bengali dominated than their surrounding neighbourhoods, as Bengalis tend to have large families and many white, and also black, families choose to send their children to church schools rather than let them be part of a small minority in a largely Bengali classroom. At the same time, some Bengali families are choosing to move out to a more suburban existence, which may have better schools and safer streets. Many go to areas where other Bengalis have gone before them, though these are more racially mixed than Tower Hamlets.

Despite this onward migration, Tower Hamlets retains a large and concentrated Bengali community. It has been possible for even the generation born in London to be brought up in a predominantly Bengali milieu, and to approach the world outside Tower Hamlets through a Bengali perspective; though that perspective has itself evolved in interaction with wider cultural changes. The East End Bengalis have created their own strong civil society with a plethora of community organisations of various degrees of longevity. These address a range of issues from the practical to the cultural and have benefited from the official support given to multiculturalism.

Religious faith

Life in Sylhet is regulated by a mystical Sufism and, although the first immigrants were not always able or inclined to observe many religious practices, very few would have forgotten that they were Muslim. For their wives, belief in the will of Allah supported them through the hardships of family separation and the men returned to a more Islamic lifestyle on family reunification. With increasing years, many of these men have discovered a new religiosity, which not only befits their position as community elders, but allows them to ask Allah's forgiveness for past sins before it is too late.[34] Some may attempt to acquire temporal and spiritual merit by investing in building mosques, either in London or Sylhet.[35] For the generation that came of age in the 1970s and 1980s, religion was generally a matter of cultural and family tradition and personal faith, but the last two decades have seen Islam come to play a more prominent role in the community generally. Many of the younger generation have been attracted to Islamist ideas, which they contrast against the Bengali Islam of their parents.

In the early years before the Second World War, services were held in the King's Hall Commercial Road and run by Jamiat-ul-Muslimin, a charity established in 1934 for the promotion of Islam. Key figures in the organisation had links with the Indian National Congress and the Hindustani Social Club, and Ayub Ali was also involved. The Jamiat played a major role in the establishment of the first permanent East London Mosque in 1941, but was dismissed from the mosque two years later after a dispute with the Board of Trustees over its running.[36] The Open University's *Making Britain* project comments – on the basis of a contemporary police report – that the Jamiat, was 'largely working class' and Asian, and the Board of Trustees 'largely elite and partly British'.[37] In 1975 the East London Mosque was forced to move out of its original home, which was compulsorily purchased by the Greater London Council, and it moved into temporary buildings until the current purpose-built mosque in Whitechapel Road was completed ten years later. This already large building has been greatly extended with the completion of the London Muslim Centre in 2004 and the Maryam Centre in 2013.

While the East London Mosque has had links with Islamist organisations since the early 1960s and preaches an Islam in which politics plays an integral part, the East End's second largest mosque, in Brick Lane, preserves a traditional Bengali Sufism. The building that houses the Brick Lane Jamme Masjid (Great Mosque) is often used as symbol of East End immigration. It was constructed in 1743 as a Huguenot chapel and before it was converted to a mosque in 1976 it had been used successively as a place of worship by the London Society for Promoting Christianity Amongst the Jews, the Methodist Church and the ultra-orthodox Jewish Machzikei Hadas, 'Upholders of the Law' (and briefly as a clothing warehouse). Tower Hamlets is punctuated by numerous mosques of varied sizes catering to different Islamic practices – in 2013 muslimsinbritain.org listed forty-six.[38] Often these occupy former houses, flats or shops, but other sites include a portakabin and railway arches. Dawatul Islam (also Islamist) occupies a former nineteenth-century school in Bigland Street[39] and Tablighi Jamaat, a revivalist movement that proselytises among Muslims, has a large mosque in a former synagogue building from the 1920s in Christian Street.

Islam has increased in importance in both private and public life, and numerous studies have testified to the growing salience of Muslim identity;[40] however, Andrew Gilligan's portrayal of Tower Hamlets as an 'Islamic republic' is a pernicious caricature.[41] Muslim identity and Islamist politics will be examined in later chapters.

The housing question

The East End is an area of endemic housing crisis. The number of homes has always been inadequate and housing conditions have long been some of the worst in London.[42] Many of the first Bengali immigrants tolerated the most basic of shared living arrangements, taking comfort in the belief that this was only a temporary stay, and spending minimal time in their lodgings. However, with the arrival of their families, housing assumed a new importance, and became a focus of campaigning action. Many families found their homes thanks to an organised squatting movement; and there have been other periods of exceptional crisis, with large-scale homelessness and Bengali families sent to distant bed and breakfast hotels.

Early immigrants had to rely on private landlords, but a large amount of council housing was built in Tower Hamlets, so, unusually for an immigrant community, a high proportion of Bengalis eventually came to live in council or ex-council accommodation. Despite all this development, there was never enough council housing, and the offices that allocated the homes were riddled with both deliberate and accidental racism.

Most Bengalis wanted to live in the area of greatest Bengali settlement around Spitalfields, but opportunities were limited and many families found themselves in other parts of the borough. Some won offers of housing in their chosen area through the housing campaigns described in Chapter 6, but families allocated accommodation under homeless legislation had little option but to accept their single take-it-or-leave-it offer, and this provided a vehicle for moving Bengalis onto some of the worst estates. So, for example, of the eight Bengali families placed on the Teviot Estate in 1984 under the Labour-controlled Tower Hamlets Council, all but one had been living for months in the grim hotels used as temporary accommodation and would have been out on the streets if they had refused.[43] Before the 1977 Housing Act made housing homeless families a legal obligation, such families had been regarded as undeserving wasters. Attitudes did not change overnight, and all homeless families were generally allocated the least popular homes. Bengalis ended up concentrated in the very worst housing of all, and a 1988 CRE report found Tower Hamlets Liberal Council guilty of allocating ethnic minorities dispropor-tionately to a poor-quality estate.[44]

Homes were often in poor condition, and were frequently also terribly overcrowded, as the housing stock had not been constructed for such big house-holds. The 2011 Census recorded that 68 per cent of Bangladeshi-headed house-holds in Tower Hamlets had dependent children, and that the average number of children in these household was 2.5. The equivalent figures for England and Wales as a whole were 29 per cent and 1.8. 35 per cent of Bangladeshi-headed households in Tower Hamlets had more than 1 person per room, and 10 per cent had more than 1 ½ persons, compared with 2 per cent and 0.5 per cent for England and Wales. Not only do Bengali families tend to have large numbers of children, but the children also tend to stay in the family home until they are married – and sometimes after that. Joint family households of various kinds are a small minority, but more common than in the general population.[45]

Competition for housing has long proved a source of social division between immigrants and the children of established residents; and this has fed into ethnic tensions and been deliberately exploited for short-term political gain. Already in 1903, the Royal Commission on Alien Immigration, which failed to find evidence for most of the social effects then largely blamed on Jewish immigrants in this same area of East London, did accept that immigration was responsible for increasing overcrowding and for displacement of the previous population.[46] The famous map of 1899 that accompanied Russell and Lewis' volume on *The Jew in London*[47] showed this in graphic terms, with large areas mottled blue to indicate streets with more than 75 per cent of their residents Jewish, and many solid blue to indicate 95 per cent Jewish residency. Even at that time, housing was an important catalyst for racist action,[48] so it is far from being a new source of tension, as was implied by Dench *et al.* in their examination of *The New East End*.[49] This much-heralded book recorded white working-class concern about the huge demand for housing, and also about housing policies that, especially after the 1977 Act, increasingly prioritised those in greatest need rather than rewarding long-term residents. The general principle of housing meeting the needs of those in the worst housing conditions had been recognised since the beginning of the slum clearances in the 1930s, but in practice it was always subject to some qualification. In Tower Hamlets, those most in need have often been large, newly arrived, Bengali families.

Dench *et al.* followed the lead of many of their interviewees in regretting the loss of older letting systems and of the strength they gave to established family networks. This is an important point, but housing for those in greatest need is important too – which is why new criteria were introduced after bitter struggle. The crucial issue, which the book did not discuss, is that the problem is not the prioritising of those in greatest need, but chronic under-investment in public housing, which has meant that those in greatest need can only be helped at the expense of those a little better off. *The New East End* developed old reactionary ideas in line with the fashionable sport of blaming the welfare state for community breakdown. It proved a headline-catching thesis, but its argument was based on ignoring wider socio-economic pressures and accepting narrow, politically imposed limits on investment in social housing. The authors rightly pointed out that 'from the beginning of Bangladeshi settlement in Tower Hamlets there has … been a contest for housing in which both groups feel badly treated',[50] but this contest will not be solved without a reversal of the attack on social housing that has been going on since the 1980s – under both Conservatives and Labour – and which, under the Conservative/Liberal coalition in the 2010s, has reached a new intensity.[51]

Work

In 1950s and 1960s London many of the Bengali immigrants found work in the garment trade, perhaps after initial unskilled jobs in hotels and catering or on the railways. Larger, more unionised clothing firms were moving out of central London, but the sweated workshops found a new lease of life providing short runs for the rationalised targeted marketing of the fashion industry. Jewish-owned firms were gradually being taken over or replaced by a new generation of immigrant entrepreneurs, including men from West Pakistan. Bengalis were slower to take up ownership roles in the garment workshops, but a new business in leather and suede appears to have been dominated by Bengalis from the start.[52] As the first male immigrants were joined by their families, manufacturers found an additional source of cheap labour, outsourcing piece-work for some of the wives to sew at home. However, despite squeezing wages and conditions, the East End industry has increasingly succumbed to even cheaper foreign competition, ordered and delivered more rapidly than ever before. Among others, London's Bangladeshi clothing workers have to compete with the booming ready-made clothes industry of their native Bangladesh, whose products may be imported and sold wholesale by men who first made their money in the sweatshops of Spitalfields.

At the same time, so called 'Indian' restaurants have expanded into an important source of wealth and employment. The 2001 Census recorded that one in three working Bengali men living in Tower Hamlets was employed in the hotel and restaurant sector and, while there has been a proliferation of fast food outlets, the great majority of those jobs would have been in Indian restaurants. For Bengali men in England as a whole, the figure for hotel and restaurant employment rose to 45 per cent.[53] Sylheti involvement in the ethnic food business is said to have its origins in the tea shops established by Bengali seamen and the eating houses that catered for the first single male immigrants. They were not the first to establish Indian restaurants in Britain, but in the post-war years they soon came to dominate the sector. Like the garment trade, it requires only a small initial investment. While the restaurant industry does not have to compete with foreign competition, it is notoriously difficult for Indian restaurants to break into the more expensive section of the market, and in order for them to make a profit at all, pay and working conditions are kept poor. Hours are long and anti-social, and few second generation immigrants have been attracted into the industry. Many restaurant workers are relatively new arrivals, glad to find work where lack of English is not a problem.

The spread of Indian restaurants has allowed Bengali families to put down roots all over the country, but Tower Hamlets has remained the Bengali capital. This large and concentrated ethnic community is able to support a host of specialist businesses, including grocers, music shops, travel agents, money exchangers, purveyors of Islamic tracts and accessories and outlets for halal fried chicken.

Much has been written about ethnic entrepreneurism. As Roger Ballard has observed, 'migration is above all an *entrepreneurial* activity';[54] that is most migrants are people with some initial means that they are prepared to stake in the hope of improving their family's future. Having made the first move they may be more open than other workers to the idea of trying different routes to achieve their hoped-for success. And members of minority groups may have to resort to setting up their own businesses as a response to the lack of available alternatives. However, while Indian restaurants have made a substantial contribution to the socio-economic development of Bengalis in Britain, and many Bengalis work in Bengali-owned businesses, the number of restaurant owners is very small.

In contrast to the entrepreneurial image, Sarah Salway's study of a more recent generation of young Bengali men in Tower Hamlets and Camden, carried out in 2003, found that most had limited career horizons. She showed how they were constrained, not only by limited qualifications, but also by the strong inclusive pulls of the Bengali community and by the exclusion resulting from actual and anticipated racist discrimination. Together, these resulted in a reliance on community networks when looking for work, and a reluctance to venture into work places with few Bengali employees or to travel far from home. While office jobs were often seen as the ideal, many young Bengali men had found work in local supermarkets and fast food outlets. Skilled trades, such as building work, were rarely considered, and little use was made of mainstream employment agencies.[55]

Overall, the Bengalis are still disproportionately in lower socio-economic groups, unemployed or not economically active, though this may hide informal employment. The 2011 Census for Tower Hamlets recorded that the percentage of Bangladeshi men in the highest rated occupations – socio-economic Classifications 1 and 2 – were 6 and 10 per cent, compared with 27 and 19 per cent for all ethnic groups in England and Wales. Among Bengali men aged over sixteen and not retired, 73 per cent were economically active, compared with 85 per cent for all ethnic groups in England and Wales.[56] And the unemployment rate for Bangladeshi men in Tower Hamlets was 22 per cent, when the national rate for male unemployment was 8 per cent (though this was an improvement on the 1991 figure of 48 per cent). Also striking were the 2001 census figures for the percentages of Bengalis with no qualifications, which rose from 21 per cent for those aged 16 to 24, to 50 per cent for those aged 25 to 34, 78 per cent for those aged 35 to 49 and 88 per cent for those aged 50 to 59. These figures were for men and women combined. The equivalent figures for all people across England were 16 per cent, 12 per cent, 21 per cent and 39 per cent.[57]

However, over the years, as the community has evolved, economic paths have diverged and occupations have become more diverse. The 2001 Census recorded 31 per cent of working Bengali men in Tower Hamlets doing jobs related to trade and business, 10 per cent in manufacturing and a further 10 per cent in the public sector (though only 1 per cent in construction).[58] And some, though still a relatively small proportion, have built up large and profitable businesses or become established in professional careers.

Racism

As the Bengali community grew, it faced similar anti-immigrant responses as had greeted the Jews at the beginning of the century; a parallel neatly demonstrated by Caroline Adams in her 1976 booklet '*They Sell Cheaper and They Live Very*

Odd', in which she juxtaposed comments from the two periods.[59] Older Bengalis recall a rise in overt racism, and some have contrasted this with much friendlier times before or just after the Second World War.[60] Racism was always there, but it could be brought uglily to the surface, especially when the immigrant population grew in size and was seized on as a scapegoat for shortages of jobs or housing or other social problems. It was stoked by the national politics of Enoch Powell and xenophobic reactions to the mass immigration of Asians expelled from East Africa, and by the local actions of far-right groups – skinhead gangs in 1970, the National Front in the late 1970s, and the British National Party (BNP) in the mid-90s. In addition to the institutional racism that pervaded many of the official organisations that the Bengalis had to deal with, more overt racism could take the form of mindless – and often vicious – attacks on the street, or of harassment deliberately aimed at driving Bengalis from 'white' estates, including regular verbal abuse, broken windows, chasing schoolchildren with knives and physical violence. This was made worse by clear police prejudice in favour of the attackers. Thus an account from 1984 describes a white woman 'accompanied by about four white thugs' forcefully entering a Bengali woman's home and hitting her on the head with a brick while she fed her baby, and the police then 'harassing the family in the front garden, while the actual fighting was going on in the back garden'.[61]

The racism reached its worst level in 1978, when comparisons were drawn with the rise of Mosley's British Union of Fascists (BUF) in the East End of the 1930s. But there were important differences. As Phil Piratin pointed out in the preface to the 1978 edition of his book describing that earlier period, the BUF had been part of a 'world wide reactionary development'[62] that had to be fought at home and abroad, but this was not the case with more recent far-right groups. The National Front and later the BNP have been able to inspire a section of alienated youth with a creed of racist thuggery and even to play the race card to win a level of electoral support; but neither of these parties has been felt as a threat beyond the groups they have targeted, and they have never been part of a significant political movement that inspired a major dedicated response.[63] However, although – and perhaps because – their power has been limited in its wider impact, they have reached a level of violence from which the 1930s escaped. At least four Bengalis have died at the hands of racist attackers:[64] Tosir Ali in Aldgate in 1970, Altab Ali and Ishaq Ali in Whitechapel and Hackney in 1978, and Shiblu Rahman in Bow in 2001. By this last date, racism was no longer such a problem in the centre of Bengali settlement, but Rahman lived in the more mixed area of Bow.

More recently – and especially following 9/11 and the London bomb attacks of 7 July 2005 – racism has been replaced by Islamophobia. Although progress had been made in developing more sensitive community policing and the local paper now tries not to incite racist sentiments, heavy handed implementation of the 'anti-terrorism' agenda has revived Bengali fears and ethnic tensions. Muslims across the UK have found themselves treated with suspicion, and a particularly dramatic example was provided in June 2006 by the armed raid of a house in Forest Gate, in the neighbouring borough to Tower Hamlets, where two Bengali brothers, one of whom was shot in the shoulder, were mistakenly believed to be in possession of a chemical bomb.

Not all racism has been one way, and as young Bengalis have become more dominant and confident, they have sometimes boosted that confidence at the expense of outsiders, or by showing they can give as good as they get. Somali refugees, who began arriving in the late 1980s, were soon made aware of the Bengalis' superior position,[65] and a Bengali former gang member, interviewed by Nick Ryan, described how his gang used to go 'honky [white] bashing' in the 1990s:

> we started attacking pubs. A man come out of the first one, he got done. It became a white and Asian thing, we thought we'd attack anyone we'd find. We were looking for trouble, 'cos they were attacking us.[66]

There has been more anti-white racism since, including a spate of attacks in 2005.[67]

Bengali women

As a political history, this book features few women in leading roles, though they have carried out the hard and often unacknowledged work of holding their families together behind the scenes. Women were required to be especially strong in the struggles to get decent housing, but women have not generally been expected to be more prominently involved in politics.

Katy Gardner noted, when she was carrying out fieldwork in a Sylheti village in the late 1980s, that 'questions concerning Islam or politics were invariably answered by telling me to "ask the men"'[68] – though she also describes the women retreating behind their mosquito nets when male relatives 'came to discuss politics late into the night',[69] so they must have been aware of what was discussed. However, politics was not part of the women's sphere. Looking at the first generation of women immigrants, Gardner observes that their lives have revolved round their role as carers: 'Ideals of nurture and caring are as central to most older women's self images as those of purity or modesty.'[70] This has often meant caring for large numbers of children and also increasingly incapacitated older husbands and other family members. The women's range of household duties left little time for anything else – including, in many cases, learning English – though some managed to squeeze in bits of sewing piecework to help make ends meet. Concepts of modesty have not generally been translated into strict purdah, but they have affected what women feel able to do, both for their own psychological comfort and to avoid the possibility of malicious rumours in a closely networked community. Women who were never allowed to shop for themselves in Bangladesh do go shopping in London,[71] however, when Naila Kabeer was researching in 1989, she found that the major weekly shop was generally done by the husbands and that, although the women she spoke to were not bothered about going to the supermarket, they avoided the Bengali male spaces of the local grocers.[72] Lack of English and very real fears of racism have compounded the constraints on these women's lives, hindering them from using public transport and leaving many isolated behind the closed doors of their flats. An anecdote from the late 1970s, told by John Newbigin, gives a sense of the constrictions under which many lived. As a community worker he had taken a group of families to Epping Forest. He recalls: 'some of the women were crying when we got to Epping because they didn't know there was countryside in England. They had not seen anything except concrete, since they had arrived.'[73]

Because family reunion has been a very slow process and, in addition, some Bengalis who grew up in Britain have chosen to bring brides over from Sylhet, there is a large proportion of first-generation women immigrants. When I accompanied political canvassers they often had to find Bengali speakers to talk to Bengali women. In 2010 I went round with a Bengali would-be Respect councillor who delegated the job to his sisters and cousin. One older lady answered the knock on her door by coming to the upstairs window, and as she talked to the modern young canvasser below she held the lace curtain like a veil to hide her face from the street. Bengali community organisations that work with first-generation immigrant women concentrate on the relatively modest task of getting them out of their homes to meet each other and build up self-confidence in a protected and safe atmosphere.

Life for the next generation is very different and girls brought up in Britain have a confidence rarely accessible to their mothers, though they are still influenced by family and community expectations. As a group, Bengali girls have been getting the best exam grades in Tower Hamlets schools and growing numbers have gone on to higher education, especially at local universities. However, they can still be pressured into accepting marriages to men brought up in Sylhet with whom they have little in common and who may retain very traditional views on a woman's role. Some have used a new awareness of Islamic texts to argue against Bengali traditions – especially regarding arranged marriage – but, although reformist Islam may help them continue in education and find their own husband, it also reinforces the idea that men and women have fundamentally different responsibilities.

By British standards, Bengalis marry young and still tend to have large numbers of children. Levels of economic activity among Bengali women are exceptionally low, though official statistics will not take account of much informal employment, including home-working. The 2011 Census recorded that only 37 per cent of Bangladeshi women in Tower Hamlets over sixteen and not retired were economically active, compared with 76 per cent for all ethnic groups in England and Wales. However Bangladeshi economic activity rates vary enormously between different age groups, ranging from 48 per cent for women aged 16 to 24, through 36 per cent for women aged 25 to 49, to 10 per cent for women over 50 and not retired. Women's economic activity is particularly low among recent immigrants,[74] but overall it has increased significantly since 2001[75] and can be expected to go on increasing. In 2001, almost half (47 per cent) of working Bengali women were employed in the public sector, especially in education, health and social work, and a third (35 per cent) in trade and business.[76]

Tower Hamlets has had some highly active female Bengali community workers,[77] but still relatively few Bengali women have chosen more overtly political paths. Those that have − including Rushanara Ali who was elected MP for Bethnal Green and Bow in 2010 − have been helped by the support of their families; but it has not been an easy journey.

Growing up in the East End

Looking at this large bustling community today the isolation of the first immigrants seems a long way off, but there have been plenty of difficulties for those brought up here too. People who left Sylhet as children suddenly had to cope with schooling in a foreign language, and even those born here have often had their schooling interrupted by long visits back to Bangladesh, or by days off to act as interpreters for mothers with little English. Many children are still expected to attend Bengali and Arabic classes on top of their school work.[78] Overcrowded homes still impact on health and homework and for many boys from large families and small homes, the street is their main recreation space.

The first generation of boys who grew up in Tower Hamlets provided the shock troops for the battles against racism in the late 1970s and 80s. This helped bring them together into a number of youth groups that have attempted to address the problems of the new British Bengali generations; but some vigilante groups morphed into less benign gangs such as the Brick Lane Mafia, which became the Brick Lane Massive. Fighting racism was still the priority for those growing up in the early 90s, who faced new attacks led by the BNP and racist violence between schools and within schools,[79] but inter-Bengali gang battles were growing too. By the late 90s, there were relatively few young whites in the main Bengali areas, and Bengali youth gangs − like alienated youth in other deprived places and times − were becoming embroiled in increasingly vicious turf wars. Also like other deprived areas, Tower Hamlets has been targeted by drug dealers. Youth gangs have become linked to organised crime, and fights can be prompted by competition between dealers.[80] Young Bengalis have found that gang membership brings with it a sense of power as well as belonging and, as Abdul Hannan at Nafas drugs project explained to me, 'for excitement you want to move onto more higher stuff. So the drugs get higher, the weapons get higher as well.'[81] I also spoke with one of the organisers of a self-help group for addicts on Stepney's run-down Ocean Estate. He found that, for some young men, drug dealing simply appeared as the most attractive career option – a way out of poverty so that they could 'buy their mum a house' and themselves a business and a nice car: 'They know somebody or they know somebody who knows someone who's a drug dealer, flash cars, loads of money, young people want all this and they want it the easy way.'[82] Hip hop culture has reinforced the message.[83] Female gangs have also made an appearance[84] and by the time I was starting my fieldwork at the turn of the millennium youth workers were reporting that Bengali girls were also experimenting with drugs and even getting pulled into prostitution to support their habit.[85] When addiction leads to crime, loyalties break down and addicts can be left more alienated than ever. Many community organisations have been concerned about what is happening, including the increasingly prominent Islamist groups who have been active in organising youth groups and attempting to attract people away from drugs and gangs. Fears of their children becoming involved with drugs and violence have helped persuade some families to leave the area, if they can. In a more positive development, average school results for young Bengalis in Tower Hamlets are much better than in the past – though the marks of white children have been particularly worrying.[86]

Bengalis and bankers

Tower Hamlets is visibly changing. The scale and nature of this change can be measured in the emergence of seven Conservative councillors in a borough that previously had none. As in so many other run-down inner-city areas, politicians and developers have realised the potential of the rent gap and the large profits to be made from land so close to the city centre, and in this case to the City of London. External pressures, especially from commercial development, were already strong in the west of the borough when Charlie Forman wrote *Spitalfields: A Battle for Land* in 1989,[87] and the 'regeneration' of the eight square miles of former Docklands through the 1980s and 90s sent shockwaves up from the south. In a pattern familiar across the world, the first years of this century were marked by widespread gentrification and redevelopment as the borough competed to attract a new wealthier class. While the overall population has expanded, previous inhabitants have been driven away from areas that have increasingly become adjuncts to the City and to the new financial centre in Canary Wharf. Neoliberal governments have promoted commercial development and home ownership at the expense of public housing and encouraged a phenomenal rise in house prices. Among the developments of executive flats there have been only a few projects that complied with requirements for 'affordable housing' and even these are not within the financial limits of most of the East End's residents.[88] The stock of housing for lower income households of all backgrounds has been drastically reduced, and the juxtaposition of new upmarket developments and older housing estates presents a landscape of stark contrasts.

Many striking physical transformations have taken place in Tower Hamlets since I first began my research there in 1998, and while some of these have been of a vast scale and involved extensive, government-sponsored gentrification,[89] the changing nature of the area can be illustrated by a couple of relatively small examples of more old-fashioned gentrification. For a while I worked as a volunteer at St Hilda's East Community Centre. On my way there I would pass an old synagogue that had been converted to a tailoring workshop, which seemed symbolic of East End history; but one day when I revisited my route I found that it had become a smart office. St Hilda's is next to the Boundary Estate, a solid and handsome example of early public housing. In the late 1990s, the estate was decidedly scruffy – I was warned to avoid the central bandstand because of abandoned syringes – and the homes were largely tenanted by Bengali families. Now, many of the flats have passed into private ownership under the tenants' Right to Buy legislation brought in by Margaret Thatcher. They have since been snatched up by aspiring professionals for prices of up to half a million pounds, and the estate has attracted upmarket boutiques.[90]

Brick Lane itself is still a place where Bengalis go to shop, pray and bump into old friends, but it has also attracted a young international crowd who enjoy the cosmopolitan atmosphere. The trendy cafés and fashion showrooms in the old Truman's Brewery site beyond the railway bridge seem as disconnected to Bengali Spitalfields as do the City developments that increasingly loom over its western edge.

Gentrification has generated opportunities for personal advancement for some individuals from all communities, including tenants who were able to buy a heavily discounted, well-positioned council flat. It has also helped some Bengali-run businesses to prosper, so contributing to a growing Bengali middle class. Although Bengalis remain disproportionately deprived, they are by no means all poor.

Some Bengali families who are able to afford it have moved away from what is still an area that scores high on indices of deprivation, settling further out from central London, where they can buy a small house with a garden and worry less about their children getting involved with drugs and gang violence. Many of these have moved to areas that already have relatively high numbers of other Bengalis; but, away from the pressures of poverty and insufficient resources, protective clustering becomes less important. Countering such forces of disper-sion, religion provides a strong cohesive pull, and the Jewish example shows that those communities that have remained inward looking and separate are those for whom religious belief has remained central.[91] In addition, the Bengali community is still increasing through natural growth, and also immigration, and many do not have the resources – financial or cultural – to move away. They tend to be more reluctant to leave Tower Hamlets than their poor white neighbours. The shortage of genuinely affordable rented housing may thus contribute to even greater ethnic segregation within the cheaper housing that remains.

Recently, the borough has also attracted new ethnic groups in the form of migrant workers from Eastern Europe, but many of these are young and single and transient, so are able to make do with relatively basic accommodation.

A snapshot of the East End today shows how complicated socio-economic patterns actually are. Bengalis are still predominantly a poor community in a deprived borough, but they have also become increasingly diffused across a wider social, economic and geographic spectrum; new immigrants and migrant workers have found work and a place to live in the East End; and inner-city regeneration and the lure of Canary Wharf have attracted a new breed of well-healed East Ender, intensifying economic competition for living space and providing everyday reminders of the economic divide. Meanwhile the economic crisis can be expected to impact disproportionately on those many areas of the borough that have suffered endemic deprivation.

Any description of a large community over many decades cannot hope to be more than a sketch, but I hope that this sketch will help to fill in the gaps in the story that follows and bring it to life.

Notes

1 Jane M. Jacobs, *Edge of Empire: Postcolonialism and the City* (London: Routledge, 1996), pp. 87 and 101.
2 The 2010 Index of Multiple Deprivation found that 40 per cent of the Lower Super Output Areas in Tower Hamlets were amongst the 10 per cent most deprived in England – the seventh highest percentage in the country, though a big improvement on the figures for 2007. See Department for Communities and Local Government, 'The English Indices of Deprivation 2010' (2011) p. 9.
3 nomis official labour market statistics.
4 Mayhew Harper Associates Ltd, 'Counting the Population of Tower Hamlets: A London Borough in Transition' (Report for Tower Hamlets Council, 2010), pp. 41–2.
5 HMRC snapshot as at 31 August 2010.
6 Or White English/Welsh/Scottish/Northern Irish.
7 The number of Bangladeshis in Tower Hamlets is up from 65,600 in 2001 to 81,400, but the percentage has fallen slightly as the population of the borough has increased even more dramatically..
8 Anne J. Kershen, *Strangers, Aliens and Asians: Huguenots, Jews and Bangladeshis in Spitalfields 1660–2000* (Abingdon: Routledge, 2005) pp. 148–9.
9 Under British rule Bengal was divided up among big landowners, or *zamindars*, and most of the people were share croppers or landless labourers. From 1874 Sylhet was administered as part of Assam, where the land tenure system divided most of the country into many small owner-run farms. Gardner claims that 86 per cent of Sylheti migrants came from landowning families (see Katy Gardner, *Global Migrants, Local Lives: Travel and Transformation in Rural Bangladesh* (Oxford: Clarendon Press, 1995), pp. 37–40).
10 A vivid picture of Sylheti village life can be found in the writings of Katy Gardner,

who researched the impact of the immigration from the perspective of the home villages at the end of the 1980s, when the village she stayed in was without metalled roads and electricity. Her academic study *Global Migrants, Local Lives* is supplemented by a more fictionalised account in *Songs at the River's Edge* (London: Pluto Press, 1997).

11 Professor Abdul Aziz told the BBC in 2005 that *Londoni* families regarded shopping malls as a safe investment and he estimated that there would soon be more than forty in the city. See Roland Buerk, 'Expat Cash Flows Back to Bangladesh', http://news.bbc.co.uk/1/hi/world/south_asia/4465203.stm, accessed 7 January 2011.

12 This outline history of the *lascars* is abstracted from Rozina Visram, *Asians in Britain: 400 Years of History* (London: Pluto Press, 2002). The number of war casualties has been estimated at 6,600, but no proper record was kept of *lascar* deaths.

13 Marika Sherwood, 'Lascars' Struggles Against Discrimination in Britain 1923–45: The Work of N.J. Upadhyana and Surat Alley', *The Mariner's Mirror*, 90:4 (2004), 438–55, p. 449.

14 Caroline Adams, *Across Seven Seas and Thirteen Rivers* (London: THAP Books, 1994), p. 61.

15 See Adams, *Across Seven Seas and Thirteen Rivers*.

16 Yousuf Choudhury, *The Roots and Tales of the Bangladeshi Settlers* (Birmingham: Sylhet Local History Group, 1993), p. 68.

17 *Ibid.*, pp. 62–4.

18 Katy Gardner, *Age, Narrative and Migration: The Life Course and Life Histories of Bengali Elders in London* (Oxford and New York: Berg, 2002), pp. 78–9, 95–7 and 100; Sarah Glynn (ed.), *The Way We Worked: An Oral History by Members of St Hilda's East Community Centre and Stepney Jewish Community Centre* (London: St Hilda's East Community Centre, 1999), p. 10.

19 Faruque Ahmed, *Bengal Politics in Britain: Logic, Dynamics and Disharmony* (North Carolina: Lulu, 2010), p. 82; Mohammad Ali Asghar, *Bangladeshi Community Organisations in East London* (London: Bangla Heritage Ltd, 1996), p. 24.

20 Chris Phillipson, Nilufar Ahmed and Joanna Latimer, *Women in Transition: A Study of the Experiences of Bangladeshi Women Living in Tower Hamlets* (Bristol: Policy Press, 2003), pp. 56–8.

21 Adams, *Across Seven Seas and Thirteen Rivers*, p. 66.

22 Interviewed 22 August 2001.

23 Quoted in Robert Miles and Annie Phizacklea, *White Man's Country: Racism in British Politics* (London: Pluto Press, 1984), p. 57.

24 In a speech to fellow Conservatives, given in Birmingham in 1968 as Labour's new Race Relations Bill was going through parliament, Wolverhampton MP, Enoch Powell, clamed that British people had 'found themselves made strangers in their own country', and he depicted a dystopian future where immigrants deliberately promoted 'racial and religious differences, with a view to the exercise of actual domination, first over fellow-immigrants and then over the rest of the population'. He warned, 'As I look ahead, I am filled with foreboding; like the Roman, I seem to see "the River Tiber foaming with much blood".' See www.telegraph.co.uk/comment/3643823/Enoch-Powells-Rivers-of-Blood-speech.html, accessed 20 November 2012.

25 For a fuller discussion on the causes of family reunification see Gardner, *Age, Narrative and Migration*, pp. 106–9.

26 Home Affairs Committee, *Bangladeshis in Britain* (London: HMSO, 1986), vol. II, p. 150.

27 Census figures from Sean Carey and Abdus Shukur, 'A Profile of the Bangladeshi Community in East London', *New Community*, 12:3 (1985), 405-17, p. 407.

28 Tower Hamlets Borough Council and NHS Tower Hamlets, 'Health and Wellbeing in Tower Hamlets: Joint Strategic Needs Assessment' (2009), p. 19. Bengalis made up the largest single group in a total number of new immigrant registrations that ranged from six thousand to just over eight thousand a year.

29 The figure is similar for both sexes.

30 Greater Sylhet Development and Welfare Council UK, www.gscuk.org/history.html, accessed 20 September 2013.

31 Ali Mohammed Abbas, autobiographical memoir (manuscript, n.d., shown to the author by his brother, Ali Mohammed Azhar), pp. 59–60. A powerful portrayal of such an arrangement can be found in the novel *Émigré Journeys*, by Abdullah Hussein (London: Serpent's Tail, 2000), which was made into a BBC drama, *Brothers in Trouble*, directed by Udayan Prasad (1995).

32 Visram, *Asians in Britain*; Adams, *Across Seven Seas and Thirteen Rivers*.

33 Charlie Forman claims, 'In 1966 a third of all adverts in the local press for privately rented rooms actually specified "no coloureds".' See *Spitalfields: A Battle for Land* (London: Hilary Shipman, 1989), p. 30.

34 Gardner, *Age, Narrative and Migration*, p. 112.

35 John Eade, Isabelle Fremeaux and David Garbin, 'The Political Construction of Diasporic Communities in the Global City', in P. Gilbert (ed.), *Imagined London* (Albany: SUNY Press, 2001) .

36 See 'Jamiat-ul-Muslimin', Making Britain Database, www.open.ac.uk/researchprojects/makingbritain/content/jamiat-ul-muslimin, accessed 11 October 2012, which also shows that protests by British Muslims against books are nothing new: in 1938, the Jamiat sent a delegation to the Indian High Commission to protest about H.G. Wells' *A Short History of the World*.

37 See 'East London Mosque and Islamic Cultural Centre', Making Britain Database, www.open.ac.uk/researchprojects/makingbritain/content/east-london-mosque-and-islamic-cultural-centre, accessed 11 October 2012. There are interesting parallels here with conflicts between the East End Synagogues and established Anglo-Jewry.

38 Accessed 19 September 2013.

39 Plans to demolish this and replace it with a new building were stalled when the school building was listed.

40 See, for example, John Eade, 'Nationalism and the Quest for Authenticity: The Bangladeshis in Tower Hamlets', *New Community*, 16:4 (1990), 493–503; John Eade, 'Identity, Nation and Religion: Educated Young Bangladeshi Muslims in London's "East End"', *International Sociology*, 9:3 (1994), 377–94; Katy Gardner and Abdus Shukur '"I'm Bengali, I'm Asian and I'm Living Here": The Changing Identity of British Bengalis', in Roger Ballard (ed.), *Desh Pardesh: The South Asian Presence in Britain* (London: Hurst, 1994), pp. 142–64; John Eade and David Garbin, 'Changing Narratives of Violence, Struggle and Resistance: Bangladeshis and the Competition for Resources in the Global City', *Oxford Development Studies*, 30:2 (2002), 137–49; Sarah Glynn, 'Bengali Muslims: The New East End Radicals?', *Ethnic and Racial Studies*, 25:6 (2002) 969–88; Justin Gest, *Apart: Alienated and Engaged Muslims in the West* (London: Hurst, 2010); Ali Riaz, *Islam and Identity Politics Among British-Bangladeshis: A Leap of Faith* (Manchester: Manchester University Press, 2013), pp. 71–3.

41 See Andrew Gilligan, *Dispatches: Britain's Islamic Republic* [Television Programme] Channel 4, 1 March 2010; Andrew Gilligan, blogs for the *Telegraph*, including, http://blogs.telegraph.co.uk/news/andrewgilligan/100060304/labour-london-

borough-becomes-islamic-republic, accessed 11 October 2012.

42 Forman, *Spitalfields*.

43 Press release by the families and community groups announcing a picket of the Town Hall, 19 June 1984.

44 Commission for Racial Equality, 'Homelessness and Discrimination: Report of a Formal Investigation into the London Borough of Tower Hamlets' (London: CRE, 1988), p. 11.

45 Elaine Kempson, *Overcrowding in Bangladeshi Households: A Case Study of Tower Hamlets* (London: Policy Studies Institute, 1999).

46 John A. Garrard, *The English and Immigration: A Comparative Study of the Jewish Influx 1880–1910* (Oxford: Oxford University Press, 1971), p. 40.

47 C. Russell, and H.S. Lewis, *The Jew in London* (London: T. Fisher Unwin, 1900).

48 David Feldman, *Englishmen and Jews: Social Relations and Political Culture 1840–1914* (New Haven and London: Yale, 1994), p. 183.

49 Geoff Dench, Kate Gavron and Michael Young, *The New East End: Kinship, Race and Conflict* (London: Profile Books, 2006), p. 4.

50 *Ibid.*, p. 164.

51 As part of the current dismantling of council house provision, needs-based policies are being increasingly reversed.

52 Ben Birnbaum, John Eversley, Tony Clouting, Dick Allard, John Hall, Cheryl Morgan, Kevin Woods, Roger Allen and Richard Tully, 'The Clothing Industry in Tower Hamlets: An Investigation into its Structure and Problems 1979/80 and Beyond' (unpublished report, Tower Hamlets Local History Library, 1981).

53 2011 figures were not available at the time of writing.

54 Roger Ballard (ed.), *Desh Pardesh: The South Asian Presence in Britain* (London: Hurst, 1994), p. 9.

55 Sarah Salway, 'Labour Market Experiences of Young UK Bangladeshi Men: Identity, Inclusion and Exclusion in Inner-City London', *Ethnic and Racial Studies*, 31:6 (2008), 1126–52.

56 Because the Bengalis are a relatively young population only a relatively small proportion are retired, so it makes sense to exclude retired people when comparing with other groups.

57 2011 figures were not available at the time of writing.

58 The relevant census categories were: wholesale and retail trade, repairs – 22 per cent; real estate, renting and business – 9 per cent; manufacturing – 10 per cent; public administration and defence, social security + education + health and social work – 10 per cent; construction – 1 per net. 2011 figures were not available at the time of writing.

59 Caroline Adams, '*They Sell Cheaper and They Live Very Odd*' (London: Community and Race Relations Unit of the British Council of Churches, 1976).

60 See several of the interviews conducted by Caroline Adams now in the Tower Hamlets Local History Library.

61 From a bulletin produced by Tower Hamlets International Solidarity and Tower Hamlets Association for Racial Justice in May 1984.

62 Phil Piratin, *Our Flag Stays Red* (London: Lawrence and Wishart, 1978), p. xi.

63 The political significance of the BNP more recently has been not so much in itself, but in its effect as a pressure group, pushing other parties towards a more racist agenda. This is not only damaging for ethnic minorities, but serves to set groups of workers in opposition to each other, and to distract attention from the real socio-economic causes of inequality.

64 These have all been recognised as racist killings.

65 http://sites.google.com/site/londonstreetgangs/borough-pages/tower-hamlets, accessed 7 April 2011; http://www.bwhafs.com/html/young.html (the website of Black Women's Health and Family Support, based in Bethnal Green), accessed 4 April 2011. Turning the tables again, one of Sarah Salway's young Bengali interviewees recounted being chased away from a new job by a group of Somalis, see Salway, 'Labour Market Experiences of Young UK Bangladeshi Men', p. 1142.

66 Nick Ryan, 'Children of the Abyss' (*Telegraph*, 2005), www.nickryan.net/articles/abyss.html, accessed 28 July 2011.

67 See Chapter 9.

68 Gardner, *Age, Narrative and Migration*, p. 62.

69 *Ibid.*, p. 136.

70 *Ibid.*, p. 130.

71 *Ibid.*, p. 139.

72 Naila Kabeer, 'The Structure of "Revealed" Preference: Race, Community and Female Labour Supply in the London Clothing Industry', *Development and Change*, 25:2 (1994), 307–31, p. 322.

73 Interviewed 21 March 2006 by Jamil Iqbal and Charlie Sen for Swadhinata Trust and the University of Surrey Centre for Research on Nationalism, Ethnicity and Multiculturalism, 'Oral History Project' (2005–06).

74 Naila Kabeer and Peroline Ainsworth, 'Life Chances, Life Choices: Exploring Patterns of Work and Worklessness Among Bangladeshi and Somali Women in Tower Hamlets' (Report for Tower Hamlets Council, 2011), Executive Summary, p. 5.

75 The 2001 Census recorded economic activity levels for Bengali women in Tower Hamlets of 37 per cent for women between 16 and 24 and 13 per cent for women aged 25–74 and not retired.

76 The relevant census categories were: education – 22 per cent; health and social work – 19 per cent; public administration and defence, social security – 6 per cent; wholesale and retail trade, repairs – 24 per cent; real estate, renting and business – 11 per cent. 2011 figures were not available at the time of writing.

77 Many of the first community workers were products of Hena Ahmed's innovative girl's club, Shejuti, which aimed to give its members confidence and boost their knowledge of both British and Bengali culture. The club was held in her house in Southeast London, where she had lived since leaving Dhaka in 1968, following her banker husband's job.

78 Language learning can prove an educational advantage even beyond its immediate benefits, but extra classes can put children under strain.

79 There were school pupils' strikes to protest against racism in 1986 and 1994. Both had support from Marxist groups: the first from East London Workers Against Racism, a Revolutionary Communist Party organisation, and the second from Militant Labour, which became the Socialist Party. (See *East London Advertiser*, 17 January 1986; Hugo Pierre, 'Stopping the BNP in Tower Hamlets' (Youth Against Racism in Europe website, undated), http://www.yre.org.uk/towerhamlets.html, accessed 9 October 2012.

80 http://sites.google.com/site/londonstreetgangs/borough-pages/tower-hamlets, accessed 2011.

81 Interviewed 5 July 2000.

82 Interviewed 6 February 2001 (asked to remain anonymous).

83 Justin Gest, *Apart*, p. 107.

84 Tower Hamlets College student, interviewed 20 July 2000.

85 Abdul Hannan and Harun Miah at Nafas, interviewed 5 July 2000, and Noore Nazneen at Step Forward, interviewed 15 October 2001.

86 Phillipson *et al.*, *Women in Transition*, p. 7.

87 Forman, *Spitalfields*.

88 A high-profile scheme for subsidised 'low-cost' rent-and-buy housing in the East End, put up by the Peabody Trust, required applicants to have an annual income of at least £28,758 (£32,644 for couples). See *Detail: Review of Architecture*, 3 (2006), p. 302.

89 Jason Hackworth and Neil Smith coined the term 'third-wave gentrification' to describe large-scale gentrification that is expanding into new areas and is being carried out by big developers actively supported by local government. See Jason Hackworth and Neil Smith, 'The Changing State of Gentrification', *Tijdschrift voor Economische en Sociale Geografie*, 92:4 (2001), 464–77, pp. 468–9.

90 The changing fortunes of Arnold Circus at the centre of the Boundary Estate were the subject of one of the six programmes that made up the Open University/BBC2 series, *The Secret History of Our Streets*. This programme was first broadcast on 11 July 2012.

91 In affluent areas, such as Golders Green and Barnet, there is no need for people to cling together for basic survival as there was in the Jewish East End, but religious Jews are still a group apart. Friends from my student days who are members of the orthodox Jewish community in North London live in a society that is structured by their religion and held together by shared practices, including dietary law and endogamous marriage.

2 *Desher Dak* – 'The Call of the Homeland'

The East End's numerous Bengali newspapers and journals – and now also other media – are witness to the London Bengalis' continued links with their 'homeland'.[1] While these provide an important source of local East End news, they have always been dominated by the politics of Bengal.[2] *Desher Dak* (The Call of the Homeland), published monthly from 1954 to 1964, was largely the responsibility of Tasadduk Ahmed, a journalist and communist activist who plays an influential role in this story, and it was closely associated with the concerns and organisations of those years. This chapter looks at the Bengalis' responses to the political call of the homeland over a rather longer period, from the sunset of the British Empire to the dawn of Bangladeshi independence.

A political journey in the heart of Empire

In an extensive interview with Caroline Adams recorded in the 1980s, Shah Abdul Majid Qureshi, who came to England from Jaganathpur in 1936 aged twenty-one, recalled his political experiences during the last decade of British rule in the Indian subcontinent. His story exemplifies the interaction of three political paths that run through immigrant politics. He told how his early interest in socialism – with its internationalist outlook – was subsumed by a movement for national liberation, and how this was later cut across by a narrower nationalism based on religious identity, and ultimately by a religious political ideology.

Qureshi was poor but well-educated – in fact his father had used up the family money educating his sons. He did not manage to jump ship till his second voyage, as he was deemed likely to desert and was kept under watch. In 1937 he got a job as a waiter, and by 1938 he had saved enough to buy his own restaurant.[3] That first restaurant, in Windmill Street near Tottenham Court Road, was destroyed by a bomb in 1940, but by 1944 he was the owner of another restaurant round the corner in Charlotte Place.

Figure 2.1 Shah Abdul Majid Qureshi

Qureshi described how pioneer settlers such as himself and the (predominantly Hindu) Indian students who ate and sometimes helped in the restaurants generated a ferment of political activity. They took part in the theoretical debates of the period and, despite his later anti-communism, Qureshi 'sometimes used to speak in favour of Russia, and all that' in Hyde Park, and was 'turning into a socialist, more or less, through the Hindu people, and the labour movement as well'.[4] However, the main focus of their activities was the campaign for independence from Britain. Qureshi was involved with the Indian National Congress and the India League, and worked with the trade-unionist Surat Alley in the Hindustani Social Club. He explained,

> in my early days in London, I used to be a Congressman because the Congress Party was the only platform for the Indian community. Mr Krishna Menon … was active on behalf of the India League, and we used to support him. In fact, myself and Ayub Ali were two of his favourite fellows. We used to preside over his meetings because he knew that we had a good following among the working class community, and with our support he could pass any resolution without difficulty … In the olden days, we used to be all supporters of Indian freedom, we never thought of Pakistan at that time …[5]

The East End branch of the India League used to meet in Ayub Ali's Shah Jolal Restaurant in Commercial Street. A contemporary police report recorded that its inaugural meeting in June 1943 was attended by around eighty people. These included leading figures from South Asia and three Europeans, but most were seamen or factory workers.[6] Besides its more obviously political role, the League organised educational classes run by students and other middle-class Indians.[7] Qureshi's description of his role in the India League demonstrates a patriarchal approach that bedevils Bengali politics. The full interview transcript makes it clear that, although he came from a relatively privileged background and by that time was owner of his own restaurant, he considered himself 'a humble working-class man'.[8] The extension of the term 'working class' to include small businessmen – the petty bourgeoisie in Marxist terms – is a common feature in accounts by Bengali immigrants who interacted with leftist groups.

Qureshi claimed to have known 'practically all' of the Indian leaders and to have had a good discussion with Subhas Chandra Bose (though he supported the war against Germany and Japan and did not support Bose's Indian National Army), but Nehru 'used to live with all the lords and ladies here' and 'we got very little chance to approach him in a friendly way'.[9] Not that he was without elite contacts himself, as 'all the Indian political workers and their associates, the English Gentlemen, MPs and all that, they used to come to my restaurant and hold meetings there'.[10] Restaurants were to continue to provide crucial meeting points for the different phases of Bengali politics.

Before the mid-1940s, in Qureshi's experience, 'nobody thought of Muslim League'.[11] The All-India Muslim League had been founded back in 1906 in Dhaka, and a branch had, in fact, opened in London two years later, but it had petered out with the death of its founder in 1928.[12] The League took on a new importance in 1940 when it passed the crucial Lahore Resolution demanding 'independent states' for Muslim majority areas, and a London branch was re-established in August 1945. The driving force behind this was Abbas Ali, who became its twenty-two-year-old president.

Abbas Ali, or Ali Mohammed Abbas as he became known, had arrived in London from Sirajganj District that January to study to be a barrister. His determination had led him to make the journey even while Britain was at war, but he soon forgot his promise to study 'under the pressure of the important political work which I conceived it my moral duty to shoulder'.[13] His dedication to social and political issues was a response to the poverty of his home village,[14] and in his passion for Pakistan he described himself as not so much a politician, but a 'missionary'.[15] His dedication to the cause kept him busy from dawn to late at night, 'my eyes firmly fixed on the map of India, always aiming at splitting the subcontinent into two'.[16] When he wasn't actively involved in the campaign he was away selling goods on market stalls to finance the political work and also to support his hand-to-mouth existence. (His family cut his allowance when he didn't pass his bar exams, and his flatmates, who had shared the rent, moved to somewhere quieter to study.) Campaign activity centred on Abbas's flat, which was damp and basic but centrally placed on Tavistock Square.[17] He gave it the grand title of Pakistan House, and it became a magnet for visiting political leaders and also a first port of call for Muslim students from the subcontinent. So as not to impede his standing he never described himself as a student, nor confessed to his other life as a market trader. Abbas later recalled that, initially, 'even most of my Muslim friends … regarded my aspiration as an idle dream'[18] and '[m]ost of the people whom we looked upon as future co-nationals spoke louder against the Pakistan ideal than the Hindu Congressites themselves'.[19] But, '[g]radually we converted most of the Indian Muslims to our way of thinking'.[20] Abbas and his 'little well-worn bag' of Muslim League enrolment forms became a familiar figure at public meetings held by the Indian National Congress and other Indian organisations.[21]

The League argued that Hindus and Muslims were irreconcilably different, and Muslims would not be safe in a Hindu-majority united India. This was a position that had emerged through long years of British divide and rule and the promotion of separate institutions for the two 'communities' in a kind of deeply conservative form of multiculturalism before multiculturalism was invented. This separatism suited the political aspirations of Muslim elites, and in further promoting it they exploited the hopes of Muslim peasants in hock to Hindu landlords and money lenders. Muslim separatism also cultivated, and flourished on, a strong emotional appeal by feeding into deep-rooted desires to live under Islamic law and revive the caliphate: ideas that are also hugely powerful today. Abbas's brother records that Abbas 'always believed that … Pakistan … was only a stepping stone towards achieving Muslim unity throughout the world'.[22]

The British section of the Muslim League kept itself deliberately independent from the organisation in India, and Abbas enjoyed the freedom that this gave them to state their own views. When Muhammad Ali Jinnah,[23] in an attempt to prevent the division of Punjab and Bengal,[24] initially accepted the 1946 Cabinet Mission Plan for a loosely federated three-part Indian Union, Abbas was insistent that nothing short of independence would do. He told Reuters that this was a 'betrayal of the Muslims of India' and the *Eastern Times* of Lahore reported on a resolution passed by the London Branch of the League after 'a heated discussion', which stated, 'the struggle now gains in intensity … The fight for Pakistan goes on'.[25]

As well as campaigning among their compatriots, the Muslim League sought to win over the British public through a mixture of talks – to social, political and religious organisations across the country – lobbying, engagement with the press and public demonstrations. In these situations it was important to show that the movement 'was not based solely on religion'.[26] In a letter to *The Times*, dated 24 April 1946, Abbas explained his position:

> The Hindus and Muslims, who, although they have lived together for a thousand years, could not be united, are fundamentally different from one another. They are two rival nations … Muslims are against the Hindu imperialism as the Indians as a whole are against foreign rule, and are determined 'to take control of their own affairs'.[27]

Figure 2.2 The Muslim League prepares to march to Downing Street and call on the Prime Minister, Clement Atlee, 1946. Ali Abbas, in the dark coat and hat, complained in his memoir: 'all we had from that quarter was his personal assurance that they would oppose any oppression of the Muslims by the Hindus'. (Sport and General Press Agency)

The League also organised and distributed its own monthly newsletter. *Pakistan News* was written in English and was aimed at both potential Pakistanis and the wider public.[28]

The League's demonstration in Trafalgar Square in March 1946 attracted a crowd of five thousand. Singing girls in saris contrasted with a banner proclaiming 'Pakistan or Muslim Revolt', and the League 'assured' their listeners 'point blank that the Muslims in India would wage a war against the British if they did not accede to our demand for division'.[29] Public interest grew with the growth of Muslim League activity in India, and Abbas – like campaigners before and after him – stressed the ability of propaganda in Britain to spread to the whole world.[30]

Qureshi claimed that he was wooed by Abbas because 'he found that we were very popular here, and mostly the Indian working-class people came under our organisation, we were leading them'. Abbas explained the League's arguments about the dangers of Hindu majority rule, but Qureshi's decision to join was aided by the reaction of his educated Hindu friends towards Jinnah. He described a discussion when, although still a member of Congress, he defended as plain truth that Jinnah was a leader of the Muslims, and one particularly large Hindu got ready to punch him, while the others did nothing to intervene. Summoning superhuman strength, and repeating, 'You have forgotten that I am the son of a Muslim', Qureshi stood up to his would-be assailant and 'it acted like a miracle'. 'Since that day', he recalled, 'I had a different belief'. With his conversion from secular nationalism to religious nationalism, he turned seriously to religion. This political shift was not good for business: 'all my customers boycotted me and in six months I had to close the place. I had to sell it at a nominal price.'[31]

The League found considerable backing among the men from East Bengal. Influential supporters included Qureshi's friend Ayub Ali – who had formed the Indian Seamen's Welfare League with Qureshi around 1943,[32] and whose house in Sandy's Row was the first stop for many a new immigrant – and Abdul Mannan, whose café in Percy Street and subsequent restaurant in the Brompton Road were popular Sylheti meeting places. When Jinnah came to London in December 1946, crowds met him at the airport with shouts of '*Pakistan Zindabad!*' – long live Pakistan.[33] Besides addressing a meeting in Kingsway Hall, he was entertained in a Punjabi café in Whitechapel's Backchurch Lane[34] and some of the Sylhetis went to talk with him at his room in the Dorchester.[35] By then Qureshi had gone back to India, where he used his political experience and connections to campaign first for the creation of Pakistan and then for the Sylhet district (which the British had administered as part of Assam and not Bengal) to choose to join Pakistan rather than India in a pre-partition referendum. The years of the freedom struggle and Second World War, culminating in the referendum and Partition, were important in politicising the people of Sylhet, including future immigrants to Britain.[36]

The Muslim League's separatist campaign seems to have encouraged Qureshi to turn towards an Islamic political outlook. He saw Pakistan as the first step towards the establishment of a 'real Islamic state' based on Islamic law[37] and he told Caroline Adams of his enthusiasm for the Bangladeshi Islamist group Dawatul Islam, established in 1978, whose belief in the inseparability of politics and religion is explored in Chapter 8.[38] However, most of those involved in the struggle for Pakistan did not travel so far down the Islamic political path (though this does not mean that they would have generally considered themselves irreligious). As this history shows, Abdul Mannan was to play an important part in the Bengali secular nationalist movement both before and during the Bangladesh War of Independence.

Pakistani politics in London

Following Pakistani independence in 1947, Bengali politics in Britain remained focused on what had become the eastern part of the new Muslim nation: then known as East Bengal and after 1954 as East Pakistan. Central to these politics was the East's fraught relationship with the West Pakistani-dominated government in Karachi and Islamabad.[39] Through the 1950s and 60s the rising tide of Pakistani politics caused ripples on the shores of the Thames. News of distant events was spread through Bengali language newspapers and by those who had taken part, especially students.

For this pioneering generation, political concerns involved the politics of their homeland alongside issues immediately relating to immigration. The two subjects were intimately connected, as Pakistani politics often impacted directly on the men in London. A crucial campaign was over the issuing of passports to enable further Bengalis to leave Pakistan. Between 1948 and 1962 there were no restrictions from the British side on the immigration of Commonwealth citizens, but the Pakistani authorities initially refused to issue passports to would-be immigrants from the eastern half of the country. The campaign for passports was co-ordinated in London by the newly formed (Bengali-run) Pakistan Welfare Association – to which it gave an enormous boost in membership – and in Pakistan by the trade union leader, Aftab Ali. When the Foreign Minister of Pakistan came to London in 1954, the meeting arranged to discuss this issue filled the Grand Palais Hall in Commercial Road, and the same year the issue was raised again at another – two thousand strong – meeting for the visit of the veteran Bengali politician, Huseyn Shaheed Suhrawardy.[40] Suhrawardy was appointed (briefly) as Pakistan's Law Minister soon after his return from London, but it was not until 1956, when he became Prime Minister of Pakistan, that the first thousand passports were granted to former seamen or their survivors or dependents.[41]

Pakistan's preferential exchange rate for foreign currency earned through business exports, but not for immigrant remittances, reflected divisions of status rather than the East–West divide. The National Federation of Pakistani Welfare Associations, formed in 1963, campaigned for equal rates and in 1964 the Pakistani government agreed to their demands.[42] This victory for Bengali organisation was not, however, without collateral damage. Before the change in policy, Tasadduk, who was one of the leading campaigners, had set up a private business, linked to *Desher Dak*, through which Bengalis could access the higher rates, and the paper became a victim of his campaigning success.[43]

Meanwhile, the behaviour of the High Commission's predominately West Pakistani staff reflected divisions of both region and status. The Bengalis vowed to bring an end to what was literally 'back door' treatment.[44] Anger was heightened by the High Commission's refusal to provide chairs for those they considered socially inferior, and Abdul Mannan recalled how this once led him to beat a particularly recalcitrant labour attaché.[45]

Of course not everyone was prepared to be openly critical. Abbas's missionary zeal led him to set up literacy classes for his uneducated compatriots in the hope that they would return to contribute to the new nation; and he established and ran a journal, *Our Home*, with the explicit aim of working with the Pakistani government, where he refused to publish the many letters received that were directed against the Pakistan High Commission.[46]

Close involvement with the politics of home was a characteristic shared with other post-colonial immigrants; however, relations with the representative high commissions varied greatly. Indian Workers' Association activists maintained close relations with the Indian High Commission, though this did not stop them protesting at the mass arrest of Indian communists in 1965. The West Indian Standing Conference was actually established on the initiative of the High Commission of the West Indian Federation.[47]

At the same time, increasingly tangible racism, manifested both in the street and in government policy, forced immigrant activists from all groups to address British politics. Bengalis joined other immigrant and labour movement activists in the campaign against the 1962 Commonwealth Immigration Act[48] and in the struggles against racist violence. In the mid-1960s, they worked with the Campaign Against Racial Discrimination (CARD), a multiethnic national umbrella group established in 1964 that sought relief through improvements in government legislation on 'race' and immigration, and focused on lobbying key figures and institutions. CARD's campaigns involved committed, generally middle-class, individuals rather than wider mobilisation, and the organisation fell apart after three years, riven by internal power struggles and disputes over the proper relationship with state organisations and the Labour Party. Martin Luther King's visit to London had provided a spur for CARD's creation, and Kalbir Shukra has compared its integrationist and legislative approach with that of the American Civil Rights Movement two decades earlier. After CARD's demise, the Pakistan Welfare Association maintained multiethnic links through affiliation to the newly established Joint Council for the Welfare of Immigrants.[49]

More politicised Bengalis also took part in the big political movements of the day, such as the Campaign for Nuclear Disarmament's Aldermaston marches[50] and international campaigns in support of struggles in Vietnam and Latin America or colonial freedom.[51] However, most political energy remained focused on Pakistan, and the increasing tensions between its East and West wings.

These tensions had been built into the structure of the newly created Muslim nation, whose two halves, separated by over a thousand miles of predominantly Hindu India, had little in common beyond their religion, and whose political and economic power was all concentrated in the West. For those with eyes to see, the problems were apparent at the outset. Sheikh Mannan – who would later play a prominent role in the Bangladesh independence movement in London, and had called out pro-Pakistan slogans with his brother as a school boy in 1940s Calcutta – told me how he underwent a rapid political awakening in post-Partition Dhaka. Towards the beginning of 1948, when only fourteen, he began to realise that Pakistan was a 'trap', and 'by the end of 1950 I had no doubts in my mind that we are a colony'. His family did not share this understanding, so, as he explained, 'very early in life, in 1950, I literally separated myself from my family'. He saw the subjugation of Bengali culture and language, and joined a 1949 demonstration for the official recognition of the Bengali language. And he saw Bengal's old Hindu elite being replaced by a new, predominantly West

Pakistani, Muslim one. In response, he allied himself with the 'have-nots' of both halves of Pakistan, arguing that 'we have got to liberate our country from the domination of this class'.[52] In developing his understanding the young Sheikh Mannan interacted with politically active students, including his family friend and near neighbour, Sheikh Mujibur Rahman, the future leader of independent Bangladesh.

Progressive politics and the Soviet Union

The political consciousness of men such as Tasadduk Ahmed and Sheikh Mannan – and also Sheikh Mujib – was not only a product of their local experiences. They and their fellow activists emerged through world-wide developments in secular socialist movements and ideas. In his survey of *Bengal Politics in Britain*, Faruque Ahmed observes that 'before 1970 most of the Bengali politicians in Britain came from the leftist student organisations'.[53] Socialism provided the focus for progressive emancipatory politics in Bengal as elsewhere, and arguments over the form that socialism should take were a constant feature of this politics. Through most of the twentieth century, wider progressive politics evolved in interaction with debates in the Soviet Union and the resulting swings in Communist Party policy. While debates within Soviet Communism may seem very distant from East Bengal or London, they impacted on the political thinking and tactical organisation of generations of activists across the world. Communists and fellow travellers were influenced directly, others through cross-fertilisation of ideas, or through the organisations and alliances that these debates promoted. A brief outline of this political background can help in the understanding of many of the developments described in this book, and these developments can themselves be seen as case studies of the significance of Soviet Communist influence.

   The fundamental issue at the core of the Communist Party debate was how and when communist internationalists could work with others who did not share their ideology. And central to this debate on tactics and strategy were arguments over the nature of the socialist revolutionary process. The difference between revolutionary success and failure was seen to depend on respecting tactical lines, so the placing of those lines became crucial and the subject of intense argument both at the time decisions were taken and in subsequent analysis. This summary can only attempt to sketch out the main shifts of position, however its purpose is not to re-examine the whole debate. It is here to provide a framework for a detailed empirical examination of some of the ideas in action, and to allow that examination to refer back to the wider tactical debates.

   Key to these debates is the argument over the need for 'permanent revolution', as opposed to the possibility of a revolution in stages, with a socialist revolution following on from a previous and separate bourgeois revolution. In the theory of 'permanent revolution' Trotsky argued that in order to achieve socialism, revolutionary workers could not rest once they had gained power and brought about democratic reform. In this view, if reactionary counter-revolutionary forces were not to be re-established, the workers' government would have to proceed immediately to socialist revolution – and that is what happened in 1917. However, for the socialist revolution to succeed, the theory required it to spread internationally. When this did not happen, the party under Stalin proclaimed the possibility of 'socialism in one country', and returned to the earlier idea of 'revolutionary stages theory'. Under revolutionary stages theory, those fighting for independence in colonial countries were regarded as allies working towards the first, bourgeois revolutionary stage.

The 'national question' was central to these debates. Lenin had argued that the communist ideal of different peoples united in a free union meant supporting 'the right of nations to self-determination' and opposing all forms of national oppression, but not actively encouraging nationalism. What this meant in practice had to be worked out in the light of actual circumstances, but Lenin insisted that the nationalist struggle must always be subordinate to the revolutionary struggle for socialism and he warned that, 'The bourgeoisie of the oppressed nations persistently utilise the slogans of national liberation to deceive workers'.[54]

Under Stalin, this warning was put aside and the Comintern instructed communists everywhere to subordinate their programme and strategy to that of the 'bourgeois nationalists'. However, following the catastrophic consequences of these policies in the Canton insurrection and Shanghai coup of 1927, when Chiang Kai-shek turned on the Chinese communists and murdered them in thousands, this strategy of collaboration was turned on its head. For the next five years, under the influence of the new policy that became known as 'class against class', the Comintern refused even to work alongside other socialists. After the dangers of this new position had been exposed by the fatal victory of the Nazis in Germany in 1933, it was abandoned in its turn in favour of another complete tactical reversal. Reverting right back to the ideas that had proved so disastrous in China, the party called for a 'popular front' of workers' parties and those of the 'progressive' bourgeois. Trotsky, who was highly critical of this position, drew a distinction between this 'popular front' and a 'united front', in which communists would remain ideologically and organisationally independent but work with others on particular issues, however, many people do not draw this linguistic distinction and the two terms tend to get used somewhat indiscriminately.

Although it was portrayed as a response to the immediate threat of fascism, popular frontism continued to be pursued after the Second World War and gained a permanent place in Soviet Communist theory. The post-war years also saw the general adoption of the idea that the second stage of revolution – the change from bourgeois democracy to socialism – could be achieved peacefully through a parliamentary road, without destroying the structural framework of the bourgeois state. Despite objections that these ideas could facilitate a revisionist backlash, the Soviet view became the new orthodoxy among communists and their sympathisers across the world. This view was especially influential on the way communists and other socialists involved themselves in the anti-imperial movements of the old colonial countries, including the struggles that brought about Indian and Pakistani independence and the later struggle that resulted in independent Bangladesh. These ideas underlie many of the relationships within and between the different political parties involved.

East Bengal and the politics of protest

At the centre of East Bengali protest politics was the Awami League, originally known, until the deliberate secularisation of its name in 1953, as the Awami Muslim League. The party was formed in Dhaka in 1949 by disillusioned members of the West Pakistan-dominated, and increasingly conservative, Muslim League. Its founders included the veteran peasant leader, Maulana Bhashani (former president of the Assam Provincial Muslim League), H.S. Suhrawardy and Sheikh Mujibur Rahman, who was then still a student (as well as Mujib's friend and neighbour, Sheikh Mannan). Their leftist programme – including land redistribution without compensation – had as its core demand the regional autonomy of the different states that made up Pakistan, in accordance with the Lahore Resolution of the All-India Muslim League of 1940.[55] Bhashani, who was made first president, could be described as combining within himself much of the idealism and many of the contradictions of Bengali radicalism. He had risen to prominence in peasant battles against oppressive Hindu *zamindars* (landlords) in the 1920s and through championing the cause of Bengali peasant immigrants to Assam, and had developed an overwhelming, but untheorised, class-consciousness that resonated with his egalitarian interpretation of Islam. As Talukder Maniruzzaman has explained:

> Bhashani ... argued that Islam enjoined everyone to the view that all properties belonged to God. He [had] firmly believed that when Pakistan was achieved all of the properties of landlords and other exploiters would be taken over by the state and distributed freely among poor peasants and workers.[56]

On the Marxist left, the East Pakistan Communist Party (EPCP) had been devastated by Partition (which the communists had opposed[57]) and the loss of most of its largely Hindu membership. In addition, the new nation of Pakistan, which had emerged out of Muslim nationalism, proved as hostile to the open propagation of Soviet Communist ideas as it was to the predominantly Hindu-origin communists who held them. However, communist activity continued behind the scenes. In the early 1950s, after an initial, disastrous attempt at fostering insurrection, the EPCP began to work through the Awami League and also through front organisations of their own creation – the Youth League and later the East Pakistan Students' Union – so spreading and consolidating their influence.

As in other revolutionary movements, students played a leading role in Bengali politics, and this was not just because the universities provided seedbeds for the growth of ideas and organisation. Institutional prejudices had a direct impact on graduate career prospects, and realisation of the personal effects of the political situation provided a powerful mobilising force, even if this might be subsequently superseded by wider, more ideological, concerns.

From the beginning, a vital demand and rallying cry of the Bengalis, and especially of politically active students, was for the recognition of Bengali as a state language alongside the Urdu of the ruling elite. Sheikh Mujib and other students were arrested in language movement protests as early as 1948. In 1952, when Pakistan's Prime Minister went back on earlier agreements with the students and declared Urdu the sole state language, mass student-led protests were met with live ammunition and baton charges from police and army. The dead included nineteen students, and 21 February – Martyrs' Day – has become an important date in the Bangladeshi calendar. Four of the twelve leaders of the 1952 Action Committee were members of the communist front organisation, the Youth League. Bhashani and the communist members of the Awami League were natural allies, and the absorption of more left ideas into the party programme included the advocacy of full political secularisation, a position that could be portrayed by their opponents as threatening the basis of Pakistan's existence.

For the East Bengal provincial election in March 1954, five parties opposed to the ruling Muslim League came together in what they called a 'United Front', which took all but nine of the 237 Muslim seats. The main components of this unstable coalition were the Awami League and Fazlul Huq's Peasants' and Workers' Party, but two religious parties formed junior partners.[58] Communists ran for election separately and also under the Awami League banner, where they were instrumental in promoting the formation of the Front.[59] The victory for pro-autonomy forces was short-lived, and at the end of May, Pakistan's central government used its power to dismiss East Bengal's provincial government.

The 'Red Maulana' at the Green Mask

A few days earlier, Maulana Bhashani had left Bengal to attend an international conference, and when the Pakistan government declared him an enemy of the state, he came, like many had before him, to London as an exile. There he joined Tasadduk Ahmed, who had gone into political exile a little earlier, in staying with Abdul Mannan. Tasadduk recalled to Caroline Adams that Abdul Mannan's house in Kensington and his Green Mask restaurant in the Brompton Road became central meeting places for 'all the political exiles of Pakistan', and that the house 'was the centre, in one sense, of opposition politics in Pakistan'. 'Over sixty' political leaders came to see Bhashani in the months that he stayed in London, including Sheikh Mujib, who stayed some time, and Suhrawardy (whose London

Figure 2.3 From left: Abdul Mannan, Aftab Ali and Maulana Bhashani

visit has been mentioned above). Bhashani's relations with Suhrawardy were already tense, as Suhrawardy had proved ready to make compromises with the Pakistan government, and Abdul Mannan spent two days persuading Bhashani to meet him at the airport and reach some sort of reconciliation.[60]

Despite his association with the left, Bhashani appears to have established no legacy of specifically left politics in London, except perhaps in the person of Tasadduk who had worked with him back in East Bengal. The 'Red Maulana' was undoubtedly a charismatic leader, and, as Faruque Ahmed put it, 'his talks sowed the seeds of Bengali nationalism among the expatriate Bengalis';[61] but beyond his appeal for justice for the Bengalis, he conveyed no clear ideological message. A glimpse into the way Bhanshani could affect a largely illiterate audience was given by Thaid Ullah, who had served in the British merchant navy in the Second World War. Ullah described to Yousuf Choudhury how he heard Bhashani at a meeting at the Green Mask, where the seamen's leader Aftab Ali was talking about the passport issue:

> After an all night meeting Moulana Bhashani led a mass prayer. In the prayer he cried and said to Allah ... 'Our brothers suffered in the war, many were killed in the seas like fish. Now the position of those that survived and are still alive, and of the sons and brothers of those who are dead, is miserable. You help to overcome their diffi-culties' ... I still remember every word of that prayer, quite a few of us, including myself, were in tears.[62]

What moved Ullah was not Bhashani's socialism, but his religious leadership.

Abdul Mannan, Bhashani's host and already a community activist, became committed to the Awami League, remaining with it even after it split with Bhashani and the left faction. He would go to Dhaka to take an active part in Pakistani politics in 1967, and then again to Bangladesh after Independence, when Sheikh Mujib himself persuaded him to stand for the legislative assembly and he spent three years in parliament.[63]

Tensions in East Bengal – the late 1950s and 60s

In the autumn of 1956, Awami-League-led coalitions took over both the provincial (East Pakistan) and central governments, and Suhrawardy, the party's national convenor, became Prime Minister of Pakistan. Political power brought differences within the party to a head. Suhrawardy rejected the League's manifesto demand for full East Pakistani autonomy, but the issue that finally split the party was over foreign policy. Bhashani failed to persuade the majority to condemn Pakistan's mutual defence agreement with the United States in favour of a non-aligned position and in the summer of 1957, together with nine other leftist members of the Executive Committee, he resigned from the party. Bhashani and other Bengali leftists joined an already existing group of West Pakistani regional and left leaders to form the National Awami Party, or NAP (pronounced 'nap'). Under Bhashani's presidency, NAP campaigned on a platform that brought together anti-imperialism, anti-feudalism and the right of Pakistan's linguistic groups to self-determination. Communists worked within NAP and at the same time continued their broader campaigning through two front organisations: one working with the peasants and the other with trade unionists.

An unedifying year of riotous politics and varied alliances was brought to an end when General Ayub Khan imposed martial law throughout Pakistan in October 1958. Opposition leaders were imprisoned, and political parties were banned until 1962, when Ayub instituted a constitutional dictatorship. The burden of protest fell on the students – the Awami-League-affiliated Students' League and the NAP-affiliated Students' Union.

Student activists in London

Reaction to Ayub Khan among the London Bengalis was also student dominated and was co-ordinated by the group around Tasadduk Ahmed – a man of almost as many contradictions as his mentor Bhashani. Tasadduk was a university-educated landowner's 'son, and a former leader of the Assam Muslim Students Federation and Muslim League organiser in the Sylhet partition referendum,[64] who had become a passionate communist when he saw how West Pakistani elites were 'using Islam for advancing their own class interest'.[65] He retained an aristocratic mien, ran a successful restaurant, championed small businesses, and was later honoured by being made an MBE – a Member of the British Empire he had so derided.[66] He was endowed with endless energy and ideas and Ken Leech recalled at his funeral that whenever he met Tasadduk 'he wouldn't necessarily say "Good morning" or "Nice to see you", he would rather say "Now the next thing is – "'.[67]

Tasadduk's organising energy placed him at the centre of a small intellectual elite that played a crucial role in the development of London Bengali politics. It was largely made up of students and also young professionals who had learnt their own politics in the persecuted left and nationalist movements of their native Bengal. Often, their parents or other relatives had been involved in the struggle against the British, and they had grown up with the background of Independence and Partition. Their sincere commitment to radical change, though heavily influenced by Marxist ideas, reflected their roots as members of rural landowning families, operating according to traditional patriarchal networks. Class analysis was generally less important to them than a sense of fairness that can be seen as a natural extension of patriarchal and religious duty, and which combined easily with popular-front politics.

One of these students was Nurul Islam, who played a prominent role in Bengali politics in Britain in the late 1950s and 60s and has since written a history of the immigration.[68] He came to London in 1956 after graduating from Dhaka University and taking active part in the Language movement in Dhaka and Sylhet. In London, he got a job as a railway clerk to support himself while he trained to be a barrister in Lincoln's Inn. He remembers going to meetings of around fifteen young students in a house in north London, where Tasadduk would tell them, 'it's no good going for capitalism, and what's the good of becoming this barrister and solicitors, and you want to exploit people? ... rather educate yourself, read Marx, Engels, Rousseau, Voltaire, Mazzini, go for Tolstoy and *War and Peace*'.[69] Sheikh Mannan explained to me that Tasadduk's discussions brought together all shades of left opinion. By the time Mannan came to London they met in the restaurant, 'And he was generous, his wife was more generous, and he never let us come without a meal'.[70] (Tasadduk had met his German wife, Rosemary, at a peace conference in Warsaw.)

Nurul Islam described how the imposition of martial law in Pakistan gave the students in London a new political importance, as they took it upon themselves to publicise information brought by their compatriots who had recently travelled from East Pakistan:

> We said, we are free, nobody can do anything to us here, it is our responsibility to shout, to tell the people of the world, to create public opinion, international opinion, what is happening in Pakistan; because Ayub Khan and the martial law people chucked out all the journalist.[71]

London-based activists formed a Committee for the Restoration of Democracy

Figure 2.4 Tasadduk Ahmed (centre right) with, from left, Fakruddin Ahmed, Nurul Islam and Bengali politician, Ataur Rahman Khan, Aldgate, 1970s (Yousuf Choudhury)

in Pakistan. They publicised their cause through meetings with speakers from both halves of Pakistan, which were attended by large numbers of East End Bengalis. As Tasadduk explained to Caroline Adams, care was taken to keep official welfare and student organisations out of politics, but when these organisations did not send the expected support to the new regime, the High Commissioner received a reprimand from Karachi;[72] and Faruque Ahmed records that in 1962 *Desher Dak* 'claimed that the Pakistani government accused the Caterers' Association of funding [an] anti-government student movement in London'.[73]

That year – 1962 – continuing political activity resulted in the creation of two new organisations in London, the Bangla Academy and Purbashuri (Pioneers), that focussed specifically on the problems faced by East Pakistan (and also of a reactionary student organisation, the Pakistan Youth Federation, founded by supporters of the Pakistani government). The Bangla Academy concentrated on the promotion of Bengali culture, but it did not shy away from more overt politics. One of their early performances raised the issue of Bengali Independence, and a play staged in 1966 put the case for armed revolution.[74] Purbashuri was a political organisation founded to campaign for Bengali liberation. Its prime instigator was Zakaria Khan Chowdhury, who had come to London in 1957 to train, like Nurul Islam, as a barrister in Lincoln's Inn. He had intended to keep his head down until he had qualified, but 'could not remain silent when all those heart-rending things were happening in Pakistan'.[75] He played a key role in establishing the Committee for the Restoration of Democracy in Pakistan, and wrote the script of the early Bangla Academy performance mentioned above. In his account of the birth of Purbashuri he described how, after several meetings and many arguments, they agreed to follow revolutionary stages theory:

> Those were long meetings, starting at 10 am and continuing up to 8 [or] 9pm. Diane, my English girlfriend (whom I married in 1966), entertained us with food and tea. I did not want independence without changing the socio-political structure of the country. My argument was only a change in geography and national flag would not ensure our people a bright future. With the independence the socio-economic structure of the country also must change ... Finally, we decided to divide our struggle into two phases. In the first phase we would struggle for independence, and once we were liberated, we would determine what the socio-economic structure would be in the future.[76]

One of Purbashuri's first actions was the production of a small book that they distributed to influential figures in the media and in the British and US governments. 'Unhappy East Pakistan' described itself as '[a] survey of inter-regional economic inequality in Pakistan, showing the methods through which the resources of East Pakistan are being transferred to West Pakistan.' It concluded that, since structural change was unlikely, the only foreseeable economic future for the East was as a 'virtual colony of West Pakistan'; and it ended with the question, 'Is this then to be the destiny of East Pakistan?'[77]

Suhrawardy came to London in the summer of 1963 in the hope of recovering his health after seven months imprisonment, and, for three weeks in August, Mujib was also in London, staying with Abdul Mannan. Both had talks with London-based student activists.

Mujib's former neighbour, Sheikh Mannan, came to Britain as a student in 1964 after graduating from Dhaka University. Financial pressures forced him to withdraw from studying law, but he found part-time work and began a course in journalism. He became an active member and later president of the Pakistan Democratic Front, a left-wing organisation of around two hundred students – almost all Bengali, but including a few from West Pakistan.[78]

Students, workers and businessmen

Bengali students in London found an immediately practical outlet for their social consciences in the East End and in the Pakistan Welfare Association, and Nurul Islam recalls that he used to give the Association part of his weekly wage packet. Tasadduk had been responsible for putting the fledgling Welfare Association on a firm footing when he became office secretary in 1953, shortly after his arrival in England, and he was also pivotal in founding the Bengali-dominated National

Federation of Pakistani Associations ten years later. Welfare work is the staple of immigrant organisation, and Tasadduk saw his work for the Welfare Association as a way of raising people's political consciousness. He was, in his own words, and in line with his Communist Party training in popular-front politics, using 'non-political organisations for political ends', whilst 'keeping my own belief to myself and to my close associates'.[79] He told the Association:

> Whether I go to Moscow, whether I go to Peking is none of your problem. So long as I am not using the platform of the Welfare Association for the political purpose, that is the main thing. And if you accept me, you have to accept me on that term.

And, when some people complained that they did not want communists organising the Muslim burial society, others responded, 'they may be communist, but they look after our money better'.[80] (Comparisons can be drawn with Indian Workers' Associations, which were similarly dominated by educated activists with links to South Asian left parties.[81])

In this way, Tasadduk and others were able to mobilise large numbers of people over major issues of concern to the community: it was the welfare associations that co-ordinated the campaign for passports and represented the Bengalis within CARD. However, the activists' socialism remained too deeply submerged in the other activities to make a lasting impact.

Another regular participant in Tasadduk's discussion groups was Shah Lutfur Rahman, who came to the London School of Economics as a law student in the late 1950s, having been involved in 'bits and pieces' of politics in Dhaka.[82] He began his life-long involvement with the East End Bengalis after being introduced to the community by 'a young Irish lady' who offered to show him 'what South Asia is' following a political discussion in the student common room.[83] In 1959 Shah took his turn as office secretary for the Welfare Association, where he would spend Sunday mornings helping his illiterate compatriots write letters home and fill in official forms; he, too, kept overt politics and welfare work separate so as not to be accused of ulterior motives.

Middle-class activism and welfare work are characteristic of this period of immigrant politics more generally,[84] but the nature of the Bengalis' political fight inspired a wider mobilisation. In Shah's view, the politically conscious students acted as 'catalysts' in bringing about the mobilisation of other Bengalis. He commented:

> The politicisation of the Bengalis … didn't happen due to the East End of London per se, it happened because some students and intelligentsia from the Bengali community, who were in various universities, started taking interest in the Bengali community in the East End of London, particularly in relationship to the movement against exploitation [by] Pakistan.[85]

The students brought a wider political analysis and administrative and professional skills, and had time that was not available to most of the hard-working immigrants. The growing force behind this mobilisation was provided by the dramatic events taking place in their Bengali homeland; the students and other activists were able to give this force direction.

However, while there was a receptiveness to the political demands that were increasingly made of the community, the level of political understanding was generally low. The Bengalis' rural roots had given them little experience of political analysis, and many of them were poorly educated or even illiterate. Nurul Islam has suggested that attendance at public meetings was partly due to the lack of other forms of recreation, and he acknowledged that even in the late 1960s 'there was hardly anything like communist or socialist education among the ordinary people'.[86] Although some restaurant owners such as Abdul Mannan came to Tassaduk's discussion groups, Shah held no illusions about the majority of his fellow Bengalis. He found that they often had to work 'from 6 o'clock in the morning until 11 o'clock at night' (like many immigrants) and 'their horizon of life was extremely limited'.[87] His social work was politically 'unproductive' until the arrival of a new generation of young men and boys in the mid-1960s, though it was some years before there was a significant number of young people.

Nurul Islam regarded the older, more established immigrant restaurant owners as the students' 'patrons', who, remembering earlier political campaigns, financed their politics, paying for such necessary expenses as printing and hiring meeting halls. Certainly the heightened political activity of this period produced, in East Pakistan House, a powerful and concrete example of a symbiotic relationship between the students and the growing Bengali business class. This large terraced house in Highbury in North London was bought in 1964 to combine the functions of student hostel and centre for Bengali political activity. The initial inspiration had come from the students and activists, but the house was largely financed and managed by the restaurant owners. Shah recalled that despite being ultimately generous, they were (unsurprisingly) initially cautious.[88]

Although by the late 60s there were contests over control of East Pakistan House,[89] its first two years saw it become an important focus of organisation with the production of a newspaper, *Purbo Bangla* (East Bengal). This publicised the situation in East Pakistan and put the case for autonomy, including serialising 'Unhappy East Pakistan'.[90] However many of the Bengalis were not yet ready for such views. Shah recounted that

> Lots of people didn't like it, they used to think we are fifth columnists, we are communists … lots of people opposed us, saying we are for the disintegration of Pakistan … Pakistan was a genuine aspiration of the Muslim of India.[91]

Mesbah Uddin was East Pakistan House's first student resident and was actively involved in the paper's production. When he went to sell *Purbo Bangla* in the East End he got beaten up.[92] In the other main centre of Bengali immigration, Birmingham, activists formed the East Pakistan Liberation Front (EPLF), which in November 1970 called for revolution against 'capitalist exploitation and colonial domination'.[93]

But the activists' radicalism was not limited to propagating ideas and rhetoric, and Faruque Ahmed gives a tantalising glimpse of activities that, had they known about them, might have seriously alarmed their more cautious sponsors. Zakaria Khan Chowdhury recorded that, alongside pushing activist candidates onto the boards of established Pakistani organisations,

> [o]ne of the objectives [in establishing East Pakistan House] was to recruit potential cadres to fight for independence. We believed we had to win the war of independence through guerrilla warfare in our country … At that time reading Mao Tse Tung and Che Guevara was compulsory for us. We also contacted some countries to train us in guerrilla fighting.[94]

One country that offered guerrilla training was Cuba, although it is unclear how much actually took place.[95]

Divisions in the left

Through the 1960s, the left everywhere became increasingly fractured, reflecting events in Peking and Moscow. The idea of 'socialism in one country' had legitimated a new nationalism and competition between the bureaucracies of the two Stalinist countries, leading to the Sino-Soviet split in 1964. This found echoes among the Pakistani communists as it did in communist parties throughout the world. The East Pakistan Communist Party (Marxist Leninist) finally split away in 1966 (and later itself divided further) and NAP followed the Communist Party lead, with Bhashani heading the pro-Chinese faction. The different tactical analyses of the two factions led them in very different directions. The pro-Moscow leaders adopted Stalinist stages theory, arguing that before there could be a communist revolution there had to be a bourgeois democratic one, and that to achieve this they had to work in a broad popular front with the bourgeois parties. Unlike the Maoists they argued for the possibility of the parliamentary road to socialism. Sheikh Mannan, who followed the line of the pro-Moscow section of a divided NAP, claimed that the majority of the students shared his pro-Moscow sympathies;[96] Shah followed a pro-Peking faction of the Communist Party, and Nurul Islam remained loyal to the Awami League.

Mass unrest

The short war in 1965 between Pakistan and India strengthened opposition to Ayub Khan. In West Pakistan it gave birth to a new opposition party, the Pakistan People's Party, led by Ayub's former Foreign Minister, Zulfikar Ali Bhutto. In the East, the war was taken as further evidence of the Bengalis' inferior treatment, as, with Pakistani forces concentrated in Kashmir, they had been left relatively undefended. East Pakistan's increasing resistance to Ayub's rule centred on the nationalist Awami League. Surhawardy had died of a heart attack at the end of 1963, and the party was now led by Sheikh Mujib. In 1966, Mujib announced his Six Point Programme for full East Pakistani autonomy, and this became the focus of a mass movement. Agitation was widespread, prompting a government clampdown, and the arrest of Mujib and other leaders. In what became known as the Agartala Conspiracy Case, after the Indian border town where the plan was supposed to have been made, they were charged with conspiring to bring about the secession of East Pakistan with Indian help. In East Pakistan, the students again took up the baton. None of the opposition groups could afford to stand idle while the government attacked the most prominent opposition leader. Together the Awami League-affiliated Students' League and the NAP-affiliated Students' Union formed an All Party Action Committee and, in January 1969, drew up an Eleven Point Programme that combined the demands for autonomy with more socialist and anti-imperialist demands. This provided the basis for massive widespread popular unrest. Bhashani, now adopting a united-front position, led protests for Mujib's release.

Demonstrations in London attracted thousands of Bengalis – including a phalanx of women from among the educated middle class who led a torchlight procession from Hyde Park to the Pakistan High Commission, pushing their children in prams. Activists managed to force their way into the High Commission and set fire to a portrait of Ayub Khan; and when Khan himself came to London, protestors surrounded his hotel so that he had to escape by a back entrance.[97] The activists and restaurateurs around East Pakistan House organised a committee, chaired by Abdul Mannan, and raised political consciousness and sufficient money from the Bengali business community to send Sir Thomas Williams QC to Pakistan to contribute to Mujib's defence team.

In February 1969, faced with mass unrest and protest against what was clearly a political trial, Ayub dropped the charges and released Mujib to a hero's welcome of more than half a million people. And when Mujib visited London that October the crowd that greeted him cried with emotion.[98]

Before that, in March, Ayub – who was also facing mass unrest in West Pakistan, led by Zulfiqar Ali Bhutto – resigned and handed control to his army chief, General Yahya Khan. Yahya promised Pakistan its first national general election, which would be held in 1970 and which became the catalyst for all-out war. The campaigns around that final battle for independence form the subject of the next chapter.

Notes

1   The Bangla Media Directory for 2013 lists eleven Bengali newspapers, three English language newspapers, three magazines, six television channels and a local radio station, all based in East London.

2   *The Asian*, an English-language journal established in 1978 with Tasadduk Ahmed as managing editor, commented in its first issue, 'The two most popular Bengali journals in the U.K. are Janomot [People's Opinion] and Jagaran [Awakening]…The vast majority of news items in these papers concern developments in Bangladesh, whether political, social or economic; and matters of public interest in the U.K. are rarely given the coverage they deserve' (May 1978, p. 8). More recently, Faruque Ahmed, who has made a study of Bengali papers, commented 'Bengali newspapers and digital media too are seen to mostly occupy themselves with Bengali politics.' See Faruque Ahmed, *Bengal Politics in Britain: Logic, Dynamics and Disharmony* (North Carolina: Lulu, 2010), p. 16.

3   Qureshi's restaurant was bought from a Calcutta Hindu.

4   Qureshi, interviewed by Caroline Adams, 1980s, manuscript transcript, p. 18 (Tower Hamlets Local History Library).

5   *Ibid.*, p. 14.

6   Quoted in 'Shah Jolal Restaurant', Making Britain Database, www.open.ac.uk/researchprojects/makingbritain/content/shah-jolal-restaurant, accessed 20 November 2012. The League was 'largely elite and predominantly British', but they hoped to attract more working-class members through the East End branch: see 'India League', Making Britain Database, www.open.ac.uk/research-projects/makingbritain/content/india-league, accessed 16 November 2013.

7   Rozina Visram, *Asians in Britain: 400 Years of History* (London: Pluto Press, 2002), p 297.

8   Qureshi, interviewed by Caroline Adams, 1980s, manuscript transcript, p. 29.

9   *Ibid.*, p. 14.

10   *Ibid.*, p. 16.

11   *Ibid.*, p. 16.

12   Ahmed, *Bengal Politics in Britain*, pp. 35–6.

13   Ali Mohammed Abbas, autobiographical memoir (manuscript, n.d., shown to the author by his brother, Ali Mohammed Azhar), p. 25.

14   *Ibid.*, p. 158.

15   As recalled by his brother, see Ali Mohammed Azhar, 'Introduction' to Ali Mohammed Abbas, autobiographical memoir (manuscript, n.d.), p. 24.

16   Abbas, autobiographical memoir, p. 29.

17   33 Tavistock Square is now marked with a plaque, erected by Camden Borough Council, that reads, 'Ali Mohammed Abbas 1922–1979 barrister and one of the founders of Pakistan lived here 1945–1979'.

18   Abbas, autobiographical memoir, p. 23.

19   *Ibid.*, p. 30.

20   *Ibid.*, p. 30.

21   *Ibid.*, p. 30.

22   Azhar, 'Introduction', p. 30.

23   Jinnah was leader of the All-India Muslim League and became the first Governor General of Pakistan.

24   P. Hardy, *The Muslims of British India* (Cambridge: Cambridge University Press, 1972), pp. 248–9.

25   Quoted in Kathleen Hunter, *History of Pakistanis in Britain* (privately published, 1962), p. 103. Kathleen Hunter was Abbas's wife.

26   Abbas, autobiographical memoir, p. 33.

27   Quoted in Hunter, *History of Pakistanis in Britain*, p. 98.

28   Abbas, autobiographical memoir, pp. 38 and 92. The paper was started in November 1946.

29 *Ibid.*, p. 37.
30 Qureshi, interviewed by Caroline Adams, 1980s, manuscript transcript, p. 16.
31 *Ibid.*, pp. 16 and 18; letter from Qureshi to Adams, dated 16 July 1983; Ahmed, *Bengal Politics in Britain*, pp. 36–9. Abbas's account, quoted by Ahmed, gives Saidur Rahman as the League's first secretary.
32 The Welfare League was ostensibly 'social rather than political', but many members felt that the welfare of Indian seamen could not be separated from politics: see 'Indian Seamen's Welfare League', Making Britain Database, http://www.open.ac.uk/researchprojects/makingbritain/content/indian-seamens-welfare-league, accessed 16 November 2013.
33 Hunter, *History of Pakistanis in Britain*, p. 105.
34 Nawab Ali, interviewed by Caroline Adams, 1980s, manuscript transcript, p. 12 (Tower Hamlets Local History Library).
35 Nurul Islam, *Probashir Kotha* [The Tale of the Emmigrants] (Sylhet: Probashi Publications, 1989), p. 933.
36 The importance of the referendum to the politicisation of Sylhet was stressed by Aziz Choudhury, interviewed February 2001.
37 Qureshi, interviewed by Caroline Adams, 1980s, manuscript transcript, p. 25.
38 *Ibid.*, p. 13.
39 The Pakistani capital moved to Islamabad in 1960.
40 Suhrawardy, a leader of the opposition Awami League, had been at the centre of Bengali politics since the 1920s. He was the last prime minister of the undivided province of Bengal under the British, and a former trade unionist colleague of Aftab Ali.
41 See Caroline Adams, *Across Seven Seas and Thirteen Rivers* (London: THAP Books, 1994), pp. 58 and 62; Caroline Adams, 'The Bangladesh Welfare Association in Great Britain' (manuscript, 1982), pp. 2–3 (Tower Hamlets Local History Library); Ahmed, *Bengal Politics in Britain*, p. 50 .
42 Mohammad Ali Asghar, *Bangladeshi Community Organisations in East London* (London: Bangla Heritage Ltd, 1996), pp. 24–5 and 127; interview with Nurul Islam, 12 June 2001.
43 Faruque Ahmed, *Bengali Journals and Journalism in the UK (1916–2007)* (London: The Ethnic Minorities Original History and Research Centre, 2008), pp. 24–5.
44 See interview with Nesar Ali by Caroline Adams, 1980s, manuscript transcript (Tower Hamlets Local History Library).
45 Abdul Mannan, interviewed by Caroline Adams, 1980s, tape recording (Tower Hamlets Local History Library).
46 Abbas, autobiographical memoir, pp. 94–3. Abbas agreed to give the High Commissioner advanced warning of any 'grievances' that might appear in the paper. Qureshi was elected as the General Manager and Secretary of the *Our Home* Advisory Board. Abbas also ran journals in Urdu and Bengali. Kathleen Hunter records that the Bengali journal was produced in a duplicated version in 1950 and in a printed form from 1958. See Hunter, *History of Pakistanis in Britain*, p. 109.
47 See Kalbir Shukra, *The Changing Pattern of Black Politics in Britain* (London: Pluto Press, 1998), pp. 10–16.
48 Abdul Mannan remembered meeting Gaitskell, see interview with Caroline Adams, 1980s, tape recording (Tower Hamlets Local History Library).
49 Ahmed, *Bengal Politics in Britain*, p. 100; Shukra, *The Changing Pattern of Black Politics in Britain*, pp. 19–26; Asghar, *Bangladeshi Community Organisations in East London*, p. 129. Birmingham Bengalis had previously been involved in a local multiethnic organisation, the Coordination Committee Against Racial Discrimination. CCARD

was set up in 1961 and counted the Pakistani Workers Association among its sponsors. See Shukra, *The Changing Pattern of Black Politics in Britain*, p. 17.

50 Interview with Nurul Islam, 12 June 2001.
51 Interviews with Sheikh Mannan, 30 March 2002 and Abul Ishaque, 11 December 2001.
52 Interviewed 30 March 2002.
53 Ahmed, *Bengal Politics in Britain*, p. 128.
54 V.I. Lenin, *Collected Works,* Vol. 22 (Moscow: Progress Publishers, 1964), pp. 143–56.
55 The resolution stated that 'the areas in which Muslims are numerically in a majority, as in the north-western and eastern zones of India, should be grouped to constitute "independent states" in which the constituent units shall be autonomous and sovereign', *Encyclopaedia Britannica* (Fifteenth Edition,1989), vol. 21, p. 105.
56 Talukder Maniruzzaman, 'Radical Politics and the Emergence of Bangladesh', in Paul R. Brass and Marcus F. Franda (eds), *Radical Politics in South Asia* (Cambridge, Mass.: MIT, 1973), p. 231. Much of the following history of the radical movements in East Pakistan is abstracted from this chapter. .
57 The party's popular-front orientation had persuaded it to work with the bourgeois nationalists and try to unite the left of the Muslim League and the Congress. See Jamil Iqbal, 'Indian independence (part 3) – Role of the Communist Party of India during Partition' (2007), www.marxist.com/indian-independence-role-communist-party.htm, accessed 16 November 2013.
58 Tahir Kamran, 'Early Phase of Electoral Politics in Pakistan: 1950s', *South Asian Studies,* 24:2 (2009), 257–82, p. 276.
59 Maniruzzaman, 'Radical Politics and the Emergence of Bangladesh', p. 232.
60 See Caroline Adams' notes on her interview with Tasadduk Ahmed (Tower Hamlets Local History Library); Abdul Mannan and Tasadduk Ahmed, interviewed by Caroline Adams, 1980s, tape recording (Tower Hamlets Local History Library); Adams, *Across Seven Seas and Thirteen Rivers*, p. 57.
61 Ahmed, *Bengal Politics in Britain*, p. 49.
62 Quoted in Yousuf Choudhury, *The Roots and Tales of the Bangladeshi Settlers* (Birmingham: Sylhet Local History Group, 1993), p. 92.
63 See Abdul Mannan and Tasadduk Ahmed, interviewed by Caroline Adams, 1980s, tape recording (Tower Hamlets Local History Library).
64 Ashfaque Hossain, 'Historical Globalization and its Effects: A Study of Sylhet and its People, 1874–1971' (PhD dissertation, University of Nottingham, 2009), p. 267, note 141.
65 Conversation with Tasadduk recalled by William Taylor in his autobiographical account, *This Bright Field: A Travel Book in One Place* (London: Methuen, 2000), p. 271. Taylor also recorded (pp. 270–1) that Tasadduk told him that his first conscious act of resistance to exploitation occurred when, as a child, he threw his father's 'thrashing stick' into the pond so that he would not be able to punish a servant girl his mother was angry with.
66 Besides his journalism and production of journals for the immigrant community, his campaigning, and his work with Pakistani Welfare Associations across Britain, Tasadduk was secretary of the Pakistan Caterers' Association in the 1960s, and Chairman of the Spitalfields Small Business Association from its inception in 1979 until his stroke in 1998. He was given an MBE for his community work in 1989.
67 Rev. Kenneth Leech, interviewed 9 March 2006 by Jamil Iqbal, Ansar Ahmed Ullah and Charlie Sen for Swadhinata Trust and the University of Surrey Centre for Research on Nationalism, Ethnicity and Multiculturalism, 'Oral History Project' (2005–06).

68 Islam, *Probashir Kotha*. Nurul Islam played a prominent role in British Pakistani organisations in the 1960s before returning to East Pakistan for family reasons in 1966 and being detained there by the Pakistan government. When I interviewed him in 2001, he was running the Bangladesh Overseas Centre in Sylhet.

69 Interviewed 12 June 2001.

70 Sheikh Mannan, interviewed 30 March 2002.

71 Interviewed 12 June 2001.

72 Abdul Mannan and Tasadduk Ahmed, interviewed by Caroline Adams, 1980s, tape recording (Tower Hamlets Local History Library).

73 Ahmed, *Bengal Politics in Britain*, p. 74.

74 *Ibid.*, pp. 76–8.

75 Zakaria Khan Chowdhury (2004), quoted in *ibid.*, p. 72.

76 Zakaria Khan Chowdhury quoted in *ibid.*, p. 79.

77 *Purbashuri* (drafted by Kabiruddin Ahmed), 'Unhappy East Pakistan' (n.d.), p. 20. (There is a copy in LSE Library.)

78 Sheikh Mannan, interviewed 30 March 2002.

79 Abdul Mannan and Tasadduk Ahmed, interviewed by Caroline Adams, 1980s, tape recording (Tower Hamlets Local History Library) .

80 *Ibid.*

81 Shukra, *The Changing Pattern of Black Politics in Britain*, pp. 15–16.

82 Shah Lutfur Rahman, interviewed 22 August 2001.

83 Shah Lutfur Rahman, interviewed 18 August 2000.

84 Shukra, *The Changing Pattern of Black Politics in Britain*, p. 10.

85 Shah Lutfur Rahman, interviewed 18 August 2000.

86 Nurul Islam, interviewed 12 June 2001.

87 Shah Lutfur Rahman, interviewed 22 August 2001.

88 *Ibid.*

89 Ahmed, *Bengal Politics in Britain*, p. 96.

90 Ahmed, *Bengali Journals and Journalism in the UK*, p. 33.

91 Shah Lutfur Rahman, interviewed 22 August 2001.

92 Ahmed, *Bengal Politics in Britain*, p. 95 .

93 EPLF leaflet, reproduced in full in *ibid.*, p. 99.

94 Quoted in Ahmed, *Bengal Politics in Britain*, p. 83.

95 *Ibid.*, p. 98. Ahmed quotes conflicting reminiscences.

96 Sheikh Mannan, interviewed 30 March 2002.

97 Ahmed, *Bengal Politics in Britain*, pp. 103–6; Nora Shariff, interviewed 16 February 2006 by Jamil Iqbal for Swadhinata Trust and University of Surrey, 'Oral History Project'.

98 Ahmed, *Bengal Politics in Britain*, p. 110.

3   *Joi Bangla!*[1] – 1971

In 1971, the battle for Bangladeshi independence galvanised the *probashi* (emigrant) Bengali community and left it not only with a new relationship to its homeland, but a new political awareness overall. The trigger was the election in Pakistan.

Pakistanis went to the polls on 7 December 1970, but before the elections finally took place, East Pakistan was hit by a cyclone and tidal wave that left three hundred thousand dead.[2] The inaction of the West Pakistan-based authorities in the face of this calamity drove a further wedge between them and the Bengalis. In Britain, collections were made for emergency relief and organising committees sprang up in the different centres of Bengali immigration. Donations were raised by the National Federation of Pakistani Associations and by the East London Mosque:[3] Peter Shore – MP for Stepney – and the Warden of Toynbee Hall helped promote and co-ordinate collection of emergency relief, students organised meetings and everyone gave money or clothes or what they could, as though in preparation for the mass mobilisation around the independence struggle.

The Awami League provided a focus for Bengali election hopes with a programme that included East Pakistani autonomy, incorporating both Mujib's Six Points and the more socialist Eleven Points. The mobilisation around the Agartala Conspiracy Case, and Mujib's subsequent visit to the UK, had strengthened the association in people's minds between Bengali liberation and the Awami League and encouraged support for the party amongst the Bengali immigrants. A UK branch of the League was formed in early 1970, which raised fighting funds for the election and personally delivered a twelve-seater mini-bus for use in the campaign.[4] Other Bengali opposition groups boycotted the elections or were politically marginal. Bhashani and much of his pro-China NAP declared a boycott at the last minute, arguing that elections should not be held when people were still starving after the cyclone. The Awami League won 160 of East Pakistan's 162 directly elected seats, and since seats were allocated in proportion to population and East Pakistanis outnumbered West, this gave them an overall majority in the National Assembly.[5] Neither Yahya Khan nor Zulfikar Ali Bhutto, whose Pakistan Peoples' Party (PPP) won eighty-one directly elected seats, would accept an Awami League government and its consequences. A period of stalled negotiations was followed by Bhutto's declaration that the PPP would boycott the National Assembly session previously agreed for the third of March; and on the first, Yahya announced that the assembly would be postponed indefinitely. In East Pakistan people poured into the streets. Radical student leaders called for independence. Mujib announced a general strike and the army further enflamed Bengali anger by firing on and killing unarmed protestors. Others were killed in communal riots.[6] However, the emphasis of Bengali protest remained non-violent non-co-operation, as the Awami League orchestrated a shutdown of all but essential economic and state functions. On 7 March, Mujib responded to mass demands and declared to a crowd of a million, 'This time, our struggle is a struggle for freedom. This time, our struggle is a struggle for independence.' Political negotiations continued while the Awami League proved its de facto control on the ground, and more and more groups and individuals demonstrated their support for Bangladesh. The 23 March, Pakistan Day, was renamed Resistance Day and the new Bangladeshi flag was flown from public and private buildings across the province. But, all the while, the Pakistan army was surreptitiously building up its troops and the Bengalis were doing what they could to prepare their defence.

Mass mobilisation

Back in London, those first days of March were filled with a rush of activity. Again and again, demonstrators gathered in Hyde Park and marched to the Pakistan High Commission, where Bengalis kept up a constant vigil. On 5 March, the High Commission flag was pulled down and burnt by activists who included members of Birmingham's East Pakistan Liberation Front.[7] There were protests in the different British cities where Bengalis lived, and those who could travelled to London to join the protests there. On 7 March, the day of Mujib's much-anticipated speech, the crowd in Hyde Park numbered over ten thousand. And that night, the demonstration outside the High Commission did not disperse until three in the morning.

The main Pakistani student hostel in Chesham Place (near Belgrave Square) was a ferment of discussion. Sheikh Mannan, then president of the left-wing Pakistan Democratic Front, tried to keep the few West Pakistani students on board: 'at first they were willing to talk, but towards the end of the discussion I realised that their sympathy ran out.'[8] The students listened to Mujib's speech broadcast by the BBC on the hostel radio,

> ... and then there [was] excitement, disappointment and frustration. So one of the

Figure 3.1 Sheikh Mannan, c1971

students got up, and he got the picture of Muhammad Ali Jinnah from the wall, and [tore it] into pieces. There was some hue and cry among the students who were still sympathetic to Pakistan, but they did not dare say anything.[9]

For the students 'normal life was suspended'. They formed an action committee, and days and nights were taken up in endless discussions and leaflet writing as they waited for directives for action from Bengal. There were meetings of Bengali doctors and Bengali women, and wherever groups of Bengalis had settled, people met to discuss and speculate and plan what they could do.[10]

In Dhaka, any hope of a negotiated agreement was definitively crushed on the *Kalo Ratri* – Black Night – of 25 March. A little before midnight, the Pakistani army launched its crackdown with an orgy of violence that left thousands of innocent people dead and turned even apolitical Bengalis into fervent nationalists. Attacks on Bengali army cantonments ensured that the remaining battalions turned against the West Pakistani troops, alongside a growing force of Bengali resistance fighters. Mujib was arrested, and other Bengali leaders, who had fled the city, set up a government in exile.

On 26 March, as the BBC relayed news of the attack, a crowd gathered at the Chesham Place hostel and marched to the High Commission, where protestors tried to take over the building and hoist the new flag of Bangladesh. In the ensuing tussle with the police, several were arrested and two ended up spending

six weeks in prison.[11] On 28 March, three thousand Bengalis, including repre-
sentatives from groups all over Britain, gathered in Birmingham's Smallheath
Park. As the barrister Zuglul Pasha, who had been chosen as president of the
Birmingham Action Committee, addressed the crowd, a group of West Pakistanis
attacked one of the Bengalis with a knife. With tensions rising, Zuglul's wife,
Badrun Nesa Pasha, found herself deputed to restore the meeting to order:

> Then I went to the microphone and addressed the people, 'Don't go, we have just
> started the independence movement … we can't go back and we can't escape. Let's
> do something, and what do we need? We need the money. Firstly we will have to
> decide how we can help our brothers and sisters, those who have engaged themselves
> in the liberation movement. We have to help them.' I donated my jewellery whatever
> I was wearing at that time. Everybody returned to the meeting after my appeal, and
> most of them listed their name with the amount of their contribution being
> announced. They were all saying, I am sending this money, and a huge list came to
> us.[12]

A small group of educated Bengali women formed a Bangladesh Women's
Association, and rapid organisation enabled them to bring out a protest of
hundreds of Bengali women in London on Saturday 3 April. Anowara Jahan
recalled: 'The information spread to all of us like fire. Everyone spread the
message to others he or she knew.'[13] The women gathered at Charing Cross,
accompanied by their children and dressed in saris to increase media impact, and
marched to a rally in Hyde Park, which was attended by sympathetic British
MPs.[14] The following day saw the first Trafalgar Square rally and buses were
booked to bring Bengalis from around Britain. Nora Shariff recalled that her
husband, Sultan, 'made a fiery speech there on that day. He was saying that he
was going and who else wanted to go to Bangladesh. As many as possible should
go and help people get freedom in Bangladesh.'[15] Memoirs recall that hundreds
were ready to go and fight, however, Bangladesh's government in exile made it
clear that the only recruits that were wanted from among the *probashi* Bengalis
were doctors, and energy was concentrated instead on campaigning in Britain.[16]
Many did brave the dangers of their war-torn homeland to find family members
and bring them back to the safety of Britain, but Yousuf Choudhury's account of
his own mission to rescue his daughter mentions meeting only one Bengali from
Britain who had gone out to fight.[17] Subsequent immigration has meant that
there are, nevertheless, now many people in Britain who did take part in the
fighting, and as I interviewed for this study I found that the horrors of those days
still bring tears to the eyes of some of those involved.

    In Britain, meetings were held everywhere Bengalis had settled, and action
committees were springing up all over the country. Committees set up for
cyclone relief transformed themselves into committees for independence. There
was an overwhelming desire to do something in response to the news coming
from Bengal and the terrible experiences relayed in letters smuggled out from

family and friends still there. People came to the restaurants to share the latest information on events in Bengal and plans for demonstrations; and the hunger for news was such that men illiterate in any language bought the British papers and took them to those who could read and translate them.[18] Of course, a few retained their loyalty to Pakistan, or preferred to sit on the fence and await the outcome of events, but most people's reactions were similar to those of Nawab Ali, whose swashbuckling adventures are recorded in Caroline Adams' collection of oral histories:

> I supported Bangladesh struggle too, [as well as Pakistan's fight for independence from Britain,] not immediately of course because we fought to make Pakistan, so we didn't want to lose it, but when we saw the newspapers, the photographs of what they had done to Bengali women, then we supported it. Eight of my family were in the *Mukti* ...[19] [*Mukti Bahini* translates as Liberation Army]

Combination and factionalism

At that time, there were some twenty-two thousand people of East Bengali origin living in Britain, of whom around three thousand lived in the East End.[20] Organising these into a coherent group was not easy, with all the usual problems that make up the realities of political struggle. There were the personal rivalries and traditional bonds that form the staple fare of accounts of community politics,[21] but there were also the much less discussed but fundamental ideological differences between many of the leading activists. Support for the Awami League had been encouraged by Mujib's various visits to London and greatly boosted by the 1970 election. But within the British branch of the Awami League, personal rivalries had resulted in a split before the first anniversary of its foundation. Many East Enders belonged to the London Awami League, whose president, Minhaj Uddin, played a prominent role in East Pakistan House. Meanwhile Gaus Khan's UK Awami League claimed more support outside London, especially among the restaurant owners and growing business class. And, beyond this, the left groups, dominated by the students and educated professionals, envisaged a very different Bangladesh from that planned by the Awami League. The British campaigns included members of East Bengal's various left groups, and although most worked together with the League and non-aligned groups, there was still underlying tension and mistrust.

Memoirs of that time record a turbulent organisational history.[22] Attempts at co-ordinating the campaign got off to an inauspicious start with two parallel meetings on 27 March. However, both agreed to work under a new Council for the People's Republic of Bangladesh, presided over by UK Awami League leader, Gaus Khan. A further meeting with activists from across Britain enlarged the controlling committee and appointed Sheikh Mannan as general secretary, but there were fierce rivalries within the council and Gaus Khan's leadership was challenged. An attempt was then made to resolve the overall leadership question by bringing in an external authority figure. Abu Sayeed Chowdhury, who was vice chancellor of Dhaka University and a judge of the Dhaka High Court, had been attending an international convention in Geneva when hostilities broke out. He had then come to Britain and been made Ambassador Plenipotentiary by the Bangladesh government in exile in Calcutta. He agreed to take on the leadership role provided the different groups could settle their differences. A fractious meeting of Bengalis from all over the country, held in Artillery Passage in Spitalfields, agreed to hold a further convention in Coventry. This convention, with two delegates from each local committee, took place on 24 April. Lulu Bilquis Banu described the meeting to Caroline Adams. Mrs Banu was then working as a school teacher and completing a PhD in London, but she had inherited a radical liberalism from her father[23] and been a student activist alongside Mujib in Dhaka in 1948:

> They wanted someone to preside over the conference, so as soon as someone's name was proposed, the others shouted, 'No, no, no, he's a thief, he's a swindler, he is so and so'. [Then someone suggested asking Mrs Banu] … and I said 'Don't be silly, in this pandemonium I am going to preside? They are breaking the chairs, hitting each other', there was so much animosity … [But she was persuaded to try.] … So suddenly Anamul Huque said, 'We have tried to start this meeting for the last one hour but no-one seems to agree who should preside, will Mrs. Banu preside?' And they all clapped … and there was absolute calm, not one protest, because I was absolutely non-political, non-partisan …[24]

She was also one of the few women present and, as Badrun Nesa Pasha had found in Birmingham, the men were reluctant to subject a woman to riotous protest.

An electoral college of eleven was chosen and they picked a national steering committee of five, including Sheikh Mannan, who much of the time acted as convener. While the committee acknowledged Sheikh Mujib as their national leader – and Chowdhury ensured they kept to a moderate line – none of the five were members of the Awami League. This committee co-ordinated the campaign but was also supposed to give birth to the election of a bigger central committee, and its failure to do so provided the basis for an attempted takeover by the UK Awami League group around Gaus Khan, which adopted the simple expedient of entering the steering committee office en masse.[25] Chowdhury claimed in his memoirs that perpetuation of the temporary steering committee was a deliberate policy on his part, with the aim of avoiding further division,[26] though it can hardly be said to have fully succeeded in this. The committee had the support of all the Moscow-orientated groups and of Bashani's Peking-orientated NAP, but the UK Awami League remained reluctant to accept its overall authority.[27]

The leaders of the different action committees also agreed that the trustees for the Bangladesh Fund should be Justice Chowdhury and two neutral non-Bengalis – Donald Chesworth and John Stonehouse MP. Despite Stonehouse's later history (he was convicted of financial fraud after attempting to fake his own suicide), the Bengali consensus was that Stonehouse's role in 1971 was honest.[28] Chesworth was chairman of War on Want and had an established record of work in East Bengal. He provided offices for Justice Chowdhury in Pembridge Gardens, Notting Hill, through Toc H, the Christian fellowship of which he was a trustee.

Despite their differences, most of the groups were fundamentally working towards the same goal; however, the followers of the pro-Peking sections of the divided Communist Party had a different interpretation of events and organised separately after the Coventry convention. They took directions from their leaders in East Bengal and produced their own paper, *Gono Juddho* (People's War), which they sent to universities all over the world. As well as rejecting popular frontism, they argued that socialism in East Pakistan would not be achieved under the leadership of the democratically organised workers' movement of Marxist theory, but through a peasants' revolution in the Maoist pattern. Shah Lutfur Rahman, who was a follower of this political line, recalled that he had no illusions about Sheikh Mujib and regarded the whole movement as run by the Indian government.[29]

Faruque Ahmed, in his *Bengal Politics in Britain*, suggests that the leftists deliberately exploited differences in the Awami League because they 'did not want the credit of forming the action committee in the UK to be enjoyed solely by the Awami League'.[30] In the event, the Awami League turned out to be the main beneficiaries of the political mobilisation in any case, but Ahmed's comment obscures the important *ideological* issues at stake here. The conflicts cannot be reduced simply to personal rivalries and desire for power. As Ahmed himself observed, 'before 1970 most of the Bengali politicians in Britain came from the leftist student organisations'.[31] The rapid rise in importance of the Awami League was a response to its success in the 1970 elections, which projected it as *the* party of independence, attracting wide support – especially, as Ahmed points out, among the less-educated business community.[32] The professionals and students who dominated the left still hoped to influence the nature of this popular nationalist wave and not be swept away by it. In fact, as this chapter argues, many on the left might more readily be accused of being over-accommodating to other parties in their attempts to pursue a popular front. And, while politicians will always try to exploit their opponents' weaknesses, it should also be noted that divisions within the Awami League have long outlasted the decline of the left.

It is not, of course, always easy to identify what is personal rivalry and what fundamental political difference. One of the steering committee members, Manawar Hussain, was barred from attending its meetings after he was accused of pro-Pakistani sympathies, but it has been suggested that in this case the political charge was a cover for more personal factional differences.[33] That May, Hussain stood as a Labour candidate in the elections for Bradford City Council. His campaign would have required him to mix with the large Pakistani population in Manningham ward, the majority of whom came from West Pakistan, but these West Pakistani voters clearly did not regard him as sympathetic to their cause, and what should have been a safe Labour seat was taken by the Conservatives.[34]

Many of the factional differences had their roots back in Bengal, but Bengali village links could play a more positive part when it came to raising crowds at demonstrations. Then the different leaders could each expect to bring a following based on traditional ties, and the competitive element served to boost overall numbers. The importance of these ties within Bangladeshi society is described by Katy Gardner, who notes that,

> In Bangladesh, commentators have long pointed out that patrilineages act as corporate groups, which include members of very different economic positions tied together by relations of patronage and economic and political dependence.

She explains, 'It is towards the *gusthi* [patrilineage] that an individual owes allegiance in matters beyond the domain of the household.' And that 'by maintaining ... patronage relations with poor kin, rich members of a lineage are guaranteed social and political support'.[35] A Tower Hamlets community worker described to me the role her father played as village elder back in Sylhet. She explained, 'The whole village is still a very sort of close-knit community, and the oldest, or the person responsible, needs to be consulted before anything goes ahead'.[36] Every day, from early morning, people came to his door with their problems – from family disputes seeking arbitration, to raising money for a poor girl's marriage. Clan loyalties are still an important feature of South Asian politics in Britain, and such traditional forces are clearly crucial; however, patronage relationships cannot all be attributed to tradition. Gardner herself notes that 'the nature of hierarchy ... is both contested and dynamic over time',[37] and patronage relationships can evolve independently from older cultural hierarchies, especially in the context of immigration, with its many examples of mutual support, exchange and exploitation. Restaurant owners had taken on a powerful role in Bengali immigrant society, and Nikhilesh Chakraborty remembered that the Bengalis used to refer to the restaurant owners who paid for the coaches to the demonstrations as 'guvnors'.[38]

Action in Britain

The British committees had two main tasks: propaganda and fundraising. They wanted to mobilise the whole Bengali community – and Sheikh Mannan remembers canvassing 'every single house and flat'. He avoided pushing his left politics and spoke 'only for liberation'.[39] Ideology was generally relegated to journals and newspapers – some transient and others more regular – which played an important role in spreading news and views within the community, but predominantly also took a popular-front line. The weekly *Janomot* (People's Opinion), whose editor supported Bhashani,[40] saw its objective as the promotion of Bengali nationalism. The steering committee produced its own papers in Bengali and in English and pushed the importance of cross-party unity; and unity was also stressed by *Mukti Juddho* (Liberation War), produce by the pro-Moscow East Pakistan Communist Party. The group around Gaus Khan produced *Bangladesh*, the pro-Peking left produced *Gono Juddho* and the Pakistan High Commission sponsored an anti-independence journal, which Bengali shops refused to stock.[41]

As in the 1940s, and like other immigrants and exiles before them, the Bengalis realised the strategic value of London as a centre of wider public pressure. Shah Lutfur Rahman emphasised to me how the British democratic tradition had made London the site of many such movements, and Sheikh Mannan observed that the Bengali activists discussed the power of British newspapers and radio and their world-wide audience: 'if we create a ripple, that will immediately be circulated in the world.'[42] To this end they kept organising demonstrations, lobbying influential people and using all means at their disposal – from films and street drama to detailed fact sheets and booklets – to publicise what was happening. Besides major London demonstrations, demonstrations were held in other British towns and cities. Students went on hunger strike outside 10 Downing Street – only stopping when Peter Shore promised to raise their concerns in the House of Commons; protests dogged the tour of the Pakistani cricket team and targeted the embassies of countries giving aid or selling arms to the Pakistani government; and in June protestors went to Paris to publicise their message outside the meeting of the Pakistan Aid Consortium of eleven donor countries headed by the World Bank. Influential people were contacted personally, with the Women's Association also targeting their wives. Support was sought from everyone, from students associations to the Pope. Every opportunity was taken to lobby British MPs and some MPs actually visited West Bengal to meet the government in exile and see the extent of the refugee crisis. Tasadduk kept up contacts with the British intelligentsia and sympathetic West Pakistanis at his Ganges restaurant (though this did lead to some unfriendly rumours).

There were, as yet, relatively few women among the East End Bengalis,[43] and these would have been restrained by tradition from taking part in public actions. But the educated middle-class women who made up the Bangladesh Women's Association (or *Mohila Samity*) kept up a busy programme of activities, ranging from more genteel fundraising to public speaking in Trafalgar Square, and sometimes they managed to coax some of the East End women to join them on women's demonstrations. Kulsum Ullah recalled:

Figure 3.2 Rally for Bangladesh, Trafalgar Square, 1971 (*Janomot*)

> ... at that time there were few [Bengali] women here and they were also unwilling to come out of their houses. That is why we had to collect people, going door to door. The husbands ... demanded their full security, and told us to bring them back home. It was our responsibility to drop them off safely.[44]

Kulsum Ullah herself was not afraid to make her voice heard and recalls standing in the road between a Bengali shop and a Pakistani shop telling people to boycott the Pakistanis.[45] Another woman went on hunger strike.[46] Lulu Bilquis Banu's teenage daughters had been allowed to join her through the help of an acquaintance in the Pakistan High Commission. Now they helped Paul Connett, of the highly active non-Bengali volunteer group Action Bangladesh, with late-night fly-posting while their mother played an important role secretly negotiating the defection of Bengali diplomats.[47] Shah Lutfur Rahman's wife, Munni, was a leading member of the women's association and Sheikh Mannan's wife, Sajeda, attended the demonstrations when she could find a lift for herself and her three-year-old twins. However, despite all this activity, most women's political involvement did not outlast the war. Faruque Ahmed has observed that:

> After Bangladesh became independent, women activists associated with the Mohila Samity and similar organisations involved themselves in various social development and cultural activities. They were not active in politics before the liberation war, and after the war it was found that they were gradually distancing themselves from politics.[48]

There were exceptions, but even those who remained involved tended to be pigeon-holed as 'women's affairs secretaries'.[49] This picture is supported by

Anowara Jahan, whose work with the *Samity* included going to the demonstration in Paris. She explained, 'I was not involved in any politics before or after the war. Generally women had no chance of getting involved in politics'.[50]

Bengali doctors and engineers in the Middle East sent donations secretly to the London organisers in defiance of threats from Pro-Pakistani Arab governments.[51] And even in London – despite the cross-class nature of the movement – some restaurant workers had to risk their jobs to demonstrate. Commercial interests triumphed as their Bengali bosses forbade them to leave work and join the protests, and occasionally even threatened to expose them as illegal immigrants.[52]

Every use was made of those who could bear witness to the scenes of devastation in Bengal, including the Banu daughters, who accompanied Paul Connett to the Paris protest where they gave their testimony to a press conference.[53]

Nurul Islam was in East Pakistan when hostilities broke out. He had gone back some time before to visit his mother who had become ill, and had soon found himself under arrest for his political activities. After two months in prison he had been released, but his passport had not been returned. When the war started, he immediately took up arms, and after about a month he found himself based with other 'freedom fighters' in India. But the liberation command knew about his former activism and felt he would be more useful back in London. He could only bear to tear himself away from the fighting for August and September, but during that time he was sent to a demonstration in Paris and a convention of socialist students in Dubrovnik, as well as speaking to Bengalis in Britain.[54]

Aziz Choudhury arrived in London in October after his political mentor, Pir Habibur Rahman of the pro-Moscow NAP, had told him to go and tell people what was happening, and a Bengali passport official had taken his life in his hands to issue him a student passport back-dated to before they were banned.[55] He travelled round Britain talking to members of the Bengali community:

> When they can hear from somebody who just came from Bangladesh, [it] was completely different … I was at gunpoint twice, so that gave people more courage to participate more, contribute more for the country.[56]

Forming the focus of all the lobbies and protests were a list of actions demanded of the governments of Britain and other countries: to put diplomatic pressure on the Pakistan government, to top selling Pakistan arms, to stop sending Pakistan aid (on which it relied for its economy and its substantial military expenditure), to expel Pakistan from the Central Treaty Organisation (CENTO), to press Pakistan to release Sheikh Mujib, to try Yayha Khan for crimes against humanity, to recognise Bangladesh, and to send aid to help with the humanitarian crisis. Bengalis in Britain did all they could to keep the war on the international political agenda and this provided vital encouragement to those living and fighting in East Pakistan, but it is, of course, impossible to measure what other impact they had. At the Paris aid meeting, the World Bank, on the basis of its own mission to a devastated and terrorised East Pakistan, 'recommended ... against new assistance to the Government of President Yahya'.[57] Alec Douglas-Home, Foreign Secretary in the Conservative government, told the House of Commons:

> No commitments of new aid of any kind were called for, nor were any given, though all expressed their willingness to contribute to humanitarian relief in East Pakistan under the effective surveillance of the United Nations. Her Majesty's Government's policy remains that projects already in hand in Pakistan must continue, in so far as this is possible, but that there can be no question of new British aid to Pakistan until we have firm evidence that real progress is made towards a political solution.[58]

The report in the *New York Times* noted that, while Britain and Canada shared the view of the World Bank officials 'that the Pakistani Government would divert funds originally earmarked for the eastern province to bolster the western economy', the Nixon administration was continuing to push through over a hundred million dollars of aid and to honour agreements for the export of military equipment.[59] Henry Kissinger and Richard Nixon ensured that the US maintained a strategic tilt towards Pakistan, which was seen as a counter to a Soviet-friendly India and as a bridge for Nixon's secret negotiations with China.[60] The British government claimed to have no outstanding arms contracts 'of any significance'[61] and dismissed suggestions that they should try to persuade the US and other countries not to ship arms to Pakistan.[62] It could, however, be argued that the Bengalis' international campaign helped create a climate where it was easier for India to intervene.

The other significant part of the campaign in Britain consisted of fundraising, which galvanised the community and produced over £400,000,[63] with everyone scraping together what they could. Many people gave regular contributions, and sometimes wage packets were handed over unopened. Ali Syed Goyas, later a member of the Toynbee Hall Pensioners Club, then lived with his father in Birmingham. He explained to me how by careful housekeeping they had managed to survive on his father's £8-a-week wage, allowing him to put aside the whole of the £25 he earned from night-time piecework in a car factory to send to the family back home. When war broke out he had just left his young pregnant wife in East Pakistan, and for months there was no news of her or his mother and brother. He had £528 saved in the bank and he gave it all to the Bangladesh Fund.[64]

Goyas had joined the Awami League in East Pakistan in 1969, when he had returned home for a period and got married, but for many it was the war that first brought them into any kind of political activity. Abdul Razzak, another member of the Toynbee Club, was then working nights in a Bradford wool mill. He had never previously been part of any political or community organisation, but in 1971 on Saturday mornings when he finished work he would have breakfast and join the coach taking Bradford Bengalis to the London demonstrations. He remembers that money was collected on Saturdays, after Friday payday, and he too became a member of the Awami League.[65]

The money was used for administration, travel expenses and publicity, and some was sent for relief work. However, the original hope of the organisers – and probably the majority of the donors – was that most would be used to buy arms for the *Mukti Bahini*, the liberation army that was organised by the government in exile and made up of regular East Pakistan army units together with some of the thousands of volunteers who had escaped across the border. The 29 April issue of *Joy Bangla*, produced by the Bangladesh Liberation Front in Leeds, included an impassioned appeal from the Prime Minister of the Bangladesh government in exile, Tajuddin Ahmed:

> Bengalis will protect the independence of Bangladesh with the last drop of blood in their bodies. Thousands of freedom fighters are facing their enemies with little more than courage and determination: they don't have enough arms. It is my conviction that immigrant Bengalis in Britain will come forward with all kinds of help to support our War of Independence.[66]

The Bengalis' plans for direct aid to the *Mukti Bahini* were immediately crushed by the Indian government. Sheikh Mannan explained, 'High hopes were raised, and everybody was thinking that his or her money was buying arms. But ... when we contacted the Indian High Commission, we were met with a blank refusal.' The excuse given was that the sums collected were too small for modern warfare:

> [T]he old man sat and laughed ... He said, 'Young man, how much money do you have?' ... I said, 'The more weapons we send the more money will come from the pockets of our people.' Then he said, 'How big is the pocket?'[67]

Undaunted, Sheikh Mannan and some of his colleagues contacted a man who had been in the Pakistani navy who said he could supply small arms privately. He produced a small sample bomb, which they tested in the hills outside Cheltenham in the early hours of the morning. But when they confronted Justice Chowdhury with their plans he was appalled:

> He banged his head against the table. He said, 'Of all the people, you did go to do this thing. You have frustrated me, you have disappointed me and you have crushed me. How on earth the British government will allow it? And if they know tomorrow that you have done this, my existence in this country will be threatened. The whole movement overseas will be stopped. Why did you do that?'

Justice Chowdhury also contacted the government in exile in Calcutta to ask that General Osmani and others stop undermining his authority by sending direct requests for arms to individuals.[68] The bulk of the money was finally handed over to the Bangladesh government after the war, and used to establish a foreign currency reserve for the new Bangladesh State Bank, though there have also been allegations of quite substantial amounts going astray.[69]

The Bengalis had realised the limits of their power to influence events. There were boundaries to what a non-governmental group could legally do, and they bowed to the pressures from international forces. As with his political campaigns, Sheikh Mannan trimmed his plans in line with the moderate majority. But this setback not only affected their ability to intervene directly in East Bengal, it damaged the credibility and strength of the organisation in Britain, as Mannan had told Justice Chowdhury it would. Mannan later observed that 'the amount of money coming every week was so encouraging, but when they heard that no weapons are sent, the flow stopped'.[70]

On the other side

Back in East Pakistan, those Bengalis who supported the other side, including members of Islamic political parties such as Jamaat-e-Islami, were armed and organised by the Pakistan army. Individuals among them used their local knowledge to perpetrate or facilitate some of the worst atrocities of the war, and some have recently been tried for war crimes.

Although the vast majority of the London Bengalis were pro-independence, there were some who held more conservative views, followed a more political form of Islam, or did not want to abandon old loyalties. Ashraf and Rezia Hussein explained to Caroline Adams that

> Both Aftab Ali [the seamen's leader] and Abbas [Ali, founder of the London Muslim League] went on supporting Pakistan, having worked so hard for it. When the Bangladesh movements started, Aftab was in Pakistan, and Dr Abdul Malik, the first governor of East Pakistan, who was his friend, asked him to come to London, and speak against Bangladesh, but when he got there and saw how people felt, he kept quiet. However, he never went home again, and he died here in oblivion.[71]

Qureshi recalled that Aftab Ali did try to persuade his 'old group' to support the Pakistan government, but his persuasion failed to work.[72] Either way his mission was not well received.

Abbas had been no supporter of military rule, but he was devastated by the potential break-up of his beloved Pakistan and had campaigned across Britain against the separation. Although he had previously planned to return to Dhaka he was to refuse ever to visit Bangladesh, even to see his mother. When he died, in 1979, the Pakistan government arranged for him to be buried in Karachi, where his gravestone describes him as 'the man symbolising the Unity of East and West Pakistan'.[73]

Abbas's Muslim League colleague, Qureshi, who was back in East Pakistan in 1971, similarly felt that he and others 'who suffered and worked and prayed for Pakistan … couldn't overnight change our principles'.[74]

Inevitably, there was antagonism between Bengalis and West Pakistanis in London. There were clashes between Bengali and West Pakistani children in Tower Hamlets schools[75] and newspapers reported street fighting and attacks on West Pakistani-owned shops.[76] In November, thousands of Bengalis arranged to say their Id prayers at local halls rather than alongside the West Pakistanis in the East London Mosque. An 'East Pakistani leader' explained to the local paper 'You have to have pure hearts to pray. But when we are with West Pakistanis all we think of is the atrocities committed against our people.'[77] A mosque spokesman insisted to the reporter that 'Religion must be divorced from politics', however this boycott has been echoed in more recent political divisions. It would not be many years before the East London Mosque was working with Dawatul Islam, an offshoot of Jamaat that argues religion should inform every part of life, including the political.

The Awami League and the left

While the Awami League ran the government in exile and the regular forces of the *Mukti Bahini*, the majority of the volunteer fighters were formed into guerrilla units and sent back to their native areas, and some of these were politically much more radical. Which group any particular volunteer ended up joining could depend very much on luck and where he first crossed the border. Pro-Moscow groups – which trained over twenty thousand people – gave unqualified support to the broader liberation struggle, as did Bhashani's NAP, but some of the so-called pro-Peking groups were more circumspect. China itself maintained good relations with Pakistan and refused to be drawn into what it described as an internal matter.[78] A significant section of the East Pakistan Communist Party (Marxist-Leninist) argued that their enemy was not only Pakistan, but Indian expansionism, Soviet imperialism and the bourgeois capitalism of the Awami League. They had their own separate guerrilla force.

Many on the left – including some within the Awami League – believed that in a long war of attrition they could defeat Pakistan and create a socialist Bangladesh,[79] but these plans were pre-empted on 3 December 1971 by India's entry into the war on the Bengali side. Just under two weeks later, on 16 December, the Pakistani forces surrendered in Dhaka to the Indian commander. Mujib returned from prison in Pakistan via London and New Delhi to a mass welcome. The decision to send him to London was made by the Pakistani government, but it provided a triumphant culmination to the campaign of the *probashi* Bengalis and an, albeit unplanned, recognition of the part they had played. When Mujib arrived in Dhaka he had already been declared President of the new People's Republic of Bangladesh at a ceremony on 8 January 1972 in Claridges Hotel in London. In fact, back in Dhaka, Mujib was not content to be head of state and soon took on the more active role of Prime Minister, appointing Justice Chowdhury as a compliant President.

While Sheikh Mujib's claim to leadership had overwhelming public support[80] – as well as the backing of the Indian government – and could hardly have been challenged, the Awami League government was not without its critics. True, they had won the 1970 election overwhelmingly, but others, including Bhashani's NAP, had not taken part, and anyway a lot had happened since then. However, the proposal for an interim national government of all parties, put forward by the pro-Moscow NAP and the Communist Party, was rejected by the Awami League out of hand, and Bhashani's public protest meetings in support of these ideas were ineffective. Sheikh Mannan recalls that Mujib's position had already been made clear to himself and his colleagues in London. (Bangabandhu, Friend of Bengal, is the honorific title often used when referring to Mujib.)

> Bangabandhu clearly indicated to me at the airport … there is no possibility of a coalition government. He told me in frank language, four of us … that I have … contested election only the other day. I even argued with him: the other day was in Pakistan … They were members of the Pakistani parliament … they are not representative of Bangladesh. But he said, no, I cannot ignore the public mandate, you come to the country and work. So, I was removed from everything. I could not associate myself with the government, so I did not go. I was provided with free tickets, I refused.[81]

First nationalism, then socialism

The dominance of the Awami League in the newly independent Bangladesh was facilitated by the popular-front tactics of much of the Bengali left. The impact of the independence movement on the London Bengalis can similarly not be understood without examining the effect of the popular-front policies pursued by the left groups who took a leading role. These allowed little room for the development of independent socialist ideas and organisation.

In 1971, in accordance with popular-front and stages theory, the majority of Bengalis, in Pakistan and in Britain, had put aside their political differences to fight together for freedom. Sheikh Mannan explained their position:

> Nationalism is a disease … if you create nation state and then you don't have internationalism, that is the contradiction here. But we were so much oppressed for 1000 years, that we needed the tag of nationalism first, otherwise you won't be able to convince the people … we thought that let us achieve liberation and … immediately after liberation we will split up, and then they will give their programme to the people, we will give our programme. If we succeed the government will be ours. That is how we work together … If the Awami League was the only party leading the liberation movement, both at home and in here as well, it would have failed.[82]

As acting convenor of the steering committee he had to be 'neutral' and 'not be bound by the party spirit, but by a nationalist spirit'. If he ever tried to put forward his political views, Justice Chowdhury would say to him, '"Liberation first or your ideology first?"'[83]

Nurul Islam threw himself wholeheartedly behind Sheikh Mujib, 'because the need of the hour is nationalism', but this did not mean that he was rejecting all the ideals raised in Tasadduk's discussion groups. He believed in socialism and in the Awami League's socialist rhetoric, and he felt that socialism would not be possible without the liberation of East Pakistan from West. He argued that a long-drawn-out battle was not appropriate to the Bengali situation, and dismissed NAP's arguments as bookish, theoretical and impractical.[84] The left's popular-front policies made such a transition to nationalism appear unproblematic.

Tasadduk himself expounded at length on the need for unity of action, and also for a popular front of political parties and activists committed to secular nationalism. He admonished both right careerists and left separatists and warned:

> Instead of taking up seriously the pressing task of politicising the masses on the basis of the present phase of our struggle if we get ourselves involved in hair splitting arguments and polemics about the long-term task, the masses will get bored and start moving away from us.[85]

His personal involvement in the details of Mujib's official declaration as President in Claridges Hotel epitomised his popular-front politics. Mahiuddin Ahmed recalled in a letter to the *Bangladesh Observer* in 1989,

> I was personal witness to the closeness between Tasadduq Bhai and Sheikh Mujibur Rahman. Tasadduq Bhai had almost developed a row with Anthony Mascarenhas [the *Sunday Times* journalist] on the 8th January '72 on the question of the security of the President of the People's Republic of Bangladesh in Claridges Hotel.[86]

Just as there was little role for the far left in the new People's Republic of Bangladesh, so the left also failed to benefit from the politicisation of the community in London. Most of the left leaders had been so busy propagating the cause of independence and avoiding anything that might discourage the broadest possible involvement that Sheikh Mannan had to admit:

> People … were ignorant about the subtle difference between the Awami League and the National Awami Party. I would not categorise them as politically immature, but they are not thoroughly informed, because nobody took the message from Maulana Bhashani, [and] went into leather factories or in a restaurant, or in garment factories – wherever our people worked … If we did go, which we did, we went for the cause of East Pakistan.[87]

The mobilisation in support of Bangladeshi independence provides a powerful example of a movement through which revolutionary socialist views might have received a growing acceptance, had those who held them not submitted themselves to a policy of self-censorship in line with the prevailing left orthodoxy. In fact, it can be argued that not only did the left fail to gain from this mobilisation, but they actually lost much of their earlier potential as the community's political leadership. Other immigrant groups may not have experienced such a dramatic example of the impact of popular-front politics, but, as demonstrated by the Bengalis even before 1971, this approach also allowed socialism to be eclipsed by the pragmatic everyday politics of general welfare activities. In the Bengali East End, the far left never really recovered its separate identity.

Notes

1 'Victory to Bengal'.
2 Estimated deaths from EM-DAT: The OFDA/CRED International Disaster Database –www.emdat.net – Université Catholique de Louvain, Brussels, accessed 24 December 2012.
3 *East London Express*, 8 and 15 January 1971.
4 Gulam Mustafa Choudhury, interviewed 10 June 2006 by Jamil Iqbal and Ansar Ahmed Ullah for Swadhinata Trust and University of Surrey, 'Oral History Project'. Choudhury was manager of the Allahabad Restaurant, owned by Gaus Khan, President of the UK Awami League, and was deputed to deliver the mini-bus.
5 Three hundred seats were directly elected and a further thirteen reserved for women, of which the Awami League had seven.
6 Urdu-speaking Biharis who had come to Bengal at Partition generally did not support autonomy or independence. Since Bangladeshi independence, this community has been largely confined to refugee camps within Bangladesh; and Biharis were denied citizenship rights until 2008, when these were only granted to people who had not reached adulthood in 1971.
7 Mohammed Israel, interviewed 25 February 2006 by Jamil Iqbal for Swadhinata Trust and University of Surrey, 'Oral History Project'. The EPLF was dissolved when the broader Birmingham Action Committee was established.
8 Interviewed by Caroline Adams, 19 March 1998, tape recording (Tower Hamlets Local History Library).
9 *Ibid*.
10 Sheikh Mannan, interviewed by Caroline Adams, 19 March 1998, tape recording, and by the author, 30 March 2002.
11 Faruque Ahmed, *Bengal Politics in Britain: Logic, Dynamics and Disharmony* (North Carolina: Lulu, 2010), p. 123.
12 Adrun Nesa Pasha, interviewed 18 September 2006 by Jamil Iqbal and Ansar Ahmed Ullah Swadhinata Trust and University of Surrey, 'Oral History Project'. See also Shahid Ali, interviewed 7 January 2006 by Jamil Iqbal for Swadhinata Trust and University of Surrey, 'Oral History Project'.
13 Interviewed 4 July 2006 by Jamil Iqbal and Ansar Ahmed Ullah for Swadhinata Trust and University of Surrey, 'Oral History Project'.
14 Ahmed, *Bengal Politics in Britain*, p. 155; interviews with Anowara Jahan and Sultan Shariff for Swadhinata Trust and University of Surrey, 'Oral History Project'.
15 Interviewed 16 February 2006 by Jamil Iqbal for Swadhinata Trust and University of Surrey, 'Oral History Project'.

16 Ahmed, *Bengal Politics in Britain*, p. 124. Badrun Nesa Pasha recalled a recruitment camp in Birmingham later in the war, with people queuing to go and fight, including 'an English barman, who came and said, "I want to fight for Bangladesh liberation movement"'. See, interview, 18 September 2006 by Jamil Iqbal and Ansar Ahmed Ullah Swadhinata Trust and University of Surrey, 'Oral History Project'. The date given for the camp was 16 December 1971, but that seems unlikely as that is the date the war ended.

17 Yousuf Choudhury, *The Roots and Tales of the Bangladeshi Settlers* (Birmingham: Sylhet Local History Group, 1993), pp. 158–64.

18 Nooruddin Ahmed, interviewed 10 April 2006 by Jamil Iqbal, Charlie Sen and Riza Momin for Swadhinata Trust and University of Surrey, 'Oral History Project'.

19 Nawab Ali, interviewed by Caroline Adams, 1980s, manuscript transcript (Tower Hamlets Local History Library), p. 12.

20 The overall figure of twenty-two thousand (which included around one thousand British-born Bengalis) was calculated by Ceri Peach, in 'Estimating the Growth of the Bangladeshi Population of Great Britain', *New Community*, 16:4 (1990), 481–91. The 1971 Census recorded 3,560 people born in Pakistan living in Tower Hamlets, and the great majority of these would have come from East Bengal. The 1981 Census recorded 9,808 people in Tower Hamlets born in Bangladesh and only 657 born in Pakistan.

21 John Eade, *The Politics of Community: The Bangladeshi Community in East London* (Aldershot: Avebury, 1989).

22 Ahmed, *Bengal Politics in Britain*; Sheikh Mannan, interviewed by Caroline Adams, 19 March 1998, and by Caroline Adams and Tasadduk Ahmed, 1 April 1998, tape recordings (Tower Hamlets Local History Library), and interviewed by the author, 30 March 2002.

23 Lulu Bilquis Banu's description of how her father made her mother abandon purdah, meet his friends and later take part in public activity is reminiscent of Tagore's novel *The Home and the World*, though without the novel's disastrous consequences.

24 Interviewed by Caroline Adams, 29 September 1990, tape recording (Tower Hamlets Local History Library) .

25 This incident was recounted by Sheikh Mannan, interviewed by Tasadduk Ahmed and Caroline Adams, 1 April 1998, tape recording (Tower Hamlets Local History Library). He was not present but had talked to numerous people who were. Faruque Ahmed claims that the take-over plan was actually leaked before it could be put into effect. See Ahmed, *Bengal Politics in Britain*, p. 138.

26 Quoted in Ahmed, *Bengal Politics in Britain*, p. 136.

27 This continued rivalry was exemplified when the UK Awami League hijacked the steering committee's plans for a demonstration in Hyde Park on 12 December by announcing their own meeting at the same time and place, forcing the Committee to withdraw to avoid damaging confrontation. See Ahmed, *Bengal Politics in Britain*, pp. 139–40.

28 See, for example, the tributes in the *Silver Jubilee Commemorative Volume of Bangladesh Independence* (London: Silver Jubilee Celebration Committee, 1997). All cheques had to be signed by Justice Chowdhury. Charges against Stonehouse in relation to the fund were investigated by the fraud squad, but no evidence was found. It has recently been revealed that Stonehouse was also denounced for spying on behalf of the Czech government. See *Guardian,* 30 December 2010.

29 Interviewed 22 August 2001.

30 Ahmed, *Bengal Politics in Britain*, p. 143.

31 *Ibid.*, p. 128.

32 *Ibid.*, p. 143.
33 Sheikh Mannan, interviewed by Caroline Adams, 19 March 1998, tape recording, and by the author, 30 March 2002 .
34 M.J. Le Lohé, 'Participation in Elections by Asians in Bradford', in Ivor Crewe (ed.), *The Politics of Race (Vol. 2 British Sociology Yearbook)* (London: Croom Helm, 1975), pp. 84–122.
35 Katy Gardner, *Global Migrants, Local Lives: Travel and Transformation in Rural Bangladesh* (Oxford: Clarendon Press, 1995), pp. 151, 30 and 156.
36 Interviewed July 2000.
37 Gardner, *Global Migrants, Local Lives*, p. 128.
38 Interviewed 30 April 2006 by Jamil Iqbal and Abdul Shahid for Swadhinata Trust and University of Surrey, 'Oral History Project'.
39 Interviewed 30 March 2002.
40 Sheikh Mannan, interviewed 30 March 2002.
41 Faruque Ahmed, *Bengali Journals and Journalism in the UK (1916-2007)* (London: The Ethnic Minorities Original History and Research Centre, 2008), pp. 58–83 .
42 Shah Lutfur Rahman, interviewed by the author 22 August 2001; Sheikh Mannan interviewed by Caroline Adams, 19 March 1998, tape recording (Tower Hamlets Local History Library).
43 Of the 3,560 people born in Pakistan and living in Tower Hamlets recorded in the 1971 Census, only 470 were female. At least 3,000 of these Pakistanis would have been from East Bengal.
44 Interviewed 1 January 2006 by Jamil Iqbal for Swadhinata Trust and University of Surrey, 'Oral History Project'.
45 *Ibid.*
46 Described by Anowara Jahan, interviewed 4 July 2006 by Jamil Iqbal and Ansar Ahmed Ullah for Swadhinata Trust and University of Surrey, 'Oral History Project'.
47 Lulu Bilquis Banu, interviewed by Caroline Adams, 29 September 1990, tape recording (Tower Hamlets Local History Library). Action Bangladesh was organised by Paul Connett and his wife and Marietta Prokope from the latter's house in Camden Town. Connett and Prokope were both lecturers and took time off work for the cause. See also discussion between the author and Sheikh Mannan, 30 March 2002.
48 Ahmed, *Bengal Politics in Britain*, p.159.
49 Lulu Bilquis Banu had a previous history of political activism but later refused offers to stand for the Bangladesh parliament because, as she told Caroline Adams, she did not like the corrupt culture of Bangladeshi party politics. See interview with Caroline Adams, 29 September 1990, tape recording (Tower Hamlets Local History Library).
50 Interviewed 4 July 2006 by Jamil Iqbal and Ansar Ahmed Ullah for Swadhinata Trust and University of Surrey, 'Oral History Project'.
51 Sheikh Mannan, interviewed by Caroline Adams, 19 March 1998, tape recording (Tower Hamlets Local History Library).
52 *Ibid.*; Sheikh Mannan interviewed by the author, 30 March 2002.
53 Lulu Bilquis Banu, interviewed by Caroline Adams, 29 September 1990, tape recording (Tower Hamlets Local History Library).
54 Interviewed 12 June 2001.
55 Discussion with Aziz Choudhury, 30 January 2001. Habibur Rahman was a NAP leader and a distant cousin of Choudhury's.
56 Interviewed 20 February 2001.
57 *New York Times*, 13 July 1971.

58 Alec Douglas-Home, Secretary of State for Foreign and Commonwealth Affairs, House of Commons, 23 June 1971, *Hansard*, vol. 819 col. 1436 .

59 *New York Times*, 13 July 1971.

60 There is also evidence that is said to suggest that Kissinger was attempting to engineer a coup within the Awami League to replace the leadership of the government in exile with others who would argue for autonomy rather than independence. See Lawrence Lifschultz, *Bangladesh: The Unfinished Revolution* (London: Zed Press, 1979), pp. 162–7.

61 Alec Douglas-Home, 26 April 1971, *Hansard*, vol. 816 col. 29. The only details given were: 'No contracts have been signed since 1967 with the exception of one for refitting a naval vessel and another for radar equipment. There is none in prospect.'

62 Alec Douglas-Home, 2 August 1971, *Hansard*, vol. 822 col. 1056.

63 Mohammed Israel, who acted as accountant for the steering committee, gives a figure of £406,856, see interview, 25 February 2006, by Jamil Iqbal for Swadhinata Trust and the University of Surrey, 'Oral History Project'. Faruque Ahmed gives £412,083, see Ahmed, *Bengal Politics in Britain*, p. 137. This would be worth over £4 million today, based on increases in the RPI, see http://www.measuringworth.com.

64 Interviewed 14 May 2001 (with Abul Kalam Azad as interpreter).

65 Also interviewed 14 May 2001 (with Abul Kalam Azad as interpreter).

66 Quoted in Ahmed, *Bengali Journals and Journalism in the UK*, p. 59. Ahmed also quotes another appeal for arms, from the first issue of *Swadhin Bangla*, produced by the Bangladesh Action Committee in Birmingham on 3 April, see *ibid.*, p. 61.

67 Interviewed by Caroline Adams, 19 March 1998, tape recording (Tower Hamlets Local History Library).

68 Sheikh Mannan, interviewed by Caroline Adams 19 March 1998, tape recording (Tower Hamlets Local History Library).

69 Some individual fundraising never made it to the bank, and Faruque Ahmed has published a list of 153 missing receipt books (Ahmed, *Bengal Politics in Britain*, pp. 149–50).

70 Interviewed by Caroline Adams, 19 March 1998, tape recording (Tower Hamlets Local History Library).

71 Caroline Adams, 16 December 1981, manuscript notes, pp. 3–4 (Tower Hamlets Local History Library).

72 Interviewed by Caroline Adams, 1980s, manuscript transcript, p. 31 (Tower Hamlets Local History Library).

73 Ali Mohammed Azhar, 'Introduction' to Abbas, Ali Mohammed, autobiographical memoir (manuscript, n.d.), pp. 29–33, 38–9; Muhammad Yousuf Akhtar, 'Ali Muhammad Abbas Bar-at-Law: "A Great Son of Pakistan"' (pamphlet published for the installation of a plaque in memory of Abbas on his home at 33 Tavistock Square, 1987).

74 Interviewed by Caroline Adams, 1980s, manuscript transcript, p. 25 (Tower Hamlets Local History Library).

75 Tunu Miah, interviewed 17 January 2006 by Jamil Iqbal and Ansar Ahmed Ullah for Swadhinata Trust and University of Surrey, 'Oral History Project'.

76 *Express*, 14 May 1971; *East London Advertiser*, 26 November 1971 and 10 December 1971.

77 *East London Advertiser*, 26 November 1971.

78 Lifschultz, *Bangladesh*, p. 23.

79 *Ibid.*, p. 25.

80 Anthony Mascarenhas, *Bangladesh: A Legacy of Blood* (London: Hodder and Stoughton, 1986), pp. 6–7.

81 Interviewed by Caroline Adams, 19 March 1998, tape recording (Tower Hamlets Local History Library) .

82 Interviewed 30 March 2002.

83 Sheikh Mannan, interviewed by Tasadduk Ahmed and Caroline Adams, 1 April 1998, tape recording (Tower Hamlets Local History Library).

84 Interviewed 12 June 2001.

85 *Bangladesh Newsletter*, 1:11, October 1971, under the pseudonym Muhit Mazumdar, reproduced in Tasadduq Ahmed (edited by Faruque Ahmed), *Jeeban Khatar Kurano Pata* (London: The Ethnic Minorities Original History and Research Centre, 2002), p. 273.

86 Copy of manuscript letter held by Spitalfields Small Business Association. (*Bhai*, brother, is a commonly used honorific.)

87 Interviewed 10 March 2002.

4 British Bangladeshis

Probashi Bengalis had shown massive support for their homeland as it struggled for independence, but after the war was over very few wanted to go back and live there. Some took up opportunities of influential positions with the ruling party, but generally the pulls were all in the other direction. This was the time when many of the Bengali men who were already working here began to bring over their wives and families – partly as a response to the traumas of separation and uncertainty that accompanied the war and the chaos of post-war devastation. There were also a number of people who had supported the Pakistan government and now found it expedient to leave Bangladesh. There were, of course, exceptions to this general rule, including Ali Syed Goyas, who we met in the previous chapter. He had applied for a British passport, but when his native country got its independence he withdrew his application, got a Bangladeshi passport instead and left to join his wife and baby son, born during the war. However, less than a year later he too chose to return to this 'civilised country', lured by a desire for law and order and the chance of earning a better income, and he was joined in 1978 by his wife and family.[1]

Rebuilding the war-torn country was a vast challenge, which Mujib and the Awami League failed to address right from the beginning. Anthony Mascarenhas described the scene in Gonobadan (Mujib's official residence) in the early days of the new nation as a '20th century parody of a Moghul court'[2] and even Lulu Bilquis Banu, who knew Mujib well and described him as a 'lovely person', criticised the culture of patronage and corruption in Bangladeshi politics.[3] However the Awami League was still riding the post-Independence wave when the first general election was held in March 1973.

The old Bengali left parties had compromised themselves out of effective power, but a new left, which looked towards China, had long been gestating within the Awami League itself. Najim Chowdhury, who came to London in the 1980s after a period as a political refugee in Germany, explains that, as a student and former freedom fighter in Chittagong, he was ready to join the new

Jatiya Samajtantrik Dal (JSD – National Socialist Party) when it was officially launched in late 1972. When he saw the Awami League government breaking every promise that they had made to the people who had been the backbone of the independence struggle, he, like many other students, followed the dissenters down the path of 'scientific socialism'.[4] It was a hard path as it set them on a collision course with the government. Repression by pro-Mujib paramilitaries was countered with further protests and increasingly with terrorism – by the JSD and other Maoist groups – which brought greater repression. In early 1975 Mujib met the rising tide of chaos by declaring Bangladesh a one-party state with himself as President. When he was murdered in a coup that August he was presiding over an economic crisis and devastating famine. The only surprise was the identity of the plot's leaders – three previously unremarkable army majors. There are many who could have been behind this attempt to take advantage of the chaos in Bangladesh. Certainly the conservative regime under Khandakar Mushtaq Ahmed, installed as a result of the coup, succeeded in pre-empting action from the powerful JSD. It was not until after Brigadier Musharraf's counter-coup on 5 November that the JSD stepped into action. Two days later Colonel Taher and his *Gono Bahini* (People's Army) ousted Musharraf and reinstated Taher's comrade-in-arms from his freedom fighting days, General Ziaur Rahman, as army Chief of Staff, the position to which he had been promoted by Mushtaq. The left's moment of power lasted just over two weeks. On 23 November police, under orders from Zia, began arresting the JSD leadership. Taher was arrested on the 24th and later tried and executed in prison. Thousands of JSD supporters were rounded up and many disappeared. The movement was relegated to a footnote of history.[5]

All this was observed from London and had its echoes among the *probashi* community, but after the great mobilisation of 1971 its impact pales in comparison. Opinions and priorities were divided. There was no big movement. Abul Ishaque, who had spent six weeks in Brixton prison for his part in the demonstrations outside the Pakistan High Commission on 25 March 1971, welcomed Mujib's new party, the Bangladesh Krishak Sramik Awami League (BAKSAL), as a 'step towards socialism' and became president of its London branch.[6] Sheikh Mannan launched a new political weekly, *Agami Bangla* (Tomorrow's Bengal), which campaigned against the growing totalitarianism. Shah Lutfur Rahman concentrated his energies on youth work among the growing population of teenagers. When Mujib was killed, anti-Mujib protestors from different political backgrounds entered the Bangladesh High Commission in London and physically attacked its national security officer. They accused him of spying on British Bangladeshis and of effecting the revocation of Bangladeshi citizenship of leading JSD organisers, including Nurunnessa Chowdhury, her husband Abdur Rob and Muhammed Nurul Huque, who was himself one of the protestors.[7] But, overall, the early 1970s was a period of consolidation and settlement in the Bengali East End, a prelude to the mushrooming of locally based political activism at the end of the decade that will be discussed in later chapters.

General Zia and the Islamic factor

The rule of General – later President – Ziaur Rahman gave a new intensity, as well as an added complexity, to secular/religious tensions in Bangladesh and in the *probashi* community. It also further eroded the already much-crossed line between democratic and military politics. The all too obvious failures of the nation's first few years had tainted the Awami League's rhetoric of socialism and secularism, allowing Zia to promote a reactionary turn towards more conservative values, underscored by a populist appeal to older religious certainties. In a fundamental policy shift, already begun by Mushtaq, Zia emphasised the country's place in the Islamic world. He rehabilitated those who had fought against liberation,[8] and he lifted the post-Independence ban on communal and religious parties. In 1977, after declaring himself civilian President, he amended the constitution to replace the original fundamental principles of nationalism, socialism, democracy and secularism with 'The principles of absolute trust and faith in the Almighty Allah, nationalism, democracy and socialism meaning economic and social justice', adding, in case of any doubt, that 'Absolute trust and faith in the Almighty Allah shall be the basis of all actions'.[9] Zia won a presidential election in 1978, and his newly formed Bangladesh Nationalist Party (BNP) won the National Assembly elections of 1979, though with the opposition parties still functioning under considerable restrictions. He attracted supporters from across the political spectrum, from religious conservatives to a section of Bhashani's NAP, united in their antagonism to the post-BAKSAL Awami League. The new political divisions extended to the *probashi* community. When Zia visited London in 1980, he helped to promote the British branch of the Bangladesh Nationalist Party. He was greeted by a crowd of several thousand, but also faced (much smaller) protest demonstrations.[10] Zia was seen as a force for stability, however he relied on a repressive regime that held thousands of political prisoners and he suppressed numerous attempted coups before he finally fell to a soldier's bullet in 1981.

The BNP ended the hegemony of the Awami League in Bangladeshi party politics and it too lays claim to the mantle of the freedom struggle. Zia's record as a brigade leader in the war, as well as his historic broadcast proclaiming the independence of Bangladesh over Chittagong's Free Bengal Radio, are central to the party's identity.[11] The importance of this legacy is displayed in Whitechapel every *Ekushey* (21st – of February), when all the Bangladeshi political parties – other than the religious ones – compete for prominence as they line up, chanting political slogans and bearing banners and flowers, to pay their respects in front of the London replica of the Shaheed Minar, the monument to the 1952 Language Martyrs in Dhaka.

Zia cut the link between Bengali nationalism (which he renamed Bangladeshi nationalism to emphasise the separation from Hindu West Bengal) and secularism, and helped to bring the politics of religion in from the cold. In Britain these changes coincided with the establishment of the new Pro-Pakistani immigrants, fertilising the growth of political religion discussed in later chapters. A new outlook was spreading through the East End community and, in the 1980s, Tasadduk Ahmed made clear the concern of the old secularists when he commented to Caroline Adams that they were winning the community back to describing themselves as Bengalis rather than Bangladeshis.[12]

The meaning of secularism

There is wide variation in understandings of what exactly is meant by secularism, and of how this should be realised in political practice, even between different Christian majority societies. Secularists share a belief in the separation of religion and state, but there are important differences as to how this is to be achieved. While British society is probably one of the most secular in the world in the sense of being least dominated by overt theology or theologians, the head of state is also head of the Church of England, bishops take part in debates in the upper house of Parliament, in English and Welsh state schools pupils must take part in a daily 'act of collective worship' that will in most cases be 'wholly or mainly of a broadly Christian character',[13] and the Church of England runs a quarter of English state primary schools and one in seventeen secondaries.[14] The First Amendment to the US Constitution, adopted in 1791, set a model of constitutional secularism by outlawing state religion and enshrining freedom of religious worship, in marked contrast to the militant institutional atheism that would come to dominate revolutionary France soon after. Thomas Jefferson famously referred to the US First Amendment as 'a wall of separation between church and State'. He believed that 'religion is a matter which lies solely between man and his God, that he owes account to none other for his faith or his worship, that the legislative powers of government reach actions only, and not opinions'.[15] However, with minimal state involvement in welfare, religious organisations are encouraged to play a major part in US civil society, and any US politician who openly admits to being an atheist has severely restricted career opportunities. Previous experience of religious persecution (a key element in the story of America's Pilgrim Fathers) can encourage a liberal approach that promotes secularism as a framework in which individuals are free to practice the religion of their choice. On the other hand, previous experience of politically powerful religious organisation can encourage a legislative secularism that attempts to limit the political role of religious organisations, as has happened in France and Turkey. This can include limiting public expression of religious affiliation. Amartya Sen has summed up these two different approaches to secularism as '*neutrality* between different religions' and '*prohibition* of religious associations in state activities', and has observed that, with respect to the former approach, the Indian subcontinent has its own long intellectual history regarding religious diversity and pluralism.[16]

In British India, the fight against imperialism became entangled with religious affiliations that were deliberately exploited by those who would gain from them, and independence was accompanied by partition of India along religious divisions. The result was an avowedly secular, Hindu-dominated India and a Muslim Pakistan where a feudal elite retained their privileges and promoted a social conservatism. Pakistan's initially ambiguous relationship to the concept of an Islamic state[17] soon hardened into a deliberate embrace, formalised in 1956 by the nation's first constitution.[18] For the people of East Bengal (as we have seen), life after partition supplied a daily lesson that being part of a Muslim nation did not provide the answer to the region's needs. The secularist politics through which many articulated their response reconnected with the socialist and liberal threads of anti-imperialism; and, in reaction to the communalist blood-letting ignited by partition, political leaders rediscovered older ideas and practices of multi-religious co-existence. This Bengali secularism followed Sen's '*neutrality* between different religions', or what Jefferson called 'rights of conscience',[19] and its supporters could themselves be people of sincere religious faith or non-believers, or anything in between. Most Bengalis who describe themselves as secular would also describe themselves as practising Muslims. Their secularism defines itself against state religion, religious intolerance and all politics that is based primarily on religious doctrines or is enacted through religious organisations.[20]

The secular religious divide remains a defining issue in Bangladeshi politics, and a source of vitriolic contention between the Awami League and the BNP, the two main political forces. But the issue has been both confused and intensified by decades of realpolitik and by the emergence of a dynastic power politics that is divorced from the needs of the people and resorts to religious populism and tactical alliances with religious parties – especially with Jamaat, the secularists' enemy from 1971. At the same time as criticising religious-based political organisation, today's secular politicians tend to emphasise their own personal religious devotion. Furthermore, their professed secularism has not prevented the Awami League from claiming Bangladesh as a Muslim nation and indulging in Islamic populism and some very surprising alliances. Ali Riaz has pointed out that in 1974 Mujib himself joined the Islamic Summit in Lahore and led the Islamic Foreign Ministers' Conference in Jeddah.[21] He notes that by the early 1990s, the League 'preferred to be portrayed as a party that valued Islam as an integral part of the culture of Bangladesh' and as a 'suitable custodian of Islam'. By the 2001 elections both main parties expressly promised to enact no laws that would be contrary to Islam.[22] He outlines how, in the period of military rule, the regimes used Islam to win popular support while the opposition parties formed alliances with the Islamists to oust the dictators, and how, when democracy was reinstated, the secular parties wooed the Islamists as king-makers or government breakers. This gave Jamaat a new political legitimacy, and – at the same time – the ideological bankruptcy and overt corruption of the main parties allowed Jamaat (despite its own role in these power games) to portray themselves as a clean alternative and to argue that the failed man-made democratic system should be replaced by the law of God. [23] The Awami League has worked with Jamaat in the past (and even made a short-lived pact, in 2006, with the Bangladesh Khilafat Majlis), but more recently Jamaat has been associated with the BNP. They were the main coalition partner in the BNP's government between 2001 and 2006 and remain, at the time of writing, their main partner in the opposition alliance.

The Awami League has taken the secularist-religious battle to the courts. In 2005, the Bangladesh High Court pronounced that amendments made to the original constitution under military rule were illegal and hence nullified. This position was upheld by the Supreme Court in 2010, and that same year saw the establishment of a special tribunal in Dhaka to reopen the cases of the men accused of war crimes in 1971. The trials were part of the Awami League's manifesto when it swept back into power at the head of a 'grand coalition' in 2008. The majority of the accused are associated with Jamaat, though two former ministers of the BNP were also included among the first indictments. The protests around these trials – which will be looked at in more detail in Chapter 8 – are a reminder of how, for the Bengalis, issues of Islamisation have an additional resonance. At the same time, and despite the trials, Awami League politicians can demonstrate a pragmatic reluctance to risk upsetting strengthened religious sensibilities, and this has resulted in them taking the logically inconsistent decision to retain the words 'Bismillah-ar-Rahman-ar-Rahim' (in the name of Allah, the Beneficent, the Merciful), introduced by Zia into the preamble of the Constitution, and not to reverse the 1988 declaration of Islam as the state religion. In defence of this position, they argue that these 'reflect the beliefs of the people'. [24]

The last three decades

Zia was succeeded by his Vice President who was subsequently elected in his own right, but it was not long before another soldier took charge. General H.M. Ershad imposed martial law in March 1982, claiming the country needed a government with military efficiency. The level of political suppression varied with time, but Ershad's hold on power was strengthened by the antagonism between the two main opposition parties. A first attempt at a united opposition front was firmly suppressed in 1984 and it was not until 1990 that, spearheaded by the students, the opposition parties again achieved real unity of action. This time they carried the masses behind them and Ershad was finally forced to resign at the end of the year in the face of huge demonstrations. Ershad's Jatiya Party (National Party), launched in 1986, was conservative and pro-Islamic like the

BNP, and it was Ershad who changed the constitution to make Islam the state religion. The party garnered appreciable support in London as the party of power, and its followers were able to point to administrative reforms that strengthened regional power structures and so increased the scope for *probashi* influence in their areas of origin. But the 1990 opposition movement produced strong echoes among the Bengalis in Britain in the form of meetings, demonstrations and leaflets.

The ensuing years have been dominated by the Awami League and the BNP and characterised by distrust, corruption and violence. Election results have reflected negative protest against the ruling regime and power has alternated between alliances based around the two dominant parties. The only exception was a two-year hiatus in 2007–08 when distrust between the parties got so bad that elections were delayed and the President declared emergency rule. Newspapers have regularly carried stories of the gunning down of political activists (often so-called student leaders) and court cases against leading members of the party out of office. There has been more politics on the streets than in the National Assembly, with parliamentary boycotts and *hartals* (mass protest strikes) as favourite opposition tactics. But through all this activity, little has been done to address the desperate economic and social needs of the majority of the population.

At the time of writing, all but one of the main Bangladeshi political parties have official branches in Britain (with disputatious organisational histories[25]). The exception is Jamaat-e-Islami, the main Islamic party, whose influence through linked Islamist organisations is explored in Chapter 8. Visiting politicians can expect a substantial audience and, while many leading figures have changed their jerseys according to the party in power,[26] Bangladeshi politics can be a source of passion and deep emotional attachment. One Awami League member described the party to me as 'like father, mother'[27] – an echo of the Bengali phrase *ma bap* (*ma baf* in Sylhet) used to refer to a paternalistic relationship. As in any politics, motives for involvement may be complex and overlapping and not necessarily reflected in explanations given in response to interviews. Bangladeshi politics can provide rare opportunities both for developing power and prestige and for affecting the lives of some of the world's poorest people.

There has always been movement backwards and forwards between Britain and East Bengal, and many people have been involved in politics in both places. The most notable recent example is probably Shofiqur Rahman Chowdhury, who after long involvement with the Bangladesh Welfare Association, the Awami League and the Labour Party was narrowly elected as a Sylhet MP in 2008. As travel and communications have improved, it has got easier to integrate political activity in the two different countries and use one to promote the other. Bangladeshi political connections can help promote the image of a potential local councillor, while credentials as a councillor will be respected within Bangladeshi political parties. Those who plan to run for office in Bangladesh must first nurse their potential constituency, playing the traditional patriarchal role of arbitrator in local disputes and being seen to give generously to local charities.[28] And, more generally, *Londoni* money plays an important part in the politics of Sylhet, with *Londoni* families enjoying the influence of their wealth and prestige at election times. London Bengalis also get direct access to those in power when they come to London on official visits. This two-centre politics can be combined with business connections (regular and irregular) to their mutual benefit.[29]

For much of the British-born generation, Bangladeshi party politics has little appeal. British branches of Bangladeshi parties do have younger members, but these are predominantly recent immigrants (often through marriage) who learnt their politics in Bangladesh.[30] The generational shift of focus is exemplified by the experience of Shams Uddin, who came to Britain in 1963, and was president of the UK branch of the Jatiya Party until his death in 2009. Shams Uddin's political awakening came with the independence struggle. As he explained:

> That time … everybody is more politically growing up, because before, nobody's interested any much politics … When started the struggle and everybody heard the Pakistani army do that and that, and after the war is finished, slowly people is involved in the politics.[31]

He joined Ershad's Jatiya Party in the mid-1980s, after hearing him speak about his government's programmes in a London meeting. When I interviewed him in 2001, he outlined the reasons for his continued involvement with Bangladeshi politics:

> I'm not much educated in the English … I'm brought up in the Bangladesh and still I want to think about for my country – because this country is all right, there is rich people, it's a rich country, but Bangladesh is poor country … That's why we want to [be] involved in the Bangladesh politics.

However, his children were not interested in Bangladeshi politics, and he could understand why:

> When I came this country first, I thought maybe I'm going to stay there five years or ten years, then I go back my country – I'm not stay here. After about ten, fifteen years then I think maybe we can't go, then I want to bring my wife, my family, children … Before, any penny we … make here we … send in the Bangladesh, and now we want to try to sell everything there and bring it here … My son and daughter, they doesn't like in Bangladesh, they are staying here, because they think their country's here.[32]

A young activist who has tried to recruit British-born youth into the women's section of one of Britain's Awami League groups confessed to me that most do not know much about the party and are put off by the nature of power politics and the way party leaders jostle for control.[33] For the British Bengalis studying A-level politics at Tower Hamlets College, corrupt Bengali politics may be just good for a laugh. One of them told me:

> All we hear is the amount of bribery that's going on, 'cos our parents talk constantly about it … And so we don't understand this stuff really, and the stuff we do understand we just laugh at it. And so, like, when we were talking about the EU in politics, it's like a couple of students will come out and say, poor Bangladesh, poor Bangladesh, just to actually lighten up the whole situation.[34]

This comment, recorded in 2000, resonates with the responses observed by Ali Riaz some seven years later. The young Bengalis he talked to were 'dismayed by the overemphasis on "home politics" at the expense of "our politics"', and sceptical about the intentions of British Bengalis involved in Bangladeshi politics.[35]

Patriarchs and professionals

Bangladesh's political and economic chaos has naturally affected the response of Bengalis in Britain to the call of their *desh* (homeland). It confirms the value of settlement in Britain and reinforces the desirability of escape by immigration into a richer more ordered world. It also dampens the potential for financial investment in Sylhet, which, despite its recent development boom, does not have the pull on *probashi* Bengalis that India now has for Non-Resident Indians. Nevertheless, the link with Britain continues to underlie the development of modern Sylhet and Sylhet is still very much present in Britain's Bengali households. Even the younger generation, which is firmly rooted in Britain, has been brought up in a society orientated towards Bangladesh, and probably with Bangla TV running in the background. Most have visited their ancestral homeland, but even if they haven't they can say, as one university student said to me without a hint of irony, 'I was born here. I haven't been back home yet'.[36] Transnational connections are always evolving but they remain strong, and this has been facilitated by new forms of communication.

Disillusionment with party politics can encourage less overtly political ways of continuing to play a role in the ancestral land, and here an important part is taken by regional associations. Considerable importance is given to a person's place of origin, and regional links can be so strong that some families prohibit marriage outside their area.[37] Regional organisations perform two principal roles: they bring together families scattered across Britain and they collect and organise funds for development work in the area of origin. Sometimes this work is a response to special needs and crises, but often the organisations help build up basic services through supporting key projects such as schools and roads. Regional organisations operate on different levels, with the larger ones more dominated by organisational meetings and the internal power struggles appropriate to their prestige. In every community people enjoy the kudos of running an organisation or giving to charity, and these things are of particular value in a patriarchal society. Motives for involvement may include personal advancement as well as genuine altruism and, while some may turn to these associations as an alternative to party politics, others will make use of their social networks to develop business connections or party political influence. Regional associations draw inspiration from traditional patterns of patronage, but also from modern Bangladesh's NGO culture, and at least one district organisation has been set up especially for members under thirty-five.[38]

The importance of regional and other charitable organisations for channelling help back to Bangladesh was demonstrated to me by Rahman Jilani, then director of Asian Studies at Toynbee Hall. He explained, 'I feel very strongly that wherever we are, we're supposed to help people within our own capacity, by politicking, or by economy, or by something, as a member of society'. After fighting for Bangladesh's independence, he was dismayed by the political path taken by the new nation and became determined to avoid political parties and offers of help from his politically powerful family. Instead, he told me that he hoped 'to retire at the age of fifty-five and then start my own charity to help people, rather than going into damned politics and create more enemies'. When we talked in 2001, he had already got together with others who had left his small home-town near Comilla at the same time as himself and were prospering around the world, and they had formed a charitable foundation. In addition, he told me that with his own money he had launched 'an income-generating project which is actually feeding 120 people a day'[39] and, on a wider scale, he had been instrumental in founding the Greater Comilla Association. Since that time he has founded a British-based charity that largely works in Bangladesh, of which he is executive director.[40] One of its main activities is home care for the elderly, following the culturally sensitive home-care model that Jilani developed for Asian elders in London.

In a similar vein, Aziz Choudhury, who we met in the last chapter, is founder president of the Sylhet Sador Association, which organises welfare work in Sylhet and 'community build up' for Sylhetis scattered across Britain. He has also established a college in his native village. He explains his inspiration through traditional concepts of patriarchal society:

> Back home we've got a different thinking, like you are not just for yourself, everybody else from your locality have a right on you, if you are doing well you should look after everybody else … Because I am here they are deprived from my help.[41]

Both the giving of general charity and of *shahajjo* (help for poorer kin) are deeply embedded in Bengali tradition.[42] As with his work at the Spitalfields Housing Co-op and the Spitalfields Small Business Association (of which he is chair), Aziz Choudhury puts greater faith in direct involvement than in party politics. Besides getting financial support from others who originated in the area and now live in Britain, he has used his experience as a community worker in London to get the active participation of people on the ground in Sylhet.

Other professionals have also been keen to use their expertise to help people in their homeland. So, for example, in 2003 the British-Bangladeshi Professionals' Association, formed by a group of young Bengalis, produced a paper entitled 'What can DFID do better for Bangladesh?' This was intended both to feed into the UK Department for International Development's (DFID's) ongoing policy review and

> to stimulate increased interaction between DFID and the British Bangladeshis and to encourage more Bangladeshis with relevant skills and knowledge, whether based in the UK or elsewhere, to engage with DFID's programme and projects in Bangladesh.[43]

Rather less conventionally, Masud Rahman, who worked as a careers advisor in Tower Hamlets, spent a working holiday on a boat travelling through Bangladesh and giving advice to young people at the places where he tied up for the night.

In 1996, the formal twinning of Tower Hamlets and Sylhet provided another vehicle for professional Bengalis in Britain – especially local councillors and council officers – to wield political influence in Bangladesh. The most coordinated example of this was provided by the European Union-funded Sylhet Partnership, in which the Danish Municipality of Horsens acted as a third partner. This two-year project, begun in January 2001, was aimed at bringing European 'regeneration' concepts to Sylhet and concentrated most of its resources on the neglected area of waste management; however it was able to do little more than dent this massive problem.[44]

The inability of relatively small amounts of regeneration funding to impact on fundamental structural problems has, of course, also been observed in Tower Hamlets, which has a long history of such projects but always seems in need of more. However, this is not the place for a critique of general concepts of 'regeneration'.[45] Rather, the next chapter turns back from these examples of Bengali absorption into currently dominant forms of governance, to look further at Bengali engagement with socialism and with those fundamental structural problems.

Notes

1 Interviewed 14 May 2001 (with Abul Kalam Azad as interpreter).
2 Anthony Mascarenhas, *Bangladesh: A Legacy of Blood* (London: Hodder and Stoughton, 1986), p. 11.
3 Interviewed by Caroline Adams, 29 September 1990, tape recording (Tower Hamlets Local History Library).

 4 Interviewed 28 February 2002.
 5 See Lawrence Lifschultz, *Bangladesh: The Unfinished Revolution* (London: Zed Press, 1979).
 6 Interviewed 11 December 2001.
 7 Faruque Ahmed, *Bengal Politics in Britain: Logic, Dynamics and Disharmony* (North Carolina: Lulu, 2010), pp. 163–4 and 174–5.
 8 Trials of war criminals were ended by Mushtaq, though they have recently been reopened by the Awami League. Under Zia, the ban was lifted that prevented those who had previously been convicted from taking part in parliamentary elections.
 9 Bangladesh Constitution, clause 8:1 and 1A, as amended by the Proclamations Order No. 1 of 1977 and incorporated in the 5th Amendment of 1979.
10 *Hackney Gazette*, 20 June 1980; *Morning Star*, 18 June 1980.
11 Mascarenhas tells the history of that broadcast and how Zia came to make it. It was not actually the first announcement of Independence, but the first that got wide coverage, and it was relayed round the world. See Mascarenhas, *Bangladesh*, pp. 118–20.
12 Tasadduk Ahmed and Abdul Mannan, interviewed by Caroline Adams, 1980s, tape recording (Tower Hamlets Local History Library).
13 www.humanism.org.uk/education/parents/worship-your-rights, accessed 5 October 2010.
14 Church of England website, www.cofe.anglican.org/info/education/schools, accessed 5 October 2010.
15 Letter to Neremiah Dodge and others, 1 January 1802, http://en.wikisource.org/wiki/Jefferson_letter_to_Neremiah_Dodge_and_others, accessed 5 October 2010.
16 Amartya Sen, *The Argumentative Indian* (London: Allen Lane, 2005), pp.18–20.
17 Pervez Hoodbhoy, 'Jinnah and the Islamic State: Setting the Record Straight', *Economic and Political Weekly*, 42:32 (2007), 3300–03.
18 Suhrawardy's criticism of this aspect of the constitution (as then leader of the opposition) pointed out the dangers of the power being given to the Ulemas to determine how the law should conform to Islam, however he also told the National Assembly: 'we believe in Islam to the core … and we hope that the combined intelligence of the representative of the people in various legislatures that will be established will be able to impress upon this country Islamic ideals, Islamic conduct, Islamic laws.' See http://pakistanspace.tripod.com/archives/56suhrawardy.htm, accessed 7 January 2011. Awami League members further to the left cannot have been happy with this careful compromise.
19 Letter to Neremiah Dodge, as above.
20 Sheikh Mujib told parliament that 'Secularism does not mean the absence of religion. Hindus will observe their religion; Muslims will observe their own; Christians and Buddhists will observe their religions. No one will be allowed to interfere in others' religions. The people of Bengal do not want any interference in religious matters. Religion cannot be used for political ends'. Parliament Debates, 12 October 1972, quoted in Amena A. Mohsin 'Religion, Politics and Security: The Case of Bangladesh', in Satu P. Limaye, Mohan Malik and Robert G. Wirsing (eds), *Religious Radicalism and Security in South Asia* (Honolulu: Asia-Pacific Centre for Security Studies, 2004), p. 470.
21 Ali Riaz, *Islam and Identity Politics Among British-Bangladeshis: A Leap of Faith* (Manchester: Manchester University Press, 2013), p. 77.
22 *Ibid.*, pp. 80 and 81.
23 *Ibid.*, pp. 79–82. Riaz also notes that religious populism in Bangladesh has been given

greater resonance because of the Islamising influence of migrant workers returned from the Middle East and the Gulf. See pp. 84–6.

24 *Daily Star*, 6 January 2010. Riaz points out that the promise to keep Bismillah was made in response to BNP scarmongering at the time of the 1991 election. See Riaz, *Islam and Identity Politics Among British-Bangladeshis*, p. 80.

25 Ahmed, *Bengal Politics in Britain*.

26 *Ibid.*, p. 233.

27 Interviewed September 2000.

28 See interviews by David Garbin in Sylhet, June 2000, and London, April 2001, carried out as part of his PhD research.

29 These political and business connections are explored in David Garbin, 'Migration, territoires diasporiques et politique identitaires: Bengalis musulmans entre "Banglatown" (Londres) et Sylhet (Bangladesh)' (PhD dissertation, University of Tours, 2004).

30 Discussion with a leader of the women's section of one of the British Awami League groups, 7 October 2001; Interview by David Garbin of a prominent member of the UK Awami Jubo [Youth] League, April 2001.

31 Interviewed 6 March 2001.

32 *Ibid.*

33 Discussion with a leader of the women's section of one of the British Awami League groups, 7 October 2001.

34 Interviewed 10 July 2000.

35 Riaz, *Islam and Identity Politics Among British-Bangladeshis*, p. 88.

36 Interviewed June 1999. I heard similar comments when interviewing college students in 2007.

37 A university graduate I was speaking with in 2001 told me that his parents had forbidden him to marry his Bengali girlfriend because she was from the wrong district. Instead he went back to his village for an arranged marriage agreed after one formal meeting.

38 Discussion with Zoinul Abidin, 27 February 2001.

39 Interviewed 13 March 2001.

40 www.beveridgefoundation.org, accessed 7 January 2011.

41 Interviewed 20 February 2001.

42 See Katy Gardner, *Global Migrants, Local Lives: Travel and Transformation in Rural Bangladesh* (Oxford: Clarendon Press, 1995), pp. 152–6.

43 'What can DFID do better for Bangladesh? A Report by the International Development Group (IDG) of the British-Bangladeshi Professionals Association (BBPA) 2 January 2003', www.amazingbangladeshis.org/uploads/IDG_DFID_Bangladesh_paper.pdf, accessed 2011, p. 2. I am grateful to John Eade, Sallie Westwood and Jamil Iqbal for allowing me to attend their focus group discussions with members of this association.

44 Stephen Jacobs, 'Sylhet Partnership Summary Evaluation Report: January – 2003' (London: SDP Regeneration Services Ltd, 2003). This project was part of the Asia Urbs Programme, and its €500,000 budget included €325,000 from the EU and €107,500 from Tower Hamlets.

45 A critique of the limits of this approach can be found in Jamie Gough, Aram Eisenschitz and Andrew McCulloch, *Spaces of Social Exclusion* (Abingdon: Routledge, 2006). The way regeneration budgets focus attention on limited projects to the exclusion of major expenditure patterns was emphasised to me by an employee of a Tower Hamlets regeneration company.

5   Socialism on stony ground

The historic example of East End Jewish radicalism encouraged many left activists to expect to see the emergence of a similarly strong left movement in later immigrant groups, but circumstances have been very different. We have already seen how popular-front politics allowed nationalism – and the everyday demands of welfare activities – to stifle the socialist ideology of the intellectual leaders of the generation of immigrants active before Bangladeshi Independence. This chapter begins by going back to look more critically at the origins of those early Bengali Socialists, at their attitude towards Islam and at their uneasy relationship with class politics.

Islamic socialists

Like the Russian Jewish revolutionaries, the first socialists in the Indian sub-continent were responding to an oppressive imperial regime, but for most of the North Indian Muslims who took up socialist ideas this did not involve a break with their cultural or even religious past, as had been so important for the Jewish leaders. Rather, the emphasis was on reform from the inside. For many of these early socialists, the road to socialism lay through the Khilafat movement, organised by Indian Muslims in 1919 to support the embattled Ottoman Caliphate, which they regarded as a final redoubt of pan-Islamic power in a world increasingly dominated by European imperialism.[1] Khilafat leaders turned for help towards the young Soviet Union, and the Bolsheviks invited the Muslim rebels to an Oriental Propaganda Bureau in Tashkent, consisting of a military school and a special communist university. Apart from isolated examples, the result was more often a broad sympathy with communism rather than a wholesale acceptance of communist ideals. This approach, which has remained as a persistent trait on the Bengali left, was exemplified in the Khilafat Conference declaration in 1920 of 'every sympathy with the Bolshevik movement so far as it is consistent with the principles of Islam'.[2]

In 1922, the Soviet Union began promoting communist organisation directly in India itself. The Indian Communist Party was established in 1925, and when it was officially banned between 1934 and 1942 it continued to work through other organisations. At Partition, the Communist Party of India claimed to have over 10,000 members in East Bengal, and in the turbulent years before Indian and Pakistani Independence the communists had a reach well beyond their numerical strength. Bengali *lascars* had plenty of exposure to communist influence. Of the principal figures mentioned in Humayun Ansari's account of *Socialism Among the North Indian Muslims*, Muzaffar Ahmad, a prominent communist leader in Calcutta from the 1920s, had strong links with the *lascars* from his native Noakhali; Abd Al-Razzaq Khan was a leader of the Calcutta Seamen's Union when he became General Secretary of the Bengal Peasants' and Workers' Party (a Communist Party front organisation) in 1927; and Ghulam Ambiya Khan Luhani worked with *lascars* in London through the pro-communist Workers' Welfare League of India in 1919.[3] In addition, Faruque Ahmed records that Jyoti Basu, the future Communist Chief Minister of West Bengal, first got involved in politics as a student barrister in London in the 1930s, where one of his activities was to help the British Communist Party (CPGB) in its attempts to provide illiterate *lascars* with some education.[4]

In the early 1920s, Shapurji Saklatvala, the Indian communist MP for Battersea, spearheaded attempts to unionise the *lascars*. By 1925, under the guidance of its energetic organising secretary, Gujarati communist N.J. Upadhyaya (or Paddy), weekly meetings of the Indian Seamen's Union at the gates to London Docks attracted a group of fifty to sixty, and by 1930, union membership had reached a peak of six thousand.[5] However, although the union was able to win cases for individual members, Rozina Visram comments that membership was 'unstable', and she records that Upadhyaya 'lamented [the *lascars*'] reluctance to exert themselves in their own interests and to strike'. She observes that, 'At a time of over-supply and under-employment their reluctance to unionise is understandable'.[6] In addition, the Communist Party failed to live up to its own resolutions and provide much practical help. Marika Sherwood has noted several occasions when the British Party was castigated for neglecting colonial workers. In 1925, the Indian communist M.N. Roy commented that 'there was much national prejudice existing even among communists ... The British Party did not like Indians coming round to head office'.[7] And in 1934, Saklatvala criticised the CPGB for its neglect of both colonial problems and 'colonials' in Britain, observing, 'There is no healthy contact between (colonial seamen, hawkers, students) and Party members'; and recommending 'an insistent education of every member of the Party'.[8]

Indian seamen were unable to win improvements in their conditions until the onset of the Second World War, but they immediately realised the opportunities – as well as the dangers – that war brought. A wave of strikes spread through British merchant ships across the world as crews refused to sail without 'reasonable wages to cover war risks' and adequate compensation for their families in case of accident or death. Several hundred *lascars* were rewarded with prison for breach of contract, but other strikes were more successful. By the end of 1939, H.S. Suhrawardy, then Bengal Minister of Commerce and Labour, had helped to negotiate a general settlement, which was accepted by Aftab Ali, leader of the All India Seamen's Federation in Calcutta; and further improvements would be squeezed from the recalcitrant ship-owners before the end of the war.[9] The *lascars* in Britain were now led by another communist, Surat Alley, originally from Cuttack in Orissa. Alley was the Federation's London representative, and although the terms of the agreement fell far short of the *lascars'* demands, he was compelled to accept them. Aftab Ali was a strong supporter of the British war effort, and also held avoidance of communism as a 'faith and a creed'. In a speech to members of the Bengal Cabinet in 1937, he used the possibility of the seamen being 'driven into the arms of Communism' as a powerful argument for employers and government to co-operate with his accommodating trade unionism. Referring to 'the steady growth of Communism' in India, he added, 'and you, Gentlemen, are all aware that the direct alternative to Trade-Unionism is Communism'.[10]

While all this may have made the former *lascars* more responsive to the call of the left activists who led the campaigns described in previous chapters, there is no evidence that the seamen who settled in London regarded themselves as players in left-wing organisations. Indeed, memories of the role of the union and of Aftab Ali can display attitudes that are more patriarchal than socialist. As one ex-seaman put it to Caroline Adams:

> He fought for us and created a union to improve our conditions … Before Aftab Ali the companies really misused their power and saw us as slaves. With him we had protection for us as workers.[11]

Developments in East Bengali communism during the Pakistan years have been outlined in Chapter 2. As in the Jewish Pale of Settlement in nineteenth-century Russia, communist ideas were taken up by an educated layer frustrated by external restrictions imposed by an unsympathetic ruler – in this case the pseudo-colonial West-Pakistani dominated government. But in Sylhet at least, there was almost no proletariat for them to work with and relations with the peasantry were still patriarchal. Conditions would have born a closer comparison to those facing the Russian revolutionary *Narodniks* who attempted to mobilise former serfs in the 1870s than to the experience of the Jews in the towns of the 1890s and early 1900s. However, unlike the *Narodniks*, the Bengali leftists were generally active in their home areas and were happy to attempt to use the old bonds rather than destroy them.

Moreover, although some people were quietly atheist, few would openly admit to atheism – and this is still true today. There was never a demand for a radical break with religious tradition even among the leadership layers; with the

'Red Maulana' as a prime example and dominating influence. When I asked if he had ever felt that his left-wing politics were incompatible with Islam, Aziz Choudhury, a former member of the pro-Moscow NAP, replied:

> those who are left-wing politician, their lifestyle is different, they're more intellectual people, so sometimes the village mullahs used to think that maybe they are the threat to Islam. But actually they were talking more about what Islam says, the equality and fairness and everything ...[12]

We have already seen how the power of the old patriarchal relationships was demonstrated in the campaign for Bangladeshi Independence. There was a well-founded expectation that people would follow their traditional leaders. As Aziz Choudhury put it, 'the general people, they don't get involved unless their community leader, or those who are activ[ists], [lead them], they don't partici-pate'.[13] Abdus Salique attributes much of the former strength of left politics in his native area to the influence of his well-respected Marxist uncle, and important elements of this patriarchal tradition have continued in London. This was clear in Salique's comment to me in 2001 that 'I always ask my people to vote for the Labour Party';[14] and when I visited Brick Lane at the time of the 2005 general election, he was described to me (exaggeratedly as it turned out) as the man who controlled politics in the area. He was chairman of the Brick Lane Traders' Association as well as active politically, and I found him in his sweetshop-cum-café presiding over a group of Labour Party councillors who he later referred to as his 'juniors'.

Active participation in radical politics in East Bengal was regarded as a luxury that could only be risked and afforded by those with some money to spare – which is why the Bengali left had previously been dominated by the largely Hindu elite. Aziz Choudhury suggests that this approach made it difficult to transfer these politics to British soil:

> Back home you don't worry, you don't have to pay rent, you don't have to earn money. You can stay in your parents' house, or you have a family house – whatever you do, you come home, you get food ... But here ... we are the first generation ... we haven't got a base to go to. Bengalis, when they get [into politics], they get very serious ... That's why I think people didn't go that far.[15]

Aziz Choudhury had been able to learn his own politics with the NAP leader Pir Habibur Rahman, who was his distant cousin. This sort of political appren-ticeship was not possible in London, though Tasadduk's discussion groups helped to fill the gap.

In London (as we have seen) the early Bengali political leaders were generally students (or ex-students) or professionals. The leaders of the Jewish immigrant left were not all ordinary workers and some had been politicised as students in Russia;[16] however, the Russian Jews came from a community that had long been barred close connection with the land and was undergoing profound physical and social upheaval, and they had learnt their socialism in an urban and industrialising setting. In contrast, socialists in East Bengal generally came from families that were deeply rooted in the land and still played a dominant part in village structures, and their definitions of class tended to become rather blurred.

In Sylheti society, pre-industrial ideas of social status retained a strong hold. In a Sylheti village, higher status is endangered by working on land belonging to a different family lineage,[17] and although work outwith the home village does not attract the same shame, labour is not easily embraced as a defining identity. Lineage links and their internal systems of patronage can also cut across potential class divisions.[18] The great majority of first-generation immigrants were proletarianised in Britain, however most still held plots of land, even if small, in Bengal, and many did not like to consider themselves part of a working class. Sunahwar Ali described to me how, when he was a Labour borough councillor, someone whose bribe he had refused retaliated by describing him as working class in a local paper.

> It's a big insult, it's like mentioning my parent is not educated … [I]f you are from [a] working-class family, and your family are uneducated, among the Bengali community this is a major obstacle for you to say or do anything.[19]

In 1991, Sylheti snobbery was strong enough to cause severe damage to the popular Bengali weekly, *Jagoron*. The paper published an article that claimed the Sylheti immigrants were descended from tea plantation workers, which, besides being inaccurate, was taken as a gross insult and met with a boycott. A rival paper commented: 'A learned friend has written that Sylheti people who come here are descendents of coolies! … such ignorance or hurling abuses, which hurt ones feelings, should be avoided.'[20]

This rejection of working-class identity – and thus of class-based organisation – cannot, however, be regarded as an automatic product of the Bengalis' retention of links to their land and villages. Indeed, as has been argued by historians of Indian labour, a village link can provide an element of extra security and so facilitate actions such as industrial strikes.[21]

Looking back at Katznelson's analysis of working-class formation[22] outlined in the introduction, we can see how the Bengalis' particular lived experience of working-class jobs and living conditions in racist Britain was additionally filtered through a sensibility rooted in quite different geographical, economic and cultural conditions. Together, this made of them a distinctive fraction of the working-class, and a fraction that didn't easily accept its class position or choose to move to Katznelson's fourth stage of class-based collective action. To understand the Bengalis' rejection of working-class identity and organisation, we need to look beyond the predispositions arising from their background and their position within a racist labour-market, and examine the nature and tactics of the left politics with which they engaged, which we have already done in the previous chapters.

Even those Bengalis who took up socialist ideas and adopted the rhetoric of class politics often used this rhetoric rather loosely. As we have already seen in Chapter 2, Qureshi described himself as part of the working class although he owned his own restaurant; Tasadduk provided the focus for left debate in the 1960s, but established an association for restaurant owners not for restaurant workers; and Nurul Islam, recalling that period, described the restaurant owners as 'the leaders of the working class' – a description that demonstrates the tenacity of patriarchal understandings.

Increasingly, Bengalis are moving out of Tower Hamlets in search of greener spaces, better schools, and more affordable and available housing (or even in order to rent out their now valuable ex-council flat). However, there are many who have made a bit of money and still live in the area and this is encouraged by the changes that have taken place in parts of the borough itself. Middle-class Jews moved out. So have some middle-class Bengalis, but this is no longer simply a poor and working-class area. Many of what could be called the second-generation activists, who cut their political teeth in the youth movements of the late 1970s and 80s, were able to build on their connections to escape from the tailoring workshops and restaurants and get white-collar jobs with the local authority or community organisations. And apart from those who have visibly moved up the social scale, the community is much less working-class than it appears. The first-generation immigrants were generally from families who owned some land in Sylhet and over the years money sent back from Britain has been built up into sometimes-substantial landholdings and other investments, although these may be tied into complicated family finances.[23] As one Bengali councillor explained to me,

> There are a hell of a lot of families who have a great deal of property back home in Bangladesh ... and here are living in severely overcrowded conditions, but still would not sell and re-jig.[24]

A British-born college student, who I interviewed in 2007, told me how uncomfortable these class confusions made her feel:

> Here we live like a working-class life, like in a council flat. When we go out there it's ... like it's a total different world; 'cos over here you're seen as, like, really low in the social class, and when you're out there you're like ... you're in the higher class ... you're treated like celebrities and stuff ... Sometimes it's OK, but once people learn that you're from London ... all they want is like money and stuff, and it's really ... difficult, life out there.[25]

There has definitely been social mobility, but all the same it would be wrong to conclude that the community is not still predominantly working class. 2001

Census figures for working Bengali men in Tower Hamlets show that only 17 per cent described themselves as managers or professionals, and only 11 per cent were self-employed. (The equivalent figures for all working men in England as a whole were 26 per cent and 18 per cent.)[26] These statistics do not, of course, acknowledge entrepreneurial activity in Sylhet; nevertheless, it is interesting to look at them alongside Andrew Godley's estimates for the proportion of entrepreneurs among Jewish men working in the East End, which rose from 11 per cent in the 1890s to 18 per cent in the period before the First World War.[27] The Jewish East End developed a strong working-class consciousness; however the Bengali's socio-economic situation has not been reflected in the growth of class politics.

The Bengalis and the unions

Although the wartime gains achieved by the *lascars* were limited – and nothing like those achieved by sailors on British articles, or even by Chinese seamen – many Bengalis who had worked on British merchant ships still had cause for grateful memories of the Indian Seamen's Union. However, the situation in which they found themselves in the London clothing workshops was different from that under the big foreign employers who ran the imperial industries and the shipping lines, and these memoires were anyway fast slipping into a distant past. In addition, and despite their socialist philosophy, the activists who dominated Bengali community politics in London from the 1950s onwards did not regard trade unionism as a priority.

One of the few who did get involved in promoting trade unionism was Salique, who worked with Dan Jones, Secretary of the Trades Council, and with the National Union of Tailors and Garment Workers. However, he still remained firmly within the old patriarchal philanthropic mould. His first acquaintance with industry was his father's biscuit factory in Bengal, which employed around seventy or eighty people:

> [L]ots of people used to work for him. I used to organise them against my father … and I was a school kid at that time … I asked my father to do the Id holiday … and he used to deny it, and I told them to go, and he was very upset with me.[28]

In London, where he came in 1970, Salique set up his own factory in Cannon Street Road making garment 'shells', which employed around a hundred people. His first attempt at trade union organisation was among his own workforce.[29]

Salique's factory was relatively large, but in general the East End rag trade had tended to revert to pre-Second World War traditions of backroom workshops. Larger firms were being encouraged to move out of London and many manufacturers, faced with growing competition from abroad, depended for their survival on subcontracting and casualisation of an increasingly immigrant labour force. As Max Levitas, who himself started in the garment trade when he left school around 1930, observed to me in 1999, 'it's all gone back to the backroom workshops which we fought against in the 30s and 40s'.[30] The Bengalis, as the most recent arrivals, found themselves in the least profitable end of the trade, making poor-quality clothes for cheap multiple stores and market stalls. They also built up a network of low-cost leather workshops. One of my interviewees experienced the leather industry first as a worker and then as a struggling small manufacturer, and well knew the difficulties of unionisation in such conditions:

> [Dan Jones] expected us to join the trade union but it was very difficult ... These were small, outdoor units they're called, like they used to get subcontracts from other big manufacturers ... If you joined a trade union then you'd have demands, and if you have demands, then this small unit, when he comes under pressure he cannot manage ... it will be a chaos.

He claimed that community bonds and personalised recruitment methods meant that his own employees did not really want to join a union – they would certainly have made it more difficult.[31]

By the late 1970s the garment trade was providing work for the majority of Bengali male school leavers, and I shall look in more detail at the activities of the tailoring union.[32] Increasing numbers of Bengalis were also finding work in the expanding Indian restaurant trade, but this area is even more notoriously hard to organise. Not only were the restaurants small family businesses where workers often had personal links to their employers, but unsocial hours kept the cooks and waiters away from political activities.[33] While – thanks, initially to Tasadduk – there have been active associations of Bengali restaurant owners, the only real success that the unions could claim in the restaurant trade was not in the 'Indian' sector but in the mainstream Steakhouse. There was a short-lived attempt in 1987 to campaign for the rights of Bengali restaurant and hotel workers through a journal, *Restora*, but this collapsed when its grant ran out.[34] Dan Jones recalls Bengali delegates coming onto the Trades Council from time to time, but these were white-collar workers – teachers and local government employees – not from the restaurants or the rag trade.[35]

Although many of those I have spoken with had no memory of union attempts to organise the Bengali workers, this is not because of a lack of trying on the part of the National Union of Tailors and Garment Workers (NUTGW) and other trade unionists. However they never managed to gain that crucial first foothold. The Trades Council recorded in 1978 that 'considerable efforts are being made now by the Tailor and Garment Workers' Union to recruit Bengalees', but that '[o]nly the larger clothing factories tend to be organised' and 'trade union membership is very low amongst the Bengalee community so far'.[36] The major drive to unionise the Bengalis could not have come at a worse time for the East End garment industry. Conditions had been steadily getting worse and from 1979 the industry felt the full force of the recession. In 1980 the *East London Advertiser* claimed that redundancies were driving significant numbers to buy one-way tickets back to Bangladesh. By January 1981 the NUTGW journal, *The Garment Worker*, recorded that 'Job losses in the East End of London alone are now in the region of seven thousand', and the following month they were describing this 'crisis in clothing' as 'the most dramatic period of decline the industry has ever experienced'.[37] Under fierce competition, tax scams and the avoidance of regulations on employment and safety came to be regarded by the subcontractors as essential for survival. Such firms did not want the union sticking their nose in. They could also cut overheads by using home-workers, and as this was the only method by which many Bengali women could contribute to the family budget, there were increasing numbers ready to take in piecework. Children could be called on to help too. Home-working is especially resistant to organisation. When I interviewed Levitas in 2000 he been helping the NUTGW visit home-workers in some five hundred households, and he explained that an added problem was the amount of illegal overcrowding and use of homes as workshops, making it impossible to involve the local authority.[38]

All this did not prevent trade unionists from attempting numerous initiatives and campaigns for unionisation, especially after racist violence in the late 1970s focussed attention on the Bengali workers. Dan Jones asked his neighbour, Salique, for ideas for propagating trade unionism and Salique, who came from a tradition of radical musicians, wrote and performed a *Trade Union song of the Bangla Deshi Workers*, which was made into a short advertising film using still photographs by Paul Trevor and played in local cinemas. The song called on people to unite to defeat the racists and 'draw the teeth of those who suck our blood and exploit us'.[39] The Tower Hamlets Law Centre in Watney Street, initiated by Jones, was involved in attempting to help the NUTGW recruit Bengali clothing workers. Rajonuddin Jalal, who was then a young member of the centre's management committee and a crucial link to the Bengali-speaking community, told me:

> There was a lot of competition for jobs. The people who were providing you with jobs, or the merchants, they could always find a way of saying to you, 'either you work on our conditions or you don't have a job.' Becoming a member of a trade union would be a last priority, I think, for somebody who was trying to earn a living and knows that they have got limited skill and therefore the choice of job that they can exercise is extremely limited as well. So we tried – I mean I was involved in that project – but it never worked.[40]

Jones also attempted some preliminary work towards unionisation through Kumar Murshid, who came from a well-connected, left-leaning Dhaka family and had arrived in London in 1982, where he worked briefly for a bank before being appointed co-ordinator of the Federation of Bangladeshi Youth Organisations.[41]

Barney Shuster, who became area organiser for the NUTGW in 1980, described to me some of their campaigns.[42] The union produced a leaflet in seven different languages,[43] though many of those to whom it was addressed would not have been able to read. However, as Shuster pointed out, the trade unionists could not have attempted to learn all the languages or 'we'd be probably professors of linguistics and very poor organisers'. Organising was what the union officials were there to do, and had they been able to get more Bengali activists on board, their own lack of the language would not have remained such a problem. They handed out the leaflet outside all factories of any size and on Friday lunchtimes outside the mosque: 'There are thousands, all milling out, and we'd go round, and they'd all take, no-one would refuse a leaflet'. However, it was not easy to penetrate the Bengali workshops, as Shuster recalled:

> I remember once I called a meeting, a general meeting, and advertised it, and the only Bangladeshi[s] that turned up were those working in our ordinary [unionised] factories – so there was a couple of blokes from Hillmans, Morris Hillman's in Hackney, which was a traditional mantle and costume factory.

Notwithstanding these organisational failures, Bengalis were not anti-union. The small number of Bengalis who worked in the few remaining larger garment factories joined the NUTGW alongside their workmates; and those who worked in the Midlands or Northern factories became union members and were glad to have the union look after their interests,[44] just as, earlier, the *lascars* had appreciated the Indian Seamen's Union. However, these were only foot-soldiers of their union. The Bengali community did not develop union activists and leaders. Older Bengali left leaders, many of whom were themselves employers, gave little practical attention to promoting trade unionism, and youth activists did not incorporate it into their fight against racism and discrimination. Without significant help from within the Bengali community to mobilise Bengali workers and develop Bengali trade union activists, union organisers were faced with an impossibly uphill task as they attempted to surmount barriers of language and culture.

Tasadduk's involvement in organising the restaurant owners into a Catering Association can be explained as part of the Bengalis' campaign to arrange immigration vouchers (see Chapter 1). However, the activity to which he devoted his later years was again concerned, not with the working class, but with the class of small capitalists to which so many of the first-generation leaders themselves belonged. This can be seen as symptomatic of the ambivalent attitude to class politics shown by the old Bengali left. The journal Tasadduk edited supported trade unionism,[45] but his own energies came to centre on Spitalfields Small Business Association (SsBA), of which he was chair from its inception in 1979 until he was paralysed by a stroke in 1998. The SsBA was set up to complement Spitalfields Housing Co-op because many buildings combined workshops and living accommodation, and housing grants only covered the residential parts.

In the foreword to the association's tenth anniversary record, Tasadduk explained: 'we have encouraged a few more business entrepreneurs by creating decent workspace for them.'[46] The association's tenants, which in 1998 ranged from craft workshops and youth training projects to shops and even a madrasa, have every reason to be grateful to this dedicated organisation, but although most are very small-scale operations, it cannot be said to have promoted socialist ideals.[47]

Despite Dan Jones' attempts to involve youth activists, younger Bengalis were influenced less by the traditional left than by pragmatic community-based organisation and the ideas of black radicalism (as the next chapter shows), and they would have been suspicious of white union leaders. Analysis by black radical leaders in *Race Today* interpreted the conservatism of union bureaucracy not as a problem innate to all trade unions, but as a racist barrier erected against the struggles of black members – and thus as an argument for separate black organ-isation.[48] Some among the younger generation identified the union officials with a white establishment they had learnt to regard as the problem. Shuster recalled a public meeting at Toynbee Hall where the young Bengalis 'were all having a go at us for not doing enough, not doing enough for them … "Why aren't we getting anything, what good are you?", that sort of thing'.[49]

Patrick Duffy commented in a report on employment and training needs compiled in 1979:

> there was little cause for Bengalis to distinguish between trades unions and other [British] institutions as (until recently) the trades union movement was not well known for taking up issues of racial equality on the shop floor, and this despite the very evident support given by trades unions on broader issues of anti-racism in public demonstrations. However, in a broader context, it must be considered that most Bengalis have endured a series of negative encounters with 'authority' (right from their first encounter with the British High Commission in Bangladesh …).[50]

A wariness of white officials would have been found across the generations, and trust in British unions may also not have come easily to older workers who were familiar with the way concern to protect British jobs tended to prevent the British seamen's unions from making common cause with their *lascar* brothers.

A much more recent example demonstrates the persistence not only of problems in unionising the ethnic restaurant business, but also of Bengali pater-nalism. In the autumn of 2011, news of the launch of a new Bangladeshi Workers' Union spread through the media. The central figure in this story was Azmal Hussain – owner of three restaurants in Brick Lane – with supporting roles being taken by members of the Labour Party, including the Labour peer, Maurice Glasman. Hussain is a scion of a wealthy Sylheti family. He first got involved in the restaurant business – and also trade-union sponsorship – in Sweden, where he went as an Awami League refugee in 1976, and has only been in the UK since 1999. While the focus of this project is clearly influenced by his experience of the strong Swedish labour movement, he described to me how he came from a tradition of charitable paternalism, which he contrasted with the self-interested involvement of the politicians with the claim that 'we are thinking of CV for the other world'.[51] Hussain told me that he had tried to establish a union before – including when he was Chair of Tower Hamlets Respect – but the difference this time was the part played by a young female Labour councillor, Shiria Khatun. Labour took up the project when Glasman, Khatun and another councillor met in Hussain's restaurant to plan Ken Livingston's mayoral election campaign and Hussain introduced the idea of the union. Union meetings were organised at one of his restaurants on Monday evenings, when most Bengali restaurant workers had a day off. Word spread through the community and there were soon five to six hundred people signed up to the group, including workers from other towns and cities. The new organisation was wooed by the trade unions (and also Shoreditch Citizens, representative of the emerging forms of civil society looked at further in Chapter 7), and it was agreed they would affiliate to the GMB (the General, Municipal, Boilermakers and Allied Trade Union). The GMB promised the Bangladeshi Union the benefits of being part of a mainstream union while allowing them to maintain a separate organisational identity to accommodate language difficulties and also other specific problems. So far so promising, but when I talked to Hussain and Khatun in January 2012 there were still only around sixty people who had signed up to the GMB, and fifty of them were Hussain's own workers, for whom he had paid the union membership. We discussed how good employment policies could be used to market the restaurants, and Khatun emphasised that the union would pursue 'round table discussions', aiming to 'engage' rather than 'anger' owners, and did not want 'the old fashioned ways of campaigning'.[52] However they admitted that many of the owners were hostile and many workers were afraid to say publicly that they were involved.[53] When I went past Hussain's restaurant in August 2013 and asked the waiter at the door about union membership he responded that that wouldn't work.

Immigrants and unions

The Bengali experience contrasts with earlier East End histories, when Jewish socialists and anarchists attempted to use trade unionism to cut across racist divisions. Their aim (if not always achieved in practice) had been to combine internationalist principles with pragmatic (but not ideological) Jewish organisation. They saw trade unionism as important for workers' solidarity, and also for dispelling working-class anti-Semitism and charges of unfair competition. As a handbill produced by the Hebrew Socialist Union in 1876 explained (in Yiddish):

> among the [Jewish workers] there is no unity and the masters can do what they please. Thus we not only suffer from disunity but also as a result draw upon us the

dislike and hostility of the English workers who accuse us of harming their interests.[54]

Jewish trade unionists responded to the Trades Union Congress's (TUC) 1895 resolution in favour of immigration restrictions with a pamphlet that ended by appealing to their 'fellow-workers',

> Whether ... it is not rather the capitalist class (which is constantly engaged in taking trade abroad, in opening factories in China, Japan, and other countries) who is the enemy, and whether it is not rather their duty to combine against the common enemy than fight against us whose interests are identical with theirs.[55]

Jewish tailors demonstrated that they could play a full role in the New Unionism of the late 1880s and in the industrial struggles that preceded the First World War. In both periods the tailors came together in a general strike with the aim of winning better working conditions and also acceptance in the wider working class. As Rudolph Rocker, the (non-Jewish) leader of the Jewish anarchists, later explained, their fight against the sweatshops was important not just in itself but in preventing them undercutting other areas of the tailoring trade and endangering working conditions for all. The 1912 general strike of East End Jewish Tailors, which won improved conditions in the workshops, was initially called in support of striking West End tailors to prevent some East End Jews acting as strike-breakers, and Rocker described it as 'even more important morally than economically'.[56] In the earlier general strike in 1889, local dockers had contributed to the tailors' strike fund. In 1912, with their own strike settled, Jewish families were able to help striking dockers by taking more than three hundred of the dockers' children into their homes.[57]

These early Jewish trade unionists saw themselves as part of the wider labour movement, but organised themselves in separate unions or in special Jewish branches of the Amalgamated Society of Tailors and Tailoresses. In those pioneering days, big unions had yet to come together, but there were also practical reasons for ethnic separation. The Jewish tailors spoke a different language and most also worked in different kinds of workshop from established English tailors. Furthermore, growing immigration and severe economic conditions encouraged growing anti-immigrant feelings among British workers and these were reflected in their trade unions, which could be very unwelcoming.[58] However, separate organisation became a habit that was hard to shift, and the last Jewish tailoring union only amalgamated with the NUTGW in 1939.[59]

By the mid 1970s, although the backstreet workshops and the restaurants where so many of the East End Bengalis worked were resistant to unionisation, Britain's black and Asian workers over all were more likely to be in a union than their white counterparts.[60] By then small unions were a thing of the past and they joined up to the large mainstream unions such as the Transport and General Workers' Union (TGWU), encouraged by organisations such as the Indian

Workers' Association and by a practical wish to fit in and to navigate the diffi-culties of the workplace. Working-class racism had been deliberately nurtured by decades of imperial propaganda as the imperialists sought to justify colonisation and to persuade workers at home that they too had a stake in the imperial project. Racism did not vanish with the end of Empire, and continued to be encouraged as a useful management tool for cutting across worker unity. In such an atmosphere, trade-union organisers were far from immune from racist ideas. Competition for jobs was not a major issue in modern racist debate before the 1970s, but the focus of TUC policy echoed establishment worries over integra-tion (with the onus being put on immigrants to accommodate to British norms) and immigration controls. Racist employment practices and racism in the workplace were rarely addressed and immigrant concerns were left unsupported. It was not till the mid-1970s that the TUC embarked on a serious attempt to attack racism, both in employment and within its own ranks. Behind this change of approach was the need to respond to the rise of the National Front and (significantly) a recognition of union failures to support major struggles by ethnic minority members, such as the strikes at Mansfield Hosiery Mills in Loughborough in 1972 and Imperial Typewriters in Leicester in 1974. By the time of the Grunwick dispute, which began in 1976, the whole labour movement was prepared to rally around a strike begun by a group of workers largely made up of Asian women. The Grunwick strike evolved into a major battle against establishment forces (protected by brutal policing and the law lords) for the right to union recognition. That this fight was ultimately lost was due not to racism but to innate conservatism within the TUC hierarchy, which – not for the first or last time – prevented the trade unions from taking all the supportive measures necessary for victory.[61]

Ethnic minority trade unionism helped unite workers across ethnic divisions and to alert the labour movement to the urgency of addressing racism. (It also shattered the stereotype of the passive Asian woman.) But by the end of the 1970s, with recession growing, the trade unions were losing their power, and this coincided with the growth of separatist 'black' politics. While some activists argued for black caucuses within the mainstream labour movement, others used union failures and examples of working-class racism to argue, not for strength-ening the more radical rank-and-file movement, but for building an alternative 'black' organisation – which is the subject of the next chapter.

The far left

None of the difficulties outlined above stopped far-left groups from trying, repeatedly, to persuade the Bengalis to fight for their rights through socialism, but although these groups attracted a few new members, they generally did not stay long, and the hoped-for breakthrough was never made. Previous chapters have shown how the Communist Party's popular-front policies allowed the socialism of the early leaders to be eclipsed first by general welfare activities and then, more importantly, by the struggle for Bangladeshi Independence. The Communist Party also failed to apply the lessons of its own grass-roots activism in the Jewish East End of the 1930s and get the post-war Commonwealth immigrants involved in its work locally, and it failed to make them feel fully accepted on an equal basis. Solly Kaye told me that one party member, Bill Pinder, 'did some work among the seamen in Cable Street',[62] however, Trevor Carter, in his account of his own and others' experiences as 'West Indians in British politics', records the party's general lack of engagement with the concerns of black comrades and its failure to give them responsibility.[63] And as far as the Bengali communists were concerned, it seems that the party made little attempt to integrate them into local organisations or address their specific issues. Sheikh Mannan, who was sympathetic to the Soviet Union, admitted:

> We demonstrated in favour of Vietnam with British student, we supported the cause of Latin American countries, we allied ourself with all liberation movement anywhere in the world. In that connection we came across the left wing student politician in this country, but personally or even collectively, we had very little affiliation with them.

He met many Communist Party members through these international campaigns, however, he explained, 'I never linked myself with them, but ... I learnt a lot from their discussions'.[64]

Shah Lutfur Rahman, who became a Maoist, commented – with some exaggeration – that the British Communist Party 'didn't have any interaction with the Asian community at all'. He blamed both sides:

> they [the CPGB] were much more involved with the wider issues, and within the Bengali community there are no reciprocal responses available at that time at all, except in very few individuals ... Racialism was never in agenda at that time in the communist movement, not in here anyway.[65]

In the 1930s, the CPGB had proved itself well attuned to the fight against anti-Semitism, which had confronted the Russian movement from its infancy. However, it seems that this time it failed to be sufficiently aware of the importance of racism and it failed to make effective connections with the new immigrants and to respond in a practical way to new concerns and opportunities.

This portrayal of failure of organisation is reinforced by accounts from two Bengalis who became active members of the CPGB: Abul Ishaque and Nikhilesh Chakraborty. Before he came to this country in 1962, Ishaque had worked in government service in Karachi, and in London he gave welfare help to less-educated immigrants, first individually and later through the Pakistan Welfare Association, where he spent some time as office secretary. The Communist Party did specifically ask him to talk to Tasadduk Ahmed, but within the party he worked through the London district office in Clerkenwell and did not make links with activists in Tower Hamlets. This was despite the fact that up to 1971 there were still two Communist local councillors – Max Levitas and Solly Kaye – both from immigrant Jewish families and both veterans of fighting racism. As a Bengali activist and member of the British party, Ishaque might have been able to help the CPGB become a bridge between the Bengali community and the more established white working class in Tower Hamlets (even though he did not live in the East End), but this possibility was not explored.[66] Levitas remembers fifteen to sixteen Bengalis in his Communist Party branch in the 1970s[67] and Chakraborty, who was elected to the CPGB Central Committee in 1974–75, did describe the Tower Hamlets councillors as 'of tremendous help to our movement'.[68] However the wording of that comment itself suggests a lack of political integration and sense of shared purpose. The CPGB and its paper, the *Morning Star*, were very supportive of the Bangladesh independence movement[69] and Chakraborty recalled that 'they invited us as guest speakers to their branch meetings',[70] but this interest does not appear to have been extended to locally based issues affecting the Bengali community, or at least not productively. When the Communists lost their two council seats in the 1971 election, Kaye gave as a reason that immigrant workers, who formed a growing part of the electorate, were 'unaware of local factors'.[71] This implies a failure to bring Bengalis into Communist campaigns and, thus, a lack of expectation of Bengali support.

In the spring of 1970, following a brutal spate of 'Paki-bashing' and the racist murder of Tosir Ali, the Communist councillor Solly Kaye was one of the speakers at a thousand-strong, mainly Pakistani, protest meeting. Writing about it in the *Morning Star*, he explained,

> … life has taught us that the purveyors of racialism can be defeated by united action … It would be the greatest error and worse, if the struggle were left to the immigrants' organisations to bear the brunt of the fight … The fight against racial discrimination and violence is part of the fight for a new and better society.

And he called for 'the most far-reaching provision of social centres where communities can meet and learn about each other'.[72] But his party did not prove capable of putting such ideas into practice, even within their own ranks.

When Ishaque took up intense political activism in response to earlier racist attacks in Camden in the late 1960s, he did so in collaboration with a small left organisation called the Working People's Party of England, who helped him form the Pakistan Workers' Union (PWU). The area around Euston has a large Bengali population, and in the summer of 1967 the PWU documented over thirty separate attacks on Bengalis, often on people coming home late after working in West End restaurants. They set up self-defence patrols and, according to Louise London's account in *Race Today*, 'they did achieve some measure of success both in reducing further incidents in the area and in actually apprehending some of the culprits'.[73] On 6 April 1970, the day before Tosir Ali's murder, the PWU announced plans to bring a similar system to the East End; and the local paper reported that on 19 April a big public meeting in the Grand Palais in Commercial Road 'ended in uproar' over the issue of vigilante patrols. While the PWU also used more traditional methods of lobbying and demonstrations, they had shown that they were prepared to ignore the more staid advice given by the National Federation of Pakistani Associations and by establishment figures such as the Stepney MP, Peter Shore, and Trevor Huddleston, Bishop of Stepney. The following day, a group met to set up 'protective gangs'. The public meeting had been called by four organisations, including the Black People's Alliance – an umbrella organisation of which Ishaque was regional convenor.[74] All four could be described as 'black' organisations and the link with a broader left seems to have gone. In the event, as Louise London recorded, 'the streets of the East End were never patrolled by squads like those which were organised by the immigrant community in Euston', and many of those involved found themselves arrested for carrying offensive weapons.[75] Although Ishaque claims that member-ship of the PWU ran into thousands, activists at that time faced a major struc-tural problem in the lack of youth (most families had not yet arrived) and also in a general desire to avoid possible trouble, which some people interpreted as inviting victimisation.[76] The following year, the pitch of racist violence had decreased, and the PWU found itself overtaken by events back in East Pakistan and the mobilisation around Bangladeshi independence.

From a socialist perspective, the PWU failed both to involve the white working class and to demonstrate that fighting racism was part of a bigger battle against inequality. Ishaque admitted to me, 'Our ordinary members were not very political you see, they're only interested about their grievance'.[77]

This first Bengali mobilisation against racism was reflected in developments later in the decade, when separate black organisation became the accepted form of immigrant politics – developments that will be explored more fully in the next chapter. This separatism did not stop numerous left groups from playing an often significant part in anti-racist campaigns and attempting to use this as a basis for recruiting the Bengalis to support their programmes for fundamental social change. Left activists argued that racism was a product and tool of capitalist control and would always recur so long as capitalism persisted, but this was not a message that was easily accepted. A history of colonialism and exploitation had induced a wariness, which cultural insensitivity – and also inter-group conflict – among the left can have done little to dispel. When I asked Ansar Ahmed Ullah, who has been active in the community since the 1970s, for his explanation of why left-wing groups had failed to make inroads, he told me:

> They thought they could come and impose their own agenda onto the local community. Some of them were fairly arrogant and aggressive in pursuing their own interest … we had our own committees here anyway that were fighting at the forefront … And in some cases they would try to hijack the whole issue.[78]

I was to hear this type of comment many times.[79] Another frequent accusation was that the left groups were only there for the demonstrations. Abdus Shukur, who at the time of my interview was a senior Labour councillor, conveyed to me his resentment as a young activist: '… at the end of the day you're going to be gone when the media disappears, we're going to have to stay.'[80] Former Labour councillor Rajonuddin Jalal explained that in the long run this benefited the Labour Party, which by the early 1980s was working with the young Bengalis and whose activists 'were people who actually lived in the community'.[81] The term 'aggressive' turned up again, in the interpretation of the conviction politics of Labour's Militant Tendency by Anamul Haque who, when I interviewed him, was also a Labour councillor. He described Militant as 'a bit aggressive … towards the people who may not accept their practical work'; however, he also observed that 'there was a time if Militant wasn't there, we cannot even protect ourselves', as the Bengalis relied on information about racist activity passed on to them by Militant, as well as by the Socialist Workers Party's (SWP's) Anti Nazi League.[82] Left activists were found to have useful organising skills, but they had obviously failed to persuade many Bengalis that they shared the *same* interest.

The Bengalis who became politically active in Britain in the 1970s and 80s had only limited connection with the old socialist traditions and many of them were not in the country when the socialists of the older generation had been practising their politics. They had grown up with the nationalism – and intense activism – of the Independence struggle, and came of age in an era when new identity-based social movements were turning their backs on old Marxist certainties. They were not inclined to interpret their position according to socialist theory. As Jalal explained:

> for the Bengalis … it was struggle for survival … I think [the link with left groups] was a temporary alliance, because young people were going through a phase in which they did not really have an understanding of the wider political picture, including myself, we were not in it because we wanted to bring down the capitalist system.[83]

Jalal's own political career, which has included eight years as a local Labour councillor and aspirations to become an MP, began, like that of many Bengali councillors, in the Bangladesh Youth Movement (BYM).[84] The main inspiration behind the movement was Shah Lutfur Rahman, one of the leaders of the British section of the Bengali pro-Peking Left in 1971. The BYM was founded in 1976 and grew out of the evening classes Shah had been running for young Bengalis since the mid-60s, which often ended in the pub – a radical step in itself. '[T]hat was our training ground', Shah recalled to me. 'We used to discuss, talk every-thing on earth until eleven, half eleven, twelve o'clock at night, and that started transforming.' They would talk about 'Why we are here … [because] without understanding how colonialism work, how imperialism work, you don't under-stand these issues'.[85] But, despite his own political beliefs, Shah did not succeed in passing on a broader socialist understanding. When I asked him about the failure of British left movements to recruit among the young Bengali activists, he told me:

> Bengalis are not easy people to be recruited in socialist, Marxist or atheist or this kind of movement, it's very rare … [P]eople from Bangladesh village who are more or less suffering from pre-monolithic religion, superstitions, from there to comprehend and understand rationalism, Marxism, is asking too much, without any disciplined education.[86]

There have been numerous examples of left movements among rural migrants (not least in Calcutta) that can be set against such a deterministic view, but Shah's comments suggest that he could have been a victim of his own self-fulfilling prophecy. As a member of an educated elite, he may have felt that some of these ideas were too advanced and that the young Bengalis should concentrate first on more basic education and the immediate and urgent concerns of combating racial violence. I cannot now ask him, as he died not long after my second interview, however he was fully aware of both the achievements and the failures of the mobilisation of which he played such a pivotal part:

> That these children have been able to sit in the council room, it itself is a great achievement. It's a great pity that much better good could [not] come out of it.[87]

Yet again, radical socialism appears to have been deferred for another day, though this time it did not really make it on to the agenda.

Shah was unusual in his generation for the extent of his involvement with the young activists.[88] After the struggle for Bangladeshi independence, many of the older Bengalis had lost their political momentum, and the fraying socialist thread became broken. While there would be no shortage of left activists attempting to inspire future generations – and even creating, in Respect, a whole new political party with Tower Hamlets as its main base – very few of these would come from within the Bengali community. And every time, as the following chapters illustrate, socialist ideas would be pushed aside by a mixture of identity politics and short-term pragmatism.

Notes

1 In its campaign against British imperial control, the Khilafat movement briefly joined forces with the Indian National Congress, but this alliance had already broken down by 1924, when Kemal Atatürk, leader of the new Turkish Republic, abolished the Caliphate.

2 Quoted in Khizar Humayun Ansari, *The Emergence of Socialist Thought Among North Indian Muslims (1917–1947)* (Lahore: Book Traders, 1990), p. 47.

3 *Ibid.*

4   Faruque Ahmed, *Bengal Politics in Britain: Logic, Dynamics and Disharmony* (North Carolina: Lulu, 2010), p. 34.

5   Rozina Visram, *Asians in Britain: 400 Years of History* (London: Pluto Press, 2002), pp. 230–4.

6   *Ibid.*, p. 234.

7   Marika Sherwood, 'Lascars' Struggles Against Discrimination in Britain 1923–45: The work of N.J. Upadhyana and Surat Alley', *The Mariner's Mirror*, 90:4 (2004), 438–55, p. 440.

8   Quoted in *ibid.*, p. 444. These criticisms were contained in a document on party work, written during a visit to the USSR in 1934, which compared the British party unfavourably to the party in the USSR.

9   Visram, *Asians in Britain*, pp. 234–53. The quote is taken from a contemporary report of a speech at a public meeting, see p. 239.

10 'Welcome Address' given at a reception for the Premier and Members of the Bengal Cabinet at the Indian Seamen's Union, Calcutta, 8 April 1937, published by the union. (Copy in Caroline Adams' papers, Tower Hamlets Local History Library.)

11 Haji Mohammed Abdul Rahman, interviewed by Caroline Adams, 1980s, manuscript transcript (Tower Hamlets Local History Library).

12 Interviewed 20 February 2001.

13 *Ibid.*

14 Interviewed 31 January 2001.

15 Interviewed 20 February 2001. In his study of Bengal in the 1920s and 30s, Tony Cox explains how the educated (and generally Hindu) *bhadralok*, or gentleman, class made up the vast bulk of Communist Party leaders and activists, and how repressive conditions encouraged the appointment of 'outside' leaders in the Bengal trade union and labour movements. See Anthony Cox, *Empire Industry and Class: The Imperial Nexus of Jute, 1840–1940* (London and New York: Routledge, 2013), pp. 51–2 and 127–30.

16 Aaron Lieberman worked as a journalist, Rudolph Rocker was a very impoverished bookbinder (as well as a Gentile) and Morris Winchevsky, after a difficult start, had steady employment (under a different pseudonym) in a bank.

17 Katy Gardner, *Global Migrants, Local Lives: Travel and Transformation in Rural Bangladesh* (Oxford: Clarendon Press, 1995), p. 139.

18 *Ibid.*, p. 135.

19 Interviewed 23 January 2001. Sunahwar himself worked as a community worker and briefly ran a small leather factory.

20 Nazrul Islam Bason in *Surma*, quoted in Faruque Ahmed, *Bengali Journals and Journalism in the UK (1916–2007)* (London: The Ethnic Minorities Original History and Research Centre, 2008), p. 98. Ahmed gives a detailed account of this episode. The Greater Sylhet Development and Welfare Council, in its letter of protest over Monica Ali's *Brick Lane*, recorded a similar outcry over a book that described the Sylhetis as servants of tea plantation owners brought back to Britain. Quoted in Ali Riaz, *Islam and Identity Politics Among British-Bangladeshis: A Leap of Faith* (Manchester: Manchester University Press, 2013), p. 51.

21 Rajnarayan Chandravarkar, *The Origins of Industrial Capitalism in India: Business Strategies and the Working Classes in Bombay, 1900–1940* (Cambridge: Cambridge University Press, 2003); Cox, *Empire, Industry and Class*.

22 Ira Katznelson, 'Working-Class Formation: Constructing Cases and Comparisons', in Ira Katznelson and Aristide R. Zolberg (eds), *Working-Class Formation: Nineteenth-Century Patterns in Western Europe and the United States* (Princeton: Princeton University Press, 1986).

23 See Gardner, *Global Migrants, Local Lives*.

24 Interviewed September 2000.

25 Interviewed 24 July 2007. This was in response to my question about whether she liked being in Bangladesh. While this student (the police cadet mentioned in Chapter 8) was remarkably socially aware, one of her classmates, in response to a question specifically about class, answered, 'I believe I do come from a working-class background ... Bangladeshis ... are from working class aren't they?' She had never thought about her class position before studying sociology – and her father had owned his own restaurant.

26 Similar statistics are not available for 2011, but the percentage of working Bengali men in Tower Hamlets who are self-employed was still below the national average.

27 Andrew Godley, *Jewish Immigrant Entrepreneurship in New York and London 1880–1914: Enterprise and Culture* (Basingstoke: Palgrave, 2001), p. 59.

28 Interviewed 23 January 2001.

29 *Ibid.* The shell is the outer layer of a garment. Salique's factory was supplied with cut cloth by a Jewish manufacturer and the shells they made were pressed, lined and finished elsewhere. This form of subcontracting became increasingly popular in the 1970s.

30 Interviewed August 1999.

31 Interviewed 12 October 2001.

32 In 1979, Patrick Duffy interviewed sixty-eight Bengali men and found that fifty-four were normally employed in clothing, though many of their fathers were employed in unskilled labouring work or as kitchen porters in hotels. Duffy's 'summary report' for the Commission for Racial Equality and the Manpower Services Commission, entitled 'The Employment & Training Needs of the Bengali Community in Tower Hamlets', presents a useful analytical account of the industry at that time.

33 I am grateful to Balihar Sangheera for telling me about his work with Monder Ram on the restaurant industry.

34 Ahmed, *Bengali Journals and Journalism*, pp. 131–2.

35 Interviewed 12 December 2000. Rajonuddin Jalal, interviewed 16 August 2000, commented that, at the time of the interview, the only Bengalis in unions would be public sector and community workers.

36 Bethnal Green and Stepney Trades Council, 'Blood on the Streets: A Report by Bethnal Green and Stepney Trades Council on Racial Attacks in East London' (1978), p. 34.

37 See Bethnal Green and Stepney Trades Council, The Joint Docklands Action Group, Tower Hamlets Branch Workers' Educational Association, and Tower Hamlets Co-op, 'Tower Hamlets: The Fight for Jobs – Tower Hamlets Unemployment Crisis Report' (1975); *East London Advertiser*, 21 March 1980; *Garment Worker*, January 1976, October 1980, January 1981 and February 1981; *Spitalfields News*, December 1985.

38 Interviewed 23 July 2000.

39 Abdus Salique, interviewed 18 May 2006 by Jamil Iqbal for Swadhinata Trust and University of Surrey, 'Oral History Project'; British Film Institute database: http://ftvdb.bfi.org.uk/sift/title/109115, accessed 20 November 2012. The song was recorded by Salique and his musical group Dishari. The words are given in the *Garment Worker*, December 1980. A recording of the song was used as the B side of Robert Wyatt's recording of 'Grass' (Rough Trade, 1981) and included in Wyatt's album *Nothing Can Stop Us* (1982).

40 Interviewed 16 August 2000. One of those involved in setting up and running the Law Centre was Shah Lutfur Rahman.

41 Kumar's mother was a leading figure in the Awami League. His father was an academic and diplomat.

42 Interviewed 21 March 2001.

43 The launch of this campaign was described in the *Garment Worker*, April 1982. Earlier leaflets in Bengali were illustrated in issues from November 1979 and December 1980.

44 See Sarah Glynn (ed.), *The Way We Worked: An Oral History by Members of St Hilda's East Community Centre and Stepney Jewish Community Centre* (London: St Hilda's East Community Centre, 1999), pp. 10–11; interviews with Abdul Razzak and Ali Syed Goyas, 14 May 2001.

45 See article by Muhit Mazumdar in *The Asian*, 1:4 (August 1978), 12.

46 See manuscript in SsBA office.

47 See SsBA 'Annual Report' for 1998.

48 Race Today Collective, *The Struggle of Asian Workers in Britain* (London: Race Today Publications, 1983).

49 Interviewed 21 March 2001.

50 Duffy, 'The Employment & Training Needs of the Bengali Community in Tower Hamlets', p. 12.

51 Interviewed 23 January 2012 .

52 Interviewed together with Azmal Hussain, 23 January 2012.

53 The situation is further complicated by the fact that, while Hussain is vice chair of one owners' association, there are others, and he has made many personal enemies through his exposure of a visa scam and through his arguments that chefs should not be brought from Bangladesh when there are so many unemployed people in the UK who could be trained to do the work. See *Sunday Telegraph*, 26 June 2005.

54 Quoted in William J. Fishman, *East End Jewish Radicals 1875–1914* (London: Duckworth, 1975), p. 112.

55 'A Voice from the Aliens' (1895), p. 8. A copy can be seen in the Wess Archive, Modern Records Centre, Warwick.

56 Rudolf Rocker, *The London Years* (London: Robert Anscombe and Co, 1956), p. 219.

57 *Ibid.*, pp. 224–5.

58 Nora Levin has noted that 'many unions refused to accept Jews as members.' See Nora Levin, *Jewish Socialist Movements, 1871–1917: While Messiah Tarried* (London: Routledge and Kegan Paul, 1978), p. 132. Before the AST opened its Jewish branch in 1884, the only Jews allowed membership were those who were English born and working in the higher end of the trade, and the subscription remained out of reach for most East End workers. See Anne J. Kershen, *Uniting the Tailors: Trade Unionism Amongst the Tailors of London and Leeds, 1870–1939* (Ilford: Frank Cass, 1995), p. 131.

59 Kershen, *Uniting the Tailors*.

60 Ron Ramdin, *The Making of the Black Working Class in Britain* (Aldershot: Gower, 1987), pp. 337–8.

61 For a fuller account of ethnic minority trade unionism in the 1950s, 60s and 70s see *ibid.*, pp. 256–369.

62 Letter to the author (n.d. 2002).

63 Trevor Carter, *Shattering Illusions: West Indians in British Politics* (London: Lawrence and Wishart, 1986), pp. 57–63.

64 Interviewed 30 March 2002.

65 Interviewed 18 August 2000.

66 Abul Ishaque, interviewed 11 December 2001.

67 Interviewed 3 August 2000.

68 Interviewed 30 April 2006 by Jamil Iqbal and Abdul Shahid for Swadhinata Trust and University of Surrey, 'Oral History Project'.
69 Ahmed, *Bengal Politics in Britain*, p. 61.
70 Interviewed 30 April 2006 by Jamil Iqbal and Abdul Shahid for Swadhinata Trust and University of Surrey, 'Oral History Project'.
71 *Morning Star*, 24 May 1971.
72 *Morning Star*, 19 May 1970.
73 Louise London, 'The East End of London: Paki Bashing in 1970', *Race Today*, 5:11 (December 1973), 339.
74 See the *East London Advertiser*, 24 April 1970. The other organisations were the Pakistan Workers' Association, which was centred in Birmingham, the Black Panthers and the Third World Party. This last was led by Brother Louis Nwaogu, who the *Advertiser* had reported opening operations in Tower Hamlets back in January (see *East London Advertiser*, 16 January and 27 February 1970).
75 London, 'The East End of London', p. 340.
76 The *Sun* quoted an H division detective: "The kids are bored. The Pakistanis are peaceable. That's trouble" (see the *Sun*, 9 April 1970). Martin Woollacott in the *Guardian* wrote that the community 'needs to develop some sinews' (see the *Guardian,* 28 April 1970). The *Sun* article actually reported mixed reactions. Besides the plans to form karate group patrols, which the policeman liked even less, they quoted a young mother of three who told them 'I'm not afraid of these louts. When Pakistani friends come to see me, I walk them home with a leg off the television set tucked up my sleeve … I'm a Moslem, but you can take the religious attitude too far. I'd give as good as I get.' (It is not recorded if the mother was herself Pakistani.)
77 Interviewed 11 December 2001.
78 Interviewed 14 November 2000.
79 See interviews with Sunahwar Ali, 23 January 2001 and Anamul Hoque, 14 September 2000.
80 Interviewed 12 September 2000.
81 Interviewed 16 August 2000.
82 Anamul Hoque, interviewed 23 September 2000.
83 Interviewed 16 August 2000.
84 The BYM was one of several youth groups that emerged in the late 1970s, and is based in Shadwell.
85 Interviewed 22 August 2001.
86 Interviewed 18 August 2000.
87 *Ibid.*
88 Shah himself was to return to Bangladesh, though he kept up regular visits to London and the BYM.

6 Black radicalism and separate organisation

Through the 1970s, families became reunited in London, the community grew and the shortage of decent housing became acute. At the same time, the recession that followed the 1973 oil crisis provided fertile ground for the growth of racist scapegoating and of racist violence encouraged by the far-right National Front. Formed in 1967, the National Front reached a peak of support nationally in 1976 and, like Mosley's British Union of Fascists before them, concentrated their activity in the East End, adjacent to the area of immigrant settlement. In establishing themselves as permanent settlers, the Bengalis mobilised to campaign for better housing and against racism. To understand the form these campaigns took, it is necessary to look again at wider political developments on the progressive left, which in this period saw a major shift from class-based organisation to separate responses to different forms of oppression. Black radicalism was a formative strand of this 'New Left'.

The New Left and New Social Movements

What began as a critique within Marxism – a more humanist reaction to the dominant economism – developed into a critique of Marxism itself. The New Left mined Gramsci's prison notebooks for more culturally based ideologies and the cultural turn away from class politics was reinforced by the events of 1968, when revolutionary students were contrasted with what was dismissed as an increasingly bourgeoisified, reformist working class. Leading roles in these theoretical and tactical changes were played by the political forces of anti-colonialism and by the American civil rights and anti-war movements. The welcome given to these movements by a large part of the left can be seen as a legacy of communist popular-frontism, which regarded the liberation activists as *progressive* bourgeois that they could work with.

When the American black leaders Malcolm X and Stokely Carmichael had visited Britain in the mid-1960s, their black and Asian audiences were experiencing the effects of growing popular feeling against immigrants, and a layer of activists was ready to turn their backs on what came to be seen as misguided ideas of integration. The early attempt at vigilante patrols described in the last chapter was just one example of the turn towards a more assertive response to racism that was inspired by events in America and the concept of Black Power popularised by Carmichael. How Black Power is interpreted depends on political predilections. For the liberal Carmichael, black organisation was needed in order to win black people a place in the existing social structure.[1] Obi Egbuna observed that within the British United Coloured People's Alliance 'there were members who believed that the answer to the Black man's problem lay in the overthrow of the capitalist system, and there were others who felt it lay in the Black man going to the House of Lords'.[2] For a growing group of radical intellectuals it provided the inspiration for a turn away from what they labelled 'Eurocentric' Marxism towards a chimeric black Marxism, in which black consciousness was to be the primary basis of political mobilisation. And, in the words of Ambalavaner Sivanandan – director of the Institute of Race Relations and editor of the institute's influential journal, *Race and Class* – 'black' was a political colour'[3] that included Asians and even, in some of the rhetoric, the Irish.

As an ideology, black radicalism was more inspirational than fully worked out. It was intended to be a basis for action and it certainly played a crucial role in the development of immigrant politics, but its effects, as Kalbir Shukra has observed, often proved more conservative than revolutionary.[4] Its main protagonists were rooted in Marxism, which dictated the language and parameters of their arguments as well as providing their principal opponent. Black radicalism disputed Marx's essential argument that the primary division in society is class, based upon ownership of the means of production, and that revolution must come initially and finally from the proletariat united against the exploiting capitalist classes. Socialist revolution remained the ultimate aim, but the autonomous black revolution had to come first and would help to bring it about. In this version of revolutionary stages theory, the majority of the working class was temporarily excluded from the equation altogether.[5]

An essential tenet of black radicalism is that the revolutionary class is much broader than the proletariat, and the main site of struggle is not the workplace but the community. In this it takes inspiration from Franz Fanon's writings on the fight against colonialism, in which he emphasises the revolutionary role of the peasantry and a loosely defined lumpen proletariat, as well as from Mao and from colonial struggles themselves.[6] This is a significant departure from Marxist argument, but it is not quite as different as some of its proponents make out. Black radicals tend to characterise 'white Marxism' as unconcerned with anyone who is not a worker and as relegating them all to Marx's 'social scum', the lumpen proletariat.[7] However, classical Marxism (and its Stalinist derivatives), while recognising the existence of a reactionary lumpen layer, does not dismiss the unemployed or non-waged workers such as wives and mothers; it regards them as part of the proletariat. Practical demonstration of this was given by the Communist Party-dominated National Unemployed Workers' Movement, set up in 1921,[8] which acted as a sort of trade union for the unemployed and organised the great hunger marches of the 1920s and 1930s; and also (after theoretical debate about the role they should play) by the Communist Party's leading part in the 1930s housing movement, which is discussed later in the chapter.[9]

The real innovation of black radicalism, and of the feminism inspired by it, was to classify the unemployed, together with black and women workers (both disproportionately in the least desirable jobs) as a separate 'sub-proletariat'[10] who, along with Marx's lumpen layer, could become the revolutionary vanguard, initially in *opposition* to the 'white, male working class'. Rather than a fraction of the working class with shared class interests they were regarded as a totally different group, and the white, male working class itself was seen as part of the problem rather than part of the solution.[11] To support this position, the integration that *had* occurred of black workers within the broader working class and the trade union movement was played down, and the individualism and parasitic nature of some of those outside conventional economic structures was obscured by their glorification as rebels. Orthodox Marxist criticism of the reactionary nature of the labour movement leadership (exemplified by some of the compromises accepted by trade union leaders) and examples of trade union racism were extended to condemn the whole movement.[12] The socio-economic causes of working-class racism and sexism were overlooked and so not addressed, and working-class unity was postponed.

For Sivanandan, writing in 1972,[13] the ultimate revolutionary struggle would only be achieved when all the oppressed came together in 'the oneness of suffering'.[14] But although he wrote that 'inside every black man there is a working-class man waiting to get out', he claimed that this ultimate unity would not be reached by attempting unity between blacks and the white working class too early. He argued that blacks would achieve class consciousness instinctively, through the development of a black political consciousness, when they realised that racism was just part of a system of oppression; and the white working class must, through its own sense of oppression, arrive at a consciousness of racial oppression. But first, the blacks had to play their historic role and set this revolution in motion with the fight against white cultural hegemony. And '[t]o integrate with the white masses before they have entered into the practice of cultural change would be to emasculate the black cultural revolution'. His position was uncompromising:

> A common understanding of racial oppression … ranges the black worker on the side of the black bourgeois against their common enemy: the white man, worker and bourgeois alike. In terms of analysis, what the white Marxists fail to grasp is that the slave and colonial exploitation of the black peoples of the world was so total and devastating – and so systematic in its devastation – as to make mock of working-class exploitation.[15]

Sivandan hoped to achieve ultimate unity through an initial position that denied the possibility or desirability of such unity, and how this would happen was never resolved. Class consciousness may not in fact be 'instinctive' after all, and if it is not, what is there in this ideology to encourage its development and to prevent the development of black racism in opposition to white and of a divided and weak working class? (How the white working class was to arrive at a consciousness of racial oppression he simply dismissed as 'the business of white radicals'.[16]) In a later article,[17] Sivanandan was scathing about the role of the black bourgeoisie who he described as disciplining black militants through the mechanism of race relations into peaceful integration within existing power structures. But, is this not the same black bourgeoisie who, through shared oppression, were the natural revolutionary allies of the black workers?

By 1978, when Stuart Hall and his fellow authors wrote *Policing the Crisis*, black organisation was being put into practice. 'As a collective solution,' they wrote, 'the option of assimilation has not only been officially closed by white society, but blacks have actively closed the door on it themselves, from the inside, and turned the key'.[18] And they explained that, 'It is through a specific kind of "black consciousness" that [black workers] are beginning to appropriate, or "come to consciousness" of their class position [as a sub-proletariat], organise against it and "fight it out"'.[19] However this 'natural and correct' response was, they acknowledged, only a 'necessary defensive strategy', which was doomed to failure because 'every time the struggle appears, once again, in its divided form, capital penetrates through and occupies the gap'.[20] Class unity was vital, but the authors were 'confronting the impossibility of developing struggle in this form at this time'.[21]

Again, the crucial question of how to move from sectional struggle to struggle as a class was not answered. In fact, the book, which is critical of some of the claims of the black radicals, ends with a warning that 'we should not mistake a proto-political consciousness for organised political class struggle and practice' or hope that 'current modes of resistance ... [will] by natural evolution ... become, spontaneously, another thing'.[22]

Hall *et al.* wrote that the argument for autonomous struggle, which 'has become the most powerful political tendency within active black groups in Britain', was 'theoretically developed' in the campaigning journal *Race Today*.[23] Activists from the Race Today Collective worked with the Bengalis in the 1970s squatting movement and the struggles against racism discussed in this chapter. Before this, at the end of 1973, the journal had had its own black revolt, which resulted in Darcus Howe's editorship. Just prior to taking over the reins he had published a seminal article on unemployed West Indian youth that argued that their 'refusal to work is a legitimate form of anti-capitalist struggle'.[24] This argument is certainly radical, but it is not 'theoretically developed' (as, in this case, Hall *et al.* admit[25]).

The first issue of *Race Today* edited by Howe featured an article by Selma

James on feminism and the black struggle that argued for the basic separatist principle of both movements,[26] claiming 'nothing unified and revolutionary will be formed until each sector of the exploited will have made its own autonomous power felt'. To James, the working class was every group exploited by capitalist society. Describing the feminist split from the mainstream left, she wrote, 'What gave us the boldness to break, fearless of the consequences, was the power of the Black movement'. James argued, in line with others on the left, that organisation must come from the oppressed themselves and not be imposed from above, but she extended this argument to claim that this organisation should be fragmented, reflecting the inherent divisions within the working class. She did not call for the different groups to come together and break down barriers from both sides, but for each group to break down its own barrier – ignoring the possibility that through this very separatism it may put up new barriers in the process. And rather than confront the big question of how this can ultimately unite the working class, she simply dismissed it. 'Strange to think,' she wrote, 'that even today, when confronted with the autonomy of the Black movement or the autonomy of the women's movement, there are those who talk about this "dividing the working class".'

In the journal's next issue, Farrukh Dhondy extended Howe's thesis to argue that black school drop-outs were in conscious revolt against a system in which they had no stake. But the nature of the revolt he describes does not seem very political, and the existence of equally alienated white school drop-outs was not acknowledged, although this is just the layer which is most likely to find their own positive identity in racist gangs.[27] Even when Dhondy mentioned strikes by Asian workers, such as at Mansfield Hosiery in Loughborough, he was careful to say that 'the animating factor was their Asian identity' and to describe the strikers as 'fending off certain sections of the left who approached them'.[28] They had to be seen as distinct from the rest of the working class, though this attitude was hardly likely to heal divisions with the factory's white workers and create a stronger united workforce.

Nowhere in all of this was the theory of black radicalism fully developed. The gaps in logic were never confronted – perhaps because they are un-crossable. And, since the theory was not developed, it could not really be passed on beyond the basic mantra of autonomous organisation. The nature of that organisation was also left somewhat vague, even by Sivanandan, who had refuted the 'romanticism of anti-organisation blacks' (giving another *Race Today* article on 'anti-employment black youth' as his example).[29] The passion and anger of the movement's leaders made sure their message was heard, but not that it was fully understood. The passion and anger of those they helped to mobilise was not directed into an ordered radical politics.

Once the black radicals – and then the feminists and other New Social Movements – had broken down the fundamental structural divisions of Marxism, rooted in economic production, there was nothing to stop a

Balkanisation of autonomous political groups that were based around different identities and responded separately to their unique experience and interests.[30] Ideas of community organisation were readily taken up by a new generation of activists and also by the state, which was ready to co-opt them into the established system, as will be discussed in the next chapter.

The Race Today Collective and the struggle for housing

By the end of the 1960s, tenants of London's worst slum areas were fighting for councils to use their powers of compulsory purchase and redevelopment to provide them with new housing, and political activists had helped to launch a major squatting movement throughout the capital. These two fights were intimately connected because the emptying of the old slums and the councils' tardiness in redevelopment meant that there were numerous places available for the squatters to move into. Sometimes council officials from both the Greater London Council (GLC) – who owned three in five local authority houses in Tower Hamlets – and Tower Hamlets Borough Council found themselves rehousing different people from the same houses and tenements again and again. By the mid-1970s a large majority of Tower Hamlets residents lived in public sector housing,[31] but very little had been built in Spitalfields, at the heart of the Bengali area, even after slums had been cleared. In the fights of both the slum tenants and the squatters, Bengalis played a significant part.

In his account of the squatters' movement of the late 1960s and early 1970s,[32] Ron Bailey described how small groups of activists such as himself (many from the libertarian left who wanted to put self-organisation into practice) worked together with families from some of the worst slums who were desperate for somewhere decent to live. Through persistent squatting and careful use of the law and the media they forced councils all over London to accept the idea of using their empty housing stock as short-life accommodation. These first squatters were generally young and white and although the availability of empty housing in Tower Hamlets certainly attracted various 'outsiders', including students, the majority of Tower Hamlets squatters were local people who had exhausted all other options.

By the mid-1970s, much of the rapidly growing Bengali community was crowded into the Brick Lane area, where the warren of workshops and privately rented old houses and tenements had deteriorated to such a state that few would live in them except those who had no other choice. When it had been just the men sharing together it had been bad enough – at least they could spend most of their time elsewhere. Now, with increasing numbers of families arriving, the situation was getting desperate. Descriptions of their cramped conditions, the inadequate and broken sanitary arrangements, the rats that bit children in their sleep, seem as if they came from the pages of Dickens.[33]

There was urgent need for more accommodation, but on top of the East

End's usual housing difficulties, the Bengalis faced additional problems when they tried to seek help from the GLC or the borough council. The nature of council-house allocation resulted in inbuilt discrimination against them, and a climate of institutional racism meant that there was little incentive for housing departments to do anything about it. For a start, there were comparatively few houses for large families and a lack of interpreters. Existing rules made it impossible to apply for family housing until wives and children were in the UK, and applicants lost their place on the waiting list if they left the UK for more than three months – which frequently happened as they battled with the red tape controlling family immigration in the British High Commission in Dhaka. On top of this, housing departments were riddled with conscious and unconscious prejudice and assumption. An independent report commissioned by the GLC in 1983–84, gives a picture of deep-seated racism in the housing bureaucracy.[34] This finding was corroborated by the squatting activist, Terry Fitzpatrick, who described to me how he accompanied a Bengali tenant to request a transfer after the man's family had been terrorised by racists on the Isle of Dogs, only to be told that the requested empty flat 'is for white people'.[35] The physical dangers from racist violence on the outlying 'white estates' meant that rehousing in or near the Spitalfields area came to be seen as a matter of survival. As a contemporary report pointed out, the housing officers' original biased allocations reinforced this racism, as they 'gave those white families the feeling that they had the "right" to keep their estates white'.[36] Bengali families who were allocated council housing on white estates were met by a reception committee of racist neighbours and many returned to the area round Spitalfields, preferring to face the extreme discomfort of a squat to the constant danger of racist attack. This was the background to the Bengali squats, which could be described as forming a second phase of the squatting movement.

At first there was no wider organisation – just individual Bengali families breaking into some of the many derelict houses that dotted the area or paying 'key money' to other squatters who were moving elsewhere. Some ended up as squatters by accident, having been conned into 'buying' or 'renting' a place in what turned out to be an empty council house.[37] Information about squatting spread by word of mouth, and people soon discovered that if they wanted practical advice the man to see was Terry Fitzpatrick of Tower Hamlets Squatters' Union in his squat in Aston Street. (Much of this account is put together from interviews with Fitzpatrick and with Mala Sen, formerly Dhondy, of the Race Today Collective.)[38] Fitzpatrick, a trained builder with 'sort of anarchist' politics of 'self-help', knew how to break into buildings and carry out basic repairs – and replace fittings often deliberately destroyed by the council – and how to get round the law. He recalls that they would break into a house with the family ready outside in a van complete with mattresses and children. Then they would change the lock, clear away their tools and put up a copy of the Forcible Entry Act of 1381, along with the phone numbers of the Aston Street squat and the

Tower Hamlets Law Centre. The medieval Act made it clear that it was illegal to break into the house to evict the new occupants.

The squats acquired a political dimension one evening in January 1975 when three members of the Race Today Collective, including Mala and Farrukh Dhondy, knocked on the Aston Street door and joined the squatters' weekly meeting. Race Today had already become involved, through their journal, in exposing a squat-selling racket in Matlock Street.[39] The Dhondys came from India. He was working as a teacher and she was with Air India. Their backgrounds had little in common with those of most of the Bengali squatters, but they could speak North Indian Languages and Fitzpatrick and the Dhondys recognised each other as serious activists. Initially Race Today was involved on an informal basis, as the squatting snowballed into a 'nightly occurrence'.[40] There was 'always a massive queue' of people waiting for an opportunity to get a home,[41] and mass Bengali squats were organised in Old Montague Street in Spitalfields and in Varden Street and Nelson Street,[42] which were owned by the London Hospital who planned to sell them to Tower Hamlets Council for demolition and redevelopment.

Race Today, as part of the vanguard of Black Radicalism, attempted to turn the squatters into a movement for black self-organisation. Like the Communist Party in the East End of the 1930s, they saw the housing struggles, together with the related fight against racism, as a step towards something bigger. Some of the Bengalis already belonged to the Squatters' Union or other squatters' organisations, but in February 1976 Fitzpatrick and the Dhondys brought together a meeting of 'seventy heads of Bengali families',[43] some of whom were already squatting while others hoped to do so. This was the official launch of the Bengali Housing Action Group (BHAG) which Race Today described in their journal as 'one of the clearest manifestations of the collective power of black workers'.[44]

During the course of the meeting Fitzpatrick was eyeing the empty bulk of Pelham Buildings through the window. This nineteenth-century tenement block had been almost emptied by the GLC, who had smashed up toilets and windows to discourage squatters but seemed in no hurry to redevelop. On Easter Saturday, Fitzpatrick, Farrukh Dhondy and six Bengali families broke into the building and within three months forty-one families were installed there. Pelham buildings became BHAG's fortress – literally so when the skinhead gangs went on the attack – though Fitzpatrick has described the well-publicised preparations to defend the block against eviction as 'bluff'.[45] Pelham Buildings also provided an inspiration to other Bengali squatters who were not formally connected with BHAG but looked to the organisation for advice. In *Spitalfields: A Battle for Land*, Charlie Forman estimated that at its peak BHAG was several hundred families strong,[46] and there may have been a similar number of squatting families outside the organisation. By the end of the year there were few places left to squat.

For most of those involved, the turn towards separate Bengali organisation seems to have been accepted as pragmatic rather than ideological. The Squatters'

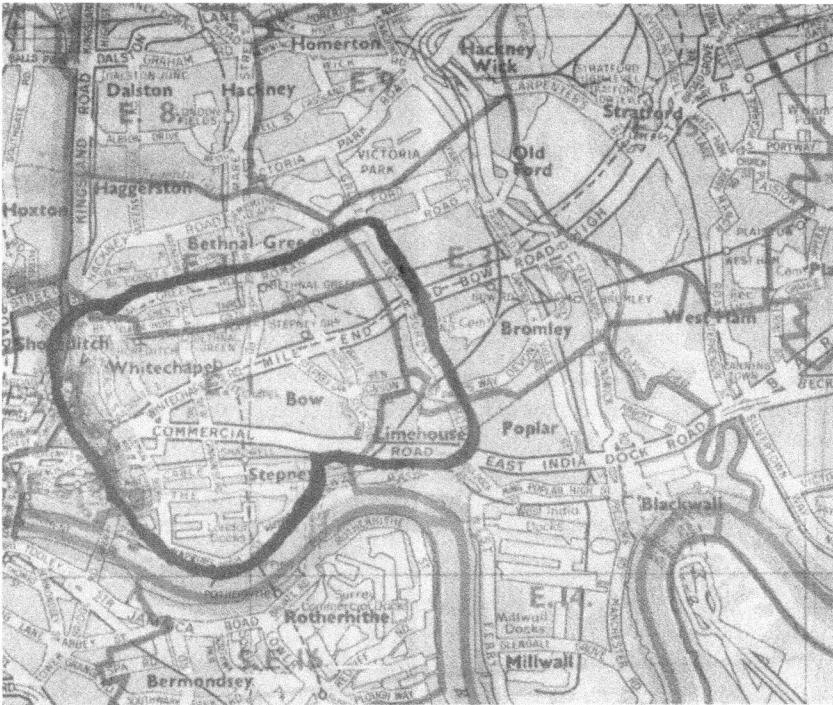

Figure 6.1 BHAG's map for the GLC outlining the area in which they would accept housing, as reproduced in *Race Today*, October 1976

Union had already been working more or less exclusively with Bengalis anyway.[47] Helal Abbas, recently leader of Tower Hamlets Council, was, with his parents, one of the first Bengali squatters and later became secretary of BHAG. He remembers that he saw separate organisation as a reflection of the Bengalis' exceptional housing need as 'one of the most disadvantaged communities'. To him,

> [BHAG] wasn't a group of radical activists who had an agenda against any particular political grouping. What we were saying is, that this is a group of people who are not currently being catered for by your local authority, which you have a legal obligation to [do]. You should listen to them. If you don't listen to them you will pay a price for it.[48]

Fitzpatrick didn't have to grapple with the anomaly of being a white organiser in a black movement because he saw it as a practical thing. He was helping people with distinctive social needs who happened to be Bengali families.

BHAG demanded not only the permanent rehousing of all its members, but also that Bengalis be given the option of housing in the safe area of the E1 postal district. Fitzpatrick 'lost count' of the number of rent books he gave back to the council as families fled the dangers of outlying GLC estates to squat in the safety of the Bengali-dominated areas. In 1977 the new Tory-led GLC announced that they would restore law and order in housing by declaring an amnesty for all squatters in their buildings who registered before a fixed date, promising that they could stay on as licensed tenants until they were given a single take-it-or-leave-it offer of GLC accommodation.[49] A BHAG deputation went to meet the council officer in charge, expecting to have to fight for their position, and were 'gob smacked' when he suggested that they draw up a list of acceptable estates.[50] A squatters' meeting agreed the idea and Fitzpatrick and two Bengali activists drew up a list of thirteen possible estates in which no reasonable offer would be refused, which was agreed at a further meeting. A similar demand was taken up by Bengali tenants campaigning for slum clearance and rehousing, though they reduced the list to eight.[51] The following year a housing association made an agreement with Tower Hamlets Council to take over Varden and Nelson streets with the squatters in place.[52]

It was the Bengalis' demands to stay in E1 that led to what has come to be known as the 'ghetto plan'. A GLC housing document dated 22 May 1978 explained about the estate lists and suggested that,

> we might continue to meet the wishes of the Bengali community by earmarking blocks of flats or, indeed a whole estate if necessary, for their community, *provided* the existing tenants wish to move away and could be given the necessary transfers.[53]

The media outcry should have been predictable[54] and most local activists reacted in horror to the idea. Ken Leech, then Rector of St Matthew's Bethnal Green, has described in his account of these events how the protest meetings that followed brought together whites and Bengalis and 'forged a new unity between various groups'.[55] Leech went on to quote a letter from the Bangladesh Youth Movement (BYM) to the leader of the GLC, in which they demonstrated their rejection of such a literal interpretation of black separatist ideology:

> We are committed to the multi-racial, multi-cultural society of which we are part, and join with other local Bengali and white groups in protesting against dangerous separatist housing policies, which would ruin existing and developing relationships between the communities and isolate the Bengali community as a target of violence.[56]

BHAG had never demanded exclusive Bengali blocks and they refuted the idea that they had asked for a 'ghetto'; however, their objection was not simply about segregation, but that this would lead to Bengalis being dumped in poor housing. In a statement issued that June, they stated, 'We will not settle for segregated slums'.[57] Despite this, Mark Phillips had observed in a study of Tower Hamlets housing struggles published the previous year that BHAG's demands were for 'what some people would describe as a Bengali Ghetto, and would be likely to attract energetic opposition from many liberal as well as anti-progressive quarters'.[58] And Mala's reaction, as she explained it to me over two decades later, demonstrates an undisguised acceptance of the separatist results of black radical organisation:

> Some people said, 'You are creating a ghetto'. We said, 'fine, we prefer the ghetto, at least you have each other to defend yourself' ... So that's what it was and we achieved it, and today you walk round Brick Lane, it's totally Bengali.[59]

Fighting racism

As the Bengalis attempted to settle into a new life in London, they came up against a wall of prejudice and racial attacks. Young skinheads were the racists' shock troops, but many of the views that they held reflected those of their older relatives, even if those relatives didn't express them in such an immediate way. A short but illuminating collection of accounts from members of the Collinwood gang, active between 1968 and 1970, shows youths driven by a visceral working-class consciousness reacting to disrupting changes in East-End community life and to growing unemployment.[60] Immigrants were the most immediate symbol of these changes, and 'Pakis' were seen as so alien that attacking them generated no sympathetic emotions, even when, in one case, the man died.[61] The mob was always on the lookout for the excitement of a bit of 'aggro', and when it came to 'Paki bashing' 'it was just like a fox hunt to go and hit one'.[62] While the callous racism and the normalisation of violence – racist and otherwise – is shocking, the gang members' own words demonstrate a strong, if sometimes confused, recognition of the overriding role of larger structural forces. It was their inability to impact these that made them turn on their immigrant neighbours.

For the Bengalis, parts of the East End were virtual no-go areas, and families faced constant and open intimidation, especially, as we have seen, where they lived apart from the nucleus of the Bengali community. Many were not even safe inside their homes, where bricks were put through windows, washing was slashed on clothes-lines and everything from shit to lighted petrol-soaked rags was put through letter boxes. From the mid-1970s, tensions were heightened by the National Front, who held deliberately provocative paper sales at the junction of Brick Lane and Bethnal Green Road during the Sunday market. These became a rallying point for alienated white youths who, after stoking up in the local pubs, would set out in groups to enjoy a spot of 'Paki bashing'. Even primary-school children were attracted into the Young National Front, and racist violence in local schools was so bad that some Bengali families withdrew their sons from school for long periods.[63]

Back in 1970, when the Bengalis were suffering racist attacks from the

Collinwood among other East End gangs, attempts to organise Bengali self-defence had petered out, but in 1976 Race Today was instrumental in organising the Anti-Racist Committee of Asians in East London (ARC-AEL). Like the earlier, short-lived Pakistan Workers' Union, they defied as useless the older generation's appeals to seek recourse through their MP and other official channels and organised their own vigilante patrols to drive round the areas where Bengalis lived. As Mala recalled:

> We had the most militant wing of organisations in the area, with the majority of the Bengali community on our side. We used to run patrol groups at night, vigilantes, to stop stray Bengalis being attacked.[64]

This movement played a significant role in mobilising the community. Caroline Adams, who as a dedicated youth-worker was an important figure for a whole generation of young Bengalis, wrote:

> ARCAEL and the activity around it transformed the consciousness of many young people ... The Bengali community had come of age and could no longer be patronised or ignored, at least not without a comeback.[65]

Fitzpatrick took an active part in this, and his recollections of the period describe how the movement's dedication to self-organisation made it resist the involvement of the organised left – though his own strong antipathy to these groups probably derives from his anarchist sympathies rather than black radical theory. Anti-racist demonstrations were organised to defend the Bengalis' right to stay in Tower Hamlets and to demand better protection. Fitzpatrick recalls helping to organise a well-attended march in June 1976 to which left activists were told not to bring placards. When Chris Harman of the International Socialist Group (which later became the Socialist Workers Party (SWP)) ignored this injunction he ended up sprawled across the pavement, and as the march progressed through the East End to protest outside Leman Street police station about their lack of action over racist violence, Fitzpatrick spent the day in a different police station.[66]

The late 1970s saw the emergence of several Bengali youth groups (including the BYM, which we met in the previous chapter) that played central roles in the fight against racism, as well as arranging social activities such as football and camping trips. Many of their members had lived through the Independence war in Bangladesh before struggling to make their way through British schools and British society. This first generation of Bengalis who came to adulthood in Britain were ready to fight for their place in their adopted country, and their nationalist consciousness from the days of the Liberation struggle became subsumed into a new ethnic consciousness. As Ansar Ahmed Ullah, who came to Britain in 1975 aged around fifteen, explains:

> Many of us witnessed the war or saw the political movement before the war and

were very much aware of political movements and what they can do in order to campaign for your rights ... And they probably felt the same when they came here. They felt it's like déjà vu ... We are being attacked, we can't get jobs, we're not given decent housing. As a community we're kind of looked down [on], that kind of stuff.[67]

Members of these groups were ready to adopt the black radicals' principles of separate organisation and their suspicions of the organised left; however few attempted to link the fight against racism to a broader political agenda. The Bangladesh Youth League included members involved with Sheikh Mujib's BAKSAL[68] and made connections to the Labour Party and lobbied MPs, but other organisations made no political claims.

The Bengali youth movements were particularly strong and active, but they were just one part of a national trend of Asian youth movements. Across the country, in different centres of immigration, boys and young men from the second immigrant generation were coming together to organise active resistance to racism, spurred on by racist attacks. 1976 also saw the foundation of the Southall Youth Movement, created as a response to the murder of Gurdip Singh Chaggar, and there were Asian youth movements in Bradford, Manchester, Birmingham, Sheffield, Luton, Nottingham, Leicester, Burnley, Pendle and Watford. Although the different groups largely concentrated on struggles in their own local areas, and there was a dearth of broader political analysis, activists could benefit from the strength that comes from being part of something bigger than the immediate community.[69]

As well as the organisational help and ideas that they received from more overtly political organisations such as Race Today and the Trades Council, the Bengali youth groups were given support and advice from a dedicated group of white community workers, funded by grants from government and charities. The approach adopted by the community workers was similar to that of the first generation Bengali activists in their work with the Welfare Association, in that it addressed immediate issues rather than fundamental political structures or approaches. The community workers promoted and were supported by multi-cultural policies and practices of group rights, which will be discussed more fully in the next chapter, and which can themselves be understood as a mainstream development of ideas generated by the black radicals.

In Bengali popular memory, the key battles in the fight against racism were those that took place in the summer of 1978, when anti-racist resistance reached a new level that translated into a qualitative change in the community's self-confidence. This period is remembered as a turning point: not just for the generation of Bengalis then coming into adulthood, who took the most active roles, but for the British Bengali community as a whole.[70] The National Front had been fomenting racist violence around Brick Lane for the previous two years, and young Bengalis had been fighting back; but it took another racist murder to trigger more radical changes. After Altab Ali, a twenty-four-year-old clothing worker, was fatally stabbed early in the evening of 4 May 1978 – a day when forty-one National Front candidates stood in local council elections – the community came together to demonstrate their right to be in Britain without suffering abuse. The thousands of Bengalis who processed with Altab Ali's coffin to Downing Street included angry young men and also the older generation that had once told them to keep their heads down and turn the other cheek. This description by Suroth Ahmed is typical of the way that those times are remembered:

> I came to Britain in 1972. To my observation we had the mindset that we, the Asian and the Bengali people don't have the right to be here. We are here only to work, not to demand any rights of our own. We have to hide ourselves from the white racist, we have to be indoors after sunset, and we have to group together to be safe … But after the killing of Altab Ali, the scenario was completely different … We never expected such huge number of people would come out to protest the killing … And I believe we never ever were unconscious of our rights after that. The Bengali community developed after that incident day by day … It was like the people were sleeping, unaware of their rights and dignity, suddenly something woke them all; they begin to realise their power of unity and so on.[71]

As Abdus Shukur put it, the struggles of 1978 were 'a point which said that we are here to stay, we are not going to be going back'.[72] 'Here to stay, here to fight' was a fundamental slogan of the Asian youth movements. Even the more cautious organisations established by the earlier generation of immigrants abandoned their opposition to self-defence.[73]

In the summer of 1978, after Altab Ali's murder, regular vigils were organised to exclude the National Front paper sellers from their favoured Sunday spot at the end of Brick Lane. The police had told the Bengalis that the only way they could keep the National Front away was to get there first, and so groups of young Bengalis and their supporters occupied the pitch through the night, playing cards, singing and drinking cups of tea brought from the Nazrul Restaurant, which stayed open specially. The chance of a fight attracted racists from outside the area as well as from local estates, and on one occasion (just after the 'ghetto plan' had been splashed across the media) as many as a hundred and fifty youths went on the rampage down Brick Lane, throwing stones and bottles through shop windows.[74] However, a generation of young Bengalis was learning to defend their community. Inevitably, comparisons were made with the 'Battle of Cable Street' in 1936, and looking back it is clear that the importance of both 'battles' was not so much their impact on the racists and their fascist leaders, but that the people the racists were attacking had proved to themselves that they could fight back.[75]

The Bengalis on the street were almost entirely male; most Bengali women would have been neither expected nor allowed to take part in activities outside the home and the family. The Trades Council noted that, 'On the huge demonstrations involving the Asian community … the number of Asian women

Figure 6.2 Sit-down protest against police racism, outside the police station in Bethnal
Green Road, 1978 (Paul Trevor)

participating can be numbered on one hand'.[76] Those women who were exceptions to this rule came from a more professional and westernised background,
such as Mithu Ghosh who worked for Tower Hamlets Law Centre from 1979
and remembers speaking at rallies, and Husna Matin who has described how,
along with her daughters and armed with steel rods, she frightened off skinhead
attackers who were beating up her neighbour and his son in Varden Street.[77] In
addition, Shah Lutfur Rahman has described how some women contributed to
the active resistance to racial attacks by firing chilli water through the window
from a bicycle pump.[78] However, the women's most important role was that of
holding the home together – for which they were expected to show extraordi-
nary fortitude. Although many had only recently been uprooted from the
familiar surroundings of Sylhet, their tenacious defence of their right to a safe
home provided a core of strength to the housing struggles.[79] Theirs was a crucial
if invisible role, but they were not generally exposed to politics beyond the
immediate struggle.

1978 brought the Bengalis a new self-confidence, but it did not end their
problems with racism. Although the violence retreated from Brick Lane, where
the authorities had eventually been persuaded to establish a police station, attacks
continued in other places where the Bengalis were in a minority, and the
situation was exacerbated by institutional racism within the police force. The
police showed themselves much more ready to arrest anti-racists than racists –
demonstrating another similarity with Cable Street – and in his original caption

to Figure 6.2, Paul Trevor observed, 'Institutional racism is regarded as a far greater menace than the racism of the National Front'.[80] The National Front moved its headquarters to nearby Shoreditch with much fanfare that September, but they had been leaching support to the Conservatives since the beginning of the year – when Margaret Thatcher began to campaign on the issue of immigration control and against Britain being 'swamped by people with a different culture'[81] – and the organisation imploded after a demoralising result in the 1979 election. This did not mean that racism had disappeared – only that some of the ideas it promoted had gone mainstream. Anti-racist campaigns continued to provide a focus of Bengali activity through the 1980s and the community faced a resurgence of racist aggression in the 90s, promoted by the British National Party (BNP), which had been formed in 1982 following a split in the National Front. The BNP were able to exploit the new squeeze on social resources – particularly housing – to scapegoat immigrant families, and the situation was exacerbated by the race-card politics of the mainstream parties, especially the Liberal Democrats, as will be discussed in the next chapter.[82] However, a new cohort of young Bengalis was ready to defend their place in Tower Hamlets.

John Rex, drawing on his research among black and Asian immigrants in Birmingham in the late 1970s, observed that growing immigrant militancy was being expressed through both community organisations and far left groups, and that

> It does seem to be the case that more and more young Asians, often educated in Britain, are taking part in Trotskyist organizations like International Socialism (now the Socialist Workers' Party) and using the organizations which they provide both for industrial struggles and for street demonstrations.[83]

Kenan Malik wrote in 2009: 'Twenty years ago "radical" meant ... someone who was militantly secular, self-consciously Western and avowedly left-wing. Someone like me.'[84] In the late 1970s and 1980s an appreciable number of British Asians joined or campaigned with far left organisations, though they might nevertheless have focussed their attention on specifically immigrant issues, or even moved away to join separatist Asian groups.[85] Malik himself was a member of East London Workers Against Racism (ELWAR), which had been established by another Trotskyist group, the Revolutionary Communist Party, and he also recalls that for his generation of young Asians, 'black' was a 'political badge'.[86] The failure of the far left groups to recruit many young Bengalis could be due to a number of factors: the Bengalis' relatively recent arrival, the impact of Bengali nationalism on their formative years, the size and closeness of the Bengali community, and the separatist claims of black radical activists.

In all the campaigns described here, left groups contributed organising skills and demonstrated their solidarity with the Bengalis, but, as observed in the previous chapter, few Bengalis interpreted their struggles according to a wider socialist vision, and left activists tended to be regarded as outsiders, working towards their own interests. Race Today activists clearly encouraged such a view. The trade unions showed public support for the Bengalis – especially in 1978, when Brick Lane became the national focus of anti-racist activity – but this was not necessarily very deep rooted. Ishaq Ali, who was killed in Hackney in the month after Altab Ali's murder, was a member of the National Union of Tailors and Garment Workers, who made a strong anti-racist statement. Some trade union leaders came to the area at the height of the racist attacks – including the TUC General Secretary, Len Murray – but there was little practical backing from the white union rank and file, who were generally employed in different areas of work and lived separate lives. Recalling one of the protests, one of my interviewees observed that Dan Jones from the Trades Council told a rally in the Naz Cinema, "'I have the support of nine thousand to ten thousand local workers ...'" But there weren't any white people. Union members weren't there actually.'[87] Cathy Forrester, who was herself very actively involved, remembers that the majority of other white East Enders were 'quite laid back, they just let things go on'.[88] On 17 July 1978, a group of organisations who had come together to form the Hackney and Tower Hamlets Defence Committee called a political strike to protest at the lack of official action against racism. The Trades Council claimed that

> More than 8,000 workers stayed away from work. Shops, factories, restaurants, even sections of the body plant at Fords closed. Although the response was largely from Asian workers groups of white workers also withdrew their labour, including trade unionists from the Brewery in Bow which had been attacked by white racists the previous week. Hundreds of youngsters from Robert Montefiore, Tower Hamlets, Clapton and other schools, stayed away from their classes or walked out of school.[89]

Speakers included Tariq Ali of the International Marxist Group (IMG) and Aloke Biswas of the SWP as well as Tasadduk Ahmed and his down-to-earth colleague, Fakruddin Ahmed. The relatively small number of local white workers actively involved would suggest that the speakers' message of 'black and white unite and fight' could have had limited resonance. On top of this, *Race Today* seems to have done its best further to confound the argument for active participation in multiracial trade union activity. Its article on the strike included dissatisfied accounts by six of those who took part, in order to support the black radical call for separate organisation.[90]

A comparison with the 1930s

Anti-racist activists like to draw parallels between campaigns against anti-Bengali racism and the National Front in the 1970s, and campaigns forty years earlier against anti-Semitism and the British Union of Fascists. Both involved conflict on the street, and both also involved a major struggle for better housing that was regarded by its organisers as a force for wider political mobilisation. But the understandings that underpinned the Communist-led movement of the 30s, determining its approach and outcome, were fundamentally different from those guiding the black radical activists of Race Today. The Communist Party used the 1930s campaigns to unite the working class across the racial divide and undercut support for fascism, and they were remarkably successful at integrating local campaigns into their wider political understanding and using them to build genuine political support for their ideas. Father Groser, the Christian Socialist president of Stepney Tenants' Defence League, recorded in his autobiographical memoir how the tenants' movement revitalised people from the defeatism of the depression years by showing them 'a possible way out of at least one of their problems'; and he described his amazement at 'the speed with which people came together, organised, and threw up their own leaders'. While assuring his readers that 'in spite of all their sufferings the masses generally were still far from accepting the Communist philosophy', he conceded,

> I sometimes wonder what would have happened if the war had not come when it did. Things were pretty desperate. It is just possible that the workers would have turned to open revolutionary activity and looked to the Communist Party for leadership. Certainly there were a great many who were thinking that way and looking in that direction for guidance.[91]

Although under Stalin the Soviet Union had reverted to new forms of nationalism and anti-Semitism,[92] and the British Communist Party was always subject to the Comintern and intolerant of those who questioned authority at any level, the communists' grassroots work in the pre-war East End was generally developed as a paradigm of Marxist internationalism. The local party's disproportionately Jewish membership was anxious to draw attention to the threat that fascism and anti-Semitism posed to the whole of the working class, and to emphasise the breadth of anti-fascist support across the class. The 'Battle of Cable Street', in which the communists played a leading role in mobilising people to stop Mosley's British Union of Fascists marching through the East End, was seen as a symbol of working-class unity, with accounts emphasising the part played by Catholic dockers and other local workers; and the major campaigns of the late 1930s for better housing conditions and fairer rents were tied into wider political struggles. The fight against fascism and the fight for better housing boosted each other. People who were drawn into the Communist Party by the fight against fascism helped to organise the concerted attack on slum housing. The fight for better housing brought everyone together, Jew and Gentile, to attack the social and economic causes on which fascism thrives.[93]

This approach is epitomised in the description of one of the early housing battles as told by Phil Piratin, who was later to become Communist MP for Mile End, and whose account of the communist-led struggles of that time is almost a handbook of grassroots activism. The events he describes took place in 1937 in Paragon Mansions, which had an active tenants' committee and communist sympathisers among the tenants; however, the immediate concern was the threat-ened eviction of two families who had no connection with the committee. Communist activists discovered that they were both members of the British Union of Fascists, which had done nothing to help them. The communists now had a perfect opportunity to demonstrate the strength of working-class unity and of their party and to discredit the fascists. Under communist leadership, the tenants united to barricade the block against the bailiffs and police, and armed themselves with mouldy flour and pails of water. During the lunch hour an impromptu meeting was held outside to explain to passing workers what was happening. The uncomfortable mixture of flour and water and public antipathy persuaded the bailiffs to hold off for a fortnight to allow further negotiations with the landlord. Most importantly, as Phil Piratin later wrote,

> The kind of people who would never come to our meetings, and had strange ideas about Communists and Jews, learnt the facts overnight and learnt the real meaning of the class struggle in the actions which now followed.[94]

Max Levitas, the future Communist councillor, lived in Brady Mansions where he was convenor of a twenty-one week rent strike in 1939. He explained to me how such strikes could also demonstrate another aspect of class unity:

> We were fighting the Jewish landlords the same way as we'd fight any landlord that increases rents, doesn't care if he repairs flats, so forth and so on: these are the enemies of the people and must be fought – if they are a Jew, black or white. And this helped to develop a much more broader understanding and [to unite] the struggle against Mosley and the fascists.[95]

The strength of the movement came from its ability to unite working-class people of different ethnic backgrounds, and the communists were always anxious to stress its inclusivity. Simon Blumenfeld's rent-strike play, *Enough of All This!*, which was written and performed at the time, has the Jewish Secretary of the Stepney Tenants' Defence League, Tubby Rosen – Tich Rose in the play – as central character, but the other characters are Father John (based on Father John Groser, the League's President), the landlord, and the Irish-Catholic residents of a housing block. In his speech at the final meeting, Rose speaks of them all, and their ancestors, as 'Englishmen', and tells the tenants, 'we ordinary people are the real England'.[96]

This could hardly be more unlike the writings of Farrukh Dhondy, which are designed to highlight difference and demonstrate the strength of separate organisation. In 'Come to Mecca', a short story for teenagers published in 1978 and dramatised for the BBC in 1982, Dhondy portrays Bengali boys separated by a cultural chasm from a young white leftist who tries to recruit them into her organisation. At the end of the story the boys tip a whole pile of socialist papers into the Thames.[97] Dhondy's preferred alternative of Bengali organisation was portrayed in his 1986 Channel 4 drama, *King of the Ghetto*.[98] The plot was built around a Bengali squatting movement with a main character based on Fitzpatrick; however, it departs significantly from actual events, not only in its detail but also in its final message. The film ends by showing newly radicalised youth in opposition to a corrupt and cynical Labour Party, but, as the next chapter shows, many of the young activists actually chose to join Labour.

In comparing the Bengali and Jewish/communist campaigns, it is important to acknowledge the different situations the campaigners faced. In the 1970s, the Bengalis were still relatively new immigrants. Many of the older men had only recently come to realise that they were truly immigrants and not temporary migrant workers, and many of the women had only just arrived. There was a huge language barrier standing between them and other East Enders, among whom there was a high level of ignorance about and antipathy towards these newest residents, making any joint action difficult.[99] By the 1930s the Jews were established in the area and although they were still resented, Jews and Gentiles shared a common experience of East End slum life. Recent immigration need not, however, preclude a level of radical outward-looking political organisation, as demonstrated by the actions of earlier Jewish socialists and anarchists described in the previous chapter.

All tenants could unite in the rent strikes against the private landlords and the campaign for more state-funded housing, but a fight for housing such as that which took place in the 1970s can easily degenerate into a scramble for the housing that is already available, and the fighters can easily be divided into competing camps. Divisions of this sort must have been welcomed by many housing officers and local politicians, even when they did not actually encourage them, as the anger became directed away from themselves. Squatters were accused of trying to jump the queue, and council house allocation has long been a huge source of conflict between Bengalis and more long-established East Enders. While Bengalis complained that they were not being given the same treatment as everyone else, there were many others who felt those who had been established in the area longer should be given preference.[100] In addition, the concentration of the Bengalis into certain areas and streets made it even less likely that they would seek common cause with their white neighbours.

However this did not stop some socialist organisations from attempting to emulate the class-based campaigns of the 1930s. ELWAR argued that defence of black people was in everyone's interest as a crucial part of the fight against wider oppression and that the key to this was mobilisation of the local white population. Workers Against Racism national organiser, Keith Tompson, explained their method:

> Our strategy is based on a simple truth: that those responsible for racial violence are always a small minority and that, as such, they can be isolated if the majority of the community is mobilized behind those under attack. Our aims in every situation are, first, to alert those who are appalled by racial violence to what is happening and to

organize them to take a stand; and second, to explain to those who don't care why they should and why they too should take a stand.[101]

ELWAR took an active role in the housing battle, and wanted to deny the racists any victories by fighting to enable Bengali families to stay on white estates where they had been allocated flats. They protected the flats and canvassed the white tenants for their support, organising protection from within the estate. Tompson gives the example of a Bengali father, Mr Ali, and his three sons who, in 1982, were allocated a flat on the all white Glamis Estate, where the racist leader of the tenants' association ensured that they were met by racist graffiti, excrement through the letter box and a hostile reception committee. ELWAR activists accompanied the family to the estate and within three days had visited all of its five hundred homes, uncovering a core of local people who were prepared to protect the family until the attacks stopped and the racists became the outcasts.[102] Others who argued against transfer as the solution to racial harassment included a Labour councillor in East India Ward, who was a supporter of Militant Tendancy and who tried to improve conditions on the Teviot Estate with a Bengali Community Centre and a football pitch.[103] However, such tactics could only have made a significant difference on a larger scale and – most importantly – with the support of the community who had to form the front-line troops. The majority of people within that community chose instead to fight for the right to stay in Bengali areas.

The legacy of black radicalism

BHAG had begun with a contradiction. It was a movement for self-organisation organised by outsiders. External leadership need not necessarily be a problem,[104] but there was resistance in the Bengali community to the idea of working with outsiders and a suspicion that they must have ulterior motives – as already observed in relation to various left groups. Sunahwar Ali, then a young activist working with BHAG and outside it and later in charge of Tower Hamlets Homeless Families Campaign, has commented:

> There was a lot of hostility ... A lot of people felt [Race Today] helped; a lot of people thought they were making name for and fame for themselves.[105]

It seems that Fitzpatrick, who moved into Pelham Buildings and was visibly giving all his time to the campaign, was more easily accepted as part of the community.

In the beginning, Fitzpatrick was sometimes viewed as the council's official housing manager for Bengalis,[106] but active Bengali involvement increased among both the squatters themselves and the newly mobilised youth. Helal Abbas recalls that Bengalis took little part in the initial running of BHAG, but by the end, when he was its seventeen-year-old secretary, 'it became a Bengali-managed organisation with support from non-Bengali members'.[107] However, it is clear that Fitzpatrick and Mala Dhondy's roles remained crucial, especially when it came to building work or dealing with the authorities or the media. Their control was challenged at one point in 1977 by Nurul Huque, an educated man from Dhaka who had set up a pioneering community school (and who we met briefly as a JSD activist in Chapter 4). Huque attempted to foment questioning of the leadership's motivation and personal morality and persuade members that BHAG needed a Bengali leader such as himself, but only a minority followed him.[108] It is not difficult to understand why the membership, demonstrating no lack of political maturity, chose to stay with their proven leaders, but this incident does illustrate a possible trap for those arguing for the self-organisation of others.

For those who promote self-organisation from the outside, nothing in their organisation becomes them like the leaving it. As Mala put it,

> When you are a political activist, you empower other people to take their chance to empower themselves. Once they have empowered themselves, you say, 'Okay sweetie, now it's your household, you look after it, I'm going'.[109]

There is no shortage of testimonies to the part played by the struggles for decent housing and against racism in the mobilisation of a generation of Bengali youth – a generation that was to occupy many of the seats on Tower Hamlets Council and run many of the local campaigning and community groups. For former council leader Abbas, his time in BHAG was 'when I became politically aware of my role and the part I can play'.[110] Even those who had not got involved with BHAG directly would have felt its influence in the campaigns of the late 1970s.

When BHAG petered out at the end of the 1970s its organisers could justifiably say they had played their part in empowering a generation of Bengalis, but was this the 'collective power of black workers' they had originally spoken of? BHAG had broken with Race Today in 1977, accusing them of a lack of practical help at a time of crisis, and Darcus Howe used the journal to pour scorn on the organisation's achievements. In a tirade in which he accused them of 'recreating, in a squalid ghetto block, some of the feudal relations of the Asian village', he blamed their failures on 'a total pre-occupation with the tactics of squatting'[111] – just the type of situation Piratin had congratulated the Stepney communists for avoiding.[112] There had been no time given to the discussion of political ideology. Every minute was taken up in routine practicalities and managing endless crises: everyone had to be persuaded to stay on board and not be tempted to sell their squat on at a profit, some people were keeping others awake machining in their flats through the night, and there were always building repairs. At squatters' meetings the correct division of the shared electricity bill had been more urgent than debates over black power.

Mala, who had played a central part until the end, later claimed only limited success:

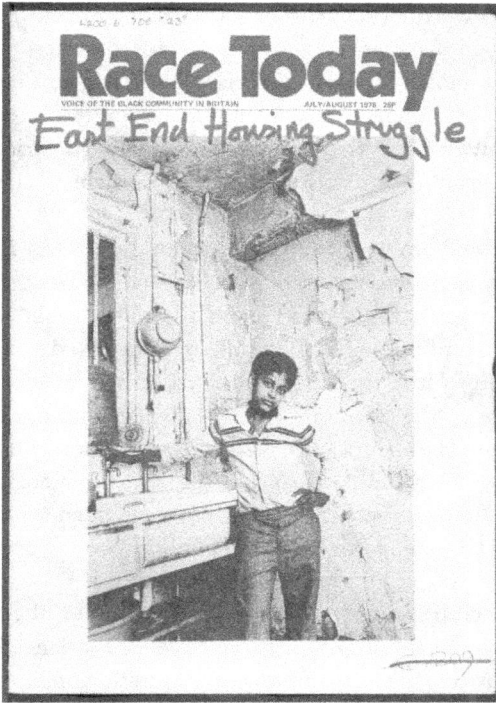

Figure 6.3   Race Today, July/August 1978

> We did change people's minds, we did make them feel … a more kind of … community sense rather than an individual sense, yes, we made strides. I don't regret that movement, I think we achieved a lot, but I think we had a limited agenda. I mean you can't create a world revolution with ghetto politics, and it was ghetto politics … After that some of us felt we'd done what we had to do and we had no more to say, they were taking over their own lives and good luck, that's what we wanted them to do anyway, and we moved onto other things.[113]

How much BHAG's demands for independent black action influenced the development of Bengali politics is impossible to say. Certainly they contradicted all the left activists' arguments about working-class unity, limited the scope of the movement, and did not encourage the sort of coming together of different groups in a common cause that occurred in the 1930s rent strikes. If nothing else, such separatist demands may have sown confusion. The separatist stance led those who followed it to ignore other movements and views and not to ask what they might learn from history.[114] The second edition of Piratin's book did not come out until BHAG was in its final phase, but there were still plenty of people around who remembered earlier struggles.

BHAG's campaign left a powerful social legacy in a relatively segregated community and ethnically distinct electoral wards, as Farrukh Dhondy has since observed.[115] Although it also helped make possible the very high proportion of Bengalis (unique among ethnic minority groups) who have been able to find accommodation in council housing, their special requirements in terms of location and house size, along with their frequent need to apply via strict homelessness legislation, have meant that it has been easy for them to be allocated the worst quality homes.

In dismissing the 'white left' and ignoring the white working class, and in not attempting to link housing problems and racism to issues beyond the Bengali community, Race Today had promoted a grassroots politics with the politics reduced to a poorly defined identification of Bengalis as a deprived and oppressed community that needed to help itself. Its youth had learned to fight, only to strive for a greater share of the establishment cake, which they then generally attempted to do through the mainstream political organisations that Race Today had turned its back on. They did not challenge the established order as the black radicals had hoped. The youth were mobilised, but the tendency for separate self-organisation appears to have led them down a political byway, and there was no new and 'progressive' way out.

The Bengali case provides a clear example of the general taming of black radicalism consequent on the contradictions within its ideology and a general tendency, despite the radical rhetoric, to focus on improving the position of black and Asian immigrants within the existing system, in line with Carmichael's more liberal approach. As Shukra put it,

> Although in processing the 'race'-class equation the black radicals sought a black Marxist position, they were unable to achieve it. This was because the particularist ideology of black consciousness which they adopted counteracted the very fusion and synthesis they were after.[116]

She goes on to observe that

> In practice the militancy of [the Asian] youth organisations, was limited to the language and direct action tactics that they used. Beyond the promise of militancy, the actual strategies remained very close to the older generation's.[117]

Embedding the radicals

On top of black radicalism's inherent weaknesses, public money helped discipline the newly mobilised activists and transform them into a new generation of community workers and public-sector professionals. In Tower Hamlets, the official response to the violence of 1978 took the form of more funding for community organisations, and this approach was boosted in the 1980s when institutional multiculturalism became the new black. By 1981, economic recession and growing unemployment was coupled with persistent racism and discrimination – not least from the police – and this resulted in unrest and riots in several areas with high ethnic minority populations, including a confrontation in Brixton between thousands of Afro-Caribbeans and the Metropolitan Police. The official response to the wave of unrest affected the course of immigrant politics throughout Britain. The report by the government inquiry into the riots, chaired by Lord Scarman, called for a two-pronged approach: hard policing coupled with measures to give ethnic minorities a stake in British society. As had happened on a smaller scale in Tower Hamlets three years earlier, older approaches of working through community leaders were given a new interpretation and impact through engagement with the new grassroots community groups, and these groups were persuaded onto a pragmatic path through the promise of substantial resources. The Conservative minister, George Young, explained to the *Sunday Times*:

> We've got to back the good guys, the sensible, moderate, responsible leaders of ethnic groups. If they are seen to deliver, to get financial support from central government for urban projects, then that reinforces their standing and credibility in the community. If they don't deliver, people will turn to the militants.[118]

Central government money was made available through the Urban Programme, which had originally been set up under Labour in 1968 to provide grants to projects in poor inner-city areas, including those with high concentrations of immigrants.[119] The programme was put into effect by the local authorities – not just by left-wing administrations but also by Conservatives who recognised its potential for neutralising potential radicalism.

The Labour left responded to ethnic minority mobilisation and the emergence of New Social Movements by embracing many of the concepts of identity politics as a fundamental plank of their progressive politics. Even more money for voluntary groups was given out by the GLC under Ken Livingston, both directly and through support for 'stressed' local boroughs such as Tower Hamlets.[120] By the time the GLC was abolished in 1986 and funding for community groups was cut back, the once-radical leaders had lost their independence and many had their feet under the council table.

Support for cultural pluralism had existed since well before the emergence of black radicalism,[121] developing in contrast and often in conscious opposition to the idea of the integrationist melting pot. While the promotion of different cultures and cultural groups is often portrayed as radical, it presents no threat to the socioeconomic system and mainstream political elites. Conservatives have liked to ridicule some of the more symbolic examples of multicultural policy as manifestations of the 'loony left', but they set up another government fund in 1987 specifically to encourage ethnic minority entrepreneurs, in tune with their own emphasis on the market and on individual social mobility.

Poor areas and immigrant communities felt the full weight of Conservative monetarist economics and all these grants could do little to ameliorate the impact of wider socio-economic conditions. But while the grants failed in their ostensible aim of securing better living conditions, they achieved the government's underlying agenda of containing and defusing potential for more radical action, and they persuaded ethnic activists and leftist community workers and councillors to help with this containment. Groups dependent on public funding soon lose their radical edge.

At the same time, the demand for funds institutionalised difference and put ethnic groups in competition with each other, and funding for ethnic-based groups provided fuel for the racists. Well-meaning lectures from liberal anti-racists could simply be dismissed as condescending. They failed to address socio-economic issues affecting the whole working class, and they ignored the argument that overcoming racist division is a first step towards fighting for better conditions.

Most Bengali activists took a pragmatic and community-centred line. They could see how much Bengalis were suffering – through racism, poor housing and a general lack of services – and they wanted to help them the most efficient way possible. When the squatters won the right to rehousing in the E1 area this was far from the end of the housing struggle, and many of those who had received their activist's training with BHAG went on to take part in other campaigns or worked with organisations such as Spitalfields Housing and Planning Rights Service (SHAPRS), set up in 1979 with grant money from the Spitalfields Project. The 1980s saw the creation of a plethora of new Bengali community groups with new sets of initials, and although individual organisations have come and gone there has continued to be a very active voluntary sector. All these groups campaigned actively for Bengali interests, but they were always susceptible to cuts in funding regimes and could never attempt to pursue a more political agenda that might jeopardise their grant.[122]

Community groups and organisations of all kinds are a vital part of Bengali culture (as we saw when looking at links with the homeland), but for many in the newly mobilised generation this was not enough. For them, the next step after the youth movements (and perhaps some further housing activism) was joining the Labour Party, because that was where the power was.

Notes

1   Kalbir Shukra, *The Changing Pattern of Black Politics in Britain* (London: Pluto Press, 1998), p. 30.
2   Quoted in *ibid.*, p. 31.
3   A. Sivanandan, 'Challenging Racism: Strategies for the 1980s', in his collected volume, *Communities of Resistance: Writings on Black Struggles for Socialism* (Verso: London, 1990, revised version of talk given on 12 March 1983), p. 66.
4   Shukra, *The Changing Pattern of Black Politics in Britain*.

5 Revolutionary stages theory was discussed in Chapter 2.

6 Stuart Hall, Chas Critcher, Tony Jefferson, John Clarke and Brian Roberts, *Policing the Crisis: Mugging, the State, and Law and Order* (Macmillan, Basingstoke, 1978), pp. 381–7.

7 Marx argues in the *Communist Manifesto* that, 'The "dangerous class" [*lumpenproletariat*], the social scum, that passively rotting mass thrown off by the lowest layers of the old society, may, here and there, be swept into the movement by a proletarian revolution; its conditions of life, however, prepare it far more for the part of a bribed tool of reactionary intrigue.' See www.marxists.org/archive/marx/works/1848/communist-manifesto/ch01.htm, accessed 20 November 2012.

8 Initially called the Unemployed Workers' Committee Movement.

9 Although Phil Piratin's classic account – in *Our Flag Stays Red* (London: Lawrence and Wishart, 1978) – presents the housing campaigns as a seamless part of the Communist Party battle plan, at the time the significance of the tenants' movement and its relationship to the class struggle was the subject of critical argument. Jack Shapiro, who I interviewed in 2002, had been a party activist and recalled campaigns organised from his family home as early as 1933, before Piratin's story begins. He also remembered a long analytical discussion in the party's London District Office as late as 1938, when the line was put forward that the movement 'could have meaning for developing people who could come into the class struggle, but wasn't the class struggle itself'.

10 This term was used by both Sivanandan and Hall *et al.*

11 See, for example, Ron Ramdin, *The Making of the Black Working Class in Britain* (Aldershot: Gower, 1987), p. 508.

12 See, for example, P. Gilroy., 'Steppin' Out of Babylon – Race, Class and Autonomy', in Centre for Contemporary Cultural Studies, *The Empire Strikes Back: Race and Racism in 70s Britain* (London: Hutchinson, 1982), pp. 305–6.

13 A. Sivanandan, 'The Liberation of the Black Intellectual', *Race and Class*, 18:4 (1977, first written for a symposium on 'immigrant intellectuals' in 1972), 329–43.

14 This phrase is from a song by Jacques Roumain, originally quoted by Fanon.

15 Sivanandan, 'The Liberation of the Black Intellectual', p. 339.

16 *Ibid.*, footnote p. 341.

17 A. Sivanandan, 'Race, Class and the State: The Black Experience in Britain', *Race and Class*, 17:4 (1976), 347–68.

18 Hall *et al.*, *Policing the Crisis*, p. 355.

19 *Ibid.*, p. 390.

20 *Ibid.*, p. 395.

21 *Ibid.*, p. 395.

22 *Ibid.*, p. 397.

23 *Ibid.*, p. 370.

24 Darcus Howe, 'Fighting Back: West Indian Youth and the Police in Notting Hill', *Race Today*, 5:11 (1973), 333–6.

25 Hall *et al.*, *Policing the Crisis*, p. 391.

26 Selma James, 'Sex, Race and Working Class Power', *Race Today* (January 1974), 12–15. The longer pamphlet version that came out of this article is discussed in Hall *et al.*, *Policing the Crisis*, pp. 369–71.

27 Farrukh Dhondy, 'The Black Explosion in Schools', *Race Today* (February 1974).

28 *Ibid.*

29 Sivanandan, 'Race, Class and the State', p. 366. The article quoted was 'Gunning for a Wage', *Race Today*, 7:10 (October 1975).

30 Shukra, *The Changing Pattern of Black Politics in Britain*, pp. 43–4.

31 The census records 67 per cent of households in council housing in 1971, rising to 82 per cent in 1981.

32 Ron Bailey, *The Squatters* (Harmondsworth: Penguin, 1973).

33 See, for example, the description of Sheba Street in the first report produced by the Spitalfields Housing and Planning Rights Service, *SHAPRS Six-Month Report*, November 1979, p. 9 (Tower Hamlets Local History Library).

34 Deborah Phillips, 'What Price Equality? A Report on the Allocation of GLC Housing in Tower Hamlets', *GLC Housing Research & Policy Report, No. 9* (1986) (Tower Hamlets Local History Library).

35 Interviewed 23 August 2001.

36 Spitalfields Housing and Planning Rights Service, *SHAPRS Annual Report*, December 1983, p. 4 (Tower Hamlets Local History Library).

37 *Race Today*, September 1974 and August 1975; BBC *Nationwide*, shown 26 September 1975. I also discussed this with Caroline Adams when I interviewed her on 13 December 2000.

38 I interviewed Terry Fitzpatrick on 23 August 2001 and 20 November 2001, and Mala Sen on 5 November 2001. I will refer to her by her first name to avoid confusion.

39 *Race Today*, September 1974.

40 Terry Fitzpatrick, interviewed 23 August 2001.

41 Terry Fitzpatrick, interviewed 1 June 2006 by Jamil Iqbal for Swadhinata Trust and the University of Surrey Centre for Research on Nationalism, Ethnicity and Multiculturalism, 'Oral History Project' (2005–06).

42 Charlie Forman, *Spitalfields: A Battle for Land* (London: Hilary Shipman, 1989), p. 81.

43 *Race Today*, March 1976, p. 52.

44 *Race Today*, March 1976, p. 53. The name, BHAG, was celebrated for translating as tiger in Bengali, though the Bengali for tiger should strictly be transliterated as *bagh*.

45 Terry Fitzpatrick, interviewed 1 June 2006 by Jamil Iqbal for Swadhinata Trust and University of Surrey, 'Oral History Project'.

46 Forman, *Spitalfields*, p. 82.

47 Mark Phillips, *Homelessness and Tenants' Control: Struggles for Council Housing in Tower Hamlets 1974–1976* (London: Dame Colet House, 1977), p. 45.

48 Interviewed 10 October 2001.

49 As Fitzpatrick pointed out, that there were few squatters in Tory areas. (Interviewed 1 June 2006 by Jamil Iqbal for Swadhinata Trust and University of Surrey, 'Oral History Project').

50 Fitzpatrick, interviewed 23 August 2001.

51 Forman, *Spitalfields*, pp. 84–6.

52 This was a period when there was increasing recognition of the value of refurbishment – in reaction against recent large-scale demolitions – and a growth of investment in housing associations promoted by the 1974 Housing Act.

53 Quoted in Kenneth Leech, *Brick Lane 1978: The Events and their Significance* (London: Stepney Books Publications, 1994), p. 13.

54 The first shot was fired by the *Observer*, see 'GLC Plans Ghetto for Bengalis', *Observer*, 4 June 1978.

55 Leech, *Brick Lane 1978*, p. 13.

56 *Ibid.*, p 14. The letter is dated 7 June 1978.

57 Quoted in *ibid.*, p. 14.

58 Phillips, *Homelessness and Tenants' Control*, p. 53.

59 Interviewed 5 November 2001.

60 Susie Daniel and Pete McGuire (eds), *The Paint House: Words from an East End Gang* (Harmondsworth: Penguin, 1972).

61 One of the boys threw a brick at a man on a boat in Hyde Park, knocking him into the water where he drowned (see *ibid.*, p. 28). Looking back at this a couple of years later, one of the gang members wrote: 'Now, you realize that it is a serious thing to take someone's life, but then you didn't think it was taking a life, you thought that it was a Paki, and that didn't matter' (see *ibid.*, p. 127).

62 One of the gang members looking back at events a couple of years earlier, in *ibid.*, p. 113.

63 See interviews with Sunahwar Ali, Aloke Biswas, Cathy Forrester, John Newbigin and Mohammed Abdus Salam in Swadhinata Trust and University of Surrey, 'Oral History Project'.

64 Interviewed 5 November 2001.

65 Caroline Adams, 'The Spitalfields Bengali Action Group and the Kobi Nazrul Centre 1974–78' (manuscript, Avenues Unlimited, 1979), quoted in Leech, *Brick Lane 1978*, p. 22.

66 Terry Fitzpatrick, interviewed 1 June 2006 by Jamil Iqbal for Swadhinata Trust and University of Surrey, 'Oral History Project'.

67 Interviewed 14 November 2000.

68 The Bangladesh Krishak Sramik Awami League, see Chapter 4.

69 See Shukra, *The Changing Pattern of Black Politics in Britain*, pp. 46–8; Anandi Ramamurthy, 'The Politics of Britain's Asian Youth Movements', *Race and Class,* 48:2 (2006), 38–60; Kenan Malik, *From Fatwa to Jihad: The Rushdie Affair and its Legacy* (London: Atlantic Books, 2009), pp. 48 and 50–2. While the majority of activists were male, Southall Black Sisters, founded in 1979, and Birmingham Black Sisters added a feminist dimension to the movement, and Manchester Asian Youth Movement had a women's secton.

70 Leech, *Brick Lane 1978*.

71 Interviewed 30 April 2006 by Jamil Iqbal, Ansar Ahmed Ullah and Charlie Sen for Swadhinata Trust and University of Surrey Centre, 'Oral History Project'.

72 Interviewed 21 March 2006 by Jamil Iqbal and Charlie Sen for Swadhinata Trust and University of Surrey Centre, 'Oral History Project'.

73 Joint Statement issued by the presidents of the Standing Conference of Pakistani Organisations in the UK, the Indian Workers' Association, and the Federation of Bangladesh Organisations, reproduced in Bethnal Green and Stepney Trades Council, 'Blood on the Streets: A Report by Bethnal Green and Stepney Trades Council on Racial Attacks in East London' (1978), p. 95 (Cambridge University Library).

74 Leech, *Brick Lane 1978*, pp. 9–10. Leech shows a photograph of the broken window of a grocery shop whose owner was 'knocked unconscious by a hail of rocks' losing 'two teeth and need[ing] five stitches in his face.'

75 Tony Kushner and Nadia Valman (eds), *Remembering Cable Street: Facism and Anti-Facism in British Society* (London: Vallentine Mitchell, 2000).

76 Bethnal Green and Stepney Trades Council, 'Blood on the Streets', p. 15.

77 Mithu Ghosh, interviewed 9 May 2006 by Jamil Iqbal; Husna Matin, interviewed 30 January 2006 by Jamil Iqbal and Ansar Ahmed Ullah, both for Swadhinata Trust and University of Surrey, 'Oral History Project'.

78 Interviewed 22 August 2001.

79 See Forman, *Spitalfields*, p. 54.

80 *Camerawork Magazine*, issue 13.

81 Margaret Thatcher, interviewed on Granada Television's *World in Action*, 27 January 1978, http://www.margaretthatcher.org/speeches/displaydocument.asp?docid= 103485, accessed 20 November 2012.

82 Liberal Democrats, 'Political Speech and Race Relations in a Liberal Democracy: Report of an Inquiry into the Conduct of the Tower Hamlets Liberal Democrats in Publishing Allegedly Racist Election Literature between 1990 and 1993' (Liberal Democrats' Tower Hamlets' Inquiry, 1993).

83 John Rex, 'Black Militancy and Class Conflict', in Robert Miles and Annie Phizacklea (eds), *Racism and Political Action in Britain* (London: Routledge and Kegan Paul, 1979) 72–92, p. 86.

84 Malik, *From Fatwa to Jihad,* p. xii.

85 *Ibid.,* p. 52.

86 *Ibid.,* p. xi.

87 Interviewed 12 October 2001. This was the same man who discussed, in Chapter 5, why the nature of the small workshops mitigated against Dan Jones's hopes for trade unionism. The Naz Cinema, which showed Asian films, took over the old Odeon on Brick Lane in the 1960s. It is now the Café Naz restaurant..

88 Interviewed 7 June 2006 by Jamil Iqbal, Riza Momin and Maliha Haque for Swadhinata Trust and University of Surrey, 'Oral History Project'.

89 Bethnal Green and Stepney Trades Council, 'Blood on the Streets', p. 58.

90 'Bengali Workers on Strike', *Race Today* (September-October 1978).

91 Father St John B Groser, *Politics and Persons* (London: SCM Press, 1949), pp. 73 and 75.

92 Stalin's 1913 article, *Marxism and the National Question,* written under the guiding hand of Lenin, remained a standard Communist text; however, Stalin cut across his own arguments both in his theories and in practice. See www.marxists.org/reference/archive/stalin/works/1913/03.htm, accessed 20 November 2012.

93 Sarah Glynn, 'East End Immigrants and the Battle for Housing: A Comparative Study of Political Mobilisation in the Jewish and Bengali Communities', *Journal of Historical Geography,* 31 (2005), 528–45.

94 Piratin, *Our Flag Stays Red,* p. 32.

95 Interviewed Autumn 1999.

96 Simon Blumenfeld, *Enough of All This! A Rent Strike Play* (London: Left Book Club Theatre Guild, 1939?). There is a copy of the play in the Unity Theatre collection in Merseyside Maritime Museum.

97 Farrukh Dhondy, *Come to Mecca* (London: Collins, 1978).

98 Farrukh Dhondy, *King of the Ghetto,* 4-part drama for Channel 4, shown May 1986. This can be viewed at the British Film Institute.

99 A series of workshops entitled Tenants Tackle Racism, held in Stepney in 1984–85, discussed the problems of 'black' involvement in predominantly white tenants' associations. One participant claimed that almost one third of their tenants' association was now Bengali, but another described going, together with three other Bengalis, to four or five meetings, and then all giving up 'due to the abuse and hostility we encountered at every meeting'. See Dame Colet House, *Tenants Tackle Racism: An Account of a Series of Experimental Workshops Held in Stepney – 1984/5* (London: Dame Colet House, 1986).

100 See, for example, *East End Advertiser,* July 1983, quoted in Forman, *Spitalfields,* p. 188. This continues to be a source of conflict.

101 Keith Tompson, *Under Siege: Racism and Violence in Britain Today* (London: Penguin, 1988), p. 189.

102 *Ibid.,* pp. 139–41. Tompson recorded that the only intervention from the police was

to demand to see Mr Ali's rent book and passport to check they had the right to move in. Kenan Malik, who was credited with a substantial part of the research for Tompson's book, has recorded that he spent much of 1984 'camped out in a house in London's East End' with a Pakistani family in Newham who were then fighting their third of six years of racist attacks and abuse from local youths. (See Malik, *From Fatwa to Jihad*, pp. 36–8.) He quoted a letter from the police to the family's MP that put all the blame on the victims: 'The arrival of a demonstrative Asian family in a predominantly whites' playground area had unpleasant effects … police do feel there is a case for rehousing this family.'

103 Described in an interview with Clive Heemskerk, who was himself a member of Militant, 6 December 2000. In a similar vein, Shila Thakor remembers helping the SWP guard a family whose house was being attacked by racist neighbours in the 1980s, when she worked as a youth worker: see interview, 9 May 2006, by Jamil Iqbal for Swadhinata Trust and University of Surrey, 'Oral History Project'.

104 As East End history had already demonstrated through the examples of Eleanor Marx in the late nineteenth century and Rudolf Rocker, the non-Jewish leader of the Jewish anarchists, before the First World War.

105 Interviewed 23 January 2001.

106 Phillips, *Homelessness and Tenants' Control*, p. 46.

107 Interviewed 10 October 2001.

108 Interviews with Terry Fitzpatrick, 23 August 2001, and with a Bengali activist who asked to remain anonymous, 12 October 2001.

109 Interviewed 5 November 2001.

110 Interviewed 10 October 2001.

111 *Race Today* (July/August 1978), p. 110.

112 Piratin wrote: 'It is not uncommon for Communists to become so submerged in the work of tenants' associations that they lose their identity. This was not the case in Stepney … we saw our main job in relation to the tenants in assisting them in every way … and explaining to the people the broader political implications of what they were doing'. See Piratin, *Our Flag Stays Red*, p. 48–9.

113 Interviewed 5 November 2001.

114 There was an article by Joe Jacobs on the police and the fascists in the 1930s in the last issue of *Race Today* before Darcus Howe's editorship, but it did not engage with wider issues or the current situation.

115 In an email to the author, dated 10 September 2002, he wrote: 'what started as the provision of a base through squatting which turned into housing associations and non-dispersed housing, became electoral voting power through providing Bengali wards.'

116 Shukra, *The Changing Pattern of Black Politics in Britain*, p. 39.

117 *Ibid.*, pp. 47–8.

118 *Sunday Times*, 10 October 1982, quoted in Tompson, *Under Siege*, p. 91.

119 See House of Commons Debate, 22 July 1968, *Hansard*, vol. 769 cols 40–9. Tompson recorded that by 1986 Urban Programme funds had risen to £38.8 million, and the proportion of the funding for voluntary groups that went to 'black' organisations had increased to over half (Tompson, *Under Siege*, p. 95).

120 Tompson, *Under Siege*, p. 103.

121 Early examples of this kind of thinking include the theories of cultural national autonomy developed by Austrian socialists responding to the cultural mix of the Hapsburg Empire at end of the ninteenth century. Ideas of cultural pluralism also developed in the US in the mid 1910s as a reaction to pressures for Americanisation. Multiculturalism has been official government policy in Canada since 1971.

122 John Eade, *The Politics of Community: The Bangladeshi Community in East London* (Aldershot: Avebury, 1989); Mohammad Ali Asghar, *Bangladeshi Community Organisations in East London* (London: Bangla Heritage, 1996). The youth groups were also sponsored to come together into a short-lived Federation of Bangladeshi Youth Organisations (with Kumar Murshid appointed as co-ordinator) because organisations such as the Commission for Racial Equality wanted a representative umbrella group that they could work with. See John Eversley, interviewed 23 March 2006 by Jamil Iqbal and Charlie Sen for Swadhinata Trust and University of Surrey, 'Oral History Project'.

7 Bengalis in the council chamber

The community-based activism of the late 1970s led to a pragmatic move into mainstream Labour politics.[1] For many activists this was the logical next step, despite the fact that party politics had been only peripheral to the struggles described in the previous chapter, and that in some of the housing battles Tower Hamlets Labour Council had been on the opposing side. These activists generally continued to see themselves as representatives of the Bengali community, but argued that they would achieve more through conventional channels. The overriding reason given by my interviewees for joining the Labour Party was to continue campaigning for better and fairer treatment for Bengalis. There were, of course, also those who thought more could be done outside organised politics, but self-organisation along 'ethnic' lines had mobilised a new generation, and now they wanted access to the mechanisms of power. As Helal Abbas (who had since become council leader) put it, 'you can only change so much from outside'.[2]

The association of ethnic minorities with the Labour Party was once a truth universally acknowledged – and repeatedly reinforced by the overt racism of the Conservatives. Immigrants were disproportionately in Labour-dominated urban centres and in working-class occupations, but support for Labour was exceptionally strong and extended across class boundaries.[3] In Tower Hamlets, this affiliation was also the best way to achieve real power within the political establishment, as – apart from a two-term Liberal hiatus – the party has dominated local politics since the 1920s. The Labour Party was the natural recipient of most Bengali votes and the natural forum for most mainstream Bengali political activity. As Manir Uddin Ahmed put it, 'everybody' was 'automatically' Labour.[4] Sundor Miah, who came to England in 1967 as a teenager, told me in 2000:

> since I came in this country, I have been taught by my father that we are supposed to vote Labour, and we're still in Labour ... I came in this country when the prime minister was Wilson ... He always ... think of immigrant people.[5]

The 1971 Independence struggle gave the Bengalis' long and increasingly intimate relationship with the Labour Party an especially firm foundation. This rested both on the active involvement of Labour MPs in support of the Bengali cause[6] and on the party's perceived ideological link with the Awami League. As Peter Shore, former MP for Stepney, observed, 'There was a feeling of some considerable overlap of values and outlook between the Awami League and the Labour Party'.[7] Recollections of the period all acknowledge the part played by a number of Labour MPs in keeping up pressure on the Conservative government to support Bangladesh, and Shore's own contribution was acknowledged officially in Bangladesh by the new government, and in London by 'an ongoing and very close relationship with the community, and indeed with their leaders'.[8] At the Awami League's commemorative meeting, held in Toynbee Hall shortly after his death, Shore was described as a *de facto* member of the Awami League and *de jure* member of Bangladesh.[9] Sunahwar Ali explained:

> his involvement given us a license; he's the friend of Bangladesh and he got a strong link with Awami League, and people in Bangladesh do respect him ... I don't agree with him lot of the thing ... but of course he got lot of motivation because of his contribution. I also got the encouragement to join the Labour Party, otherway I wouldn't be there.[10]

Personal support for Shore extended to his reselection battle, when he was challenged by Jill Cove from the left in the mid-1980s.[11]

Developing links with the Labour Party had been cemented following the Independence war, when future hopes were focused increasingly on a settled life in Britain, and the Bengalis made use of their newfound channel to power and political assertiveness to keep their constituency MP busy with immigration problems and all the other difficulties that beset an immigrant community in a poor neighbourhood.

By the early 1980s, while some of the newly mobilised generation felt ideological ties to Labour,[12] for others the link was natural or simply pragmatic. When I asked a prominent Labour councillor to explain his choice of party, he told me:

> we thought, OK, the fastest way to get in, in this area, will be through the Labour Party because that's the party in control of the local mechanisms at the time ... it wasn't for any political ideals ... because all of them were just as bad ... the Labour Party had brought some of the worst immigration policies and procedures of that period ... The Tories were far too right for us to even consider ... and to get the voters to vote for it in an area like this; and the Liberals we thought would never get into power.[13]

Sunahwar Ali simply explained, 'I'd rather work with people who can deliver thing[s] for the community ... because sometime[s] ideology doesn't work'.[14]

Entering Labour's stronghold

At first, though, many of this newly politicised generation found the Labour Party far from welcoming. Some early Bengali immigrants appear to have had no problems in joining their ward parties,[15] and Manawar Hussain became an alderman in Bradford City Council as early as 1972,[16] but many East End Bengalis who hoped to join the party were faced with a blank refusal. John Eversley remembered, from when he was a local community worker in the late 1970s, talking with a member of Spitalfields Ward Labour Party, which was at the heart of Bengali settlement, and being told 'quite explicitly', 'we will not elect them in the Labour Party'.[17] Sunahwar Ali recalled that when he and two or three others applied to join the party in Spitalfields they were told, 'Sorry, we don't have vacancy, we've got too many member, we cannot allow'.[18] The situation was changed by the intervention of Labour left-wingers, but Sunahwar's explanation exhibits the prevailing distrust of their motives:

> a group of certain people … those who believe in left policies on the Labour Party side, they thought, 'This is the time we can utilise them.' They came and said, 'Why don't you become a member we'll help you?'[19]

The inclusion of people from all ethnic backgrounds can also be seen as flowing directly from leftist ideology – both from socialist universalism and from the developing support for identity politics – and the view of these events from the left is a little different from many Bengali perceptions. At that time, Labour ruled over Tower Hamlets almost unopposed and its entrenched, relatively right-wing leadership clung fiercely to power. Jill Cove, one of a small group of Labour left-wingers, explained that it was not only Bengalis who had difficulties breaking into the party fortress. She applied to join Spitalfields Ward Labour Party, together with her partner George, in the late 1970s, and they were also told there was a waiting list and were given no further information. In 1979, after more than a year, they got hold of application forms, found out when the ward meeting was being held, marched in, slapped the forms down on the table and demanded membership. There were many others in a similar position and every month the meetings were lobbied by a crowd of would-be members. On one occasion, when there were some twenty people outside, Jill and George found there were only three other members present, and they proposed opening up the party. The new members admitted that day – who could be described as belonging to various ethnicities and social backgrounds – included Abbas and three other future Bengali councillors.[20]

The 1982 council elections added a new dimension to the Bengali sense of exclusion, and this was met by radical action. The Labour Party had chosen to stand one Bengali candidate in St Katherine's ward,[21] but they had nominated no Bengalis in Spitalfields, where the community was most concentrated. John Eade has recorded in detail how, in protest, four Bengalis (two of whom 'claimed to have been members of the Labour party'[22]) put themselves up for election as independents, and a fifth stood for the newly formed Social Democratic Party (SDP). Two of the independents were chosen and supported by the People's Democratic Alliance (PDA), which was created for the purpose of the election by delegates from different Bengali community groups. The four independents were of varied ages and experience, but their action was a natural outcome of the politics of self-organisation that had been promoted in the 1970s, even if in this case it was not the preferred option. Spitalfields elected three councillors. When the results were announced, Nurul Huque of the PDA topped the poll, while the other PDA candidate missed third place by twenty-six votes. (We last encountered Huque making an unsuccessful leadership challenge in the Bengali Housing Action Group. When Eade interviewed him he accused local Labour leaders of excluding Bengalis through racist hiring policies, explaining that they had responded to his demand for Bengali doctors, social workers and teachers by describing him as racist.[23])

Abbas had accepted his party's choice of candidates and campaigned for Labour, but he confirmed that Huque's election had the desired impact:

> we lost ... a safe Labour seat to the independent. We could have lost more. I think from that [the] party took the message clearly at the following elections: we saw Bangladeshi candidates – people who were capable and able to represent the local community – were given opportunities to stand as Labour Party candidate[s].[24]

This was also the year following the 1981 riots, when the neglect of black constituents had been brought abruptly to the notice of politicians of all kinds.

In fact, Abbas himself was soon to be selected by the Labour Party to stand in the 1985 Spitalfields by-election. Somewhat perversely, the PDA could not resist putting up their own candidate, who squeezed the Labour majority down to just nine votes. The PDA candidate was able to make use of strong Bangladeshi village networks to mobilise support.[25] Non-party ties and networks have always been exploited by politicians of all backgrounds, but in the close and patriarchal communities created by immigrants from Bangladesh and Pakistan they can be a significant force.[26] Traditional patterns of patronage were used, reinforced and extended. New networks were formed around entrepreneurs who had achieved success through business ventures or illegal money transfer,[27] and communication difficulties gave a position of power to those who could translate to and from English and understood political procedure. In ward meetings, leading Bengalis would refer to others as 'my members';[28] and when I asked Shofiqur Rahman Chowdhury – who was a long-established Labour Party (as well as Awami League) member – if he had ever thought of becoming a councillor he told me, 'I create councillor. I don't want ... to be a councillor'.[29] Labour canvassers going round Spitalfields did not bother to knock on every door as Bengali party members knew where to find the community leaders who would be able to deliver a score of votes.[30]

Figure 7.1 Rajonuddin Jalal demonstrating against the British National Party, c1984 (Phil Maxwell)

The first Bengali Labour Party members were quick to recruit more. Rajonuddin Jalal, who became a prominent councillor, recalled:

> by the mid 80s, I think, we realised that there is a need to capture political power if you're going to change policies in the town hall. And that's what we did. We started recruiting Bengalis actively, and there was a time when the Labour Party got fed up, they did not want any more Bengalis.[31]

Jill Cove commented that it was 'like opening the flood gates'. She observed that it was nothing to get a hundred and fifty membership applications at a ward meeting, often with the forms filled up in the same handwriting. At AGMs it was possible to sign up at the door and Bengali members would be outside ready to pay for others to join. Ward party coffers were full. Mass memberships were accepted in principle, but subjected to random checks that exposed many names that were invalid – people who had not been aware of what was happening or were away in Bangladesh or even no longer alive. This did not exempt Cove from having to refute allegations of racism for questioning these lists.[32] There were claims that ward parties were being packed with supporters to secure election of certain Bengalis to party positions, or their nomination for council elections. One of my (Bengali) interviewees described how this worked:

> [A] few people, they got some money together and asked all the village people, all the people that they know, to become Labour Party member of … a particular [ward]. And so if you got fifty or two hundred members and if you can pay two

hundred times £5 per year [membership] for couple of years, then you can be chosen for whatever you want to be in that particular party.[33]

Such political tactics are not actually illegal (providing the paper members do exist and are willing participants). Nor, though South-Asian kinship links can be used to make them spectacularly successful, are they confined to ethnic minority communities. At the same time, white politicians are not above making use of Asian patronage systems when they work to their own advantage.[34] Eade noted that the local Labour leader liked to 'work through informal links with local activists', 'largely on a personal basis',[35] and politicians today all seek out ethnic minority 'community leaders'.

Eade's 1989 study provides the main published account of the Bengalis' early relationship with the Labour Party. It is concerned with the mechanisms of local politics and their interaction with community groups and networks, and the picture he paints is complex and at times Machiavellian. His account is not set against an analysis of political practice more generally, and so risks being hijacked by those who present a 'racialised political discourse'[36] in which it is predominantly ethnic minority, and especially South Asian, politics that is perceived to be associated with corruption.

White politicians are also objects of racialised discourse, notably in 'the perception that the left have used black representation in order to fulfil their own objectives'.[37] This discourse was common to many of my interviewees, as demonstrated by the comments above on getting party membership. It was encouraged by the separatist ideology of black organisation, and by a generally pragmatic (as distinct from idealistic) political understanding. When such discourses operate, every action can be ascribed an underlying racist or supremacist motive, whether or not it actually exists, with the risk both of obscuring actual racism and of perpetuating a division into 'them and us'.

Despite these feelings, and the legacy of black separatism, the national debate on Labour Party black sections does not seem to have played a very significant part in Tower Hamlets. Nationally, an unofficial Labour Party Black Section had been formed in 1983, though it had not been recognised by the party conference. This type of autonomous organisation was rejected as separatist not just by the party leadership but also by those on the far left, such as Militant Tendency, who saw it as divisive of working-class unity. Debate raged throughout the 80s, but in the 'new realism' of the 90s it was settled with the compromise of a Black Socialist Society in 1993. In Tower Hamlets these discussions resulted in the formation of an Ethnic Minorities Group in 1986, co-ordinated by Jalal, which was meant to represent ethnic minority members within the Bethnal Green and Stepney Constituency Labour Party and pushed for more ethnic minority councillors.[38] Peter Shore observed, with respect to the demand for black sections in his constituency,

On the whole I think, yes, there was support, but there was always a kind of concern that it could lead to division rather than the other way round ... It wasn't a matter of furious debate as far as I can remember in the Tower Hamlets party.[39]

Abbas told me in 2001:

> I think there was sympathy and support for black section[s], there's no doubt about it, but people obviously have felt what the black section had to offer wasn't the most appropriate for us, in this part of London ... We had a black section but it wasn't as active as in the other parts of the country.[40]

He explained, 'by having a higher concentration of Bangladeshis in a borough like Tower Hamlets, people felt we had the numbers, we had the influence to bring about changes'. It seems that, with Bengali activists already operating as an ethnic lobby, there was no strong desire for a broader 'black' organisational structure, though politicians are always attracted to potential channels of power and influence. Abbas also noted, 'Some of my colleagues are still actively involved in black caucus groups'.

Bengali representation

The selection of a Labour parliamentary candidate to replace Peter Shore on his retirement in 1997 generated inevitable expectations that there would be a Bengali MP. Competition was bitter. Jalal, one of the main contenders, was suspended from the party after being accused of sending a fax to the press that charged the local Labour group leader with racism and was made to look as though it came from his rival Pola Uddin.[41] He denied involvement, but it has been suggested that the unseemly struggle and the lack of Bengali unity were instrumental in preventing a Bengali from being chosen. However, the selection was also seen by many as an example of party racism, and anger and frustration over Labour's 'failure' to put forward a Bengali candidate was reflected in the 1997 election results. Oona King was safely elected for Labour, but the Conservative's Kabir Chowdhury bucked the national trend to celebrate a 5 per cent swing in his favour.[42] A Bengali MP is seen as a symbol of community achievement and recognition of community entitlement, and before the election of Rushanara Ali in 2010, the lack of this type of ethnic representation was commonly interpreted as a denial of democratic rights. Jalal gave voice to these frustrations in an interview recorded in 2006:

> I think Tower Hamlets was the right platform for us to have produced member of parliament, members of the Greater London Authority, and of course one or two MEPs as well. We have not succeeded. That is partly because the authorities were not interested in letting the Bengalis succeed. They were happy to import other people to suppress the rightful demands of the Bengali community. But the battle goes on and I am sure we will win.[43]

As councillors, Bengalis have generally regarded themselves as fighting for the betterment of their community, as raising the community profile and as role models. When I interviewed him in 2000, Abdus Shukur recalled:

> I put down on a piece of paper about fifteen years ago what I wanted to achieve. One ... was to have Bengalis in political structures in the borough, to ensure that those structures were taking in the issues of concern to that community, and to ensure that Bengalis' needs were being recognised on a London-wide basis: to ensure that the political structures are aware of the Bengali community ... And I think to a large degree we have achieved that.[44]

However, councillors will also emphasise that they are there to represent all their constituents and, as former councillor Nooruddin Ahmed put it, involvement in mainstream Labour politics was a means not only to achieve improvements for his community, but also to contribute to his adopted country.[45] Catherine Neveu, who researched Bengali electoral representation in 1989, commented on the contradictory attitudes (from Bengalis and others) that both 'expect Bangladeshi councillors to be representatives of the Bangladeshi population and ... accuse them of acting so'.[46] Abbas, as the first Bengali leader of the council, attempted to satisfy both views:

> By having a Bengali leader now on the council, I think we are sending very clear messages about equality ... but also able to demonstrate that as a Bengali leader you can represent not only the Bangladeshi community.[47]

This problem is as old as ethnic minorities in British politics. Dadabhai Naoroji, who in 1892 was elected to represent Finsbury, so becoming Britain's first Indian MP, declared when he was earlier adopted as a prospective parliamentary candidate for the Liberals in 1886:

> Standing as I do here, to represent the 250,000,000 of your fellow subjects in India, of course, I know thoroughly well my duty: for if I am returned by you, my first duty will be to consult completely and fully the interests of my constituents.[48]

Naoroji, three times president of the Indian National Congress, wanted to get an Indian perspective heard in parliament and had had to take on bitter resistance, including within his own Liberal Party. The Indian communist, Shapurji Saklatvala, who was elected as Labour MP for Battersea in 1922 and elected again under the CPGB banner in 1924, argued that the Indian and British working classes shared common interests. Krishna Menon, a popular and dedicated Labour councillor in St Pancras from 1934 until he became High Commissioner for newly independent India in 1947, saw his work for London's slum dwellers and for India's independence as different parts of the same fight against exploitation and oppression.[49] All three men represented working-class constituencies.

By the time of the 2010 general election, the demand for a Bengali representative was so strong, and the Bengali electorate so significant, that all the major parties chose to field a Bengali candidate. Indeed, in the previous election (which will be discussed in more detail in Chapter 9) George Galloway, standing for Respect, had exploited this demand with the argument that a vote for him and against Labour's Oona King would be the best way to ensure a Bengali MP next time around; and Azmal Hussain told me that his aim and objective in becoming chair of Tower Hamlets Respect was to ensure the election of a Bengali MP.[50] One of the consequences of having Bengali candidates and active Bengali language media is that more interviews and debates are carried out in Bengali. These can communicate directly with voters who have little English, including many Bengali housewives, but put a section of discussion out of reach for the major part of the electorate.

Rushanara Ali, elected for Labour as the first Bengali MP, is well aware of the different demands that her role entails. She carefully explained to me:

> I'm first and foremost British. I was brought up here, and I have Bengali origin and heritage, and I was born in Bangladesh. So I have strong connections with my country of birth, and I'm very proud of that … And I think it's really important … that parliament and local government … reflects the kind of diversity that we have in the country … [S]ymbolically it's quite a powerful thing … I meet a lot of parents who say to me that they find it really helpful to be able to say to their children, look, if she can go and be an MP, then anything is possible. And that's really encouraging, that's really nice. So I think from my point of view, I don't mind the community highlights that I'm the first British Bangladeshi MP to be elected to our parliament … if it helps encourage their children. But, obviously, as you know, as a member of parliament, a third of my constituents are of Muslim origin, majority Bangladeshi, the rest of my constituents are from other communities, white middle class, white working class, Somali. So I'm not a representative of one community, even though I recognise that that's obviously a big deal for the community that I come from. And it's important for me to ensure that I am accessible to everybody, and I am speaking up for all the different groups of people who make up my constituency.
>
> I have a constituency boundary, even though I obviously straddle constituencies in terms of identity … there aren't special rules for me just because I happen to be the first person of Bangladeshi origin, and nor should there be. But at the same time … I recognise that there are people around the country who are of Bengali origin and heritage – first and second and third generation – they are very proud to see me in Parliament and feel they can identify with. And so I take that responsibility seriously; but … my first priority are my constituents, just like for any other MP.[51]

Returning to local politics, most Bengali Labour councillors voted with left-leaning party members on measures aimed at lessening deprivation, in which, to quote Abbas, the Bengalis and the left shared a 'natural common agenda',[52] but there was no especial affinity with left issues more generally. Thus, there was a lot of Bengali support for the fight against the Poll Tax, which impacted heavily on

Figure 7.2 Rushanara Ali MP speaking at the 2012 commemoration of the murder of Altab Ali in the park now named after him. She is standing in front of the Shaheed Minar, a memorial to the Bengali language martyrs that is a smaller version of the memorial in Dhaka (M-Kollective)

the poor and especially on overcrowded households with several adult members, but no particular Bengali consensus on campaigning for the miners during the pivotal 1984–85 strike. Within the general give and take of political bargaining, Bengali party members could group together quite independently of more orthodox left/right divisions, leading to strange changing alliances.[53] Links to different Bangladeshi political parties have also played a crucial part in individual political careers and added another layer of bonds and influences.

Liberals and Tories

While there will always be accusations of ethnic voting to ensure the election of Bengali councillors (or of members of a particular *gusthi*) and accusations of white voters not voting for Bengalis, the major electoral battles have been between the politics of the different parties, and the major fight for Bengali representation has been *within* the parties. Resistance to ethnic minority involvement can come not only from direct prejudice but also from fear of the electoral impact of standing ethnic minority candidates, however this becomes less significant – or even reversed – as the ethnic minority vote itself increases. In Tower Hamlets, the fight for representation within the parties has long been won. Although there was no Bengali Labour parliamentary candidate until 2010, the 1997 general election saw Bengalis standing across the political spectrum from

the Referendum Party to Socialist Labour, and they have occupied a disproportionate number of council seats for several years – in Autumn 2013 there were
twenty-nine Bengalis out of fifty-one councillors.

Before the eruption of Respect (which will be discussed in Chapter 9),
those who had had enough of Labour could choose between the Conservatives,
who until recently had not had a single councillor elected, and the Liberals (or,
later, the Liberal Democrats), who came to power locally for eight years from
1986 after the former Labour leadership broke with their party and split the
Labour vote. Anthony Messina has pointed out that, although Liberal policy was
historically favourable to immigrants, this was not generally well known, and nor
was it always reflected in their politics at local level.[54] The racism of Tower
Hamlets' Liberal administration became national news on more than one
occasion.

Most Bengalis could be guaranteed to vote Labour anyway, so, for the Tower
Hamlets Liberals, appealing to the white working class made electoral sense;
indeed, the Labour party also succumbed to similar tactics when circumstance
suited. There was plenty of scope for political groups to play the 'race card', and
this became a particularly potent practice from the mid 1980s. Conservative
housing policies – especially the council tenants' 'Right to Buy' introduced in
1980, and the accompanying restrictions on investment in council housing –
were putting pressure on councils' housing waiting lists throughout the country.
In the East End, this coincided with rising Bengali demand as family reunification brought wives and children from Bangladesh. Other inner London boroughs
had larger numbers of homeless families, but in Tower Hamlets more and more
of the homeless were Bengali – half of the total in 1981 and nearly 90 per cent
in 1987.[55]

The conduct of the local Liberals became so notorious that the national
party was forced to hold an inquiry into their publication of 'allegedly racist
election literature between 1990 and 1993'[56] and to suspend the three men most
involved. Tower Hamlets Liberals had actually been practising their populist
politics from the time of their election to office in 1986, when they caused
widespread outrage (and publicity) with proposals to put hundreds of homeless
families into a ship moored on the Thames.[57] Their continued focus on local
housing consciously encouraged the idea of different housing entitlements for
different ethnic groups.

Charlie Foreman has shown how such policies allowed the Liberals to shift
the blame for housing shortage onto the homeless (predominantly Bengalis),
while they continued to sell off housing and building land.[58] Under the previous
Labour administration, housing policy had been both inefficient and discriminatory; however, the Liberals made discriminatory procedures the centre of their
community politics, establishing the idea that the Bengali families were a threat
to the existing community and did not belong in Tower Hamlets. One of their
first acts was designed to garner popular support for this approach. They asked

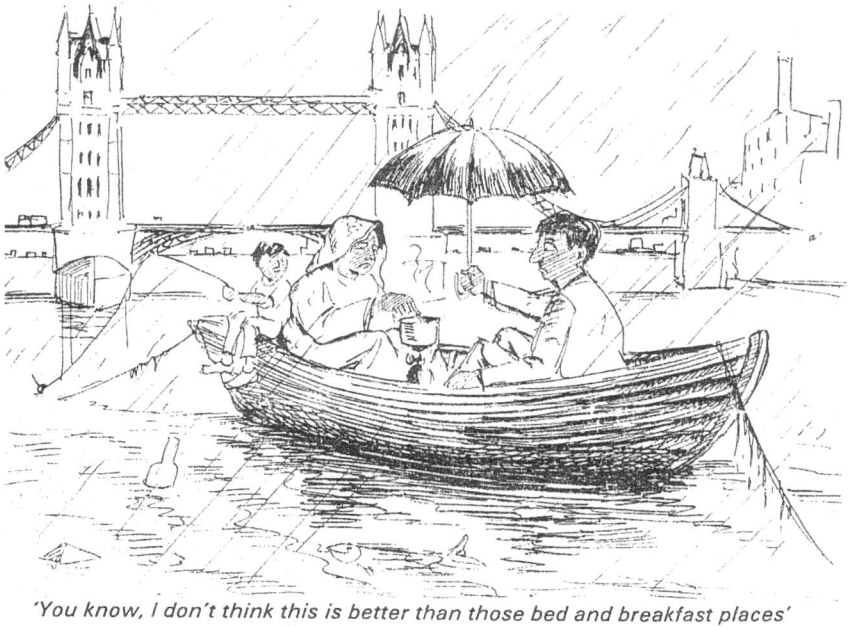

'You know, I don't think this is better than those bed and breakfast places'

Figure 7.3 Jubo Barta, a journal for Bengali youth, protests against Tower Hamlets' Liberal council's plans to house homeless families in a ship on the Thames, 1986

existing council tenants to endorse proposals that limited still further the options available to homeless families requiring more than two bedrooms, almost all of whom would be Bengali.[59]

In 1987, Tower Hamlets council stopped paying for accommodation for dozens of homeless families where wives and children had recently arrived from Bangladesh, and succeeded in getting the courts to support their argument that the families had made themselves intentionally homeless when they left Bangladesh and so were not entitled to housing.[60] This was a practice that had previously been attempted by Labour, and although they had not succeeded in implementing it in Tower Hamlets, a Labour council in Camden was offering 'Irish and Bangladeshi families … air tickets as an alternative to homes'.[61] At the same time, Tower Hamlets Liberals reintroduced housing policies that favoured sons and daughters of long-established existing tenants – policies that had been scrapped in the early 1980s as inherently racist, but which today seem to be creeping back again. Although the number of allocations made under this scheme was relatively small, the ideas it embodied provided a rallying cry for a white community that saw itself as under siege. Between 1989 and 1992 sons and daughters legislation was used to place a hundred and seventy tenants, of whom 73 per cent were white, 11 per cent black and 6 per cent Asian,[62] but the policy allowed the Liberals to present themselves as champions of the local (white) community and to paint the Bangladeshis, and their Labour defenders, as usurpers of local homes.

For the 1990 local council elections, the Liberals made this point through a provocative fake leaflet that purported to be an edition of Labour News and announced 'HOMES FOR LOCALS – RACIST! SAYS LABOUR'. It continued,

> In the last 4 years Bangladeshi people in Tower Hamlets have been discriminated against by Liberals' racist housing policies, like the Sons and Daughters scheme and their decision not to house homeless families because they had left homes abroad…
> If Labour is elected the homeless will go to the top of the list, EVEN IF THIS MEANS ALL EMPTY FLATS BEING ALLOCATED TO THEM.[63]

The next year, newly elected councillor Jeremy Shaw, who had written the leaflet, took advantage of his position on a post-cyclone charity mission to Bangladesh to take his message to the Bangladeshi Government and the British High Commission in Dhaka. Before leaving he informed the *East London Advertiser*,

> I will tell them that Tower Hamlets is full to bursting, and that for anyone to leave Bangladesh and come to Tower Hamlets and expect the Council to house them is totally irresponsible – both to their own families and to the rest of the community … I will want to know what procedures are followed by the British High Commission before they give people permission to settle in the U.K.[64]

Populist abuse of housing politics reached an infamous peak in Millwall on the Isle of Dogs, where it enabled the brief reign of BNP Councillor Derek Beackon. It was no accident that this racist politics thrived next to the Thatcherite reincarnation of the former Docklands as a new financial centre, which could be seen to be consuming money and land while providing no benefits to its poorer neighbours. Unemployment was high and housing scarce and neglected, and there were good socio-economic reasons for local residents to be angry. The 'Island's' relatively small Bengali population provided an easy scapegoat. In her analysis of these events, Janet Foster quoted the local vicar, who commented that the arrival of yet another set of newcomers was 'one more bit of change that people didn't like but which they felt they could kick against'.[65]

The Liberals had divided Tower Hamlets into administrative neighbour-hoods, and the Isle of Dogs was Labour-run and had not adopted the sons and daughters schemes that operated in Liberal-run areas. This became the main plank of the Liberals' 1992 Millwall by-election campaign, which adopted the slogan, 'Island homes for Island people'.[66] Housing allocation in Masthouse Terrace, the first social housing to be built in the area for many years, provided a focus of debate and anger, especially as the scheme included some larger units that were commonly perceived as purpose-made for large Bengali families. The xenophobic atmosphere allowed the BNP to pick up 20 per cent of the vote, but instead of taking this as a warning, both Liberals and Labour chose to pander to populist racism when Millwall held a second by-election the following year.[67] The left-wingers who had dominated the ward Labour Party in the 80s had been ousted and the new ward leadership attempted to outflank the Liberals on their own ground. Rather than campaign for more housing for all, they issued a clearly coded call to 'house the hidden homeless … your children who have to sleep on the couch, your brothers and sisters who want a place of their own, your grand-children without space to grow up in'.[68] The crucial boost to the BNP was, however, provided by a dishonest tactical blunder. The Labour Party chose to put out false canvas returns suggesting that it was the BNP that was the main threat to a Labour victory. It seems they had intended to frighten people into voting Labour to keep the BNP out, but populist sentiments had been aroused and the effect was a boost in BNP credibility that made their imagined threat a reality.[69] Beackon got in with 1,480 votes to Labour's 1,473, and although he lost the election the following year, that was only after a major effort to bring out the anti-racist vote and trump a BNP vote that had actually risen by 561.

Despite this history, some Bengalis have chosen to pursue their political path through the Liberal Party. Sajjad Miah, a Liberal councillor from 1990–94, joined the party along with a group of other Bengalis when its political star was on the rise. His motivation was very similar to that of many Bengali Labour members – to help his community achieve more equal treatment in areas such as housing – and he later excused his part in this notoriously racist administration by arguing, 'if you don't involve with them in the decision making, you can't change them'. He told me:

> I was a member of Labour Party as well, once a long time ago, but then we discuss ourselves and thought that to be in a society we should be involved with every political party … I think in mainstream if you don't involve with the politics, if you don't involve with the decision making process, you will not have any say.[70]

An added attraction of the Liberals was that the Labour Party was already crowded with Bengalis jostling for community leadership, and here he was more likely to be able to achieve a position of influence:

> Everybody said Labour and Labour. There was too many competition … even if you want to become a councillor, if you want to become … more actively involved in ward committee or anything, there are several people coming and you have to fight and all those things.

For Anamul Haque, who stayed with Labour and later became a Labour councillor, community-based pragmatism extended to encouraging his fellow Bengalis to join the Liberals and SDP[71] because, as he explained, 'We want every corner of the politics, we must know the information what is happening and what our community can get the best interest of out of the whole system'.[72]

Sabine Drewes, writing in 1994, observed that Tower Hamlets Liberals had a 70 per cent Bengali membership on paper, but that this was based on traditional village patronage politics, and that 'the interplay of white domination of central party committees and of the [Bengali] community leader's personal career aspirations … prevented effective representation of ethnic interests'.[73] The community leader in question was Syed Nurul Islam who stood for the Liberal Democrats in Bethnal Green and Bow in the 2005 general election when he came in fourth on 11 per cent of the vote.

Although it now has a new support base in the predominantly white, gentrified areas of the former Docklands, the Conservative Party has always been relatively ineffective as a route to power in Tower Hamlets. However, it has also attracted Bengali members and fielded Bengali parliamentary candidates. (In Autumn 2013 there were no Bengalis among the seven Conservative councillors. The Bengali Conservative elected in May 2010 defected in 2011 to the independent group around the ex-Labour elected mayor.) Shahagir Bakht Faruk, who stood for the Conservatives in the general election in 2001, described himself to me as born a Conservative, with a natural affinity to Conservative family values.[74] In this he echoed an argument, put by some party strategists, that Asian society is (as Disraeli had said of the Jews) naturally conservative, and that Asians (like many Jews) would with time come to their 'natural home'.[75] Muslim voters were particularly sympathetic to the Conservative stance on 'Clause 28' (outlawing the promotion of homosexuality), but the main reason that Bengali support for the Conservatives has increased – apart from specific votes for a Bengali parliamentary candidate, and protest votes against the ruling Labour Party – is, as it was for the Jews, changes in socio-economic circumstances.

Women in a man's world

The British-born generation has produced more female activists and at the time of writing Tower Hamlets is represented by a Bengali woman MP, but there have been relatively few Bengali women in politics. A combination of language problems, fear of racial attack and a 'modesty' inspired and sometimes enforced by both religion and tradition still prevents some women from so much as leaving their homes, and even when they are backed by a supportive family, women with political ambitions can have problems. When I began interviewing for my research in 2000, the one female Bengali councillor was a young barrister, Jusna Begum. She told me that, although she received tremendous cross-cultural support for her political activities, there were always some Bengalis, especially men, who disapproved of such behaviour in a young unmarried Bengali woman, and they were not above trying to sabotage her chances. On the morning of her first Labour Party selection meeting an anonymous letter went out accusing her of having had a white boyfriend at law school, an (unfounded) charge that was enough to damage her reputation with the older generation and temporarily prevent her selection.[76]

Jusna Begum claimed that she was a victim of smears again in the 2002 council election, with Labour party members being told 'Muslim Bangladeshi women should not be involved in politics', and that these pressures did eventually manage to force her out.[77] Her successor as lone female Bengali councillor, Mumtaz Samad, resigned from the council and the Labour Party in July 2004, accusing her fellow Labour councillors of sexism and harassment.[78]

At the time of writing there are five Bengali women on the council, but Shiria Khatun (who we met in the previous chapter setting up a Bangladeshi workers' union) was recently harassed by an eighteen-month campaign of threatening and obscene anonymous phone calls criticising her for her western clothes and tight jeans. There were several different callers and strange cars began following her. She didn't want to show that she was bothered, but when one caller threatened to exhume her parents' bodies and bury her in their graves, and then followed this with a threat to her four children, she called in the police.[79] No-one was ever caught, but the threats stopped. Shiria Khatun told me:

> I was not just worried about myself but I was worried about my whole family, because of the threats that were being made to me. And I didn't know who was making those threats. The police were very, very good and supportive. My family were very supportive. Without their support I probably would not have stuck – you know – stood for re-election. My family gave me the strength to go on. They were with me – my cousins, my nephews, my nieces. They said to me that if I think about standing down then I'll have them to answer to. And they were out with me campaigning.[80]

When I then asked her if she would advise a young Bengali woman to go into politics, she immediately responded, 'Oh yes, absolutely. I'm doing it!'

For Pola Uddin, who became the first female Bengali councillor in 1990, the main barrier appears to have been the assumption by institutions, starting with her grammar school, that Asian women have no ambitions beyond raising a family. Her political career has taken her to the House of Lords as a New Labour Peer – some claim this was her consolation prize for missing the party nomination to stand for parliament – and provides a striking example of the interaction of community-based pragmatism with the wider political climate. She lived through the Bangladesh war as a child and told me 'I don't understand any Bengalis … of my generation who wouldn't be interested in politics'. When she saw the restrictions on what women and Bengalis could do in Britain, joining a movement 'to fight for changes was just as natural as breathing air',[81] and Jill Cove persuaded her to join the Labour Party.[82] We have already seen how a female speaker could diffuse a highly charged Bengali political meeting; as an outspoken and thick-skinned Bengali woman in a political environment obsessed with identity and with demonstrating diversity, Pola Uddin found herself much in demand, and 'often being pushed to represent "the community"'.[83] Unfortunately, her pragmatism also allowed her to conform to the general lapse in parliamentary ethics, and she was one of the politicians exposed in the 2009 expenses scandal. A House of Lords Select Committee found that, by mis-describing a house that she used as an occasional 'bolt hole' as her main residence, she had wrongly claimed over £125,000.[84] Her credentials received further public questioning when it was pointed out that although the family owned the bolt hole in Kent and a luxurious home in Bangladesh, they still lived in subsidised social housing.[85]

Provided things don't go wrong, political women can be important role models for Bengali girls, however it would be naïve to think that their involve-ment is either symptom or cause of more fundamental *political* change. Pola Uddin fitted comfortably into the market-based politics of Blairism and the superficially radical choice, in 2007, of a young Bengali woman as Labour parlia-mentary candidate was seen as a strategic victory for the established Labour leadership.[86]

Rushanara Ali – elected as MP in 2010 – exemplifies New Labour's politics of aspiration. Her own career is a model of the kind of social mobility that she herself has promoted through the UpRising leadership programme established by the Young Foundation, a 'centre for social innovation' that continues the work of the late Labour peer Lord Young,[87] for whom she worked while at university. Educated at local state schools, she went on to read Philosophy, Politics and Economics at Oxford, and then became parliamentary assistant to Oona King. This was followed by jobs in the Foreign Office and the Home Office and as a research fellow for the Institute of Public Policy Research, and then five years as Associate Director of the Young Foundation. As Ali told the *Huffington Post*, on her first day as King's assistant 'she kept introducing me to people saying, "You know, one day she's going to be the MP for Bethnal Green and Bow", to which my heart used to sink'.[88] Ali admits that she has been incredibly lucky in the opportunities she has had, but insists that 'you also have to make your own luck and you've got to put the work in'.[89]

Her selection battle for parliamentary candidate was predictably bitter but, as she explained to me, the compelling argument that persuaded her to put herself forward was that, 'regardless of what the outcome was going to be … it was just going to change a lot of attitudes within the community … and more widely'. A generation of women would be looking at her experience, so that 'even if I failed, the next time, someone was going to succeed'. In the event, she found that

> many of the people who were the first to support me and stand up for me were people of my father's generation, the kind of elders, if you like … I was so impressed, and actually just totally inspired by their ability to stand up to people who were peddling just absolute garbage about me.

There was also the inevitable boyfriend rumour at the time of the election in 2010,[90] but Bethnal Green and Bow had reverted to a safe Labour seat.

Despite an obsession with issues of class, Ali's focus is on mentoring and supporting individuals rather than on structural changes. And when I asked if she would call herself a socialist, her response was carefully measured:

> I'm not ashamed to call myself [that] – if you want to label me … But obviously the nature of my party is very different from the classic socialist parties that you might be thinking of or that the Labour Party might have been historically.

A second Bengali woman has been chosen to stand in the 2015 election as Labour's parliamentary candidate for the marginal seat of Hampstead and Kilburn. As granddaughter of Sheikh Mujib and niece of Awami League leader Sheikh Hasina, Tulip Siddiq comes from a family where political involvement is expected and she acknowledges, 'I was lucky that I had the means to intern for free for a whole year … After my internship, I immediately walked into a paid job in Parliament'. Despite the huge differences between her background and that of most of Camden's large Bengali community, she embraces the idea of ethnic self-representation and writes, 'Often BAME [Black, Asian Minority Ethnic] communities feel (and maybe wrongly so) that a BAME MP is more likely to understand and appreciate their concerns'.[91]

The new establishment

As the young Bengali activists of the late 1970s and 80s developed into hardened politicians, Bengali councillors began to be criticised in much the same way that they themselves had once criticised the older council regime and their more cautious seniors in the Bangladesh Welfare Association. When I was carrying out interviews for this study in 2000, one young Bengali woman described them to me as a powerful network of middle-aged Bengali men whose petty politics disgusted many of her generation.[92] And local councillors (along with politicians in Bangladesh) had become figures of fun for the politics class at Tower Hamlets College, where some students argued that the councillors were only interested in a good name and staying in power.[93] For older Bengalis, or recent immigrants, who may have little English, Bengali councillors still provide a vital link to local power structures, but for many others, the presence of Bengalis on the council has made little difference. Some Bengalis expressly told me they would choose to see a white councillor if they had a problem.[94] Distrust of politicians is a general phenomenon, but when in 2003 Nasir Uddin, a young Bengali Labour councillor, was caught sequestering regeneration money from a youth charity,[95] the case was perceived as a symptom of a wider malaise.

By that time, like all Labour Party representatives, Bengali Labour councillors were having to work within the ideological and structural restrictions of

Tony Blair's New Labour. As a leading councillor complained to me when I interviewed him in 2000:

> it's become far more stage managed than ever before. Everybody is into the scenario of 'we must get in'. Of course we must get in ... but you then don't forget what you came in for.[96]

Multiculturalism, neoliberalism and local governance

Identity politics has fed into the new forms of local governance that have been created to support the neoliberal state and that build on practices developed in numerous regeneration projects. Through the 1980s and 90s, Conservative governments deprived local authorities (which in urban areas were often Labour-run) of many of their powers, contracting out their services and forcing them to work with private business. And 'regeneration' programmes multiplied, reflecting the growing number of areas that were becoming casualties of free-market economic policies and deindustrialisation. Increasingly, whole sections of local governance, as well as specific regeneration programmes, were being controlled by what were described as 'partnerships' of different organisations. Proponents of multiculturalism welcomed such arrangements, which appeared to chime well with Bhikhu Parekh's vision of a 'community of communities' and Tariq Modood's view of pluralised national identities.[97] New Labour took up the partnership model and made it its own, and the Conservative coalition government has claimed it back as part of its 'Big Society'. Tower Hamlets has been held up as an exemplar of partnership governance.[98] The – far from equal – partners consist of local authorities, public agencies (such as the police, health authorities and local colleges), private businesses, voluntary organisations and community groups. (Notably, partnerships generally include no role for trade unions.) While businesses may not always find it worth their while to play an active part in neighbourhood partnerships (unless they involve an opportunity for property development) the whole system is set up and monitored by central government according to criteria dictated by the demands of the market. In line with this market ethos, competition is at its core: competition for funding between different neighbourhoods, and competition for funding within neighbourhoods between different community groups.

Critics point out that, despite the rhetoric about 'stakeholder' participation and local control, important decisions have been centralised and power has been taken from elected councillors and passed to a system that is opaque and not democratically accountable. (The recent introduction of directly elected local mayors in some authorities, including Tower Hamlets, has simply concentrated powers in a single person, which is likely only to increase the democratic deficit.) Community groups attracted by the rhetoric of partnership soon find they have no impact over important decisions. They are needed to give a semblance of democracy, and when community activists are incorporated into official partnerships they are unlikely to protest about official actions. In fact activists can find themselves so weighed down with bureaucratic paperwork that it takes all their efforts just to keep up to date with meetings.[99]

While community involvement along this communitarian model is able to contribute little to democracy, partnerships provide plenty of scope for patronage and for inter-group rivalry, especially where large sums of money are being distributed and community organisations are being called on to help provide public services.[100] Ethnic-based organisations are always included among the 'stakeholders', both because this ensures their support and because, by the 1990s, multiculturalism had come to be accepted as the epitome of Western liberalism. The densely networked Bengali community has been well placed to take advantage of this system and use it to promote selected organisations and personal careers.

Competition between organisations can be intense and bitter, and millions of pounds have been committed to projects specifically supporting black and minority ethnic groups. The November 2000 issue of *Banglatown News* announced the award of £5 million regeneration money to a partnership of about fifty Black and Minority Ethnic (BME)-led groups, as well as reporting on the Ethnic Minority Enterprise Project that had been newly set up to assist ethnic minority businesses in Tower Hamlets. Such policies can contribute to resentments and perpetuate division. Gillian Evans has observed that the emphasis on multiculturalism has also forced the white working class to 'think of themselves as a new ethnic group with their own distinctive culture' but that this has not been legitimated by middle-class recognition.[101]

The furore that surrounded the building of a sheltered housing block for 'Asian Elders' in Shadwell in 2004 demonstrated just how divisive an ethnic-based approach can be, especially when there is huge competition for limited resources.[102] In this instance, it can be argued that the Sonali Gardens scheme responded to very specific needs that would not have been met in a more general development. However, the promotion of BME-led housing associations could have more serious implications for inter-ethnic tensions and segregation. BME housing associations are defined as those with 80 per cent or more of their governing body drawn from BME communities. They also tend to employ many more BME staff and house a much higher proportion of BME tenants.[103] Restrictions on tenants' ethnicity are only possible in exceptional circumstances (to meet special needs, as in Sonali Gardens, or in accordance with charity obligations),[104] but BME-led associations may be more ready to address what is lacking in the general market from the point of view of a particular ethnic group (such as larger houses for Bengalis), and tenants from that group may be more attracted by the housing.

Bengali elders, such as the residents of Sonali Gardens, often still have language restrictions (as well as specific religious and cultural needs); and the generation that came of age in the 1970s, 80s and early 90s argued the need to organise separately for defence. Now, separate organisation is no longer claimed as a necessity, but multicultural policies have helped ensure that the tradition of separation has continued through to today's youth. Although Dench *et al.* were not quite accurate in stating that, in the 1990s, there were no mixed youth clubs in the borough[105] (I helped at a girls group with one white member), there are still many specifically Bengali youth organisations and even a Bengali football league.[106] Combined with a growing Bengali population, such separatism can easily encourage the feeling among white working-class families that there is little left for them and that they are better off moving out of the East End. Other ethnic minorities may be able to use multicultural policies to achieve a degree of recognition, but remain in the shadow of Bengali dominance.

That dominance was given official recognition in the, not uncontroversial, restyling of the former Spitalfields ward as Spitalfields-Banglatown. This branding of the core area of Bengali immigration demonstrated the strength of the Bengali presence on the borough council and was aimed at boosting the many Bengali businesses, especially the restaurants, that crowd into the area now marked by specially designed Bengali lampposts and Bengali street signs. Banglatown is an example of place-marketing and at times Brick Lane resembles a theme park, but it clearly stakes Bengali claims to this part of London.

In the mid-2000s, a small group of Bengalis, led by the Labour patriarch Abdus Salique, who we met in Chapter 5, tried to extend this claim and control how the area and its Bengali residents were represented in fiction – specifically in Monica Ali's *Brick Lane*. Taking to the street and the national media, they portrayed themselves as spokesmen for a Sylheti community outraged by its portrayal in the novel (published in 2003) and subsequent film.[107] Although they could not stop the filming, the remaining shots were completed away from Brick Lane and Prince Charles pulled out of the planned royal film performance, illustrating how sensitive society has become to the risk of offending ethnic minority sensibilities.[108]

Increasingly, the community groups playing a prominent role and linking into official partnerships have been based around religious faith. Government recognition of religious identity as a primary organising principle has responded to, but also reinforced, the new emphasis on religious identity within ethnic minority groups, and the turn towards faith groups has allowed governments to promote more reactionary forces that are in tune with dominant political thinking. It is no accident that Britain appears to be following a US model in increasing the role of faith groups in the maintenance of civil society.

Multiculturalism and progressive politics

The prioritising of 'community'-based objectives has divided the working class along ethnic lines and promoted cross-class ethnic bonds, so discouraging the development of a more class-based politics that might threaten elite interests. Multicultural policies have furnished politicians with a progressive veneer with which to cover their purposeful eradication of traditional labour-movement politics – following the defeat of the left in the 1980s – and their consequent failure to address fundamental socio-economic inequalities. As Floya Anthias put it in 1990:

> The attention to ethnic divisions which is current in British society … serves to mask the essentially divided nature of Britain's indigenous population [and she could have added increasingly also the immigrant population], the haves and have-nots, the employed and the unemployed, capital and labour. The constituency of class inequality has been pushed to the back of the agenda and blacks have become the new proletariat of both the liberal conscience and its more and less progressive allies.[109]

The more recent turn towards faith groups has especially tended to favour social conservatism, even allowing that individual 'community' or faith groups may support progressive as well as more conservative ideas.

Multiculturalism as a political system thus distracts attention from fundamental socio-economic problems and divisions and holds back progress towards greater social equality, but this is an argument with which the main proponents of multiculturalism seem reluctant to engage. So, for example, despite acknowledging that the effects on life chances of parental class and education 'are usually much greater than the effects of race or ethnicity',[110] Tariq Modood simply dismisses the view that class identities are a primary form of political mobilisation that should not be divided by 'assertions of race, political femininity, gay pride politics and so on'.[111] He ignores the achievements of those who have addressed multiple inequalities through a unified socio-economic perspective and, without bothering to argue his case, deems it sufficient to relegate class-based politics to a past that 'soon gave way to an understanding that these [other] positions were a genuine and significant part of a plural centre-left egalitarian movement'.[112] (Debates around multiculturalism will be looked at more fully in the final chapter.)

Bengali involvement in mainstream British politics developed in parallel with the growth of identity politics and the waning of the politics of class. The challenges of establishing an immigrant community in one of the most deprived areas of London were met through pragmatic community-based organisation and this continues to be the basis of British Bengali politics today – even if the community may be referred to as Muslim rather than Bengali. In a limited sense, this strategy has succeeded. Bengalis have taken their place at all levels of Tower Hamlets society and Bengali children top the borough's school league tables, but this is still an area of multiple deprivation with socio-economic problems affecting people of all ethnic backgrounds, especially the Bengalis and other minority ethnic groups.

Notes

1   This was the first serious attempt to get into mainstream British politics, though Ali Abbas, founder of the London branch of the Muslim League, had stood as in independent parliamentary candidate for Holborn and St Pancras South in the 1964 general election, where he got just 226 votes.

2   Interviewed 10 October 2001.

3   Anthony M. Messina, 'Ethnic Minorities and the British Party System in the 1990s and Beyond', in Shamit Saggar (ed.), *Race and British Electoral Politics* (London: UCL, 1998), 47–69.

4   Interviewed 22 September 2000. Manir Uddin later became a Labour councillor and mayor of Tower Hamlets.

5   Interviewed 22 September 2000.

6   Some Conservative MPs were also supportive of the Bangladeshi cause, see interview with Labour MP Michael Barnes, quoted in Ashfaque Hossain, 'Historical Globalization and its Effects: A Study of Sylhet and its People, 1874–1971' (PhD dissertation, University of Nottingham, 2009), p. 269.

7   Interviewed 15 February 2001.

8   Shore, interviewed 15 February 2001.

9   Shore died on 24 September 2001. The meeting was held on 7 October.

10 Interviewed 23 January 2001.

11 As Shore put it when I interviewed him on 15 February 2001: 'There was no question of the Bengali[s] as a group, as it were, being turned against myself or in favour of anyone else.' There was also a Bengali candidate, but Jill Cove was seen as the main rival contender.

12 See, for example, interview with former councillor Nooruddin Ahmed, who was a member of the Bangladesh Youth League, 10 April 2006, by Jamil Iqbal, Charlie Sen and Riza Momin for Swadhinata Trust and University of Surrey, 'Oral History Project'.

13 Interviewed 12 September 2000 .

14 Interviewed 23 January 2001.

15 Sheikh Mannan (interviewed 30 March 2002) joined on his arrival in England in the mid-1960s, though that was not in Tower Hamlets; Abdul Malik joined in 1968 and was active on his EC (see Caroline Adams, *Across Seven Seas and Thirteen Rivers* (London: THAP Books, 1994), p. 125); Ashik Ali was welcomed into St Katherine's Ward Labour Party in 1976 (see interview with Ashik Ali, then Tower Hamlet's only Bengali Labour councillor, in *Labour Herald*, 26 November 1982).

16 After twice losing out in council elections due to the impact of Pakistani politics (see Chapter 3), Hussain was selected by the other councillors to join the council as an alderman on 3 October 1972, and was subsequently elected to the new Metropolitan District Council in 1974. See unattributed news cuttings in Bradford City Archives; M.J. Le Lohé, 'Participation in Elections by Asians in Bradford', in Ivor Crewe (ed.), *The Politics of Race (Vol. 2 British Sociology Yearbook)* (London: Croom Helm, 1975), 84–122, pp. 113–14. Furthermore, as Le Lohé observed, by 1970 Bradford's Manningham Ward Labour Party was 'predominantly Asian' (see *ibid.*, p. 106). There was also a Bangladeshi councillor elected in Waltham Forrest in 1978. (See Faruque Ahmed, *Bengal Politics in Britain: Logic, Dynamics and Disharmony* (North Carolina: Lulu, 2010), p. 251.)

17 Interviewed 23 March 2006 by Jamil Iqbal and Charlie Sen for Swadhinata Trust and University of Surrey, 'Oral History Project'.

18 Interviewed 23 January 2001. Abdus Shukur (interviewed 12 September 2000) recalled a similar reaction.

19 Interviewed 23 January 2001.

20 Jill Cove, interviewed 16 October 2001.

21 Ashik Ali, who was not from Sylhet, and who described himself as hard-working and on the left, topped the poll for the ward. See *Labour Herald*, 26 November 1982.

22 John Eade, *The Politics of Community: The Bangladeshi Community in East London* (Aldershot: Avebury, 1989), p. 46.

23 *Ibid.*, pp. 47–8. Huque was also not from Sylhet.

24 Interviewed 10 October 2001.

25 See comment by Robbie McDuff in Eade, *The Politics of Community*, pp. 76–7; *New Life*, 26 July 1985.

26 George Galloway's by-election win for Respect in Bradford West in March 2012 was reported to be partly due to a reaction by the younger generation against the clan politics of the Bradford Pakistani establishment, who had become dominant in the Labour party and expected their biradari to deliver block votes for their preferred candidates. (The Urdu term *biradari* is equivalent to the Bengali *gusthi* and refers to patrilineage.)

27 The traditional *hundi* system is used for sending a high proportion of remittances to Bangladesh.

28 See interview with Jill Cove, 16 October 2001.

29 Shofiqur Rahman Chowdury, interviewed 7 February 2001. Chowdhury chose instead to become an MP in Sylhet.

30 Jill Cove, interviewed 16 October 2001. White and Bengali members canvassed together. For the white members this removed language problems, and it also dispelled the natural fears encountered by immigrants who opened their door to find a stranger with a clipboard.

31 Interviewed 16 August 2000. Jalal no longer lives in the East End and defected to the Liberal Democrats in 2007.

32 Cove also rejected Eade's suggestion (see *The Politics of Community*, p. 73) that the left used membership disputes to delay entry of Bengalis not sympathetic to their views, claiming that this would anyway have required a greater knowledge of Bengali community politics than they possessed. She explained that, for her, it was a question not of whether people were left or right, but whether they actually existed. Former councillor Sue Carlisle (in phone discussion with the author, February 2001) also described the problems of mass membership applications, including one cheque for a hundred and twenty people.

33 Interviewed April 2001. He decided to do community work outside the political arena.

34 Kalbir Shukra, 'New Labour Debates and Dilemas', in Shamit Saggar (ed.), *Race and British Electoral Politics* (London: UCL, 1998), 117–44, pp. 128–9; John Solomos and Les Back, *Race, Politics and Social Change* (London: Routledge, 1995), pp. 72–4, 80, 99, 103–4 and 106–7.

35 Eade, *The Politics of Community*, p. 41. Paul Beasley led the Majority Group in Tower Hamlets Labour Party from the early 1970s until 1984.

36 This term was used and explored by Solomos and Back in *Race, Politics and Social Change*, pp. 95–113.

37 Solomos and Back, *Race, Politics and Social Change*, p. 157. Although they do not actually use the term this way round, this perception can be described as a racialised discourse too.

38 See *Hackney Gazette*, 21 March 1986; Eade, *The Politics of Community*, pp. 78–9.

39 Interviewed 15 February 2001.

40 Interviewed 10 October 2001.

41 *Evening Standard*, 20 February 1995; *East London Advertiser*, 23 February 1995 and 2 March 1995; *Independent*, 27 May 1995.

42 Pippa Norris, 'Anatomy of a Labour Landslide', http://www.hks.harvard.edu/fs/pnorris/Acrobat/landslide.pdf, accessed 20 November 2012, p. 7. Interestingly, the only other seat to show a similar pattern was Bradford West, which also had an Asian Tory candidate, and which in March 2012 gave a surprise win for George Galloway and his Respect Coalition, seven years after Galloway's historic defeat of Labour in Bethnal Green and Bow.

43 Interviewed 11 March 2006 by Jamil Iqbal and Charlie Sen for Swadhinata Trust and University of Surrey, 'Oral History Project'. The appointment, in 2004, of a British Bengali as British High Commissioner to Bangladesh, while not as significant as having a Bengali MP, provided a source of satisfaction to British Bengalis.

44 Interviewed 12 September 2000. The importance of role models was confirmed by Masud Rahman, who I interviewed on 24 April 2001 when he was working as a careers advisor. He told me that the young people he discussed with did not want to do jobs that they had not heard of other Bengalis doing.

45 Interviewed 10 April 2006, by Jamil Iqbal, Charlie Sen and Riza Momin for Swadhinata Trust and University of Surrey, 'Oral History Project'.

46 Catherine Neveu, 'The Waves of Surma have Created Storms in the Depths of the Thames – Electoral Representation of an Ethnic Minority: A Case Study of Bangladeshis in the East End of London', paper given to APSA 85th Annual meeting, Atlanta Georgia, 1989 (manuscript copy in Centre for Bangladeshi Studies, Roehampton), p. 10.

47 Interviewed 10 October 2001.

48 Quoted in Rozina Visram, *Ayahs, Lascars and Princes: The Story of Indians in Britain 1700–1947* (London: Pluto Press, 1986), p. 248, note 45.

49 Rozina Visram, *Asians in Britain: 400 Years of History* (London: Pluto Press, 2002), p 304–40.

50 Interviewed 23 January 2012.

51 Interviewed 25 January 2012.

52 Interviewed 10 October 2001.

53 Compare, for example, *East London Advertiser*, 27 April 1995 and 2 May 1996 .

54 Messina, 'Ethnic Minorities and the British Party System in the 1990s and Beyond', pp. 57–9. He also noted that the Liberal Democrats' emphasis on Europe and electoral reform held little appeal to ethnic minorities, and that the party was not generally strong in areas where most minorities lived, so its relevance to ethnic minority politics tended to be peripheral.

55 Charlie Forman, *Spitalfields: A Battle for Land* (London: Hilary Shipman, 1989), p. 231.

56 Liberal Democrats, 'Political Speech and Race Relations in a Liberal Democracy: Report of an Inquiry into the Conduct of the Tower Hamlets Liberal Democrats in Publishing Allegedly Racist Election Literature Between 1990 and 1993' (Liberal Democrats' Tower Hamlets Inquiry, 1993). The local party campaigned as the Liberal Focus Team.

57 *East London Advertiser*, 31 October and 7 November 1986.

58 Forman, *Spitalfields*, pp. 249–51.

59 *Ibid.*, p. 250.

60 *Ibid.*, p. 244; *New Statesman*, 11 December 1987.

61 Keith Tompson, *Under Siege: Racism and Violence in Britain Today* (London: Penguin, 1988), p. 129.

62 Liberal Democrats, 'Political Speech and Race Relations in a Liberal Democracy', p. 26.

63 A copy of the leaflet is in Tower Hamlets Local History Library.

64 *East London Advertiser*, 15 November 1991. Similarly, just over a hundred years earlier, the Jewish Board of Guardians had put notices in foreign papers warning of the depressed British labour market in order to try and stem further Jewish immigration. See Vivian Lipman, *A Century of Social Service* (London: Routledge and Kegan Paul, 1959), p. 93.

65 Janet Foster, '"Island Homes for Island People": Competition Conflict and Racism in the Battle over Public Housing on the Isle of Dogs', in Colin Samson and Nigel South (eds), *The Social Construction of Social Policy: Methodologies, Racism, Citizenship and the Environment* (Basingstoke: Macmillan, 1996), p. 162.

66 Liberal Democrats, 'Political Speech and Race Relations in a Liberal Democracy', pp. 37–40.

67 *Ibid.*, pp. 40–2.

68 *New Statesman and Society*, 18 February 1994, p. 20.

69 *Ibid.*, p. 19; Liberal Democrats, 'Political Speech and Race Relations in a Liberal Democracy', pp. 54–5.

70 Interviewed 17 January 2001.

71 The Social Democratic Party (SDP) was formed in 1981 by Labour Party members who split from their party to take a more centrist position. They formed a tactical alliance with the Liberals later that year, and in 1988 the two parties merged to form the Liberal Democrats.

72 Interviewed 23 September 2000.

73 Sabine Drewes, 'Ethnic Representation and Racist Resentment in Local Politics: The Bangladeshi Community and Tower Hamlets Liberal Council 1986–93' (manuscript, 1994, Centre for Research on Nationalism, Ethnicity and Multiculturalism, University of Surrey), p. 30.

74 Interviewed 1 August 2001.

75 See Shamit Saggar, 'Analyzing race and elections in British politics: some conceptual and theoretical concerns', in Shamit Saggar (ed.), *Race and British Electoral Politics* (London: UCL Press, 1998), 11–46, pp. 40–2. Disraeli – Conservative prime minister, friend of Queen Victoria, and baptised Jew – asserted that 'all the tendencies of the Jewish race are conservative. Their bias is to religion, property, and natural aristocracy … The native tendency of the Jewish race … is against the equality of man', quoted in Arthur Liebman, *Jews and the Left* (New York: John Wiley and Sons, 1979), p. 10.

76 Jusna Begum, interviewed 19 September 2000 .

77 *East London Advertiser*, 8 July 2004.

78 *East London Advertiser*, 29 July 2004.

79 *Sunday Express*, 7 March 2010; *Evening Standard*, 8 March 2010; interview with Shiria Khatun, 23 January 2012.

80 Interviewed 23 January 2012.

81 Pola Uddin, interviewed 17 January 2005.

82 Jill Cove, interviewed 16 October 2001.

83 Pola Uddin, interviewed 17 January 2005.

84 www.publications.parliament.uk/pa/ld201011/ldselect/ldprivi/39/3903.htm#a15, accessed 7 November 2012.

85 *The Sunday Times*, 17 May 2009.

86 *East London Advertiser*, 9 May 2007.

87 www.youngfoundation.org, accessed 20 September 2012. Michael Young was one of

the authors of *The New East End*, which was discussed in Chapter 1. For more on the UpRising leadership programme, see Rushanara Ali, 'Let power reflect the people', *Guardian*, 20 February 2008.

88 www.huffingtonpost.co.uk/2012/01/17/rushanara-ali-ken-livingstone-bethnal-green-labour_n_1210617.html, accessed 18 January 2012.

89 Interviewed 25 January 2012.

90 A friend told me that he was shocked to hear a ten-year-old girl observe that if she had a vote she wouldn't vote for Rushanara because she was a bad role model as she had a boyfriend.

91 See Tulip Siddiq's blog, 'Engaging the Black, Asian, Minority Ethnic (BAME) Community', 20 May 2009, http://www.tulipsiddiq.com/engaging-the-black-asian-minority-ethnic-bame-community, accessed 7 November 2013.

92 Interviewed October 2000.

93 Separate interviews with two students, July 2000.

94 This view was put by three separate interviewees.

95 *East London Advertiser*, 4 March 2005 and 15 March 2006; BBC News, April 2006, http://news.bbc.co.uk/1/hi/england/london/4873312.stm, and 31 July 2006, http://news.bbc.co.uk/1/hi/england/london/5231340.stm, accessed 20 November 2012.

96 Interviewed 12 September 2000.

97 Bhiku Parekh, *Rethinking Multiculturalism: Cultural Diversity and Political Theory* (Basingstoke: Palgrave, 2000); Tariq Modood, 'Multiculturalism and Integration: Struggling with Confusions', in Hassan Mahamdallie, *Defending Multiculturalism: A Guide for the Movement* (London: Bookmarks, 2011), 61–76, p. 76.

98 In 2003–04, Tower Hamlets Council was awarded Beacon Status for Community Cohesion, which it credited to its partnership strategy. See Alastair King, Head of Policy and Partnership, Tower Hamlets, 'Strength in Diversity', *Local Government Chronicle*, 22 July 2004, www.lgcplus.com/lgc-news/features-strength-in-diversity/1232490.article, accessed 20 November 2012.

99 Jamie Gough, Aram Eisenschitz and Andrew McCulloch, *Spaces of Social Exclusion* (Abingdon: Routledge, 2006), p. 205; Mike Geddes, 'Partnership and the Limits to Local Governance in England: Institutionalist Analysis and Neoliberalism', *International Journal of Urban and Regional Research*, 30:1 (2006), 76–97; Chris Allen, *Housing Market Renewal and Social Class* (London and New York: Routledge, 2008).

100 For Gough *et al.*, the distribution of resources to different interest groups 'reinvents the long tradition of local pork-barrelling politics and clientalism, dressed up with a postmodern "celebration of difference". It tends not merely to cater for but reinforce the differences between the different constituencies, and to disguise their common interests'. See Gough *et al.*, *Spaces of Social Exclusion*, pp. 200–1 .

101 Gillian Evans, quoted in Owen Jones, *Chavs: The Demonization of the Working Class* (London and New York: Verso, 2012), p. 102. In July 2013 Tower Hamlets Council held 'The borough's first ever Cockney Heritage Festival', but the emphasis was nostalgic: see www.towerhamletsarts.org.uk/?cid=51260, accessed 31 July 2013. Councillor Rania Khan in her headscarf surrounded by pearly kings and queens made a striking multicultural image.

102 *Evening Standard*, 27 April 2004; *Daily Mail*, 28 April 2004; *East London Advertiser*, 29 April, 6 May, 13 May and 10 June 2004.

103 Bob Blackaby and Raj Patel, 'Black and Minority Ethnic Housing Associations: The Shape of the Future of the Sector, Chartered Institute of Housing Case Study Report' (London: CIH, 2003), p. 17.

104 Commission for Racial Equality, 'Statuary Code of Practice on Racial Equality in Housing (England): Consultation Draft' (London: CRE 2006), pp. 23–4.

105 Geoff Dench, Kate Gavron and Michael Young, *The New East End: Kinship, Race and Conflict* (London: Profile Books, 2006), p145.

106 Bengali football is now co-ordinated by the Bangladesh Football Association (UK), which was established in 1996 and currently has a membership of forty teams. They also support Sporting Bengal, made up of the best players from their summer league, which gained semi-professional status in 2003 and played in the FA Cup in 2005. See www.bfauk.com, accessed 22 October 2012.

107 Salique told the *Guardian* (18 July 2006), '[young people] are willing to blockade the area and guard our streets. Of course, they will not do anything unless we tell them to, but I warn you they are not as peaceful as me.' In a robust defence of free speech, Ali has berated the role of the journalists: 'As seems to be the way with these things, press coverage began (in this newspaper) with the reporting of the views of a couple of self-appointed "community leaders". I love it when a journalist does this. I think of him stumbling around Tower Hamlets, waving a notebook and echoing the old colonial cry from down the ages: take me to your leader.' See Monica Ali in the *Guardian*, 13 October 2007.

108 For a critique of this new censorship see Kenan Malik, *From Fatwa to Jihad: The Rushdie Affair and its Legacy* (London: Atlantic Books, 2009).

109 Floya Anthias, 'Race and Class Revisited – Conceptualising Race and Racisms', *The Sociological Review*, 38:2 (1990), p. 39.

110 Tariq Modood, *Multiculturalism: A Civic Idea* (Cambridge: Polity Press, 2007), p. 58.

111 *Ibid.*, p. 69.

112 *Ibid.*, p. 69.

8   Mobilisation through Islam

We have become so used to hearing about British Muslim identity and British Muslim politics that it can be difficult to remember that up until the end of the 1980s relatively few people thought in those terms. Of course the growing Muslim populations had generated growing numbers of mosques, but identity was largely associated with a person's place of origin and ethnic minority politics was increasingly being played out through ethnic groups as well as through mainstream political parties. Organisations that promoted a specifically Islamic approach to politics existed, but they were still of only marginal importance. The growth of political Islam, or Islamism, is a world-wide phenomenon, and the foregrounding of Islam as the system that encompasses every aspect of life has set itself up against the secular idea of separating politics from a personal religion. Islamism has become a topic of popular debate only in recent years, but it became a strong and strengthening force in Britain's South Asian communities through the 1990s – well before 9/11. It is impossible to say how many people have adopted an Islamist perspective, but that is not the point. These ideas have absorbed the energies of some of the most politically active young members of the community, allowing them to have an effect well beyond simple numerical strength.

Islam and Islamism

Only a small number of Bengalis of any age have abandoned their religion, but the form of worship practised by today's Bengali 'elders' is mainly that of their families back home. Like the majority of British Muslims, they follow the Barelwi tradition, which preserves the mystical Sufism of medieval India. An important part of their devotions is mediated through *pirs* – saints or spiritual masters. This practice was rejected as un-Islamic by the nineteenth-century Deobandi reformers – as well as by twentieth-century modernisers – and the Barelwi tradition was actually a reactionary response to the Deobandis. Worship

at the Brick Lane Mosque, which is particularly patronised by the older generation, is very similar to that in Sylhet, and the maintenance of Bengali cultural
traditions forms an important element of their practices. For the Islamists, many
of these traditions are trimmings that serve only to obscure the real importance
of Islam and to divide its followers along ethnic lines. There is a strengthening
belief in the importance of turning back to the fundamentals of religion below
the cultural accretions and a desire for a more active identification with Islam in
every aspect of life, including the political.

Interpretation of the Islamic ideal is a function of time, place and socio-
political context, and also of their interaction with different schools of thought
over the nature of Islam's sacred texts. Islamic evolution has centred on debates
over whether their meaning is literal or allegorical, over which texts are authentic
and over the acceptability of going back and reinterpreting original texts, as
distinct from relying on the superstructures of jurisprudence built up over the
centuries. *Ijtihad* – the inferring of new religious rulings through the examination of fundamental religious sources[1] – has been crucial to the development of
Islamic responses to western modernism, allowing clerics to build on the existing
body of jurisprudence, or, in more radical movements, to go back and re-
examine primal texts.

There are also large conservative or reactionary groups that resist the use of
ijtihad at all and these tend, as well, to discourage overt political action. The
Barelwis fall into this group, as do the powerful Tablighi Jamaat, whose emphasis
on revivalist missionary work among the Muslim grassroots makes it especially
inward-looking. (Tablighi Jamaat is not related to Jamaat-e-Islami – *jamaat* simply
means party or group.) At first glance this emphasis on personal religiosity may
seem to tie into European notions of secularism, with their separation of the
personal and the political, but in the way of life promoted by such groups,
religion remains the overarching force and broader political activity may not
feature at all, so their impact on Muslim politicisation may be somewhat
negative.

In complete contrast are those Muslims who would describe themselves as
secular, and whose engagement with Enlightenment thought and cultural
practices has resulted in attempts to 'rationalise' Islam and to open the door to
the development of social and political thought that is independent of their
faith.[2]

Others have responded to the Enlightenment and to modern social and
political challenges by counterpoising an Islamic political solution. Central to the
evolution of this Islamist approach are organisations allied to the Muslim
Brotherhood – founded by Hasan al-Banna in Egypt in 1928 – and to Jamaat-
e-Islami (Islamic Party) – a political party and ideological movement founded by
Abul A'la Mawdudi in Lahore in 1941 and now working separately in each of
the countries of the Indian subcontinent. Because of the South-Asian inheritance, many British Islamist organisations are allied to Jamaat. Mawdudi (who

lived from 1903 to 1979) built on traditional Islamic jurisprudence, but used *ijtihad* both to purify Islam from 'perverted dogmas' absorbed from other cultures[3] and to address the problems of modern life. His insistence that the gates of *ijtihad* are always open has allowed those who follow his teachings to reinterpret them in response to later changes in society and to different geographical settings. While the spread of Mawdudi's ideas has been facilitated through links with the subcontinent, Islamism is internationalist and ideas cross organisational boundaries. The Muslim Brotherhood has achieved world-wide influence and writings by its leaders – especially Sayyid Qutb's *Milestones*[4] – have become standard Islamist texts. (An exploration of the political position of these groups with respect to economic structures and attitudes towards capitalism and socialism is included in the next chapter.)

Jamaat organisations are rooted in South Asia, but they have links with sympathetic movements across the world, and see themselves as part of the *Ummah*, the international Muslim community – an internationalism encouraged by globalisation and transnationalism.[5] Their ultimate aim is an Islamic state, but their strong core framework and outer flexibility allow them to adapt to different political and social situations. In Britain, Jamaat-inspired Islamists concentrate on *dawah* – spreading the word of Islam – on winning support through grassroots welfare work and on providing a living example of a righteous community, and they have created a formidable network of organisations. Outer flexibility has allowed them to develop organisations and literature in English designed to address the concerns of the British-educated generation. As early as 1988, Francis Robinson predicted that support for Jamaat in Britain would be proportionately greater than in Pakistan because of its ability to address the 'challenges of Western civilisation' and its history of growth 'amongst those who are in a state of transition from one type of society to another'. He also foresaw that its high level of organisation and 'traditions of welfare provision' would allow it to 'work with some success towards creating a high level of Islamic organisation within the British state framework'.[6]

Jamaat and related organisations have developed a gradualist approach and work within the wider political system. They see this as the most practical way of pursuing particular issues of concern to Muslims, as a civic duty and as a way of building respect for their movement. The thinking behind this approach was clearly spelled out by Azam Tamimi of the Muslim Brotherhood in an interview for a documentary on *Muslims & Politics* made for the 2005 general election.

> [L]iberal democracy consists of two components: a procedural component, which is compatible with Islam, and a philosophical component, which we have problem with ... I call on Muslims ... to pay attention to the procedural component, which involves electing a government, making a government accountable, upholding the rule of law and equality before the law, respecting human rights. Now the philosophical component is to do with a world view: how we see ourselves, how we see the world. We Muslims have a world view of our own.

Tamimi argued that a Muslim can join a political party 'provided it is not at the expense of a Muslim faith and a Muslim code of morality'; and, along with Iqbal Sacranie, then Secretary General of the Muslim Council of Britain, he stressed the importance of voting, after taking account of key issues affecting Muslims.[7] Jamaat and the Muslim Brotherhood stress the importance of Muslims playing a full role in civil society, and the concluding message to a well-attended convention on 'Muslim Priorities in the West' in York Hall in August 2001 was for Muslims to impress non-Muslims with their actions wherever they were.[8] While right-wing blogs[9] like to 'expose' Islamist sympathies among members of the Tower Hamlets Labour Party and accuse them of entrism, there is nothing secret about the Islamists' aims.

For some, this approach is too cautious, too slow, too compromising. For them there are more radical and revolutionary groups that set aside centuries of Islamic scholarship to take their message straight from the Quran and *sunnah* (the practice of the Prophet as recorded in the *hadith* (sayings and actions) and *sira* (histories)). They see themselves as walking in the footsteps of the first Muslims, trusting in God to help them today as they believe He did in the past. Some radical groups describe themselves as *Salafis* in reference to those Muslim pioneers, the *salaf* (ancestors), and follow a strict conservative regime. But the radical movements that have had the biggest impact on British Bengali politics are Hizb ut-Tahrir and its offshoot Al Muhajiroun.

Hizb ut-Tahrir – Party of Liberation – was established in Jerusalem in 1953 as 'a political party whose ideology is Islam'.[10] (It expressly states that it is not priestly and not educational.) It functions as a revolutionary vanguard party with the aim of restoring the *Khilafat* or Islamic state and then expanding it to encapsulate the whole world, and it readily endorses the neoconservative 'clash of civilisations' thesis as 'inevitable'.[11] It draws parallels between the situation today and that which existed before Muhammad, so justifying the following of Quranic example. As a first stage in its revolutionary programme, the Hizb creates activist cells and attempts to spread its ideas through the *Ummah* or wider Muslim community, but the achievement of a *Khilafat* is regarded as an imminent possibility, so much consideration is given to its structure and workings. They argue that, eventually, an aggressive *jihad* must be fought against all those who refuse to convert to Islam or to submit to the authority of the *Khilafat*, but that this is to be done by the *Khilafat* army, so a Muslim's duty today is to work towards the creation of that Islamic state. Already, Muslims whose lands are under attack have a duty to repel their enemy, and others have a duty to ensure they have sufficient help.[12] The Hizb is very clear that since only Allah has the right to make laws, any association with parties that do not promote an Islamic programme is prohibited, and that includes voting. Although it is now very careful not to step outside British law, its views are uncompromising. In a small book produced to explain its position, it states that under the Islamic system for which it strives, a Muslim is not free to 'have an opinion other than that of Islam' or to behave in

Figure 8.1 Al-Muhajiroun poster telling Muslims that voting is *haram* (forbidden), 2001 (Sarah Glynn)

ways prescribed by Islamic law, and that '[t]he Muslim is not free in the matter of his belief because if he apostasizes from Islam, he is asked to return. If he does not, his punishment is death.'[13]

Islamism in Britain

The Jamaat-linked UK Islamic Mission was set up in the old East London Mosque in Commercial Road in 1962. In 1978 Dawatul Islam was formed as a separate Bangladeshi organisation, and they started up their Young Muslim Organisation (YMO) that first year. This specifically Bangladeshi youth organisation followed in the footsteps of the Islamic Youth Movement, founded by Jamaat in Bradford in the early 1970s, which, as Philip Lewis has explained, 'gave [young Muslims] space to retain pride in their Islamic identity, while able to distance themselves from and critique aspects of their Pakistani culture in the name of Islam'.[14] Muslim university students also had long-established student societies and the Federation of Student Islamic Societies, formed in 1963. By the late 70s, Asian youth movements were springing up everywhere but, as we have seen, these were predominantly secular organisations. The YMO first came to more general notice when it took part in the 1981 elections for the Bangladesh Welfare Association and persuaded the Association to add the preamble *Bismillah-ar-Rahman-ar-Rahim* (in the name of Allah, the Beneficent, the Merciful) to its constitution:[15] an echo, perhaps, of the political changes in Bangladesh described in Chapter 4.

The Iranian revolution of 1979 gave Islamic politics a new prominence. Iran's is a Shia Islamism, of less immediate relevance to the majority of Britain's South Asian Muslims, but the revolution also began a competition between Iran and Saudi Arabia for British Muslim hearts and minds. Saudi money helped boost Jamaat (and also Deobandi) organisations. By 1985, Dawatul Islam had taken control of the East London Mosque, and their new building, which was opened that year, had received a donation from the Saudis of £1.1 million. This was a mosque for a growing congregation, including second-generation immigrants who benefited from their publications in English and for whom the YMO was providing an increasingly busy schedule. The YMO's anniversary souvenir for 1988 lists a range of activities from *dawah* (spreading the Islamic message) through education and training to football and kung fu. The late 1980s also saw a bitter and prolonged battle for control of the mosque, fomented, according to Ed Husain, by issues around 'Bangladeshi regionalism'.[16] YMO members helped oust Dawatul Islam and replace it with a new organisation named Islamic Forum Europe, but not before violent clashes in which the police were called.[17]

At the end of the 80s, Islamic politics was galvanised by the protests surrounding the publication, in September 1988, of Salman Rushdie's novel, *The Satanic Verses*. The campaign to ban the book as offensive to Muslims was started by Jamaat in India before being promoted by Jamaat and the Saudis in Britain. It became mainstream news in January 1989 after the Bradford Council of Mosques (an organisation originally established in 1981 and a beneficiary of municipal multiculturalism) videoed their mass protest and burning of the book and sent the pictures round the world. Tensions were ratcheted up the next month when Iran's Ayatollah Khomeini issued his *fatwa* calling for Rushdie's death. The protests in the Bengali East End were far from the vehemence of those in Bradford, which Yunas Samad has attributed to Bradford's particular history of Muslim embattlement and mobilisation along religious lines.[18] However there were public meetings in both the East End's main mosques and two large marches to Hyde Park. Although British Muslims were first alerted to Rushdie's book by a Jamaati organisation – the Islamic Foundation – the subsequent role of Jamaat-linked groups was small. It has been suggested that this was a by-product of the Iranian-Saudi struggle for Muslim hegemony, in which groups connected to the Saudis did not want to give too much support to a campaign hijacked by the Iranian *fatwa*.[19]

The Satanic Verses provides a symbolic start to the new era of Islamic politics, but much more significant politically was the collapse of the Soviet Union, and with it a generation of hopes for an alternative socialist future. This was the culmination of a decade of socialist defeats, beginning with the elections of Margaret Thatcher in 1979 and Ronald Reagan in 1981. In his analysis of 'the Rushdie Affair' in Bradford, Tariq Modood concluded that, 'the demonstrations and book-burnings were above all working-class anger and hurt pride',[20] but his explanation for this anger taking a religious outlet is unconvincing. He traced the cause to the vacuum created by the 'desertion of the secular intelligentsia', which 'does not understand and/or feel responsible for its own ethnic working class'.[21] There was certainly a vacuum and lack of secular leadership, but that vacuum was not due to the absence of a middle class. It was left by the virtual extinction of class politics. When socialism is no longer thought to be able to offer a way out, working-class anger will turn to other movements. The 1980s had demonstrated that the alternative politics of ethnic mobilisation and municipal anti-racism led to a dead end and were unable to address the causes of social deprivation or even prevent racial discrimination, but the seeds of identity-based organisation had been sown. Islamic identity and Islamic politics were ready to capture people's hopes and energies.

In *Young, British and Muslim*, Philip Lewis quotes an interview with the writer Hanif Kureshi from 1995, in which Kureshi observed the big change that had occurred among British Pakistanis in further education colleges from when he had been a student twenty years earlier:

In my day we were mostly leftists of some variety, but the collapse of Eastern European Communism has made that very difficult. Now they are turning to religion.[22]

It is not just Eastern European Communism (which had its own problems) that has collapsed, but an effective left movement of any kind.

In the same way that – as Marx predicted – the growth of socialist and Marxist societies was accompanied by a decline in religion, so the perceived failure of the Marxist humanist solution and the widespread abandonment of secular socialism has encouraged people to look for comfort and answers in old and new religious certainties. Islamist politics is expanding through the Muslim world and many of the countries where it is now dominant were once strongholds of Marxist and secular-nationalist movements.

The linking of the rise of Islamism with the decline of the left is an argument with which few people who do not themselves support left politics seem prepared to engage.[23] I noticed, for example, that a review of research into Muslim political mobilisation that was commissioned by the British government and produced in 2007 includes long quotes from a paper I wrote in 2002,[24] but makes no allusion to this link, which was the paper's main argument.[25] The liberal establishment does not want to accept that people are looking for major structural changes and that, with the absence of a left alternative, people may turn to other ideologies. (This situation encourages far-right nationalism as well as Islamism, and these different radicalisms can each be boosted by the growth of the other.) An extreme example of blinkered establishment complacency is provided by Will Hutton, who argued in a British newspaper that some strands of Islamic thought were simply provoked into being by the 'self-evident superiority' and success of modern western values.[26] In contrast, as will be seen in the next chapter, radical Muslims have long been aware of the potential competition from left ideas.

Islamist organisations have been able to draw on substantial financial resources, which have been important in facilitating their growing religious and social programmes. British Muslims have received large donations from foreign sources, which naturally seek out sympathetic recipients and expect ideological and political loyalty in return.[27] In recent years these organisations have also become very effective at raising large amounts of money from the local Bengali community, both for projects in the UK, such as the London Muslim Centre, and for projects back in Bangladesh. The fundraisers have been able to combine traditional attitudes towards Islamic charity with the advertising power of community television, especially during Ramadan. Ali Riaz notes that 'According to the weekly *Jonomot*, the Bangladeshi community in Britain has been annually contributing £5 million to charity'.[28]

The turn to religion has been boosted by western governments, who have always preferred to deal with more conservative forces than allow the development of alternative groups that might challenge elite interests. They have given support to religious organisations at all levels, from local government to foreign policy – where they have promoted traditional tribal and religious leaders in Afghanistan and Iraq. Anyone tempted to doubt the deep-seated resistance that has been maintained by ruling elites towards left ideas only had to listen to the horror that greeted the suggestion, during the 2008 US presidential election campaign, that Barak Obama might introduce redistributive taxation, or to observe the almost universal anti-Chavez bias shown by all mainstream media in the coverage of the 2012 Venezuelan election.

Earlier studies of Jamaati Islamism in Britain emphasised that 'essentially the organisations attract the educated middle-classes',[29] which contributed to their slowness in getting established.[30] Modood, writing in 1990, commented that Jamaat had 'negligible working class community links',[31] but he saw the potential for this to change as Muslim youth grew up and were educated in Britain.[32] This has now happened. By the time I was carrying out fieldwork at the start of the millennium, leadership of the movement was still associated with young educated professionals, but it had developed a strong foothold among British-educated working-class Bengali youth – a hold that was enhanced by their recognition that these professionals shared their own working-class roots. The growth of Islamic organisations has been helped by the widening of university education, which has brought an influential layer of young people into contact with well-organised pan-Islamic student societies.[33]

While Jamaat-based organisations have been the main political beneficiaries of the rise of Islamism in Britain, the 1990s also saw the growth of more radical groups that appealed to those seeking a more revolutionary solution, of which Hizb ut-Tahrir was most significant. During the early years of the decade, when they gained a new young following, the Hizb was lead by Omar Bakri Muhammad.[34] In 1996, he split from the main group and set up a separate organ-isation, Al Muhajiroun – literally 'emigrants', the term used to describe those who went with Muhammad from Mecca to Medina.[35] Bakri's grand statements and ambitious plans were always guaranteed to attract a shocked media, and after 9/11, Al Muhajiroun attained a notoriety out of all proportion to its support on the ground when he gave vocal support to the terrorists. Although he dissolved the organisation when it was banned in 2004, members continued to be involved in successor groups. Meanwhile, Bakri's departure has enabled Hizb ut-Tahrir to acquire a degree of public acceptance. Although their aims are unchanged, their spokesmen try not to alienate their listeners when interviewed by the media, and they have publicised their condemnation of 'violent attacks on civilians like 9/11 and 7/7'.[36] This more tactical approach was exemplified by the Hizb member I talked with after the public showing of the *Muslims & Politics* documentary at Queen Mary University of London in 2005. Ruksana Rahman told me that she carried out her activism within the Muslim community, which should be self-reliant but also interact with wider society.

Some radical groups have recruited young British Muslims to train as *jihadis* and fight in foreign wars, which came to be perceived as more of a problem when they found themselves on the opposite side to British soldiers. A notorious few have extended their fight to include terrorist actions against civilian targets. For those who wanted to commit to *jihad*, organisations such as Azzam Publications used the web to give not only detailed instructions on how to deliver money to the Taliban, but also advice on joining the *muhajideen* in Chechnya. Those who wanted to fight were instructed to contact, in confidence, 'members of their own communities and countries who are known to have been for jihad' and get training first. And they were also helpfully told that 'Anyone unable to go and fight in Chechnya should refrain from attacking innocent people in countries outside the land of fighting. Any such energy should be translated into actually fighting in Chechnya, or obtaining training in other parts of the world.'[37]

Despite well-publicised examples, *jihadis* remain an extremely small propor-tion of those who follow Islamist thinking, and it is both incorrect and dangerous to argue, as some have done, that 'extremist' violence is a natural destination for all Islamists. This argument, which was promoted in Paul Berman's best-selling *Terror and Liberalism*, published in 2004,[38] was given ammunition by Ed Husain, cofounder of the Quilliam Foundation, a government-supported anti-extremist organisation.[39] Drawing on his own experience (outlined below) as a now-reformed Islamist, Husain claimed that Islamism dehumanises non-Muslims and that 'extremist rhetoric' is 'the preamble to terrorism'.[40] In fact, most British Islamists pursue their goal through active involvement in British institutions and they can be inspired by their faith to work for a fairer society. Even those who reject all secular politics are generally careful to keep within British law. Husain's conflation of critical ideas and political dissidence with their expression in violent political action encourages a dangerously authoritarian response, which could easily be extended to attack all critical ideologies. However much we may disagree with someone's political ideas, or with the concept of a system in which the ultimate frame of reference is interpretation of scripture, this does not make the person who holds those ideas a terrorist, and political ideology should be debated with, not outlawed.[41] It can also be argued that, while the British state will hardly be sympathetic to people who take up arms against its soldiers, those who go to help fight against an occupying army are doing a very different thing from those who take part in terrorist attacks against unarmed civilians.

If 'Islam is the solution',[42] what is the problem?

Islamism especially appeals to the generation who have been brought up in Britain, and since Bengalis and Pakistanis tend to have large families, these young people make up a large part of Britain's Muslim communities. Although most young Bengalis maintain a strong attachment to their parents' native land, often referring to it as 'home', their daily lives and probable futures are spent in the grey brick and concrete of Tower Hamlets, where the culture of Bengal can seem increasingly irrelevant. As described in so many anthropologies of diaspora, many have felt stranded between two cultures, rejecting the traditions of their parents and yet not feeling fully part of wider British society.

In the late 1970s and 80s, individual and community frustrations had been channelled into the fight against racism.[43] These battles gave the Bengalis a new confidence but could not prevent a resurgence of racist violence in the early 90s, including, in September 1993, a brutal attack on a young Bengali student, Quddus Ali, and the election of the BNP's Derek Beackon in the Isle of Dogs. The emergence of a significant Islamist movement in Tower Hamlets took place against the backdrop of violent and institutional racism, and in a political culture that encouraged the Bengalis to respond by asserting their separate identity. (White Marxist activists recall older Bengalis deliberately trying to prevent the Marxists' mixed-race organisation working with Bengali youth in the fight against this racism, though the Bengalis' hostility might also have been prompted by the Marxists' outspoken politics.[44]) The – by then familiar – prescription of liberal anti-racism and ethnic politics had failed to break down racist antagonisms and had also failed to deliver prospects for a better socio-economic future. By the turn of the millennium, violent racism was largely banished from the heart of

Tower Hamlets, where Bengalis made up a major proportion of the population. However, the racist murder of Shiblu Rahman in the more mixed district of Bow in the spring of 2001 was a cruel reminder that it had not disappeared,[45] and hidden racism and institutional racism continue to be deep-rooted. Even where racism was no longer a significant factor in everyday life, it left a legacy of distrust and separatism, so that many Bengalis perceived the economic attacks of neoliberalism as an attack on their community.

In neoliberal Britain, the prospects for most young Bengalis have looked drear, with little hope of them being able to do anything about it. The generations who came of age in the 1970s and 80s believed they were struggling for a better future: later generations have no longer had that faith. They are the losers in an increasingly materialist world that appears to have little use for them; and it doesn't help that the proximity of the City exposes them continually to visions of unattainable wealth. Tower Hamlets, like many other areas where ethnic minorities have been able to settle, offers them few prospects for finding well-paid and satisfying work or decent accommodation. At the start of the millennium, when I carried out most of the interviews quoted later in this chapter, the borough's male unemployment rate was approaching 15 per cent, and in five of the seventeen wards it was over 18 per cent. This compared with a British average of 6.5 per cent.[46] Since the 1990s, the alienation of young Bengalis has been only too evident in its brutal symptoms of drug addiction, drug-related crime and gang violence.

Islamism responds to modern individualised notions of identity,[47] but then transcends them to emphasise new concepts of community. Islamic brotherhood may be embraced as a potent antidote to alienation, and being part of the *Ummah* can make local gangs seem trifling. Jamaat-based groups around the East London Mosque can be seen to be addressing community concerns such as gang violence and drug addiction with focussed and persistent grassroots work,[48] and they have been able to offer a relevant structure to a generation for whom more traditional mosques have little appeal. They have achieved this through providing their own versions of standard youth-club activities and combining these with Islamic teaching, in English, especially directed to the concerns of the British-educated generation. Young Islamists discover a purpose and discipline in their lives and are made to feel they have a valued role in the organisation. The fight against real (and perceived) Islamophobia can unite young Muslims in a common purpose in the same way that the fight against racism did previously, and Islam can be embraced as something to be proud of. Poor and victimised residents of a borough known for social deprivation become members of an international community with a proud history and promises of future glory. For young women, Islamism has also been embraced as a safe way of rebutting some of the expectations and restrictions of Bengali tradition.

It may be contended that arguments about social deprivation cannot account for the large number of middle-class Muslims attracted to Islamist movements, but radical and revolutionary movements always attract a section of middle-class support, especially among students, and this is particularly true for minority groups facing a level of discrimination that cuts across the classes – as exemplified by the high number of Jews in Russian revolutionary movements in 1917.

With the left in retreat, more radical Islamist movements can appeal to those searching for an alternative to hedonistic capitalist materialism who might otherwise have looked towards radical socialism. Kenan Malik has observed that many recruits to Hizb ut-Tahrir were former left activists,[49] though this will have been less true among the Bengalis where socialist movements never had much hold. In joining a radical Islamist group, young Muslims can escape the confines of traditional community and family structures and feel that they are making history.

Following the call of Islam

These different Islamist responses to the numerous problems of life in Tower Hamlets are exemplified by the experiences of the young Bengalis who followed Islam's call. The best known of these young Islamists must be Ed Husain, whose book, subtitled 'Why I joined radical Islam in Britain, what I saw inside and why I left', became a best seller.[50] His is hardly a scholarly analysis – indeed Husain's experiences did not cure him of a tendency towards a naive tunnel vision – but as a deeply personal account it captures the heady atmosphere of movements that attracted a significant proportion of Tower Hamlets' young Muslims. It also provides an important picture of the organisational workings of these movements on the ground. By the time Husain was writing his book he had returned to a more private Sufi Islam. From that perspective the organisational activities he describes appear wrong and senseless, but if they are understood as part of a political programme they are not unusual. Indeed anyone who has been involved in far-left politics will find much that is familiar. The method of organisation and training adopted by Jamaat is even referred to by them as a 'cadre system',[51] suggesting a debt to the organisational methods developed by the communists.

When Husain first encountered Islamist ideas in 1991 he was a sixteen-year-old school misfit. Although many Islamists had not previously been particularly religious, Husain's family had given him a strong grounding in the Barelwi Islam of their native Bangladesh. They had also instilled in him an interest in the Gulf War. Now he was seeking greater knowledge of his religion and the direction this search took was first set by his local state school. There, separate Muslim assemblies were run by the Jamaat-linked Muslim Educational Trust, who had also produced the textbook used in his religious education class. Another student introduced him to the YMO and the East London Mosque, and he was immediately impressed. He saw people who were committed, organised and dynamic; people who he could relate to as role models and who were interested in him and took him into their fold. He also admits that the YMO was generally looked up to by his fellow school students, partly as a result of its involvement in the internecine fights in the mosque: 'They were as bad and cool as the other street gangs, just without the drugs, drinking, and womanizing.'[52] The YMO constantly assured him of Islamism's political superiority over the west, and engaged him in its highly structured, time-consuming and competitive training programme. By the summer his evenings had become filled with YMO events and meetings and he was spending much of his school day organising and leading prayer meetings and promoting the YMO. When his distressed father gave him an ultimatum to leave Islamism or leave home, he chose to take refuge in the mosque, until one of the YMO leaders negotiated his return to his unhappy family. He had proved his dedication to the cause.

With his determination strengthened, he became active in the YMO-dominated Islamic Society at Tower Hamlets College, where he had gone to study for his A-levels and was soon elected its president. Husain claims that they 'ran the Islamic Society like a military operation' and that in the space of six months they 'had changed the entire atmosphere at college'.[53] While it is always difficult for someone caught up in a political movement to evaluate that movement in a wider perspective and envisage life beyond its bounds, even those not involved can recognise this as a time when Islamist ideas were winning a new generation of followers. Strengthened by the uncompromising message of Qutb's *Milestones*, the Islamic Society exalted in high-profile and deliberately provocative campaigns that won the support and admiration of their peers and wrong-footed their liberal teachers.[54] Their posters calling for 'Islam: The Final Solution'[55] gave a nasty twist to the Muslim Brotherhood's famous slogan ('Islam is the Solution'). They forced the college to provide a larger prayer room, frightened students away from the disco and pressured Muslim girls to wear the *hijab*. Husain claims that society membership exceeded two hundred.

The YMO was not the only Islamist group seeking to attract the college's young Muslims. Some of the girls, for whom the YMO then had little to offer, had chosen to follow a dogmatic Wahhabi sect that demanded they cover themselves completely and emulate the first Muslims, the *Salaf*; and Husain admits that a shortage of Jamaat speakers led the Islamic Society to invite Islamists from other groups. Dynamic *Salafi* speakers from JIMAS[56] persuaded some of his contemporaries to enlist for *jihadi* training in Afghanistan, but Husain himself was drawn to the all-encompassing political logic of Hizb ut-Tahrir, whose call for an Islamic state seemed to provide a tangible solution to all the world's problems, including the massacres of Bosnian Muslims then dominating television screens. The Hizb's urgent, confident internationalism made the YMO's focus on Bangladeshi politics and grassroots work in the local community appear parochial and timid. The Hizb was concentrating recruitment efforts on Tower Hamlets' large Muslim community and Husain was welcomed into their secretive cell structure (the product of an organisation that had been outlawed in many countries in the Middle East). His cell leader, the co-founder of the British branch of the Hizb who had moved on to Islamism after student membership of the Socialist Workers' Party (SWP), 'was convinced that he was participating in the making of a new world order'. 'To us,' Husain explains, 'the emergence of the Islamic state was simply a matter of time. The caliphate by next Ramadan was not a slogan; it was a statement of intent.'[57]

The Hizb exploited every opportunity for debate, both formal and informal, and adopted political campaigning techniques learnt from radical socialist groups. Their approach was even more bullish and confrontational than the methods he had learnt with the YMO, especially towards competing Islamist groups. When Husain was removed from the presidency of the college Islamic Society, the Hizb set up a rival group.

The rise of this new force across the UK drew the attention of the media, which helped boost its image. However Husain concedes that when they organised a march through Whitechapel for Bosnia in the summer of 1993, they were disappointed that they had only mobilised 'just under a thousand people'.[58] And the Hizb's international conference, ambitiously organised in the twelve thousand-seat Wembley Arena to coincide with the seventieth anniversary of the end of the Ottoman Caliphate in 1924, proved a 'shambolic failure' and left a profound sense of anti-climax among the young activists who had learnt to expect imminent revolution. Even their attempts to knock on the doors of Muslim homes to inform people of the conference were often met with 'hostility'.[59]

By this time Husain had moved to the more racially mixed Newham College, where the Islamic Society was run by *Salafis*. Initially he kept out of college politics but in 1995, together with his Hizb friend, Majid Nawaz,[60] he set up a debating society and began a recruitment drive that was to see students increasingly divided between Muslims and non-Muslims, even when socialising in the common room. In their campaign for a prayer room, he responded to the Hizb's call to link local issues to global ones with the provocative slogan, 'They slaughter us in Bosnia, expel us from our homes in Palestine, and refuse us the basic right to pray in Britain'.[61]

However, the Hizb's immediacy and energy, which at first sight had appeared to give it an irresistible strength, were endowing the growing organisation with a vital weakness. With everything focused on political tactics, little time was left for developing the Islamic knowledge and practices that that politics was supposed to be defending and promoting. Members were learning to run before they could walk. There was little help for those without a religious background and even Husain found that he was 'no longer an observant Muslim',[62] often going to bed exhausted with no time to pray. The Hizb regarded radical politics as a religious duty, but it had allowed that politics to replace all other religious duties. He found that smoking and profane language were usual, and segregation of the sexes was more honoured in the breach than the observance. (The high-octane lifestyle was also matched with a taste for fast cars, which religious scruples prevented their owners from insuring. As natural events were deemed acts of God, they considered insurance *haram*.) Husain began to feel the general lack of religiosity as a hollowness at the centre of the Hizb, and this was one of the reasons for his ultimate abandonment of Islamism. A more abrupt wake-up call was provided by a murder outside the college, which he believed to have been an indirect result of the Islamic supremacism they had fostered.

If Husain had been shunned by his school fellows for avoiding the dominant gang culture, this was not the case with Abdul Rahman,[63] who I interviewed in early 2001. By that time he was an articulate young man in his twenties who worked locally in a government office, and an active member of Al Muhajiroun, which he had moved on to from Hizb ut-Tahrir in 1997. We had arranged to meet at the School of Oriental and African Studies (SOAS), where he attended evening classes in Arabic and, to avoid offending religious law by being alone with a woman from outside the immediate family, he brought with him a friend who sat silent throughout our discussion. (No neglect of religious laws here.) Thus chaperoned, I asked him to tell me about his personal Islamic journey. Abdul had been raised to be a Bengali Muslim integrated into British society, but was left feeling in between communities, neither Bengali nor English. Like so many of his peers, he sought a role in street culture and became infatuated by gangster movies. When a lecturer at Tower Hamlets College introduced him to revolutionary socialism he felt, in his own metaphor, like a drowning man to whom a hand had been held out. He identified from personal experience with the arguments about working-class oppression and began to take part in campaigning for bigger student grants and distributing SWP leaflets. Although he then regarded Islam as only old-fashioned ritual, he could not reconcile his belief in God with the theories of dialectical materialism, and when a college friend took him to debates organised by Hizb ut-Tahrir, new horizons opened up for him. For the first time he encountered his religion as a way of life, a complete ideological and practical system. His quest for the true path took him travelling around the world and especially the Middle East, abandoning the degree he had started at university, and he tried to 'correct' his parents' religious practices. For Abdul, rigorous political Islam filled both an emotional and an intellectual need; and it was his belief that Islam liberates from oppression. He told me that *jihad* training was an obligation, but for him the most important battles were clearly the intellectual struggles through which they were spreading Islamist understanding.

When I attended an Al Muhajiroun public meeting in Ilford the following year,[64] I was able to observe first-hand how idealistic young British Muslims were persuaded to take action on behalf of their Muslim brothers and sisters. Tony Cox, who was with me and who worked for the far-left Militant Tendency in the 1980s, observed that despite the obvious differences, especially in the proposed solutions, it reminded him of Militant meetings. It was not just the young men – some in their work clothes – in the stark hall, but the serious and focussed class-based rhetoric and the promise of being part of a structured resistance. The speaker's condemnation of hoarding money, his denouncement of interest as the 'ball and chain of economic enslavement' and his repeated references to Muslim oppression all appealed to a radical instinct for a fairer society. (He also delighted in expounding on the inadequacies of the *kufrs*, or unbelievers, including that Queen Victoria only bathed once a year – which, apart from its historical confusion, was a difficult criticism to make in a distinctly dirty Muslim centre.) We were told that the 'clash of civilisations' was inevitable and no-one could erase *jihad* from the Quran. While physical support for Muslims under attack is the highest assistance, most of us there had not reached that height. However, financial support for the *muhajideen* is the same as fighting. People invest money in *kufr* financial schemes, but this is the best investment and will be rewarded in the hereafter. And more specifically – one pound can buy three bullets for a Kalashnikov. When we had asked two men before the start of the meeting why they had got involved with the organisation, they replied, what would you do if your family was attacked? – meaning, of course, not their relatives but the *Ummah*.

That radical Islamic groups can respond to many of the same sources of discontent as radical socialists is also illustrated by the leaflet distributed by Hizb ut-Tahrir at the big anti-war march in London in 2003. The main focus of its attack is capitalist colonialism and it is not until the final sentence that it invites the reader 'to study the Islamic Ideological solution'.

While members of the Hizb (and formerly also Al Muhajiroun) regard Jamaat and the YMO as provincial and ultimately un-Islamic due to their compromise with western democracy, the Jamaat organisations dismiss the radicals as unrepresentative fringe organisations that give Islam a bad image. The more revolutionary groups cannot match Jamaat's rigorous organisation, nor have they found time for the kind of grassroots issues through which the Jamaat organisations have been able to retain their membership and recruit from a broad constituency.

The East London Mosque has built its strength on the basis of solid community work, and this approach can be compared with that of the Communist Party in the East End of the 1930s, as well as of other Islamic organisations such as Egypt's Muslim Brotherhood or Turkey's Justice and Development Party. It contrasts with the Brick Lane Mosque, which refers social welfare problems to the secular Bangladesh Welfare Association next door. Young Muslims have been attracted to the East London Mosque through the YMO or its newer female counterpart, Muslim Aat, and they have received encouragement through the example of those who have found in Islam the motivation to take control of their lives and improve their position in society. (The East London Mosque would certainly discourage its young brothers and sisters from dropping out of university.) Abdul Miah, a youth worker with Brick Lane Youth

Development Association, described the mosque as like a second youth centre.[65] Islamic discussions are well publicised and can even attract street-wise kids with little else to do. Thus a boy at the Crowder Youth Club, who described himself as not particularly religious, told me that he went to 'talks and things like that' because 'just, it's interesting, innit, to hear about and find out more'.[66]

For Nazmul, discovery of the YMO when he was at Tower Hamlets College helped him turn his life around. He had been involved with gangs and crime and more than once got kicked out of school. He emerged from college with high A-level grades and when I interviewed him in 2000 was reading law at university (and a leading member of the organisation). He explained how this transformation came about:

> I don't think they spoke to me directly about education, they talked to me about Islam. What is Islam? Islam is a way of life ... After that I suppose I had role models, I saw in YMO ... which I [had] never met before, people who were lawyers ... teacher[s] and so on. [These] role models give you a motivation; you want to be like them ... We can look up to them, because we know that they were once taking drugs and in gangs and doing other things ... One of the fundamentals of Islam is to bring about change, change for the benefit of everyone ... The best way to make a change in the community is to do something and be something.[67]

Clearly, for Nazmul personally the role of Islam in the form of the YMO has been immensely beneficial. In his words, 'it gave me a life-line'.

Abdul Hannan, at Nafas drugs project, told me that he used the appeal of Islamic brotherhood for youth outreach work:

> A lot of things have been achieved ... through the path ... of religion, basically. 'Cos the majority of us who are Bangladeshis ... our roots are ... Islam, at the end of the day ... This is the only thing that binds our community together ... I mean, I feel confident where, like, if I was on the street, rather than preach that I'm Bengali ... if I preach Islam to them, they would more adhere to me ... They would try to listen.[68]

In a close community in which older boys are already respected as 'brothers',[69] a more specifically Islamic brotherhood becomes an extension of existing ties. Less romantically, *Insight*, a bi-monthly magazine produced by Islamic Forum Europe, argued that 'a deep sense of fear and belief in the hereafter' is the best deterrence to criminality.[70] And Sabina, who I interviewed at Women's Relief where she worked, justified the severity of parts of *shariah* law with the observation that 'maybe if there was more stronger punishments, people wouldn't commit those crimes in the first place'.[71] Harun Miah, a student who was helping Hannan, explained that, for them, 'Islam is not a religion but it's a guideline for us to follow. Everything and everyone should have a guideline so they know where they're going wrong and right'.[72]

The highly structured Jamaat-based groups give their recruits an extensive organisational training that helps boost their overall confidence (as Ed Husain discovered). Nazmul told me how the YMO turns school children into young activists:

> They learn skills, how to organise a circle. I mean sounds simple, but for young people it's quite a bit – the chair, the secretary, how to arrange a meeting, how to arrange a public meeting, how to demand something to the college through the students' union … Once they go to college they can use that skill as a tool to live at college.[73]

Nazmul acknowledged that organisations that (as he put it) 'believe in revolutionary change', such as Hizb ut-Tahrir and Al-Muhajiroun, can be more attractive to rebellious students than the YMO, which believes in 'evolutionary change'. Indeed, he compared the appeal of the 'revolutionaries' to that of socialist revolt against the government, but he assured himself that such student allegiances were only temporary.[74]

Unlike traditional, all-male Bengali mosques, the East London Mosque has a women's prayer room and women's talks and discussions, and at the York Hall conference mentioned above the women's section was noticeably fuller than the men's.[75] Although their black *jilbabs* and *hijabs* may look intimidating – to Bengali women as well as to western ones – girls who follow the Islamic revivalist path stress the freedom that their religion gives them. They compare their position to that of their mothers, who are often restrained by Bengali cultural mores that give little importance to women's education and restrict their movements outside the home. In fact they may use their new-found Islamic knowledge to demonstrate to their parents that such restrictions have no basis in religious law. While they would not dispute that 'the husband has been given the position of head of the family',[76] they explain that men and women are equal in importance but have different roles, and that the idea of a woman having no say over whom she marries is anathema to Islam.

Women's Relief, the advice centre at the East London Mosque, is not afraid to tackle sensitive issues such as domestic violence and female genital mutilation,[77] as well as helping in general areas such as training and job search. When I talked to the young woman who ran the centre in 2001, she was juggling her job with teacher training and looking after her small child. The new Islam wants to see its children's mothers well educated, religiously and otherwise, and recognises that women may want or need to work – child-care is not so much of a problem when many Bengali grandmothers are at home close by. In this they have updated Mawdudi's view that 'Women have been ordered to remain in their houses and discharge the responsibilities assigned to them', only going out 'when necessary'.[78]

Aisha Miah, a community worker who I interviewed in 2000, was not part of the Jamaat movement. She prayed at home rather than at a mosque because she held the traditional belief that that earns a woman more reward in heaven,

Figure 8.2 Women's gallery, public meeting for young Muslims, York Hall, August 2001
(Sarah Glynn)

and she wore a traditional Bengali shawl rather than a *hijab* – but her approach
to her religion was in many ways typically modern:

> A lot of people say, we don't believe that our children should go on to education and
> stuff like that. As soon as they're sixteen they should be at home, whatever, specially
> the girls ... and then married off. But in our religion this is for illiterate people. Our
> religion says, right, knowledge is the biggest thing that you could ever have, so it
> doesn't matter how much education a woman takes in, the better it is for her ... The
> best professions for women in Islam is teaching because you're actually sharing the
> knowledge that you've got. And that's the most beneficial one. That's where you'll
> get the most reward [in heaven] ... In this society and this day, right, [men and
> women] have to work together ... [But] as long as your mind is clean and clear
> whilst you're actually doing the job, you can do whatever you want; and as long as
> you're dressed appropriately as well.[79]

Ruksana Rahman, from Hizb ut-Tahrir, told me that Islam says that women
should be politically active but also have other roles and responsibilities as
mothers and daughters.[80] And even groups who expect full veiling can

encourage girls to take part in public protest, protected behind their veils. One of the strangest sights of my fieldwork was a lobby of a meeting of Tower Hamlets Labour Group by around a hundred schoolgirls hidden under black *jilbabs* and *niqabs* so only their eyes were visible. They carried poster-painted placards demanding that their Muslim School be allowed to purchase a disused Victorian school building and were gathered on one side of the atrium to the modern council offices, while the men who had organised the protest occupied the other side.[81]

The adoption of visible Islamic symbols such as the *hijab* has been further encouraged as part of a defiant response to prejudice and Islamophobia and as a way to reclaim Islam from those who would use it to justify terrorism.

Following 9/11 there was a predictable upturn of interest in the meaning of Islam among non-religious Muslim youth. Already by 20 September, Junaid Ahmed at the YMO was able to tell me that,

> those who are not practising … have realised that they ought to practise, and they need to at least show their identity as a Muslim … A lot of people have come to us to find out about this situation in the light of Islam.[82]

Through formal meetings in the mosques and youth clubs and informal contacts on the street, the YMO put forward their interpretation of events. In November, Ahmed reported that,

> As far as the Muslims who are not practising, yes, when we go and approach them there is … more interest in listening to us, rather than saying, 'Oh, these are the practising brothers again, they're going to say the same thing.' … They're listening and they're saying, how can we help?'[83]

If, in the excitement, their listeners proposed going out to fight, then the YMO would tell them, 'that's not our duty and responsibility here. Our responsibility is to pray for them, to speak out against any injustice, be it in Afghanistan or in America, and that's what we should do.'[84] In its 2001 Ramadan message, the YMO advised members to 'be pro-active and speak out gently but confidently for peace and justice in the world'.[85] Public statements and government lobbying were orchestrated through the umbrella of the Islamist-dominated Muslim Council of Britain (MCB), and Ahmed was careful not to pre-empt the decisions of its leaders. For its part, the Council was anxious to draw a line between itself and some 'vocal groups', through which the Muslim community was 'threatened from within'.[86] Ahmed put this more directly when he told me shortly after 9/11 that Al Muhajiroun 'have a few individuals who have big mouths and they shout'.[87] The reaction of British Jamaat-linked groups to both the terrorism in New York and the war in Afghanistan was firm but measured – in fact very much in line with the wider anti-war movement, but with greater emphasis on the lack of incontrovertible legal proof of bin Laden's guilt. They regarded Afghanistan under the Taliban as a sort of failed Islamic state in the same way that Trotskyists have both criticised and defended the Soviet Union as a failed workers' state. Articles in *Insight* analysed the realpolitik of gas pipelines and containment of rival powers, as well as looking at the stresses on the community from the point of view of a clinical psychologist.[88] There were none of the suggestions of Jewish conspiracy found in the speeches of Jamaat's Ameer in Pakistan.[89]

Members of Al Muhajiroun – the principle 'vocal group' from which the MCB was anxious to distance themselves – told us outside their Ilford meeting that bin Laden had achieved more for the growth of their movement in a few months than they had achieved in ten years recruiting at universities.

Debate and discussion travel rapidly through the Muslim world, aided by modern media. A plethora of books and leaflets have provided a crucial tool for spreading the Islamist message, but these have been increasingly supplemented by videos and websites. Islamist groups were early users of the internet and British Muslims are in touch with ideas from across the *Ummah*. This has made it easier for young Muslims to develop their own understandings of Islam, independent of their local mosque and 'community leaders', and has also provided a platform for the growth of some wilder ideas and conspiracy theories, especially following the attack on the twin towers. As in so many areas of the net, Islamic web discussions can sometimes prove disturbing reading.

United *Ummah* or divided community?

For the older generation, whose political consciousness was moulded by the secular nationalism of the Independence struggle, this turn to Islamism is a source of deep unease, and especial concern has been concentrated around the dominant position of men accused of war crimes in 1971. This was expressed in protest demonstrations at the many visits of the Jamaat-e-Islami MP and charismatic preacher, Delwar Hossain Sayeedi. Ali Riaz notes how Sayeedi has played a leading role in turning traditional public gatherings for scriptural commentary, known as *waz mahfils*, into a vehicle for expounding on contemporary politics; and he has described how the preacher's speeches fired his listeners with hatred for the secularists, which could erupt in violence against the protestors. *Waz mahfils* have been organised for the British Bengali community since the late 1980s and Sayeedi's speeches are also available as recordings in Brick Lane shops.[90]

The UK branch of the Nirmul Committee, which campaigned for prosecution of war criminals and the resumption of a legal process that was interrupted by the 1975 coup, published detailed allegations of Sayeedi's involvement in a reign of terror that included the murder of intellectuals, supplying young women to the Pakistani army and looting Hindu homes.[91] The Nirmul Committee also publicised the Channel 4 *Dispatches* programme of 3 May 1995 that, in the words of the Channel 4 press release, revealed 'exclusive evidence of how three prominent British Muslims are guilty of inciting torture, mutilation and murder'.[92] One of the three, Chowdhury Mueen Uddin, was vice chair of the East London Mosque and a trustee of Muslim Aid and has since also become Director of Muslim Spiritual Aid Provision in the NHS and Chair of the Multi-Faith Group for Health Chaplaincy. Another, Abu Syed, was head teacher of a Muslim school and a co-opted member of Tower Hamlets Education Committee. The next section looks at how the long-awaited prosecution of Sayeedi, Mueen Uddin and other alleged war criminals has reignited old hatreds in Bangladesh, and also among the community in Britain. However, for many years these issues had had relatively little impact on the emerging generation of British Bengali activists.

Stephen Barton, who studied the Bengalis in Bradford in the early 1980s when Dawatul Islam supported the splitting off of a new separate Islamic centre, commented on Jamaat's support for Pakistan in the 1971 war and concluded, 'Membership of the Dawat al-Islam is liable to remain small, at least in Bradford, until these memories fade'.[93] For the younger, British-educated generations, those memories soon faded. In fact the Jamaat-linked organisations seemed to have managed to separate themselves from historic ties more easily than their political rivals. In keeping with their internationalist vision, Jamaat-e-Islami Bangladesh, unlike the other main Bangladeshi parties, does not have foreign branches and the refusal of its international sympathisers to limit their attention to Bangladeshi (or Pakistani) politics only strengthens the appeal of Jamaat's ideology in London. By contrast, the emphasis that the London secularists often give to the legacy of the independence movement has not helped their cause, especially among the post-1971 generations, who associate Bangladeshi politics primarily with corruption.

For many Bengali Muslims brought up in London the politics of Bangladesh were not relevant. Although some young people could be called upon to come out and support Sayeedi in demonstrations, when I interviewed Junaid Ahmed back in 2001 he explained, 'with all due respect to Sayeedi,' that,

> the Young Muslim Organisation UK never invited Sayeedi to Britain in the recent past, and we don't plan to invite him because he doesn't speak English; and he's dealing with the senior, older generation of the Muslim community, and we're concentrating with the British Muslim youth here in Britain, and they have different agenda, they have different interests, they have different way of thinking.[94]

Nazmul noted, 'We do identify ourselves as part of the global Islamic movement … [but] I don't have any links with Jamaat, because I don't know anyone in Jamaat'.[95] He saw the protests against Sayeedi as due to a combination of Bangladeshi politics and the vested interests of those Sayeedi criticises, such as people who make money from selling alcohol, or who follow the traditional Bengali *pirs*, or saints, of which his revivalist Islam did not approve. (There is a grain of truth in this as the protesters also emphasised Sayeedi's insults to the community, which he portrayed as uneducated and immoral:[96] criticism especially unacceptable in coming from a non-Sylheti. But this was not the primary concern.)

Bangladeshi politics were not relevant to Nazmul in London; however his explanation revealed an even deeper division between his views and those of Sayeedi's secular critics. When he talked about vested interests he categorised the protesters as un-Muslim. And he was similarly dismissive when I asked him about *Ekushey*, the 21 February Language Martyrs' Day, which (as we saw in Chapter 2) commemorates a defining moment of Bengali struggle against West Pakistani dominance. Commenting on the organisers of the *Ekushey* commemorations, he stated, 'most of them are atheist, who don't like Islam'. Most Bengalis who describe themselves as secular are religious people who believe it is possible to separate religion and politics (see Chapter 4) – the Nirmul Committee leaflet actually quotes Prophet Muhammad – but, when questioned, Nazmul only qualified the comment with, 'If they're not atheists some of them are at least minimum; they're atheist supporters, or people who are not supportive of us.' Ironically, the justification given for these divisive views is the Islamist aversion to dividing the Muslim people, which gave Jamaat's opposition to the separation of East and West Pakistan a religious intensity.

For those within the Islamist movement, Islam is a force that brings people together, but at the same time, as Nazmul's comments demonstrate, it can be a source of bitter division between them and those outside it.[97] Few can feel these divisions more strongly than the young British Bengalis trying to find their way among the different forces acting on their lives. Radical Islam may divide its adherents from their traditional parents – and the Sayeedi demonstrations saw parents and children facing each other across the barriers. It also puts those who do not conform to its moral code under strong pressure to join the group, or risk being categorised among the drug takers and tarts. Interviewing students at Tower Hamlets College in 2000, I found that the old parental fear over 'what will the community say?' had been supplemented by the new moral policing of the College Islamic Society. Amina was a serious bookish student and a believing Muslim, who liked to wear a denim jacket over her modest but modern dress and trousers, although she had been told that the way she dressed made people wrongly assume that she was 'the type' who went out with boys.[98] She explained that 'the moment the Islamic Society are around ... everybody's quietened down, and they're just aware that they're there, so you've got to behave well'. If they saw an Islamic Society boy the girls would 'run a mile' to avoid charges of 'free-mixing'. Amina had used the Islamists' pro-education arguments with her parents when they questioned her decision to go to university, but her failure always to keep to a strict Islamic code in her busy life of friends, work and study was a source of real fear for her:

I get scared when people ask me about my religion because I think I am really neglecting Islam ... If I'm giving myself excuses ... that's a sin ... That's saying you're a ... non-believer, and to say that, that I'm a non-believer, I think is the most harsh thing you can do to yourself.

As has been noted before,[99] a girl's 'empowerment' by religion has its price. Some respond to such pressures by adopting a hypocritical double life. Others may simply feel ostracised by a society that would classify them as sinners, and be left with little alternative guidance with which to replace the traditional morals of their parents. The Islamist movements profess their universality, but those who refuse to be enlightened according to their ideology will not be helped by them.

Of course the pressures on students will vary as different cohorts make their way through the college. When I talked to one of the teachers in 2007 she told me that the Islamic Society had been particularly strong about four years earlier, when a group of boys took it on themselves to reprimand others about unsuitable behaviour, but that it had since become less dominant, although some girls were putting pressure on others to conform to Islamic mores. Interviewing four of her female Bengali students, I was reminded how difficult it is to generalise. Two had been covering their heads since their school days and spent their spare time at the College Islamic Society and at the London Muslim Centre attached to the East London Mosque; the other two were tomboys who enjoyed music and dancing, did voluntary work outwith the Bengali community, and had put off becoming more religious for an unspecified future. One of the latter had surprised everyone by becoming a police cadet and planning to be a police officer. She told me that she had got dragged into gang wars when at school, her cousin and her mate had both got shot, and she wanted to do something to end the violence.[100]

Islamism doesn't just affect people at an individual level. At the same time as encouraging their adherents to play an active part in civil society, and criticising isolationism, Islamist groups such as those around the East London Mosque provide the means for Muslims to live in an increasingly separate social sphere, almost from the cradle to the grave. In Tower Hamlets there is an Islamic playgroup, and even for those who do not attend the (all still private) Muslim schools, there are evening classes, Saturday school and numerous Islamic summer schemes. While there is a strong emphasis on Islamic knowledge, it is recognised that children need more than this, and organisations such as the Junior Muslim Circle ensure that football, camping, trips and other activities can all take place in 'a sound moral atmosphere'.[101] Youth groups – run separately for boys and girls – are extremely active, as are Islamic student societies. At Ramadan, Muslim Community Radio invites listeners to 'tune in with the whole family'.[102] The London Muslim Centre arranges regular sessions that provide help in finding and applying for jobs, as well as opportunities for serious Islamic study. Alongside advice services, Women's Relief organises sport, art and social activities, and the centre includes a gym and spa. For the old, there is a day centre and sheltered flats. The funeral service was, of necessity, one of the first institutions established.[103]

The rise of Islamism has emboldened a few troublemakers to take up a new form of Islam-inspired hate crime, however serious incidents have been few and isolated, and the picture painted in Andrew Gilligan's *Telegraph* blog, and widely disseminated, is an inflammatory distortion. Thus, for example, although much publicity has been given to cases of homophobia, police figures for homophobic incidents recorded in different London boroughs show that, for the twelve months up to September 2012, the worst borough was Westminster, which recorded a hundred and twenty-one incidents to Tower Hamlets' seventy-one.[104] Nevertheless, the previous chapter did record how local councillor, Shiria Khatun, was threatened for wearing western dress, though this could be as much a product of a more general misogyny as of religious intolerance.

The secularist generation has been left to wonder at the way the tide has turned and how to stop it. Ansar Ahmed Ullah, who came to this country in 1975 aged around fifteen, observed to me in 2000: 'They're obviously providing a service that's missing in the community ... So I think it's [more] to do with our failure than anything else that they've been able to attract [a] large number of young people.'[105] With like-minded colleagues, he has attempted to keep alive the old spirit through the UK Nirmul Committee; but even at the turn of the century, when Bangladesh had not yet reached its thirtieth anniversary, he confessed: 'Because [the] Nirmul Committee was fairly political in its makeup it wasn't appealing to all the young people.'[106] His colleague, Sunahwar Ali, commented:

> If you ... talk to [the] younger generation [of] the Bengali community ... if you say 'what is '71, what's happened? There was war between Bangladesh and who?' [They will say] 'Oh maybe the British or something.' People don't have a clue.[107]

To try to reach a new generation, the Nirmul Committee established a cultural organisation, the Swadhinata [Freedom] Trust, to propagate Bengali secular culture in a way that would appeal to British-born Bengalis and serve as a source of both personal and community strength.[108] However the link with 1971 may prove a liability as either irrelevant to Britain, or – now – as connected to the discredited Awami League. More importantly, cultural politics can hardly compete with the pull of Islam, which has behind it the power of an over-riding ideology.

Old wounds reopened

The establishment of an International Crimes Tribunal (ICT) to prosecute men accused of war crimes in 1971 was a widely popular Awami League manifesto promise in the 2008 election, and the Tribunal began work in 2010. However, far from closing this chapter of history, the ICT has succeeded in opening up old wounds, fanning the flames of religious conservatism and bringing Bangladesh to a new level of violent unrest. The first indictments were issued to nine leaders and former leaders of Jamaat and two former ministers from the Bangladesh Nationalist Party; and the Bangladesh Nationalist Party was quick to brand the trials as an attack on Islam. At the time of writing (October 2013) the ICT had resulted in six death sentences (one of them in absentia) and one sentence of ninety years imprisonment. Sayeedi had been convicted and condemned to death and proceedings had begun against Mueen Uddin, although he remained in England. In addition, the Bangladesh High Court had declared Jamaat unfit to contest the forthcoming election because, as the *Economist* explained, 'its charter puts God above democratic process'.[109]

Perhaps, given Bangladesh's poisonous history of self-seeking tit-for tat politics, the tribunal was doomed to failure, but the sometimes-blatant abandonment of due legal process is, nevertheless, disappointing. Serious criticisms have been made by the Bar Human Rights Committee of England and Wales, Human Rights Watch and the *Economist*, none of which has any reason to favour the Islamist leaders on trial.[110]

Some of the biggest protests around the trials have actually been by supporters of the tribunal process. These were called in response to the life sentence initially given to Abdul Quader Mollah. The protestors believed that this meant that Jamaat's Assistant Secretary General, who greeted his sentence with a 'V' for victory, would be released as soon as there was a change of government. On 5 February 2013, young activists converged on Dhaka's Shahbagh, a traditional site of protest, calling for a death sentence for all convicted war criminals. After initial surprise, the government welcomed the movement and changed the rules to allow a retrospective change of sentence.

In contrast, the protests in opposition to the trials have drawn support from the rural hinterland. They have often been destructive and violent and sometimes murderous – David Lewis records that after Sayeedi was sentenced to death on 28 February, Jamaat supporters attacked 'government offices, police stations and minority communities around the country'[111] – and the government response has been condemned as massively and brutally disproportionate. Human Rights Watch has recorded killings of police and Awami League supporters and also killings of protestors and bystanders by the security forces.[112]

An increasingly prominent role in protest organisation has been played by the recently formed Hefazat-e-Islam (Protectorate of Islam), a madrassa-based organisation created in 2009 to oppose plans to equalise women's inheritance rights.[113] For Jamaat, this provides a convenient front organisation and army of foot-soldiers. For the Hefazat, the protests are an opportunity to demand a new regime based around a conservative Islam that would impose severe restrictions on women and introduce capital punishment for blasphemy. They characterise the secular Shahbagh protestors as atheists.[114] On 5 May, Hefazat-e-Islam organised its supporters, including tens of thousands of white-clad madrassa students, to come to a 'Siege of Dhaka' to put forward their demands. They were met by police and paramilitary forces who broke up the gathering using often-indiscriminate violence, with the worst attacks taking place in the small hours of the morning when many protesters were sleeping. While dismissing claims of hundreds or thousands of deaths as unfounded, Human Rights Watch has estimated that 'at least 58 people died on May 5 and 6, seven of whom were members of the security forces'.[115] In a further twist, the Awami League government's integrity has been diminished even more by its attempts to pander to religious populism by jailing 'atheist bloggers'.

All this has had its echoes in Tower Hamlets where, as in Bangladesh, it has reinforced the secular-religious divide. Many secular Bengalis have allowed their abhorrence of the crimes committed in 1971 to blind them to criticism of the trial process. There have been protests in support of Shahbagh, and even a small protest outside the office of Human Rights Watch, which was accused of succumbing to powerful Jamaati lobbying and (with post-colonial sensitivity) of interfering in Bangladeshi affairs.[116] Islamist groups, especially those with links to Jamaat, have used the flaws in the trial process to protest the innocence of accused Jamaati leaders. They have combined this with a potent attack on government violence and human rights abuses and on government corruption (including the corruption that allowed the Rana Plaza garment factory collapse that killed over eleven hundred workers), and with the unsubstantiated branding of their opponents as *nastik* – atheists.[117] Both sides compete for the symbolic community space of Altab Ali Park (named after the murdered garment worker), where the proximity of the East London Mosque and London Muslim Centre gives the Islamists an organisational advantage. The most active Shahbagh supporters have found themselves considerably outnumbered, and they have complained of intimidation and violence from their opponents. They have received threats and harassment in person and online, pro-Shahbagh demonstrators were attacked outside Altab Ali Park, a UK Awami League leader found men breaking into his home, a female television reporter was assaulted and an Awami League journalist was beaten up in Greatorex Street.[118]

However, despite some large and angry demonstrations, involvement may not have been as widespread as these might imply. Abjol Miah – who we will meet properly in the next chapter and who has been very active in protesting against the trials and the Awami League government – claims to speak for 'third-generation British Bangladeshis',[119] but a telling post on his Facebook page suggests that the protests were not getting the resonance among the local Bengali youth for which he had hoped. Following a comment on press bias, he observed, 'No wonder the British Bangladeshi 3rd generation are not interest in Bangladesh!'[120] The initial high-intensity activity has not been maintained, but, with Bangladeshi politics degenerating into further violence, it is too soon to know what the long-term impact will be. So far, most other Bengalis with

Figure 8.3 Supporters of the war crimes trials protesting opposite Human Rights Watch, who have been highly critical of the trial process, August 2013 (Sarah Glynn)

political positions in Britain have restricted themselves to appealing to people to behave peacefully and have refrained from getting actively involved on either side.

Faith as government policy

The last chapter concluded by looking at the growing role of community groups, and especially faith organisations, in local governance.[121] The prominence being given to 'faith communities' at all levels can be seen to be a tactical choice for those who wish to preserve existing structural hierarchies – even if it is not presented that way. Faith groups may also see a mutual benefit in such a system, and this lay behind the Archbishop of Canterbury's ill-fated support for greater recognition of *shariah* law.[122] Recognition of 'faith communities' has been encouraged by co-ordinated lobbying by different faith groups – including through the Inter Faith Network[123] – and the lobbying has fallen on receptive ground. As early as 1991 the Conservative government established an Inner Cities Religious Council, with representatives of five major religious faiths, and a new Faiths Branch of the Department of the Environment; and the role of faith groups was strengthened under New Labour. A report for the Home Office Faith Communities Unit in 2004 observed that, 'Some areas of policy are now routinely recognised by Departments as requiring the input of the faith communities, for example as partners in urban regeneration', and it put forward recommendations 'designed to make [existing] processes even more effective across government'.[124] A Faith Community Capacity Building Fund was set up in 2005 explicitly to provide funding for faith-based groups.[125] There has also been funding at local level.

Before the London Muslim Centre was built there was a passionate two-year battle to secure the site beside the East London Mosque for Islamic use, against opposition from a private developer and more secular Muslim councillors. David Garbin and John Eade have pointed out that this marked a major shift from the prioritisation of cultural to religious identity, and they note that for the Mosque activists this 'demonstrated their strengthening position both within the community representation sphere and in the struggle for local resources'.[126]

By the time it came to the actual construction of the eight thousand square metre centre, the council were fully on board, and ready to advertise their involvement. Their website described the London Muslim Centre as 'the result of innovative joint working between the Council and its partners in the Tower Hamlets Partnership, the East London Mosque, the Greater London Authority and the European Development Fund', and portrayed it as 'promoting racial equality and community cohesion'.[127] The centre has an open door policy and is anxious to engage with non-Muslims; however, it has to be asked if giving the mosque such a pivotal role in civil society is really contributing to community cohesion, and this question concerns not just non-Muslims but also Bengalis who do not share Islamist Muslim beliefs. At the opening ceremony for the centre in 2004 the crowd of fifteen thousand spilled across the road outside,[128] and five years later the mosque embarked on a further large expansion. Mass fundraising has included a record-breaking £1¼ million pounds in a single night during Ramadan 2010.[129]

Besides their wide range of more general social functions, the East London Mosque and London Muslim Centre are used as a channel for the provision of public services by authorities ranging from the health service to the jobcentre. Between 2006 and 2011 this accounted for an average of £480,000 of public money each year.[130] From the perspective of the service providers, this gives them a route to a large section of the population. It also ties that population more closely to the Mosque. A visit from the imam as part of the Improving School Attendance Partnership may persuade families of the importance of getting their children to school,[131] but it also increases the authority of the Mosque as arbiter of all aspects of life. Similarly, drugs advice given by a fellow Muslim may hit home, but it can also present an Islamic lifestyle as the only valid alternative to drug dependency.[132] At the same time, youth groups and holiday projects run by enthusiastic young Islamists have received funding from the borough council and other secular bodies.[133] And Tower Hamlets Borough Council holds regular discussions with the local Council of Mosques, which it helped establish in 2001.

This is all in line with the observation in the Home Office document quoted above that 'Central Government is increasingly exploring ways of using the experience and resources of faith communities "on the ground" to deliver services';[134] and it encourages division along faith lines.

While expansion of the East London Mosque has been dramatic, mosques following other Islamic traditions have also grown and benefited from the official patronage of faith communities. In 2009 the Brick Lane streetscape acquired a new Islamic marker when the former Huguenot church that is now the Brick Lane Mosque built a controversial, council-funded, modern minaret.[135] More recently, Tower Hamlets' independent (ex-Labour) mayor, Lutfur Rahman, set aside three million pounds to be spent on improvements and repairs to faith buildings between 2012 and 2015. Of the first round of grants, totalling £595,000, £388,000 went to Muslim organisations and £140,000 to Christian ones.[136]

One of the more surreal examples of this faith-orientated policy was provided by Islamic Forum Europe's annual Community Fair in Mile End Park (supported by the borough council), which I attended in the summer of 2007. Alongside the usual roundabouts and ghost train were tents for Islamic exhibits and talks, stalls selling T-shirts with slogans such as 'Muslims do it 5 times a day', and a bookstall where my eye was caught by a small volume entitled *Women who Deserve to go to Hell*.[137] In line with equalities policy, a council employee was approaching members of the crowd with a questionnaire that asked whether they thought that the fair encouraged community mixing and included a question about the respondent's sexual orientation.

If government bodies want to work through faith organisations, this naturally raises questions about which groups they should work with. There have been many attempts to bring together different Islamic traditions into wider representative bodies, both locally and nationally. Tower Hamlets Council of Mosques is a relatively recent creation, but an important early example was provided by the Bradford Council of Mosques, founded in 1981 to cut across Muslim sectarianism and provide a vehicle for interaction with the public authorities on issues such as education. It received grant funding from Bradford City Council and (from 1983–88) its community workers were supported by central government.[138] Increasingly, attempts were also made to create a national organisation, especially following the mobilisation around *The Satanic Verses*. By the mid-1990s, Philip Lewis was able to observe that 'There is now a plethora of bodies presuming to speak for all British Muslims',[139] and – despite Bradford Council of Mosques' lead role in the book-burning – government took an active interest.

By the late 1990s, with the support of the Conservative Home Secretary, Michael Howard, the Muslim Council of Britain (MCB) had emerged as the most significant link between British Muslims and the British government.[140] The product of years of negotiations, it was officially inaugurated in 1997, six months after the election of the New Labour government, with whom it developed a strong working relationship. This umbrella group has brought an impressive number of Muslim organisations under its cover, but is by no means representative of all branches of Muslim opinion. However, unlike its critics – who were unhappy with the Islamist approach of the leadership and their links with groups such as Jamaat – the MCB proved a well-organised lobbyist. It seemed all set to take on a role similar to that of the Board of Deputies of British Jews.

9/11 – or, more specifically, British government reactions following 9/11 – threw developing relationships into a turmoil. Over the last decade, policy towards British Muslims has been characterised by confusion and deep contradictions, which have continued across the change of government. New Labour kept constructing and promoting new, less ostensibly political, organisations for government to do business with. The MCB, sidelined in 2006 but too important to be excluded, found themselves walking a difficult tightrope between not upsetting government and not alienating their own base. Their different roles of helping Islamic organisations and representing Muslims to the outside world can prove difficult to combine, and if the Council are thought to be bending their principles in any way so as to conform to government expectations, they lose support among the Muslim communities. Public statements are received very differently by young working-class Muslims and the mainstream press, and internet blogs from all viewpoints are ready to pick up and spread every possible innuendo.

The government's widely criticised Preventing Violent Extremism programme, introduced in 2007, talked about 'addressing the grievances that ideologues are exploiting';[141] however this was not reflected in government actions. They presided over growing inequality; they continued with a foreign policy that had been widely criticised for taking a neo-colonial approach and for bringing more problems to the areas in which they had intervened; and they introduced anti-terror laws that encroach on long-established civil liberties and that, because these are more often targeted at Muslims, encourage Muslim alienation from the political system – just as the old stop-and-search on suspicion, or 'sus' laws alienated a generation of young blacks. In addition, governments have generated a plethora of ill-thought-through experiments designed to promote an alternative 'moderate' Islamic movement and leadership. These interventions, based around an elusive search for 'proper' Islam, demonstrate a simplistic view of religion, and repel those they seek to reach. By blurring the distinction between multicultural policy and the prevention of terrorism, government schemes have managed to alienate both the Muslim communities they gave funds to and the non-Muslim communities who received nothing.[142]

Of course faith-group politics is not limited to government organisations: faith-based multiculturalism has found a firm place in community organisation too. Nowhere has this been more clear than in The East London Citizens'

Organisation (TELCO), a powerful alliance of community groups, established in 1996, that has been a pioneer of the communitarian model in Britain. TELCO has run some successful campaigns on social justice issues, and includes secular organisations such as trade unions, but it is predominantly made up of faith organisations – of which the East London Mosque is much the largest, followed by the Catholic churches. Because TELCO works through religious organisations rather than individuals, it strengthens their position in civil society.[143]

The political promotion of faith groups of all kinds, and the emphasis on people's religious affiliation, is helping to consolidate the power of religious organisations and foreground religious identity. The official argument that the incorporation of faith-based bodies contributes to 'social cohesion'[144] and that 'Muslim identity politics can support and encourage integration'[145] seems, at best, ingenuous, if not dangerously sophistic. Religious mobilisation may, indeed, encourage participation in the political process and many Islamist groups do encourage their followers to become exemplary members of civil society. However, they become involved first and foremost as Muslims, and this approach seems designed to perpetuate and institutionalise their religious difference.

Forces of conservatism

Apart from providing fertile soil for the seeds of future ethnic and religious tension, faith-based politics can hold back progress in reaching the radical solutions urgently needed to tackle fundamental social and economic problems. We have already seen how new forms of governance are being used to cut across progressive movements, and how governing elites deliberately promote more conservative religious groups as a counter to leftist organisations. The promotion of religious organisations is being used by neoliberal regimes as an important method of social control through a combination of encouraging social conservatism and strong hierarchical organisation, and through the old colonial practice of divide and rule.

The Islamist organisations themselves are deliberately drawing a generation away from seeking any other form of radical change. As Jamaat-e-Islami (Pakistan) put it in their website:

> [Jamaat's] greatest contribution lies in saving millions of Muslim Youth ... It has offered before them Islam as an alternative to the contemporary ideologies of secularism, liberalism, nationalism, capitalism, socialism and the like.[146]

Islamists believe that the ultimate ideal would be to live in a world governed by Islamic Law, and that 'so far, as the teachings of the Quran and the *sunnah* are concerned, they are eternally binding'.[147] While the great majority stress that the ideal of a Muslim state is to be achieved through democratic evolution and not bloody revolution, the complete Islamic society is the ideal to which their community and educational work is ultimately aimed. Their idealism, their

sincerity and their organisational skills are admirable and enviable. The contributions that they have made to social work and youth work are very real. But those
who do not believe that the route to a better society can be found through
Islamic Law and Islamic ethics and charity, and who do not share their ultimate
aim of an Islamic society, have reason to be concerned at this Islamic revival.

Notes

1 Tariq Ramadan, *Western Muslims and the Future of Islam* (Oxford: Oxford University
   Press, 2004), pp. 43–8.
2 Malise Ruthven, *Islam in the World* (Harmondsworth: Penguin, 1984).
3 Abul A'la Mawdudi, *Towards Understanding Islam* (Leicester: The Islamic Foundation,
   1981), pp. 96–7.
4 Sayyid Qutb, *Milestones* (1964), www.youngmuslims.ca/online_library, accessed 24
   March 2005.
5 See S. Sayyid, 'Beyond Westphalia: Nations and Diasporas – the Case of the Muslim
   Umma', in Barnor Hesse (ed.), *Un/Settled Multiculturalisms: Diasporas, Entanglements,
   'Transruptions'* (London: Zed Books, 2000), 33–50, p. 36.
6 Francis Robinson, 'Varieties of South Asian Islam', *CRER Research Paper*, no. 8
   (Warwick: CRER, 1988), p. 20.
7 IQra media, *Muslims & Politics*, DVD written and presented by Wakil Ahmed,
   directed and edited by Shofiquez Zaman (London, 2005).
8 This final speech was given by the British Iraqi, Anas Altakriti. The conference was
   organised by the Young Muslim Organisation, its female counterpart, Muslim Aat,
   and Islamic Forum Europe, and attracted around a thousand young Muslims.
9 Lead by Andrew Gilligan at the *Telegraph*, who also produced a TV documentary on
   these themes for Channels 4's *Dispatches*, broadcast 1 March 2010. (The transcript is
   available here: http://blogs.telegraph.co.uk/news/andrewgilligan/100060409
   /britains-islamic-republic-full-transcript-of-channel-4-dispatches-programme-on-
   lutfur-rahman-the-ife-and-tower-hamlets-the-full-transcript, accessed 20 November
   2012.)
10 Hizb ut-Tahrir, *Hizb ut-Tahrir* (London: Al-Khilafah Publications, 2000), p.1.
11 Hizb ut-Tahrir, *The Inevitability of the Clash of Civilisations* (London: Al-Khilafah
   Publications, 2002). The idea that Islam is intrinsically antipathetic to Western civilisation has been popularised in recent years by Bernard Lewis and Samuel
   Huntington and become an accepted view on the American right.
12 Hizb ut-Tahrir, 'Jihad in Islam' (2008), www.english.hizbuttahrir.org/images/
   pdfs/JihadinIslam2.pdf, accessed October 2012 .
13 Hizb ut-Tahrir, *Hizb ut-Tahrir*, p. 38.
14 Philip Lewis, *Islamic Britain: Religion, Politics and Identity Among British Muslims*
   (London: IB Tauris, 1994), p. 107. By the late 1970s the Islamic Youth Movement was
   in decline, but Bradford gave birth to another Jamaati youth organisation, Young
   Muslims UK, in 1984.
15 Abdur Razzaq Siddiqi, 'Reflections', in *YMO 8th Anniversary Souvenir* (1988), p. 12.
16 Ed Husain, *The Islamist: Why I Joined Radical Islam in Britain, What I Saw Inside and
   Why I Left* (London: Penguin, 2007), p. 166.
17 *East London Advertiser*, 22 May 1987; *Docklands Recorder*, 7 January 1988; *East London
   Advertiser*, 4 May 1990.
18 See Yunas Samad, 'Book Burning and Race Relations: Political Mobilisation of

Bradford Muslims', *New Community*, 18:4 (1992), 507–19, pp. 512–18; Yunas Samad, 'The Politics of Islamic Identity Among Bangladeshis and Pakistanis in Britain', in Terence Ranger, Yunas Samad and Ossie Stuart (eds), *Culture, Identity and Politics: Ethnic Minorities in Britain* (Aldershot: Avebury, 1996), 90–8, pp. 94–6.

19 See Samad, 'Book Burning and Race Relations', pp. 510–11; John Rex, *Ethnic Minorities in the Modern Nation State: Working Papers in the Theory of MultiCulturalism and Political Integration* (Basingstoke: Macmillan, 1996), p. 235.

20 Tariq Modood, 'British Asian Muslims and the Rushdie Affair', in James Donald and Ali Rattansi (eds), *'Race', Culture and Difference* (London: Sage, 1992), 260–77, p. 261.

21 *Ibid.*, pp. 270–1.

22 Kureshi, interviewed by *Newsweek*, 29 May 1995, quoted in Philip Lewis, *Young, British and Muslim* (London: Continuum, 2007), p. 129.

23 Kenan Malik, whose work is discussed in Chapter 10, provides a notable exception, but he spent formative years in left politics.

24 Sarah Glynn, 'Bengali Muslims: The New East End Radicals?', *Ethnic and Racial Studies*, 25:6 (2002), 969–88.

25 T. Choudhury, 'The Role of Muslim Identity Politics in Radicalisation', paper commissioned by the Department for Communities and Local Government, London (2007).

26 *Observer*, 17 June 2007.

27 Salma Yaqoob, a Muslim and anti-war activist in Birmingham, and at that time leader of Respect (see Chapter 9), told the BBC's *Panorama* in August 2005, 'Funding is always an issue and it has been tempting for groups to take up offers of foreign sponsorship. Invariably, money which comes from foreign governments, for example despotic regimes like Saudi Arabia, comes with strings attached (e.g. not to engage in criticism or politics).' See http://news.bbc.co.uk/1/hi/programmes/panorama/4172000.stm, accessed 1 November 2013.

28 Ali Riaz, *Islam and Identity Politics Among British-Bangladeshis: A Leap of Faith* (Manchester: Manchester University Press, 2013), p. 125. The Janomot articles he quotes were published in autumn 2006.

29 Ron Geaves, *Sectarian Influences Within Islam in Britain – With Reference to the Concepts of 'Ummah' and 'Community'* (Leeds: Department of Theology and Religious Studies University of Leeds, 1996), p. 223.

30 See Lewis, *Islamic Britain*, pp. 105–6.

31 Modood, 'British Asian Muslims and the Rushdie Affair' p. 268.

32 See *ibid.*, p. 271.

33 Riaz, *Islam and Identity Politics Among British-Bangladeshis*, p. 14.

34 While Ed Husain, as a former member of the Hizb, later described Bakri as 'charismatic' and 'pugnacious' (see *The Islamist*, p. 80), Jon Ronson's Channel 4 documentary, *Tottenham Ayatollah*, shown 8 April 1997, presented him as 'likeably clownish'. However Ronson never shared Bakri's undoubting faith, nor his conviction of the significance of what they were doing. Ronson observed that Bakri exhibited the 'optimism of the devout'. Had he felt that Bakri's optimism had any justification he would have found him rather less likeable. (Ronson's documentary was re-shown on 5 September 2005 under the title *Tottenham Ayatollah Revisited*.)

35 The split appears to be a result of disagreement over the relative importance of political activity in the West as opposed to the Arab world, where the central leadership wanted to focus resources.

36 www.hizb.org.uk/solutions/report-the-future-for-muslims-in-britain, accessed 10 October 2012.

37 Downloaded December 2000. The BBC reported on the popularity of Azzam.com in February 2002, see http://news.bbc.co.uk/1/hi/uk/1823045.stm, accessed 15 October 2012.

38 See Arun Kundnani, 'Islamism and the Roots of Liberal Rage', *Race and Class*, 50:2 (2008), 40–68, pp. 47–52.

39 For a critical analysis of the role of the Quilliam Foundation, see Sarah Glynn, 'Liberalising Islam: Creating Brits of the Islamic Persuasion', in Richard Phillips (ed.), *Muslim Spaces of Hope: Geographies of Possibility in Britain and the West* (London: Zed, 2009).

40 Husain, *The Islamist*, pp. 264 and 278.

41 Pragmatically, too, driving an ideology underground can encourage the development of violent protest. It is also unnecessary as we already have laws in place to deal with incitement to violence. Tony Blair proposed a ban on Hizb ut-Tahrir following the London bombings in 2005, but was ultimately dissuaded by the Home Office and police, who argued that a ban 'would serve only as a recruiting agent if the group appealed against the move'. See the *Observer*, 24 December 2006.

42 Slogan of the Muslim Brotherhood.

43 See Kenneth Leech, *Brick Lane 1978: The Events and their Significance* (London: Stepney Books Publications, 1994).

44 Hugo Pierre, 'Stopping the BNP in Tower Hamlets' (Youth against Racism in Europe website, undated), http://www.yre.org.uk/towerhamlets.html, accessed 9 October 2012. YRE was set up by Militant Labour, which became the Socialist Party.

45 www.guardian.co.uk/uk/2001/dec/15/race.world, accessed 9 October, 2012.

46 These figures are from the 2001 Census. The adjacent boroughs of Newham and Hackney had similar rates, but only six of the remaining thirty boroughs had rates exceeding 10 per cent. I have given male unemployment figures because these are the most significant for a community in which a large proportion of women still do not enter the labour force (see Chapter 1).

47 Kenan Malik, *From Fatwa to Jihad: The Rushdie Affair and its Legacy* (London: Atlantic Books, 2009), p. 27.

48 In the late 1990s the Islamist-run Brick Lane Youth Development Association even used the 'neutral ground' of the East London Mosque to hold a 'peace conference' between large and violent warring gangs. See quote from one of their social workers in Nick Ryan, 'Children of the Abyss' (*Telegraph*, 2005), www.nickryan.net/articles/abyss.html, accessed 28 July 2011. Ryan has interviewed several Bengali ex-gang members and drug dealers over the years. Some 'reverted' to Islam in prison, though going straight didn't always last. See also, Nick Ryan, 'Soldiers of God' (*Esquire*, 2009), www.nickryan.net/aticles/soldiersofgod.html, accessed 28 July 2011.

49 Malik, *From Fatwa to Jihad*, p. 22.

50 Husain, *The Islamist*.

51 Interview with a Jamaat member working at Islamic Forum Europe, 25 February 2001; Jamaat-e-Islami (Pakistan) website, www.jamaat.org, downloaded February 2001.

52 Husain, *The Islamist*, p. 33.

53 *Ibid.*, pp. 56 and 65.

54 A woman who had been a teacher in the college at that time told me that the experience had resulted in her having a breakdown.

55 Husain, *The Islamist*, p. 54.

56 *Jamiat Ihyaa Minhaaj al-Sunnah*: Movement for the Revival of the Prophet's Way.

57 Husain, *The Islamist*, p. 95.

58 *Ibid.*, p. 120.

59 *Ibid.*, pp. 137 and 136.
60 Nawaz was later to become a co-founder of the Quilliam Foundation.
61 Husain, *The Islamist*, p. 141.
62 *Ibid.*, p. 146.
63 Pseudonym, interviewed 10 February 2001.
64 This was a weekly meeting held in Eton Road Community Centre on 11 January 2002. All those who came were young – most seemed to be in their early twenties – and most were Asian. There was a small group of women and children sitting (or playing) separately at the back.
65 Interviewed 12 June 2000. He gave a similar description to the Special [i.e. *halal*] Fried Chicken outlets where the boys liked to hang out. The organisers of the BLYDA have links with the East London Mosque.
66 Interviewed 28 July 2000.
67 Pseudonym, interviewed 29 November 2000.
68 Interviewed 5 July 2000.
69 Interview with youth worker, June 1999; and see Claire Alexander, '(Dis)Entangling the 'Asian Gang': Ethnicity, Identity, Masculinity', in Barnor Hesse (ed.) *Un/Settled Multiculturalisms: Diasporas, Entanglements, 'Transruptions'* (London: Zed Books, 2000), p. 142.
70 *Insight* editorial, September/October 2001.
71 Pseudonym, interviewed 16 January 2001.
72 Interviewed 5 July 2000.
73 Pseudonym, interviewed 29 November 2000.
74 Pseudonym, interviewed 29 November 2000.
75 Regional convention on 'Muslim priorities in the West', Saturday 11 August 2001.
76 Mawdudi, *Towards Understanding Islam*, p. 109.
77 This is not practised in Bangladesh but is common among Somalis.
78 Mawdudi, *Towards Understanding Islam*, p. 109.
79 Interviewed 5 July 2000.
80 Conversation after the showing of the *Muslims & Politics* documentary in Queen Mary University of London, 23 April 2005.
81 This lobby by Madani Girls' School took place on 25 September 2000. In 2008 Madani finally purchased a different disused school building from the council, leading to well-publicised claims that the Labour council had agreed the sale at below market price. See www.telegraph.co.uk/education/education-news/8038820/British-schools-where-girls-must-wear-the-Islamic-veil.html, accessed 10 October 2012.
82 Interviewed 20 Sept 2001.
83 Interviewed 29 Nov 2001.
84 Junaid Ahmed, interviewed 29 Nov 2001.
85 YMO Ramadan Message, 'Ramadan – in the midst of global darkness', www.ymouk.com/publications/prints/ramadan.htm, accessed 25 November 2001.
86 MCB press release, 'Islamic values are our guide – Statement of British Imams and Scholars', 7 October 2001.
87 Junaid Ahmed, interviewed 20 September 2001.
88 *Insight*, November/December 2001.
89 'Implicating the Muslims in this incident was part of a long term Jewish conspiracy', Qazi Hussain Ahmad, quoted on Jamaat-e-Islami (Pakistan) website, www.jamaat.org, 15 September 2001.
90 Riaz, *Islam and Identity Politics Among British-Bangladeshis*, pp. 55–8. Riaz also gives an

indication of the subjects of some of his speeches, see pp. 54–6. Nirmal Committee publications document incidents of violence against anti-Sayeedi protestors.

91 Nirmul Committee, *Public Informer: Defenders of Bangladesh*, issue 13 (1999).

92 David Bergman (director and researcher), *War Crimes File*, television documentary (Twenty Twenty Television, shown on Channel 4 *Dispatches*, 3 May 1995). The producers hoped that it would persuade the British authorities to try the men in Britain.

93 Stephen Barton, *The Bengali Muslims of Bradford: A Study of their Observance of Islam with Special Reference to the Function of the Mosque and the Work of the Imam* (Leeds: Department of Theology and Religious Studies, University of Leeds, 1986), p. 71.

94 Interviewed 29 November 2001.

95 Pseudonym, interviewed 29 November 2000.

96 Nirmul Committee, *Public Informer*, 13.

97 Tensions between Islamists and secularists were explored by Eade *et al.*, who used the concepts of 'imagined communities' and the 'Islamisation of space' to look at conflicts over the Baishakhi Mela – which celebrates the secular Bengali New Year – and over the development of the London Muslim Centre. See John Eade, Isabelle Fremeaux and David Garbin, 'The Political Construction of Diasporic Communities in the Global City', in P Gilbert (ed.), *Imagined London* (Albany: SUNY Press, 2001), and John Eade and David Garbin, 'Changing Narratives of Violence, Struggle and Resistance: Bangladeshis and the Competition for Resources in the Global City', *Oxford Development Studies*, 30:2 (2002). However, they never question the desirability of identity politics, preferring simply to celebrate 'the resistance of these imagined communities to the corrosive force of national assimilation', see Eade *et al.*, 'The Political Construction of Diasporic Communities in the Global City'.

98 Pseudonym, interviewed 20 July 2000.

99 See Nira Yuval-Davis, 'Fundamentalism, Multiculturalism and Women in Britain', in James Donald and Ali Rattansi (eds), *'Race', Culture and Difference* (London: Sage, 1992), 278–91, p. 289; Claire Dwyer, 'Contradictions of Community: Questions of Identity for Young British Muslim Women', *Environment and Planning A*, 31 (1999), 53–68, pp. 63 and 65.

100 Interviewed on 24 July 2007. The police cadet told me she had not experienced racism in the police force.

101 www.eastlondonmosque.org.uk; www.islamicforumeurope.com, accessed 30 June 2006.

102 *ELM News*, October 2005.

103 The Indigent Moslems Burial Fund (whose trust deed is dated 1927) was run from the East London Mosque, and the current funeral business behind the mosque was established in 1950 by Taslim Ali and his Welsh wife. The business is now run by their son and granddaughter. See *Express*, 29 December 1967; Rosie Dastigir, 'Gulam Talsim, Funeral Director', *Spitalfields Life*, 8 January 2013, http://spitalfieldslife.com/2013/01/08/gulam-taslim-funeral-director, accessed 12 November 2013.

104 Westminster (which has a slightly smaller population than Tower Hamlets) also had the worst figures for incidents of racist and religious hate. See www.met.police.uk/crimefigures/index.php, accessed 13 October 2012. See, also, the East London Mosque's refutation of Gilligan's homophobia stories: www.eastlondonmosque.org.uk/archive/news/328, accessed 13 October 2012 .

105 Ansar Ahmed Ullah, interviewed 14 November 2000.

106 *Ibid.*

107 Sunahwar Ali, interviewed 23 January 2001.

108 See interview with Ansar Ahmed Ullah, 14 November 2000; Sarah Glynn, 'The Spirit of '71 – How the Bangladeshi War of Independence has Haunted Tower Hamlets', *Socialist History Journal,* 29 (2006), 56–75.

109 *Economist,* 10 August 2013.

110 Bar Human Rights Committee of England and Wales, 'Statement', 4 March 2013; Human Rights Watch, 'Bangladesh: Stop Harassment of Defense at War Tribunal', 2 November 2011, www.hrw.org/news/2011/11/02/bangladesh-stop-harassment-defense-war-tribunal, accessed 19 October 2013; Human Rights Watch, 'Bangladesh: Azam Conviction Based on Flawed Proceedings' 16 August 2013, www.hrw.org/news/2013/08/16/bangladesh-azam-conviction-based-flawed-proceedings, accessed 19, October 2013; *Economist,* 19 November 2012, 15 December 2012, and 23 March 2013. David Bergman, who made the War Crimes documentary shown on Channel 4, has summed up the situation and his frustration with those who would overlook the attempts to bypass due process: 'I am and have been a supporter of war crimes accountability and understand resentment of years of impunity … but I also think it is important to consider the actual process of accountability in the tribunals, which do raise very serious questions indeed.' See David Bergman, 'My response to Tahmina Anam's article on "Shahbag", 1971 war crimes trials in Bangladesh, and demands for hangings', *Bangladesh Chronicle,* 15 February 2013, www.bangladeshchronicle.net/index.php/2013/02/my-response-to-tahmina-anams-article-on-shahbag-1971-war-crimes-trials-in-bangladesh-and-demands-for-hangings, accessed 12 November 2013..

111 David Lewis, 'The Paradoxes of Bangladesh's Shahbag Protests', 21 March 2013, http://blogs.lse.ac.uk/indiaatlse/2013/03/21/the-paradoxes-of-bangladeshs-shahbag-protests, accessed 19 October 2013.

112 Human Rights Watch, 'Blood on the Streets: The Use of Excessive Force During Bangladesh Protests', August 2013, pp. 12–19, www.hrw.org/reports/2013/08/01/blood-streets, accessed 3 March 2014.

113 Toufique Imrose Khalidi, 'Behind the Rise of Bangladesh's Hifazat', *Al Jazeera,* 9 May 2013, www.aljazeera.com/indepth/features/2013/05/201356134629980318.html, accessed 19 October 2013.

114 See the Hifazat's 13 demands, www.thehindu.com/todays-paper/tp-national/the-13point-demands/article4590494.ece, accessed 19 October 2013.

115 Human Rights Watch, 'Blood on the Streets', p. 23.

116 I witnessed this demonstration on 27 August 2013 and spoke to the protestors afterwards.

117 A '*nastik*' list was posted on Facebook.

118 Protestors have kept a list of incidents. The attack in Greatorex Street is described in the *Docklands and East London Advertiser,* 2 July 2013.

119 Speech given to a protest demonstration on 5 May 2013.

120 6 March 2013.

121 The significance of these new forms of governance for the growth of local faith-based community organisations has also been explored in Les Back, Michael Keith, Azra Khan, Kalbir Shukra and John Solomos, 'Islam and the New Political Landscape: Faith Communities, Political Participation and Social Change', *Theory, Culture & Society,* 26 (2009), 1–23. Back *et al.* argue that, while many of those involved may regard such organisations – which coexist with transnational Islamic politics – as alternatives to mainstream politics, they must be considered an important form of political participation. However, they do not attempt to investigate the impact of this form of politics either on democracy or on the 'communities' involved.

122 Rowan Williams, then Archbishop of Canterbury, put forward his ideas in a Lecture at the Royal Courts of Justice on 7 February 2008, entitled 'Civil and Religious Law in England: A Religious Perspective', see www.archbishopofcanterbury.org/1575, accessed March 2008.

123 Interfaith Network for the United Kingdom, *20 Years: Milestones on the Journey Together Towards Greater Inter Faith Understanding and Cooperation* (London: The Interfaith Network for the UK, 2007).

124 Home Office, *Working Together: Co-operation Between Government and Faith Communities* (London: Home Office, 2004), p. 8.

125 Riaz, *Islam and Identity Politics Among British-Bangladeshis*, p. 156.

126 Eade and Garbin, 'Changing Narratives of Violence, Struggle and Resistance'. See also David Garbin, 'Immigration, Territoires et Identités: Enquète dans un quartier de l'East End de Londres' (DEA Dissertation, University of Tours and University of East London, 1999).

127 www.towerhamlets.gov.uk, accessed 2006.

128 *East London Advertiser*, 17 Jun 2004.

129 www.eastlondonmosque.org.uk/news/270, accessed 21 November 2012.

130 Data from reports filed with the Charity Commission, published on line at http://hurryupharry.org/wp-content/uploads/2012/02/Public-funding-of-the-East-London-Mosque-to-2011.pdf, accessed 21 November 2012.

131 *Guardian*, 6 Aug 2002; www.eastlondonmosque.org.uk, accessed 2006.

132 www.eastlondonmosque.org.uk, accessed 2006.

133 Brick Lane Youth Development Association Bi-Annual Report, 2002/4; Interview with Shazid Miah, president of the YMO, August 2004.

134 Home Office, *Working Together*, p. 8.

135 Earlier controversy about the impact of even a detached minaret on this historic building was compounded by concerns over the decision to use public funds, and by the (aborted) proposals to erect arches to Brick Lane that were reminiscent of *hijabs*. See Anne J. Kershen, *Strangers, Aliens and Asians: Huguenots, Jews and Bangladeshis in Spitalfields 1660–2000* (Abingdon: Routledge, 2005), p. 107; Audrey Gillan, 'Brick Lane Plan for Hijab Gates Angers Residents', *Guardian*, 15 February 2010.

136 http://moderngov.towerhamlets.gov.uk/documents/s45861/0032%20-%20Community%20Faith%20Buildings%20Support%20Scheme%202012-2015%20Round%201.pdf, accessed 2 November 2013; www.towerhamlets.gov.uk/lgsl/601-650/646_faith_buildings_grant.aspx, accessed 2 November 2013.

137 Mansoor Abul Hakim (trans. Rafiq Abdur Rahman), *Women who Deserve to go to Hell* (Karachi: Darul Ishaat, 2004). Reasons given for a woman to go to hell (which is described in gruesome detail) include grumbling, quarrelsomeness, disobedience towards her husband, and cutting her hair short. When I asked the polite stall holder if I deserved to go to hell, she replied that she was sure not, and no-one could say who would go as it was up to Allah.

138 Lewis, *Islamic Britain*.

139 *Ibid*., p. 207.

140 Hansard, 19 July 2007 Col 169WH, http://www.publications.parliament.uk/pa/cm200607/cmhansrd/cm070719/halltext/70719h0006.htm, accessed 12 November 2013. Mr Goodman observes: 'The Muslim Council of Britain was, for a long period, the main Muslim partner of Conservative and Labour Governments. The legend is, and I have no reason to doubt it, that the MCB was partly put together by my right hon. and learned Friend the Member for Folkestone and Hythe (Mr. Howard) when he was the Home Secretary.'

141 HM Government, *The Prevent Strategy: A Guide for Local Partners in England* (London: HMSO, 2008), p. 6.

142 For more on the government's relationship with British Muslims, see Sarah Glynn, 'Liberalising Islam'.

143 Lina Jamoul and Jane Wills, 'Faith in Politics', *Urban Studies,* 45:10 (2008), 2035–56. Both authors had high-profile roles in TELCO. They celebrate and promote this political and civic involvement through religious organisation and seem happy to accept that it strengthens the power of the institutions involved. The unquestioning welcoming of faith-based organisation in general, and TELCO in particular, is shared by John Eade and Halima Begum, who claim that TELCO provides an example of 'faith acting as social glue for organising around social justice initiatives'. See Halima Begum and John Eade, 'All Quiet on the Eastern Front? Bangladeshi Reactions in Tower Hamlets', in Tahir Abbas (ed.), *Muslim Britain: Communities Under Pressure* (London and New York: Zed Books, 2005), 179–93, p. 187. Begum and Eade's account, which is short of both empirical evidence and critical analysis, also presents an extraordinarily sanguine view of Tower Hamlets' politics, claiming that 'the overall embedded community structure within a mainstream regeneration regime prevents the alienation of young Bangladeshi Muslims from finding a home in Islamic extremism', see p. 193.

144 Home Office, *Working Together,* p. 3.

145 Choudhury, 'The Role of Muslim Identity Politics in Radicalisation', p. 5.

146 Jamaat-e-Islami (Pakistan) website, www.jamaat.org, accessed February 2001.

147 *Ibid.*

9   The Respect experiment

We have seen how, for many young Muslims, political Islam, or Islamism, has become the new opposition to capitalist materialism, attracting a generation away from seeking secular solutions through socialism, as well as from the leftist-derived New Social Movements. This chapter looks at how some socialists, predominantly in the Socialist Workers' Party (SWP), have tried to rebuild links with young Muslims through an unlikely political alliance that attempted to bring together two completely separate ideologies in what was tantamount to a single political party. This experiment in popular front politics (a politics whose dangers, from a left perspective, were examined in Chapter 2) was brought into being by the protests against Britain's involvement in the wars against the Taliban in Afghanistan and then against Saddam Hussein's Iraq. It was a product of a weak left that was seeking new allies, and a growing Islamist movement who no longer saw the left as a threat and was ready to accept a tactical alliance against joint enemies.

Respect was able to achieve a brief flowering on the back of the double failure of what is still referred to as the mainstream left. The Labour Party, remoulded and not simply rebranded as New Labour, had failed to bring the long-awaited fairer society, abandoning its core supporters along with its socialist policies. And it had taken the country to war in Iraq against massive popular opposition and on grounds that were increasingly being questioned. New Labour's failures were felt especially strongly in Tower Hamlets. Not only had the Labour government presided over continued social deprivation in the shadow of the booming centre of finance capital, but both local MPs had supported the war in Iraq, and members of the local Labour Party were facing charges of corruption involving the misappropriation of large amounts of regeneration money. The earlier generation of secular Muslim activists who had chosen to work through the Labour Party were regarded as compromised by their association with an authoritarian and increasingly unpopular government and a discredited local administration. The Labour council failed to win back support when, despite declaring themselves officially anti-war, they took no active role in the anti-war movement. The council leader, Helal Abbas, excused this to me on the grounds that, as a Muslim-dominated group, it would have left them open to negative media stereotyping.[1]

Part of the anti-war movement

The reaction to 9/11 by the United States and its allies accelerated Muslim politicisation and gave a new urgency to anti-capitalist and anti-imperialist movements everywhere. Many Muslims had been unhappy about the previous Gulf War. This time there was no mitigating invasion of Kuwait, and there was a widespread groundswell of discontent and of organisation against the war. Muslims who might have stayed away from political involvement in the past were encouraged to take their part in the wider movement and to add their voices to protests against what many saw as an attack on their Muslim brothers and sisters. Across the UK, Muslim groups mobilised and Muslims took part in public demonstrations in numbers out of all proportion to their share of the population.

From September 2002, the major London protests against Britain's involvement in the war in Afghanistan and then in Iraq were organised by a partnership of the Stop the War Coalition – dominated by the SWP – and the Muslim Association of Britain (MAB).[2] The well-organised MAB, which took on the role of co-ordinating Muslim participation in the anti-war movement, is an Islamist organisation affiliated to the Muslim Brotherhood[3] and one of the many groups under the Muslim Council of Britain umbrella – though few of the thousands of Muslims from many different traditions who participated in the anti-war movement were themselves members of the Association. Richard Phillips has recounted how the MAB rejected the Stop the War Coalition's invitations to affiliate, and opted instead for a partnership of equals;[4] an astute political move that allowed them to avoid assimilation into a left-led organisation and gave them a strong voice in key decisions, such as who should speak at the mass public rallies.

Left activists were glad to share platforms with a minority community that was represented disproportionately in lower socio-economic groups and that was under attack from an increasingly Islamophobic right wing. During the 1999 war in Kosovo, the left had also opposed British government intervention, which on that occasion had been on the same side as Muslim fighters. This provided a source of occasional confusion; but it was quickly forgotten.

In fighting alongside those whom society has oppressed, socialists have often found themselves shoulder to shoulder with Muslims. That they should have found themselves on the same anti-war platforms and that, as the two most active organised groups, they should have developed a joint leadership structure, is not surprising. What seems to many to be rather less logical is that alliance over one issue – even one as important as war – should be enough to form the basis of a political coalition, especially given the ideological barriers to such a union. This chapter analyses the history of this experiment, and shows that many of its failures had their roots in a marriage that was based on opportunism rather than on a shared vision for the future. It then steps back from the immediacy of events on the ground, with their own compelling logic, to look at the fundamental differences between the two underlying ideologies, and to ask whether these made failure inevitable. This is not a new question. There have been numerous attempts to bring together Muslim and leftist groups, and as many failures. But the fact that attempts continue to be made makes it important to look again at both the underlying issues and at their manifestation in a well-documented example.

The rise of the Respect Coalition

The catalyst that turned a tactical combination of Muslims and leftists into (effectively) a new political party was George Galloway, who would be elected Respect MP for Bethnal Green and Bow in the May 2005 general election, after a bitter, closely fought and high-profile campaign. A long-standing left Labour rebel with a passionate interest in the Middle East and a gift for oratory, Galloway was a leading figure in the Stop the War Coalition, and while the Labour Party prepared for his expulsion he was already discussing plans for a new organisation.[5] For Galloway, Respect provided a new political platform. For the SWP, the inclusion of a well-known MP with no links to themselves made the organisation appear broader and much more electable. As the biggest organisation on the British far left, the SWP had previously ventured into electoral politics under the banner of the Socialist Alliance, a left alternative to New Labour launched before the 2001 election. However, this had already been allowed to peter out, with the SWP demonstrating an unwillingness to allow the growth of anything that it could not control and so stifling initiatives that came from outwith their organisation and excluding other leftists from playing any significant role.[6]

Respect: the Unity Coalition was launched in January 2004. Its '"postmodern" name ... invented by an eight-year-old'[7] officially stands for respecting equality, socialism, peace, the environment, community and trade unionism.

In its determination to be inclusive – and despite that 'S' – Respect was only minimally socialist. Furthermore, Galloway explained, 'we don't bind a Muslim candidate ... to the explicitly socialist parts of our programme'.[8] The dilution of socialist values was resisted by many Respect members, but the SWP committed themselves to popular frontism and consistently used their majority to ensure that this line was adopted, even to the extent of alienating a large section of their own membership.[9] The launch conference was told that they could not be 'more socialist' because they wanted to 'reach out' to Britain's large Muslim communities. After pushing through Respect's very minimal programme, the National Secretary explained:

We … voted against the things we believed in, because, while the people here are important, they are not as important as the millions out there. We are reaching to the people locked out of politics. We voted for what *they* want.[10]

The SWP was trying to appeal to a Muslim constituency, but what was the role of their anti-war partners, the MAB? Were they even part of the new coalition? George Galloway told me when I interviewed him in January 2005,

They are fully part. They have two members on our national council, specially delegated by them, to sit as full members … And two other of their prominent activists are on our national council in their own right … as individuals elected at the meeting … [S]ince our annual meeting, which took place a month or two ago, they have concretised their relations with us.[11]

However, Azam Tamimi, then official spokesperson for the MAB, had made clear to me two days earlier that council membership did not in fact equate with full support. The MAB position, as he explained it, is that shown by the majority of Islamists who engage with secular politics:

Our choice in the Muslim Association of Britain is not to give our 100 per cent support for a single party. It's going to be constituency per constituency, person per person. And therefore, it's not a question of agreeing fully, or disagreeing fully, it's a question of where we see eye to eye on about three or four major issues … But, we're not going to talk about all the other things that we would love to see in the world as Muslims, because that is unrealistic.[12]

While the MAB were fully behind Galloway in the 2005 general election, they supported Labour's Ken Livingston in the 2004 London mayoral election, and Anas Altikriti resigned the presidency of the MAB in order to stand as an individual under the Respect banner for the 2004 European parliamentary elections, held the same day. The semi-detached nature of the main Muslim organisational group did not, however, prevent Respect from putting a Muslim in first or second place on all their Euro-election slates.[13]

Winning elections

Respect did not win any seats in those elections, but in Tower Hamlets they took more votes than any other party; and it was here, seven weeks later, that they had their first election victory. Oliur Rahman, a twenty-three-year-old Bengali, was elected councillor in the St Dunstan's by-election following the dismissal of Labour's Nasir Uddin for corruption.[14] It was on the basis of a series of promising electoral results that Respect decided to concentrate a high proportion of its efforts for the 2005 general election on East London, and especially on Galloway's battle with Oona King for the formerly safe Labour seat of Bethnal Green and Bow.

King, along with Jim Fitzpatrick in the other Tower Hamlets constituency of Poplar and Canning Town, had voted in favour of the war. She was regarded as a New Labour loyalist and her original selection had been resented by many Bengalis who had hoped that a Bengali would be chosen. What is more, Respect estimated that the electorate of Bethnal Green and Bow was 55 per cent Bengali Muslim.

Leaflets distributed outside the mosques for Galloway's earlier European election campaign had described Respect as 'the Party for Muslims'; and now, although Respect was promoting some traditional left issues – especially concerning housing – debate focused on the 'Muslim vote'. When I interviewed Galloway three-and -a-half months before the general election,[15] he was anxious to make clear that Respect also had wide non-Muslim support, but he told me that he expected a 'very good percentage' of his vote to come from the Muslim community. He explained, 'We are not only not embarrassed about being seen by Muslims in Britain as a champion of their interests, we are exceedingly proud of that'. Galloway is a Scot of Irish Catholic descent, but he refuses to discuss his religious beliefs and there has been well publicised speculation that he has converted to Islam.[16] (His election leaflets for the Bradford West by-election, which he won in March 2012, even portrayed him, albeit ambiguously, as a better Muslim than his Pakistani opponent.[17]) In the 2005 election, as noted in Chapter 7, he also appealed explicitly to a Bengali ethnic vote by claiming (correctly) that voting for him was the best way to get Oona King out and prepare the ground for a Bengali next time, and his election campaign included a visit to Bangladesh.

When campaigning in the predominantly white end of the constituency, Galloway was careful to stress his old-Labour values, but his most active local helpers were young Bengali men and his main support was always going to come from the Bengalis. The Iraq war was Respect's main campaigning issue and was portrayed as an anti-Islamic war. Galloway told a packed public hustings, 'If you make war against Muslims abroad, you are going to end up making war against Muslims at home'.[18] In portraying the war as a crusade, Galloway ignored most serious left analysis, which saw it in terms of wider economic and political strategies.

Oona King insisted that she was 'working for the whole community' in contrast to Galloway's 'single-issue campaigning',[19] but Labour responded to the challenge from Respect by going out of their way to demonstrate their own support for Muslim interests. A *defeated* motion at the Respect national conference in the autumn of 2004, calling for an end to state subsidies for faith schools, prompted a press release from Tower Hamlets Labour Group in which Oona King not only boasted of the government's support for state-funded Islamic schools and other pro-Muslim legislation, but branded Respect 'an enemy of religion'.[20] And the following month she was publicly chastised in the local paper for sending out Eid cards to non-Muslims by mistake.[21] Helal Abbas told me that his Labour council did a lot of work with local mosques during the Iraq war,[22]

Figure 9.1 George Galloway celebrates his election victory, 2005 (Guy Smallman)

and during the election campaign Labour leaflets were worded differently for distribution in Muslim areas, allowing their opponents to draw attention to the inconsistencies.[23]

After a high-drama campaign, Galloway was elected as Respect's only MP. Salma Yaqoob managed a close second for Respect in Birmingham Sparkbrook and Small Heath, where the 2001 Census had recorded that the population was over 50 per cent of Pakistani or Bangladeshi origin.

One of the results of all this was that many among the white working class felt increasingly excluded. During the election campaign, both Oona King and the Labour council became the target of angry letters to the local paper by white constituents drawing on a legacy of them-and-us politics. This one is from a Mrs King of Poplar (no relation):

> I see more and more people writing in to say how badly the real East Enders are treated in Tower Hamlets … People born and bred in the East End who went through a war like me are forgotten. The real East Enders come out as second class. What do we expect when Tower Hamlets council offices are run for foreigners. Let's have fairness, treat all people the same – not foreigners first![24]

There were many letters after the election critical of Galloway, often along similar lines to this one from Janet Parker:

> Perhaps if he spent less time travelling around the world talking about Iraq, and more time in his constituency – if he can remember where it is – he might realise there is

more to the East End than Brick Lane. The man's a 'one trick' pony and his party is only interested in votes from one community. As for the rest of us, it seems we're on our own now.[25]

Although Respect have campaigned on key social issues – especially against the transfer of council housing to housing associations – they have failed to persuade a section of white voters that they are more than an ethnically based or single-issue party. They had high hopes for the local council elections in May 2006 but, despite a hugely unpopular Labour council and chaos among the Liberal Democrats, the only Respect candidates elected were twelve Bengalis, and there was a strong correlation between the percentage of votes cast for Respect in each ward and the percentage of Bengalis in the population.[26]

The fall of Respect

Labour was still in control of the council, but Respect's new prominence as the main opposition group had made it a focus for the same sort of pragmatic, community-based politics that had previously concentrated on the Labour Party. The MAB and other Muslim organisations had proved too politically astute and too pragmatic to tie themselves to a small and volatile opposition movement;[27] however, Respect attracted large numbers of individuals and families who identified themselves politically as Muslims, and those who came to the fore were often people who, through their business and family connections, were regarded locally as 'community leaders'. Among Bengali activists and small businessmen, Respect began to be perceived as a possible new route for community uplift and personal ambition. This essentially pragmatic approach recognised shared interests, but not necessarily shared values, and was very similar to how a previous generation had regarded the local Labour Party. There were defections both from and to Labour and traditional community networks that had previously been used by Labour were activated in support of Respect candidates. The organisation also attracted the familiar problem of mass-membership applications as wealthy and ambitious members enrolled and paid for their own supporters – though there were protests when personal vote banks meant that the SWP's preferred nominees lost out in selections of candidates or officers.[28] After one of the new Respect councillors had resigned his position and poured venom on the organisation in the local press, I asked a Respect activist who was campaigning in the consequent by-election how the councillor had been selected in the first place. I was told, without a hint of concern, that he was well connected and could deliver a lot of votes.[29]

While the fate of the Socialist Alliance should make us wary of laying all blame for the eventual collapse of Respect on its reliance on a broad coalition, such a collection of different interests was inherently unstable. The coalition came together because its various elements needed each other. When their leaders began to doubt that need, it soon and messily fell apart. Galloway felt that the SWP was holding back the development of Respect through a less than full commitment to the project, and Peter Manson claimed in the *Weekly Worker* that the SWP had provoked the split because the coalition was 'costing it members',

> And, far from being able to ride on the backs of (mainly muslim) 'community leaders' and businessmen into the council chambers, the opposite was the case. While the SWP provided the foot soldiers, it was the businessmen and their patriarchal networks that reaped the benefit.[30]

Galloway expressed his concerns over Respect's organisational failures in a long letter to National Committee members at the end of August 2007, setting off weeks of increasingly acrimonious exchanges.[31] That October, after some particularly stormy local meetings, the four Tower Hamlets councillors who had been most closely associated with the SWP resigned the Respect whip. The following week Galloway retaliated by changing the locks on Respect's national office and by mid-November remaining supporters could choose between two rival Respect conferences-cum-rallies. 2008 saw Galloway's residual Respect group reduced to just six councillors. Of the four breakaway councillors, who were facing certain defeat at the next election, Ahmed Hussain moved straight to the Tories in February, despite having signed up to the SWP, and in July Lutfa Begum — who had also become an SWP member — her daughter Rania Kahn and Oliur Rahman all joined Labour, with the first two putting their names to statements that the local paper dismissed as 'Labour spin'.[32]

When it came to selecting candidates for the 2010 general election, Galloway left Bethnal Green and Bow to Respect's leader in the council, Abjol Miah, and stood instead for Tower Hamlets' other constituency, now redrawn as Poplar and Limehouse. Despite an energetic campaign, both Respect candidates came only third in their constituencies, with around 17 per cent of the vote. Bethnal Green and Bow was easily regained by Labour, with Rushanra Ali winning a 43 per cent share. Within the council, the 2010 elections reduced Respect to a single councillor, a man first elected as a political ingénue in the 2007 by-election on the strength of his position as a popular local shopkeeper.[33] However, a ghost of Respect has re-emerged in the independent group of councillors — including the three ex-Respect councillors above — who were expelled from Labour in September 2010.[34] The reason for their expulsion was that they continued to support the local party's choice of candidate for the new post of elected mayor of Tower Hamlets after he had been deselected by Labour's National Executive Committee and had declared that he would stand as an independent. Despite the accusations of Islamist infiltration and countering socialist rhetoric in which this dispute has been dressed, personal ambition and bureaucratic heavy handedness seem to have played a substantial part.[35] Lutfur Rahman, the deselected candidate, was accused by Helal Abbas, who originally lost out to Rahman but was then imposed in his place, of being involved in

Islamic Forum Europe, which Abbas described as 'a fundamentalist organisation which is gradually infiltrating the Labour Party'.[36] Whilst the theme of Islamist 'infiltration' has been pursued relentlessly by the journalist Andrew Gilligan, New Labour had previously openly worked with and encouraged Islamist Jamaat organisations, as they had done with other faith groups. Indeed the London Muslim Centre had worked as a 'partner organisation' with the council when Abbas was council leader, and he told me when I interviewed him in August 2004 that they were proud to be associated with it. Respect had campaigned actively for the creation of the post of mayor but, when it came to the mayoral election, they did not put up their own candidate. Instead they gave their backing to Rahman, who was elected on 21 October 2010 with a large majority on a very low turnout.

When George Galloway confounded the political pundits and was returned to parliament at the Bradford West by-election in 2012, he was able to embody the hopes of voters disillusioned with the neoliberal politics of the mainstream parties and with the community politicking of Bradford Labour Party's Pakistani-dominated election machine. But this revival of Respect's fortunes was built on shaky foundations. There was little established activist base; Galloway's ill-judged comments on rape in association with the Julian Assange case have since lost him support and, significantly, prompted the resignation of Respect's widely admired national leader, Salma Yaqoob.[37] After Galloway announced he was thinking of leaving Bradford and standing for London mayor, the city's five Respect councillors who had been elected in the wake of the by-election all left the party.[38]

Hopes and beliefs

Many of those who rose to a brief prominence through Respect had little previous political experience and, for most, the business of organising and campaigning – and perhaps later reading council minutes – took priority over political theory. Respect members were encouraged to come to talks at the SWP's annual 'Marxism' week, but when I interviewed Galloway in 2005 he admitted that they were too preoccupied with elections to give proper attention to the political education of new members.[39] For a large number of Respect activists, as well as Respect voters, the coalition was simply regarded as another vehicle for pursuing the many needs of an underprivileged community in a poor borough and a continuation of the anti-war movement. However some have attempted to engage with more fundamental issues concerning the underlying aims of their political experiment.

The two principal players among the Tower Hamlets Respect (and former Respect) councillors were seen as belonging to opposing factions, but an examination of what they have in common can help throw light on the organisation. Oliur Rahman and group leader Abjol Miah are both young and had little political experience before joining the anti-war movement. Both had community-based employment, Rahman in a job centre and Miah as a youth worker, and both stress their connections outwith the Bengali community. Rahman is careful to emphasise his trade-union credentials (he was branch chair of his union), while Miah is a graduate of strikes and fights against school racism and had previous organisational involvement with the Young Muslim Organisation (which he first joined for the football) and with the mosque, though both go to the Islamist East London Mosque. In addition, both stress that they are on the political left; however, neither has stepped far outside the instrumentalist Labour Party mould occupied by previous Bengali councillors. Although Miah stayed with Respect and Rahman moved (temporarily) to Labour, Miah admitted to me,

> If Labour didn't take us to a war, then I think my point of view could have been a bit different. I still have friends in the Labour Party, and they argue the case that you can bring change from within the party.[40]

When I talked to him in the summer of 2007, he seemed relatively unfamiliar with the language of class politics. He relied, instead, on the moral strength afforded by his faith, believing that actions here will be rewarded in the world to come.[41]

In the protests against the Bangladeshi war-crimes trials in 2013, where he took a prominent role, Miah's interpretation of events merged class divisions into his Islamist narrative. Speaking to a demonstration outside the Bangladeshi High Commission, timed to coincide with Hefazat-e-Islam's Siege of Dhaka on 5 May, he contrasted the 'rich sons and daughters of Shahbagh' who have 'declared war on Allah and on our Prophet' with 'the real people of Bangladesh' who 'are coming from the ground, coming from the villages'. He warned 'if you take politics with Islam, then you will see that the people will rise'.[42] Others have been happy to accept this rose-tinted view of the Hefazat. Galloway retweeted Abjol's comment that 'the real people of Bangladesh have come out and spoken' and, on 10 May, the Bradford West MP used a speech at an East London rally to call for the peaceful overthrow of Bangladesh's 'gangster government'. [43]The SWP have also tended to show uncritical support for the Islamists, and their national secretary addressed the High Commission demonstration.[44]

At the ward meeting after Rahman's election to the council,[45] Galloway introduced him as 'a Bengali, Muslim, Trade Unionist', and when I had asked Rahman before the meeting if he would describe himself as a socialist he had said yes. This multiple identity remained how he saw himself;[46] alongside support for working-class issues, he promoted the campaign for a local schoolgirl's right to wear the all-covering *jilbab*[47] and told me that faith schools were 'obviously' good and that it was 'vital' to have a Bengali MP.[48] Both men have attempted to engage to some extent with the very different traditions that came together in Respect, but how much is this possible?

Figure 9.2 Abjol Miah speaking at a protest outside the Bangladesh High Commission, timed to conincide with the Hefazat-e-Islam 'Seige of Dhaka' on 5 May 2013. The man in the turban is Mufti Sadruddin, who claimed that the majority of Bangladeshis want an Islamic state (Feb28).

To answer this question it is necessary to look more closely at both socialism and Islam. This theoretical debate may seem far away from the often opportunistic and petty politics of Tower Hamlets, but it impacts directly on the understanding of growing numbers of British Muslims. While no-one would suggest that the majority of Respect's Muslim voters live their lives under the guidance of Islamic political theorists, what is important here are the understandings of those in a position to have an impact on wider political developments. People who come to active political involvement through their Muslim identity and want to develop their political understanding beyond the petty politics of the town hall will soon encounter Islamist ideas, either directly or from local leaders inspired by them. This is especially true for younger Bengalis who are searching for an alternative to neoliberal capitalism through Islam. In Miah's experience,[49] few in the Muslim world would admit to not having read Qutb or Mawdudi, there are numerous Muslim study circles, conferences and internet discussion groups and people do 'talk about Islam'. And while this description may only apply to that corner of the Muslim world that he knows best, it is that corner, and others like it, that has been mobilised by Respect.

If we are to understand what it means to people to be politicised through Islam, we need to turn, as they do, to look at the fundamental ideas within Islamism.

Can a Muslim be a socialist?

As Galloway was preparing to stand for election in Bethnal Green and Bow, I asked Azzam Tamimi whether a Muslim could be a socialist. I wanted to hear his view both as a scholar of Islamic politics and as official spokesperson for the MAB. He told me, '[T]here are within capitalism and within socialism values that are compatible with some of the values of Islam', but 'those Muslims who became socialists departed from Islam. Those Muslims who became capitalist departed from Islam. Because we are talking about different visions, different world views.'[50] The Quran, he explained, revealed 'a set of values' rather than a model of governance; and how these were interpreted depended on 'the experience and perception of people at a given time and at a given geography.' He, and his generation of Islamic political thinkers, claim influence from social democracy, and he constructs, as an ideal paradigm, an 'Islamic democracy' where the 'divinely revealed' *shariah* remains an immutable frame of reference and the elected government, legitimised by the people, has 'no room for anti-Islamic parties' because 'the people will not want it'. He illustrated this point with the example of the US, where 'a communist party is outlawed'. This is, of course, just one view among many, and Tamimi's comments are part of a continuing dialectic between Islam and post-Enlightenment political science.

The previous chapter looked at the evolution of various movements within modern Islam and especially at the development of Islamism. But how have Islamist theoreticians and organisations responded to the challenge of socialism? Like many religions, Islam contains both powerful conservative forces and a strong radical thread, and has a long history of reformist movements that have attempted to rediscover an original purity in the face of moral decadence and social oppression. These have been inevitably impacted by external socio-political changes but, looking inwards, the creation of a just society through political action can also be supported through the example of the Prophet himself, with the first years of Islam providing a paradigm of the ideal Muslim social system. And, despite the temporal power of Sunni legal establishments and Shia clerics, central concepts of Islam can be interpreted as arguments for a universal classless society. The unity of God can be extended to man; divine justice applies to all; the *Ummah*, or community of believers, transcends tribe and nation; the hoarding of wealth is regarded as sinful; monopoly and usury are banned; and Islam prescribes a welfare system based on taxing both income and capital.

The founder of Jamaat-e-Islami, Abul A'la Mawdudi, rejected both capitalism and socialism in favour of what he understood as an Islamic economic solution. In his attack on socialism he was responding to Soviet Communism, and he condemned it for its tyranny and violence and its lack of moral order. However, although he enumerated the evils of even reformed capitalism, he admitted that its underpinnings 'are the true principles of human economy, provided they are shorn of exaggerations incorporated with them by the bourgeoisie of the West because of their selfishness and extremist nature'.[51] Mawdudi's economic prescription reads as capitalism with an Islamic face: a sort of Islamic welfare state.

Hasan al–Banna, founder of the Muslim Brotherhood, wanted Egypt to become an Islamic state, but the Brotherhood was forged in a period of revolutionary upheaval and in spreading the Islamic message they responded to contemporary political concerns. They had mass working-class membership, were active in the formation of trade unions and played a significant role in the widespread labour unrest. However, while Banna wanted to resist foreign companies, he did not welcome class conflict. The Brotherhood argued that the employment relationship should be based on mutual 'respect and sympathy', including respect for the rights of management. Banna was reported as lecturing to union groups on their duties towards 'God, himself, and the owner of the plant'. The Communist Party and other left groups, active in the same pool of discontent, regarded the Brotherhood as playing a dangerously divisive role in labour politics, and the Brotherhood's hatred of communism extended to informing on communists during government round-ups in the 1940s.[52]

Sayyid Qutb, who joined the Brotherhood in the early 1950s, regarded the man–made systems of both capitalism and communism as 'rebellion against God's authority and the denial of the dignity of man given to him by God'. Marxism, he argued in his widely read *Milestones*, had initially attracted large numbers of people because it was 'a way of life based on a creed', but it was a 'system which is against human nature',[53] based on 'exciting animalistic characteristics'.[54] He warned Muslims not to be tricked by their enemies into believing that their struggle was economic, political or racial; their struggle was between 'unbelief' and 'faith'.[55]

Greater equality played an important part in Qutb's vision and he claimed that, 'Only in the Islamic way of life do all men become free from the servitude of some men to others'. However, he explained that the purpose of this freedom was to devote themselves to the worship of God.[56] Despite his emphasis on creating actual political structures, he argued that the important rewards are not in this world, but in the praise of angels and the Hereafter.[57]

Yusuf al–Qaradawi spent long formative years with the Muslim Brotherhood and twice turned down offers to take on its leadership.[58] Thanks to a combination of modern media and personal charisma, he is one of the most influential Islamist thinkers active today. At the centre of his message he stresses the importance of *wasatiyya*, the balance or middle way between extremes – including between capitalism and socialism, between individualism and collectivism and between tradition and reform.[59] While his religious rulings have upset both religious orthodoxy and Western secularists,[60] politically his Islamic judicial approach is not so much a middle way between capitalism and socialism as a system of living that can function within an essentially capitalist economy. There are echoes of Mawdudi here, and indeed Mawdudi was a great admirer of Qaradawi's jurisprudence.[61]

Qaradawi's social philosophy centres on *zakah* – the Islamic tax on wealth and savings to support the poor and religious causes – and the IslamOnline website that he supervises praises the tax for the way 'It frees society from the ill feelings arising out of class hatred. It opposes an individualism that is blind to the travails of one's neighbors and stands against a socialism that shackles individual freedom.' As with Banna, class-based politics was specifically rejected, and this article also pointed out that *zakah* is a 'profitable investment ... because it will establish economic balance and social justice, and at the same time earn an immense reward in the Hereafter'.[62]

The legalistic approach exemplified by Qaradawi and Mawdudi appeals to a conservative desire for moral certainty rather than a wish for progressive radical reform.

While these movements are forthright in their rejection of socialism as a political ideology, there is also a frequently encountered belief that the best of socialism is contained within Islam. As Abjol Miah put it to me, 'fighting for your rights [and] social justice' are 'part of the *shariah*'.[63] This approach regards Islam as the truth that gives life its meaning and purpose and so cannot accept a Marxist materialist understanding of the world. It was exemplified by the Awadh Khilafat Conference declaration in 1920 of 'every sympathy with the Bolshevik movement so far as it is consistent with the principles of Islam',[64] and by the arguments put forward by the Movement of God-Worshipping Socialists, formed in 1940s Iran, who claimed that Marxists demonstrate an idealistic view of human values that could only come out of faith in God and is contradicted by their materialist understanding of society.[65]

Ali Shari'ati, often referred to as the ideologist of the Iranian revolution, joined the successor of this latter group as a young man and built on this argument to explain why he regarded Marxism as a 'Western fallacy'.[66] Although the Shia tradition of which he was part has no direct links with the majority of British Muslims, his writings can help illuminate to what extent a Muslim can be a socialist. Like Muhammad Iqbal,[67] who was an important influence on him, Shari'ati stressed the failures of both bourgeois liberalism and communism, and blamed them on their shared materialist roots.[68] But he saw Marxism as an irreconcilable enemy. This was not only because Marxist views were attracting the same youth that he was appealing to with reformist Islam, but also because, unlike capitalism, it provided an alternative world view. Qutb had recognised Marxism's attraction as a creed; Shari'ati emphasised that:

[C]ontrary to the beliefs of those who look for shared modalities in Islam and the communism of Marx, these, as two comprehensive ideologies, are altogether opposed ... the only comparable modality of the two schools is that each is a complete, comprehensive ideology.[69]

Instead of socialism, Shari'ati campaigned for a 'Red Shi-ism' in which Islam would become a revolutionary force for a fairer world, inviting the common people to rebellion and armed struggle against oppression, ignorance and poverty.[70] In this view, the next world should not distract from engagement with worldly life, but it remained the ultimate reward or punishment for 'the respective services or disservices done by each person for his society'.[71] Socialist ideas were kept firmly contained within an Islamic discourse.

Views from the left

Marxists[72] would agree with Shari'ati that Marxism and Islam are based on different, and mutually incompatible, understandings of ultimate truth. In the Marxist view, 'Man makes religion, religion does not make man'.[73] Shari'ati's criticisms seem to be directed at an Althusserian Marxism that interprets historical materialism as structuralist determinism, but other Marxists have rejected Althusser's views and re-emphasised the role of human agency.[74]

Marxists believe the world will be changed by human action, but in order to change the world for the better it is necessary first to interpret it correctly. That is why they will argue against what they believe to be a wrong interpretation of the world and why, for Marx, 'the criticism of religion is the prerequisite of all criticism'.[75] Explaining his famous comment that religion 'is the opium of the people', Marx wrote:

> The abolition of religion as the illusory happiness of the people is the demand for their real happiness. To call on them to give up their illusions about their condition is to call on them to give up a condition that requires illusions.[76]

Religion, he argued, is a dangerous illusion. It can be, and often has been, used as a conservative force in support of existing authority, persuading people to accept their lot meekly in the hope of rewards beyond the grave. Even where there is no manifest exploitation, its controlling mechanisms can be internalised, helping people to accept inequalities rather than to fight against them, as when Luther 'freed the body from chains because he enchained the heart'.[77] Shari'ati adapted the first part of this argument to condemn not religion, but the 'narcotizing and benumbing' effect on the masses of reactionary and corrupt forms of religion, which he claimed can only be eliminated by 'true religion'.[78] However, the core of Marx's argument is that religion obscures objective truth and understanding, which are the necessary first steps for real progress. Religious interpretations of the world, as governed by an all-powerful deity (or deities) whose acts (while mysterious) respond to our imperfect attempts to keep to a divinely ordained moral code, can lead us to get lost down byways of theological speculation. Marxists argue that this prevents us from seeing the world as the product of human society, only able to be changed through human understanding and action; the realisation that this world is all we have should lead people to try and make this life as fulfilling as possible. Fundamentally different interpretations of the world lead to fundamentally different programmes for righting the world's wrongs.

Marxists understand the values by which we live as human – made not by individuals[79] but by the actions of human society. As such, these values are not immutable, but neither are they arbitrary nor inevitable. There have been many creative and inspiring movements that have set out to generate a better society, and before the French Revolution their aims were generally interpreted according to a religious understanding of the world, because that was the way people knew how to think. However, Marxists understand all these developments as the products of interacting human minds and actions and argue that, while religion provided a framework that helped in their evolution, it ultimately proved a constraint on both understanding and action.

There is no place for religious belief in the Marxist world-view and no place for dialectical materialism in a world ruled by God. A religion such as Islam may incorporate ideas that can be interpreted as socialistic, but the very name Islam means submission to the rule of God, as revealed to Muhammad. All followers of religious faith are bound ultimately by divine authority as mediated through worldly religious authorities.

The Bolsheviks recognised the intrinsic incompatibility of Marxism and religious faith and argued that workers needed to be freed from religion. Despite later developments under Stalin, the first Bolshevik government understood that religion could not be legislated out of existence,[80] but they thought that people could be persuaded, through 'widespread scientific education and anti-religious propaganda', to give up their reliance on old beliefs as they participated in making society fairer through human action, and religious escapism became unnecessary. At the same time, they retained and expanded the Provisional Government's law allowing freedom of religious expression, and their draft programme of 1919 acknowledged the need 'to take care to avoid hurting the religious sentiments of believers, for this only serves to increase religious fanaticism'.[81]

The problems of promoting Marxism in a devoutly religious environment had been addressed a little earlier, in Ireland, by James Connolly, who was executed for his part in leading the Easter Rising in Dublin in 1916. Connolly was concerned that the aggressive atheism of his fellow Marxists was alienating the ordinary Irish Catholic workers. He believed it was possible to put forward a materialist argument for Marxism and criticise the actions of the Catholic hierarchy without asking people to renounce their private beliefs. He argued that socialism was not against religion, but emphasised socialism's fundamental importance as 'a bread and butter question'.[82] Connolly's own religious belief is disputed,[83] and other Marxists have criticised his prohibition on all discussion of theology,[84] but his position would not challenge the Marxist atheist understanding that, as socialist ideas and society take root, so religion will become redundant and wither.

Combining religion and socialism

There are, of course, religious people from all faiths who have tried to combine religion and socialism and have worked alongside non-religious socialists: people such as Father Groser, who helped to form the Christian Socialist movement, and who we met in Chapter 6 as president of the Tenants' Defence League in 1930s Stepney.[85] Groser, a socialist but not a communist, was inspired by Jesus's teachings and saw this active involvement as his Christian duty, like the priests and nuns who turned to liberation theology in Latin America, or the widely respected Labour MP, Tony Benn, who came to socialism from a Protestant perspective.

On the other side of the world, many Bengali Muslims were moved to follow Maulana Bhashani, the religious and political leader with Maoist sympathies who played an important role in the fight for Bangladeshi independence, but whose appeal to a religiously inspired morality inhibited development of more materialist understandings.

Religion may provide the motivation for an egalitarian commitment, but is unlikely to lead to socialist understanding without a secularist separation of private faith from the public political world. Arguments such as Connolly's about the compatibility of religion and socialism could appeal to 'secular' Muslims – who would accept the separation of religion from 'bread and butter' questions – but would be of limited use among those who argue that faith should underlie every aspect of life and thought and whose ultimate aim is an Islamic state.

That there is no place for secularist separations in Islamist ideology, Qaradawi makes very clear:

> Since Islam is a comprehensive system of ʿIbadah (worship) and Shariʿah (legislation), the acceptance of secularism means abandonment of Shariʿah, a denial of the Divine guidance and a rejection of Allah's injunctions … The acceptance of a legislation formulated by humans means a preference of the humans' limited knowledge to the Divine guidance: 'Say! Do you know better than Allah?' …
>
> For this reason, the call for secularism among Muslims is atheism and a rejection of Islam. Its acceptance as a basis for rule in place of Shariʿah is a downright apostasy.[86]

This is a severe charge. At the very least an apostate can be certain of eternal damnation. While Qaradawi does not speak for all Islamists, and interpretations of *shariah* vary, Islamism has no sympathy for the secularist position.

A third way?

The idea that Islam supports neither capitalism nor socialism but provides an alternative system has become something of a cliché, but what might this actually mean in practice? We have seen how Mawdudi's economic prescription was for a sort of Islamic welfare state. In his book on Western Muslims, Tariq Ramadan (the thinker who most inspired Abjol Miah[87]) adopts a much more radical approach to Islamic law but arrives at a very similar construction. He describes this as 'an economy with a human face'.[88] Like Qaradawi, Ramadan is looking for a 'middle way', and the way he finds 'fixes clear and distinct conditions for involvement in the dominant economic system'.[89] Like New Labour's 'Third Way', this offers little challenge to hegemonic capitalism (though it is not wedded to free-market neoliberalism). Ramadan's 'liberation by stages', through building up ethical businesses,[90] might allow those involved to sleep better at night, but it would make little impression on wider economic structures.

Lessons for the future

In considering the collapse of Respect, it is important to acknowledge both the previous failure of the Socialist Alliance and Respect's general opportunism, of which the attempt to unite socialists and Islamists was both a symptom and further cause. The Socialist Alliance had already exposed organisational failings within the SWP, and the opportunism led the coalition to rely on networks of people whose interests were rather closer to home. However, the ideological incompatibility highlighted by this chapter formed a fundamental fault-line at the heart of the Respect project, forcing it to fall back on short-term tactical alliances. Basic differences in world-view influence even those who would not describe themselves as Islamists and who have not consciously applied the ideas discussed here to their own political actions. They may still be affected, at some level, by the belief that they do not have to engage fully with socialist ideas because all that is good in socialism is already contained within Islam, and they may be wary of the materialist approach.

Respect liked to portray itself as part of the East End socialist tradition and to draw parallels with the powerful Communist Party of the 1930s, with its significant ethnically Jewish membership. But the Communists would have been appalled at the emphasis given by Respect to Muslim identity and to encouraging political and community action through religious organisations. Their strength and their ability to stem the growth of fascism were due to an emphasis on class politics that cut across ethnic and religious difference.[91]

The Communist Party built on years of grassroots work to develop not only electoral success, but also a solid base of politically conscious supporters. Later, the compromises with capitalism that characterised post-war Communist policy disillusioned many supporters long before they had to face revelations about the nature of Stalin's rule;[92] however, Respect sidelined left arguments from the start, precluding development of a left political consciousness. A socialist organisation that campaigned for greater economic equality – and against discrimination on the basis of religious (as of other) differences, and against the wars in Afghanistan and Iraq – could have appealed to Muslims as well as non-Muslims; or at least to those Muslims who might have helped build an organisation according to the socialist principles Respect's founders claimed to support. Instead, by jettisoning those principles, Respect has bequeathed a legacy of disunity and distrust amongst what remains of the left and encouraged a politics that builds on and reinforces ethnic division.

Respect consciously appealed to a specific faith and ethnic community and jettisoned so much socialist ideology in order to do so that it lost members from its founding organisations. In its opportunistic focus on election gains, it proved as ready as the mainstream parties to make use of patriarchal Bengali village networks to bring in the votes, and its eventual decline and split had long been predicted.[93] Rather than promote working-class unity, it further encouraged a politics that builds on and reinforces ethnic division. The increased emphasis on ethnicity was observed by the political reporter of the *East London Advertiser*, who noted at the time of a council by-election in October 2008,

> As soon as the by-election was called … activists from all parties called me seeking an inside line on whether their opponents were going to select a Bengali or someone white.[94]

It was no coincidence that in the 2010 general election the main candidates in Bethnal Green and Bow were all Bengali.

This political attention may indeed have helped to give Tower Hamlets Muslims greater public confidence and, to use a favourite New Labour term, 'community cohesion', but, as Dench *et al.* observed with respect to the East End's strong white communities, such cohesion can be at the expense of relations with those outside.[95] A sense of group strength can sometimes be expressed in violence against outsiders. The 2005 general election campaign exposed elements of anti-Semitism among Bengali youth[96] (Oona King is proud to be half Jewish), and there were reports of a spate of 'Asian' anti-white racism, ranging from racist taunts to extreme violence and even murder.[97] At one particularly troubled estate in Bethnal Green the local paper reported 'gangs hurling racist insults like "white trash"'.[98]

There has been no significant right-wing backlash in Tower Hamlets itself, but the 2006 council elections saw the British National Party (BNP) become the second biggest party in Barking and Dagenham council, and it is to places such as Barking that many white East Enders have gone to live. This time, far-right councillors proved a temporary phenomenon, and a combination of BNP disarray and mass anti-fascist mobilisation saw all twelve councillors lose their seats in 2010. However, in the absence of an effective left movement, far-right political groups are able to appeal to the neglected interests of local white communities at the same time as Islamists appeal to Muslims.

While Respect's leftist leaders had shown themselves ready to abandon fundamental principles in pursuit of an elusive short cut to socialism, Islamist organisations remained detached from Respect, kept their ideological positions uncompromised, and avoided the political backbiting. At the same time, they benefited from the focus on Muslim identity, and we have seen how Islamist movements have grown in strength. Tamimi made clear that the MAB's readiness to work with secular socialists was actually a consequence of the socialists' relative political weakness. He told me, 'when we criticise socialism as a world-view we don't depart much from what Mawdudi or Sayyid Qutb had said'. However he went on to explain, 'the socialists of today, especially in Britain, are not seen by us as the enemies of yesterday … now increasingly capitalism is becoming a more dangerous thing than socialism'.[99]

When weak leftist organisations campaign alongside religious groups, they inevitably risk helping to boost those groups and religious ideas at the expense of themselves. People are encouraged to take political action through their religious identity, religious morality supplants potential socialist understandings and religious loyalties cut across class-based organisation. This type of political mobilisation provides no basis for the development of a socialist political consciousness and actually encourages left political ideology to be sidelined as destructive of consensus.

Despite their respect for their new comrades, many on the left have failed to learn from them the important lesson of not compromising on fundamental principles, and as a result have weakened their own position and that of the left more generally.[100] At the root of this failure is a misunderstanding of the nature of religion. Whilst it is possible to imagine 'secular' Muslims practising forms of socialism and working alongside non-religious Marxists, Islamists have a fundamentally different political understanding; it is impossible to combine the two different and complete worldviews of Marxism and Islamism. This does not mean that Marxists and Islamists (or other religious people) cannot or should not work together when, as is often the case, they share similar immediate aims. It is often possible for Marxists and Islamists to find a common minimum programme and a reasonably sensitive *modus vivendi*. However, their ultimate aims are very different. Joint action over shared issues is one thing. A formalised relationship that requires the suspension of ideological debate and the abandoning of fundamental principles is quite another.

Notes

1 Interviewed 6 August 2005.
2 CND soon became a third partner.

3   www.pewforum.org/Muslim/Muslim-Networks-and-Movements-in-Western-Europe-Muslim-Brotherhood-and-Jamaat-i-Islami.aspx, accessed 21 November 2012.

4   Richard Phillips, 'Standing Together: The Muslim Association of Britain and the Anti-war Movement', *Race and Class*, 50:2 (2008), 101–13, pp. 103–4.

5   George Galloway, *I'm Not the Only One* (London: Penguin, 2004), p. 154.

6   See the *Weekly Worker*. This is the journal of the CPGB, a marginalised junior partner in both the Socialist Alliance and the Respect Coalition. It is a relatively open chronicler of events on the left, and is widely read by left-watchers of all kinds.

7   Galloway, *I'm Not the Only One*, p. 150.

8   Marc Shoffman, 'Galloway: Respect Candidates can be Anti Gay', *Pink News*, 21 February 2006.

9   S.W. Kenning, 'Decline, Paranoia and Discontent', *Weekly Worker*, 2 December 2004; Peter Manson, 'Gerrymandering, Exclusions and the Farce of Three-minute Democracy' and John Nicholson, 'SWP in Denial', *Weekly Worker*, 4 November 2004.

10 John Rees, quoted in Peter Manson, 'No Respect for Socialist Principle', *Weekly Worker*, 31 January 2008.

11 Interviewed 19 January 2005.

12 Interviewed 17 January 2005. Tamimi's defining issues were: opposition to the war in Iraq and the subsequent occupation, support for Palestinian rights, opposition to anti-terrorism measures that victimise Muslims, and absence of racist and Islamophobic tendencies. He made a similar statement on IQra media, *Muslims & Politics*, DVD written and presented by Wakil Ahmed, directed and edited by Shofiquez Zaman (London, 2005).

13 Galloway, interviewed 19 January 2005.

14 The corruption scandal had also led to the closure of the local community centre. Kumar Murshid (who we met in Chapters 5 and 6) was charged alongside Nasir Uddin, but was subsequently acquitted and joined Respect.

15 19 January 2005.

16 www.pakistan.tv/videos-george-galloway-a-muslim-convert-you-%5BiJEK27GodEs%5D.cfm, accessed 13 October 2010; www.guardian.co.uk/politics/2012/apr/29/george-galloway-interview-bradford-west, accessed 21 November 2012.

17 His 'important message' to 'voters of the Muslim faith and Pakistani heritage' pointed out, among other things, that he didn't drink and had always fought for Muslims. 'God KNOWS who is a Muslim', it stated, 'And he KNOWS who is not.'

18 Hustings held by The East London Citizens' Organisation (TELCO), at Queen Mary University of London, 20 April 2005.

19 *East London Advertiser*, 4 March 2005.

20 The press release was dated 7 November 2004. Respect's SWP leadership ensured that any motions that might put off potential Muslim voters would not be passed.

21 *East London Advertiser*, 2 December 2004.

22 Interviewed 6 August 2005.

23 Where one leaflet said 'Oona voted to protect Muslims from hate crime' and that she had made a promise to 'Iraqi Muslims', the other said she 'voted to make incitement to religious hatred a crime' and had made a promise to 'Iraqis'. This was pointed out by John Rees at a Respect canvassers meeting.

24 *East London Advertiser*, 18 February 2005.

25 *East London Advertiser*, 23 June 2005. Many of the letters to the paper are from party hacks or a few regular grumblers, but there are significant numbers of genuine complaints.

26 R squared = 63% and P<0.001 – i.e. 63 per cent of the variation can be explained by the percentage of Bengalis.

27 A new, more traditional leadership, wary of the association's oppositional public profile, eventually ended the MAB's partnership with the Stop the War Coalition itself, but active members continued their involvement under the banner of the British Muslim Initiative. See Phillips, 'Standing Together', p. 107–09.

28 Huw Bynon, 'Chaos in Tower Hamlets Respect', *Weekly Worker*, 6 July 2006; Peter Manson, 'It's Not What You Know But Who You Know', *Weekly Worker*, 8 February 2007; Socialist Workers' Party, 'An Appeal to Respect Members', 24 October 2007, www.swp.org.uk/respect_appeal.php, accessed 25 October 2007.

29 Informal discussion, 24 July 2007. Nick Ryan spent time with one of the Respect candidates on the eve of the 2006 council elections and has described watching 'as promises and deals were struck with family members and friendly elders'. See Nick Ryan, 'In the Shadow of the City' (*Observer*, 2006), www.nickryan.net/articles/city.html, accessed 28 July 2011.

30 Peter Manson, 'Choosing Between Opportunists', *Weekly Worker*, 24 April 2008.

31 The letter can be viewed here: http://socialistunity.com/galloway-on-respect, accessed 14 November 2013 .

32 Ted Jeory, 'Labour Spin Insults the Intelligence', *East London Advertiser*, 7 July 2008.

33 Respect candidate Harun Miah, interviewed in Peter Manson, 'Respect – The Party for Everyone', *Weekly Worker*, 2 August 2007 (this is not the same Harun Miah as was quoted in Chapter 8); discussion with by-election canvassers.

34 The 2010 council elections left Labour with forty-one out of fifty councillors, but the breakdown in November 2013 was: Labour 27, independent 14, Conservative 7, Respect 2, Liberal Democrat 1.

35 Christine Shawcroft, 'Report of the NEC meeting held on 21 September 2010. Emergency Item: The Tower Hamlets Mayoral selection', www.christineshawcroft.co.uk/nec, accessed 13 October 2010.

36 Quoted in www.guardian.co.uk/politics/davehillblog/2010/oct/08/tower-hamlets-mayoral-campaign-faith-and-democracy, accessed 21 November 2012.

37 www.birminghampost.net/news/politics-news/2011/07/07/salma-yaqoob-to-stand-down-as-birmingham-councillor-65233-29007875, accessed 19 October 2012.

38 *Independent*, 16 August 2013; *Guardian*, 25 October 2013. Two were suspended for being critical of Galloway and the others left in sympathy.

39 Interviewed 19 January 2005.

40 Interviewed 25 July 2007.

41 Interviewed 24 and 25 July 2007.

42 www.youtube.com/watch?v=yChTKzegK7Y, accessed 19 October 2013. Miah was clear who he blamed for the growing violence. His Facebook post of 3 March 2013 stated, 'The anti Muslim blogers who insulted Allah and his Prophet have inflamed the country'.

43 Report of the previous day's rally on blog dated 11 May 2013, www.votegeorge galloway.com, accessed 20 August 2013.

44 http://socialistworker.co.uk/art/33271/London+protest+in+solidarity+with +Bangladesh, accessed 19 October 2013.

45 Held on 6 August 2004.

46 Peter Manson, 'Fighting Over the Corpse', *Weekly Worker*, 1 November 2007.

47 A Muslim version of the school uniform had already been agreed with parents and there was concern that, in defending the rights of this one girl, campaigners were supporting a situation where girls would be under peer pressure to conform to more

and more strict religious dress codes. See Pola Uddin, 'Once, Muslims and Labour were Natural Allies. Not Now', *Guardian*, 19 June 2004.

48 Interviewed 19 January 2005.

49 Interviewed 25 July 2007.

50 Interviewed 17 January 2005.

51 Abul A'la Mawdudi, *Capitalism, Socialism and Islam* (Kuwait: Islamic Book Publishers, 1995), p. 74.

52 Richard Mitchell, *The Society of the Muslim Brothers* (Oxford: Oxford University Press, 1993), pp. 278, 253, 254 and 39.

53 Sayyid Qutb, *Milestones* (1964), http://web.youngmuslims.ca/online_library/books/ milestones, accessed 24 March 2005, Introduction.

54 *Ibid.*, Chapter 3.

55 *Ibid.*, Chapter 12. Al-Qaradawi has departed from this view in describing the Palestinians' war with Israel as 'a battle of land, rather than one of belief', see www.islamonline.net/English/News/2002-06/04/article12.shtml, accessed July 2008 .

56 Qutb, *Milestones*, Introduction.

57 *Ibid.*, Chapter 12.

58 *Al Jazeera*, 12 January 2004, source AFP, http://www.aljazeera.com/archive/2004/ 01/2008410145045889729.html, accessed 11 January 2012.

59 Soage, Ana Belén, 'Shaykh Yusuf al-Qaradawi: Portrait of Leading Islamic Cleric', *Middle East Review of International Affairs*, 12:1 (2008), 51–68, p. 58.

60 His suggestion, as reported in Soage, 'Shaykh Yusuf al-Qaradawi', p. 59, 'that 'apostates should not incur the death penalty but "only" social ostracism' upsets both.

61 Soage, 'Shaykh Yusuf al-Qaradawi', p. 51.

62 www.islamonline.net/english/introducingislam/Worship/Zakah/article01.shtml, accessed 21 November 2004.

63 Interviewed 25 July 2007.

64 Quoted in Khizar Humayun Ansari, *The Emergence of Socialist Thought Among North Indian Muslims (1917–1947)* (Lahore: Book Traders, 1990), p. 47.

65 Ali Rahnema, *An Islamic Utopian: A Political Biography of Ali Shari'ati* (London: IB Tauris, 2000), p. 26.

66 Ali Shari'ati, *Marxism and Other Western Fallacies: An Islamic Critique* (Berkley: Mizan Press, 1980), p. 29.

67 Muhammad Iqbal, *The Reconstruction of Religious Thought in Islam* (1930), www.yespakistan.com/iqbal/reconstruction, accessed 21 November 2012.

68 Shari'ati, *Marxism and Other Western Fallacies*, p. 21.

69 *Ibid.*, p. 64.

70 Ali Shari'ati, *What Is To Be Done: The Enlightened Thinkers and an Islamic Renaissance* (Houston: The Institute for Research and Islamic Studies, 1986), p. 43; Ali Shari'ati, *Red Shi'ism (the Religion of Martyrdom) vs. Black Shi'ism (the Religion of Mourning)* (n.d.), www.iranchamber.com/personalities/ashariati/works/red_black_shiism.php, accessed 11 January 2012.

71 Shari-ati, *Marxism and Other Western Fallacies*, p. 57.

72 While many different schools of thought would describe themselves as 'Marxist', the ideas described in this section would, I believe, be widely accepted.

73 Karl Marx, *Introduction to A Contribution to the Critique of Hegel's Philosophy of Right* (1844), www.marxists.org/archive/marx/works/1843/critique-hpr/intro.htm, accessed 21 November 2012, para. 3.

74 Shari'ati regarded Marx's comments on religion as mere stylistic embellishments on Feuerbach (see Shari'ati, *Marxism and Other Western Fallacies*, p. 56) but, in his *Theses*

on Feuerbach, Marx made clear that Feuerbach's argument was incomplete precisely because it did not take account of man's active role in changing society: see Karl Marx, *Theses On Feuerbach* (1845), www.marxists.org/archive/marx/works/1845/theses/index.htm, accessed 21 November 2012, para. 3.

75 Marx, *Introduction to A Contribution to the Critique of Hegel's Philosophy of Right*, para. 1.

76 *Ibid.*, paras 4 and 5.

77 *Ibid.*, para. 32.

78 Shari'ati, *What Is To Be Done*, pp. 31 and 48; Shari'ati, *Red Shi'ism*.

79 Marx, *Theses On Feuerbach*, paras 6 and 7.

80 V.I. Lenin, *Draft Programme of the R.C.P.(B.)*, 'Section Of The Programme Dealing With Religion' (1919), www.marxists.org/archive/lenin/works/1919/mar/x02.htm, accessed 11 January 2012.

81 *Ibid.*

82 James Connolly, 'Workshop Talks' (1909), www.marxists.org/archive/connolly/1909/talks/shoptlks.htm, accessed October 2012.

83 In a letter dated 30 January 1908, Connolly wrote, 'For myself, though I have usually posed as a Catholic I have not gone to my duty for fifteen years, and have not the slightest tincture of faith left. I only assume the Catholic pose in order to quiz the raw freethinkers whose ridiculous dogmatism did and does dismay me as much as the dogmatism of the orthodox. In fact I respect the good Catholic more than the average freethinker.' (Quoted in J.W. Boyle, book review of *The Life and Times of James Connolly* by Desmond Greaves, *Labor History*, 14:1 (1973). However, Father Aloysius recorded that he heard Connolly's confession and gave him Holy Communion before his execution: see www.bbc.co.uk/history/british/easter-rising/witnesses/personalrecollections.rtf, accessed 19 October 2012.

84 The Socialist Party of Ireland prohibited 'discussion of theological or anti-theological questions at its meetings, public or private', see James Connolly, 'The New Evangel', *Workers' Republic*, 17 June 1899, www.marxists.org/archive/connolly/1901/evangel/socrel.htm, accessed 21 November 2012 .

85 Groser, Father St John B., *Politics and Persons* (London: SCM Press, 1949); *Christian Socialist*, 32, May 1966, www.stgite.org.uk/media/boggisongroser.html, accessed 11 January 2012.

86 Qaradawi, 'How the Imported Solutions Disastrously Affected Our Muslim Nation', quoted in his own *fatwa* of 22 June 2002, see www.islameonline.net, accessed March 2005. See also footnote 58 above.

87 Interviewed 25 July 2007.

88 Tariq Ramadan, *Western Muslims and the Future of Islam* (Oxford: Oxford University Press, 2004), p. 188.

89 *Ibid.*, p. 197.

90 *Ibid.*, p. 198.

91 Sarah Glynn, 'East End Immigrants and the Battle for Housing: A Comparative Study of Political Mobilisation in the Jewish and Bengali Communities', *Journal of Historical Geography*, 31:3 (2005), 528–45; Sarah Glynn, 'Marxism and Multiculturalism', *Human Geography*, 3:1 (2010), 108–27. Although Father Groser was made president of the Stepney Tenants' Defence League, he was not there as a community representative. His presence would, however, have helped cut across Catholic anti-communist sentiment.

92 Sam Bornstein and Al Richardson, *Two Steps Back: Communists and the Wider Labour Movement, 1935–1945* (Ilford: Socialist Platform, 1982).

93 The unravelling of Respect was closely dissected in the *Weekly Worker*.

94 Ted Jeory, 'Reflections on a Stint in London's East End', *East London Advertiser*, 23 October 2008.

95 Geoff Dench, Kate Gavron and Michael Young, *The New East End: Kinship, Race and Conflict* (London: Profile Books, 2006), p. 187. Bengali Muslim cohesion can exclude secular Bengalis as well as non-Muslims.

96 There are well published accusations – see *Guardian*, 12 April 2005; *East London Advertiser*, 15 April 2005; BBC Today Programme, 5 November 2005 – and I talked with Oona King's Bengali assistant when he was clearly shocked at the hostility he had encountered campaigning outside a mosque, where several people had called her a 'Jewish whore'.

97 *East London Advertiser*, 10 March, 7 April, 19 May, 6 July, 4 August, 11 August, 15 September, 6 October, 27 October and 24 November 2005. While this seems to have been a particularly bad period, there had been anti-white racism before. Chapter 1 quotes someone who took part in this in the 1990s and the *East London Advertiser* for 24 January 2004 quoted Jim Fitzpatrick, MP for Poplar and Canning Town, speaking about gangs of Asian kids who were attacking white women. He told the journalist, 'I have had increasing numbers of reports of white women of all ages experiencing everything from abusive comments, to being stoned.'

.98 *East London Advertiser*, 10 March 2005. The problems occurred in the Jesus Hospital Estate off Columbia Road.

99 Interviewed 17 January 2005.

100 I first wrote about this in an academic paper and my intended audience was people who would describe themselves as progressive or on the left. I put a draft version on the web and was glad to find that it had been appreciatively quoted. However, I was a little taken aback when I clicked on the link and found that my admirer was a Muslim columnist who was quoting my argument over the incompatibility of Marxism and Islam to upbraid Salma Yaqoob for her closeness to the SWP. Now I don't think that Yaqoob did compromise her Islamic position – she is a practicing Muslim with conscientious left-liberal politics who chose to go with the non-SWP wing after Respect split – and my own concern was over what is happening to the British left, but it was disconcerting to find myself a character in my own story.

10 Diverging paths

I quoted in the preface the old call, 'black and white, unite and fight'; however, the common theme that runs through this history is not unity but segregation. Segregation not just in the sense of measurable physical separation – as expressed in separate housing patterns and school rolls – or even of cultural segregation that can allow people to live parallel lives. There has also been a tendency for Bengalis to engage with wider civil society – in which many are very active – specifically through their separate identity as Bengalis or, increasingly, as Muslims. All these forms of segregation and separateness are interconnected and are products both of wider political and social forces and of developments in progressive left politics that have had an especially critical impact on the political mobilisation of the Bengalis themselves. An initial separation of immigrant communities is to be expected. Immigrants cluster together for mutual support in an alien environ-ment and to escape hostile responses from existing residents, which are fuelled both by popular racism and by fear of competition for jobs and resources. But segregation and the racism that encourages it have both been enhanced by political action, even though this has often not been the intention.

Before looking at the debates on why segregation matters and at what can be done, this final chapter will summarise, briefly, how it has been affected by the political developments described in previous chapters. The focus of this account has been on Bengali political mobilisation, so I will first look at the impact of this, before going on to the impact of more mainstream politics.

This is a history of political actions, but these actions take place in and are conditioned by their socio-economic and geographical surroundings. Some of the many remarkable changes to those surroundings have already played a part in this story, but I want to go back to the statistics included in the very first paragraph of Chapter 1. Despite all the changes that have happened, despite all the wealth that has been made and despite the arrival of a new middle-class immigration that would have had no place in the old East End, Tower Hamlets continues to be an area of exceptional deprivation. All this political activity –

including developments within the political mainstream – has achieved little improvement in the life chances of a large proportion of Tower Hamlets residents of all ethnicities, and the borough's large and growing Bangladeshi community still suffers disproportionately by most socio-economic indices.

Segregation through Bengali mobilisation

The early immigrants of the 1950s and 60s were brought together by shared concerns over their homeland and over immigration. Campaigns over these issues encouraged a Bengali solidarity, but made few links with their non-Bengali neighbours. Political engagement with those outside the Bengali community was largely limited to lobbying on behalf of specifically Bengali interests. Many of the leading Bengali activists were involved with or influenced by the Communist Party, and Stalin's revolutionary stages theory and popular-front politics guided their actions, both in their powerful campaign in support of national liberation and in their community welfare work. They set aside their long-term aims for a socialist society, and concentrated on immediate demands for national independence and on resolving the nitty-gritty of community problems. Popular-front tactics submerged socio-economic analysis and prevented them from engaging in wider economic struggles. Far from providing the first step towards a socialist future, this approach contributed to marginalising the socialist aims that most of the principle activists claimed to support. Attention was concentrated on unity within the Bengali community (bringing together socialists and bourgeois nationalists, restaurant owners and kitchen staff) rather than unity with British workers.

The mass mobilisation around Bangladeshi Independence in 1971 politicised Britain's Bengalis, but, despite the important role played by left activists, popular-front tactics ensured that the legacy of this politicisation was a pragmatic politics, focussed on the *probashi*, or emigrant, Bengali community. At the same time, much political and organisational activity, as well as considerable financial investment, was (and continues to be) directed towards Bangladesh.

The development of socialist class-based politics was further hindered by the elitist origins of the Bengali socialist leaders. These relied on old patriarchal bonds, and tended to use terms such as 'working class' in a manner that had little relationship to a person's position in capitalist economic structures.

There was also remarkably little practical help from the Communist Party, although it was active in the East End in the 1950s and 1960s. In line with other accounts of the CPGB's failure to engage effectively with communist or politically sympathetic post-war immigrants, the party seems to have missed the opportunity to build links with like-minded members of the Bengali immigrant community or to attempt the kind of grassroots work that had enabled it to build its strength among East End Jews before the Second World War.

By the late 1970s, struggles for better housing and against racism saw the

Bengalis influenced by arguments that expressly promoted separate organisation along ethnic lines, pioneered by black radical organisers from the Race Today Collective. Black radicalism, which became the politics of a generation of immigrant youth, was at the forefront of the New Social Movements that reacted against economistic versions of Marxism by jettisoning Marx's basic principle that class was the fundamental division in society. Black consciousness became the basis for political mobilisation, and the white working class was seen as at best irrelevant and at worst part of the problem. While a more ideological commitment to black radicalism remained fairly peripheral to most of those involved, this movement succeeded in developing separate organisation and a general distrust of the 'white left', and in cutting across possibilities for linking with wider working-class issues. Instead, the young generation mobilised by these campaigns adopted a community-centred pragmatism whose main focus was the fight for Bengalis to get their fair share of existing resources; and this became a principle aim of their subsequent entry into, and eventual dominance of, local Tower Hamlets politics. The housing campaign, with its insistence on Bengalis being able to live in areas of existing Bengali settlement, also left a legacy of physical segregation.

Black radicalism and the identity politics of the New Social Movements morphed into theories of multiculturalism that were taken up by the liberal-left – especially by the GLC and other Labour councils – and were then institutionalised by the liberal establishment. And once Bengalis had breached the resistance of the remains of the local Labour right wing, their community-based politics thrived in this new environment. In Tower Hamlets Council Bengalis continued to make use of patriarchal and village links, and although Bengali councillors acknowledge that they represent everyone in their ward, the main focus of much of their activity has been on addressing the problems that beset the Bengali community. This has often found them fighting alongside their left-wing counterparts, but the legacy of anti-imperialism and then black-radicalism, and the continued emphasis on community encouraged by multiculturalism, has all contributed to a dismissal of socialist universalism as the product of a self-interested 'white left'.

The main vehicle for this community politics was the Labour Party, which itself was soon moving rightwards, though some Bengalis sought to pursue a similar approach through other parties. Ethnicity has played a growing role in the selection of political representatives, and the natural culmination of the focus on Bengali representation became the election of a Bengali MP. So important was this seen to be that in the 2010 general election the candidates chosen by all the main parties were Bengali.

With socialism on the retreat since the 1980s, and even its social democratic variety off – and deliberately removed from – the agenda, some of those who once looked to socio-economic solutions are increasingly turning to other ideologies. Ethnic and community politics has not achieved its promised changes and a new generation is attempting to take strength from the old certainties of religious faith. In Islamism, they find a comprehensive view of the world and their place within it, and an authoritative structure for their lives. This foregrounding of Islam as the power that encompasses every aspect of life, sets itself up against the secular idea of separating politics from a personal religion. The young Islamists – and most are young – are welcomed into an international community with a proud history and promises of future glory. It is not hard to understand how Islamism can be seen as a potent antidote to alienation, socio-economic disadvantage and lack of opportunity, and how it has been effectively counter-posed as an alternative to hedonistic capitalist materialism and (more specifically) to Tower Hamlets' drug and gang culture.

Islamist ideas have been strengthened whenever external events have awakened people's Muslim identity and their sense of Islamic brotherhood, from the publication of *The Satanic Verses* to the persecution of Muslims in Bosnia and, more recently, the international responses to 9/11, and the wars in Afghanistan and Iraq. They have been further reinforced as people have responded to growing Islamophobia by visibly strengthening their Muslim identity.

Radical groups such as Hizb ut-Tahrir and (the now-banned) Al Muhajiroun, have been able to attract those who believe a better future will only be achieved through revolutionary change. Meanwhile, more mainstream organisations linked to Jamaat have established their strength through disciplined structures (inspired by Communist Party organisation) and by concerted social-work activity that has built them a firm base in the wider Muslim community. They self-consciously provide examples of responsible civic engagement that impress themselves on Muslim youth as well as on their non-Muslim interlocutors. They have been able to build on the new and growing role that has been given to faith groups in civil society, and this has helped them consolidate their influence.

The new importance given to Muslim identity and organisation has made it possible, for those who wish it, to live much of daily life in a Muslim environment as well as to engage with politics through Muslim identity and guided by Islamic ideals. As with any group based around strong religious faith, the certainty that their way is the right way can alienate those who do not share these views. Despite Muslim involvement in civil society and local politics, Islamism sets up a fundamental divide between those who interpret everything through Islamic law and everyone else, including Bengalis who have a different approach to their religion and to its relationship with secular understandings. Although it contains its own vision of a fair society, Islamism draws people away from commitment to wider secular movements that address social inequalities from a materialist perspective.

Despite socialistic ideas within Islam, Islamists regard their faith-based politics as an oppositional alternative to secular socialism and Marxism. However, that did not stop anti-war activists attempting to unite followers of these different ideologies under a single political banner. Islam means submission to the rule of

God, while Marxism rejects faith-based views as obstructions to genuine understanding and therefore to the ability to implement progressive change. While secular Muslims may be attracted to forms of socialism, Islamists will always be guided by a 'higher' power. Respect's brief and unproductive flowering demonstrated the limits of this opportunistic approach to political organisation, which sought to ignore history and create an instant radicalism. While Islamist organisations remained organisationally detached and ideologically uncompromised, left activists, led by the Socialist Workers' Party, were prepared to reduce their agenda to a minimally socialist programme in an attempt to appeal to a Muslim community that was often socially conservative but politicised by the war in Iraq. Their version of popular-front politics was based on the marginalisation of socialist understanding and could make little headway in developing a serious campaign on socio-economic issues or in attracting support from the wider working class. Respect came to be regarded by many as a party for Muslims and its moment of success made it another vehicle for pragmatic community politics and personal political ambition. (The 2006 council election showed support for Respect was much stronger in wards with large numbers of Bengali voters.) In addition, Respect's emphasis on the 'Muslim vote' encouraged a matching response from Labour. Contrary to their rhetoric of unity, Respect succeeded in consolidating separatist attitudes.

Segregation through mainstream political action

Before looking at specific policy developments, it is important to contextualise these within the wider decline of the left. Developments in far left politics and their impact on the nature of Bengali political mobilisation have been central to this history, but on top of these, the last three decades have seen the corrosion of British social democracy, and with it any mainstream attempts to address underlying socioeconomic inequalities. Indeed, the neoliberal policies pursued by New Labour as well as Conservative governments have entrenched and deepened inequality, and unequal societies are fertile territory for ethnic and other divisions. People seek scapegoats for economic failure, and ethnic divisions can be used and hardened by those who want to draw attention away from any questioning of economic structures and to block any possible resurgence of a united working-class politics, as well as by the racist far-right. Inequality can be exploited to encourage division and a defensive retreat into separate communities, and the absence of any credible force addressing this inequality leaves room for the growth of destructive separatist visions.

Beyond this, it is not easy to isolate effects of individual policies. However, national and local government policies have had an influence on all the different stages and forms of segregation. While some of these policies have been expressly directed at ethnic minorities, others may seem superficially to be unrelated – such as housing legislation, or even going to war – and some have been expressed as plans to reduce division but have ended up making it worse. Even during periods when government policy would be described as assimilationist, mainstream politics has often acted to encourage segregation.

Immigration legislation can be seen both as a response to popular racism and, despite its avowed opposite intent, as a spur to greater racism and 'racial' division. Since the 1962 Commonwealth Immigration Act, immigration rules have been constructed so as to restrict non-white immigration,[1] and it soon became the accepted view that limiting such immigration was key to improved 'race relations'. This legitimised the idea that racist violence could be blamed on the growth of the black and Asian population, which, along with the discriminatory immigration laws themselves, poured oil on the racist flames. This racism encouraged the perpetuation of defensive clustering by immigrants and the movement of white families out of what were becoming regarded as immigrant neighbourhoods.

In addition, the way immigration legislation worked promoted chain migration, which itself encouraged ethnic clustering. Chain migration was an inevitable consequence of immigration through work vouchers (which were organised by earlier immigrants) and through family reunification. Immigration rules applied to the majority of non-white immigrants, but especially impacted on settlement patterns of ethnic groups such as the Bengalis that were only just getting established in Britain when the laws came in.

The politics of housing has been crucial to 'race relations' and to segregation, and nowhere more so than in Tower Hamlets, where the housing available has always fallen far short of what is required and housing issues dominate councillors' surgeries. Chapter 6 described how racism combined with ethnic mobilisation around housing issues to create both organisational and physical separation, with a clustering of Bengalis in the E1 postal district, but external politics has created divisive forces too.

In her 1989 study of segregation, Susan Smith showed that apparently aracial policies 'have effectively (if apparently unintentionally) denied black people full access to the welfare and property rights associated with state-subsidized housing'.[2] Chapter 6 described how the nature of council house allocation resulted in inbuilt discrimination against the Bengalis over a long period, while a climate of institutional racism meant that there was little incentive for housing departments to do anything about it. Chapter 1 showed how growing numbers of Bengalis who had to be found homes through homeless legislation were moved into some of the borough's worst estates. Through no wish of their own they had become colonisers of new areas, and the political climate ensured the development of new segregated spaces through racism, defensive separatism and 'white flight'.

Chapter 1 also outlined how, over the last thirty years, government policies have reduced social housing and so further increased demand for the homes that remain, adding more pressure to a situation that is commonly interpreted as competition between ethnic groups. When attempts were made to address Bengali needs – by rehousing squatters, by giving priority to homeless families or those suffering severe overcrowding, or by building larger housing units – this was seen as queue jumping and discrimination against longer-established residents. Governments have been adept at presenting inadequate resources as the result of robbing Peter to pay Paul rather than as due to an overall lack of government investment, and the interests of different ethnic groups have been set against each other. Chapter 7 showed how the competition for housing has provided plenty of scope for political parties to play the race card and indulge in populist exploitation of resource division in pursuit of the white working-class vote. These self-serving political tactics built on and promoted separatist mentalities, encouraging racist attitudes and the popular linking of ethnicity and territory.

The institutional promotion of multiculturalism or faith groups, though often presented as benefiting ethnic minorities, can, too, be seen to be perpetuating division[3] – as also shown in Chapter 7. This has provided a distraction from fundamental economic issues and a barrier to the creation of unified resistance to attacks on the working class as a whole. Instead, it has encouraged different groups to turn inwards on themselves and to compete against each other along ethnic lines. Ethnic-based organisation has become standard practice in many spheres with no particular cultural requirements, such as youth clubs and football teams; and competition between organisations for limited financial resources can provoke bitter resentments. When it comes to physical segregation, Black and Minority Ethnic-led housing associations may encourage greater concentration of certain ethnic groups, and multiculturalism has acquired a growing geographical dimension through the promotion of Bengali or Muslim public spaces, such as Banglatown and the dominating bulk of the London Muslim Centre.

Chapters 7 and 8 showed how official encouragement of faith groups evolved through multiculturalism and through changes in local governance and how this has developed in a dialectical relationship with the growth of Islamism. Islamist ideas have become increasingly influential, especially as Muslims have found themselves at the centre of government policies, though by no means all Muslims who have become politically involved through faith-based groups would consider themselves Islamists and their political interests may be relatively parochial. All kinds of mosques have been able to grow in importance as a result of government promotion of faith communities and the significance of Muslim identity has been strengthened.

Chapters 8 and 9 looked at how government responses to 9/11 served to inspire Islamic consciousness and mobilisation through Islamic identity. The 'War on Terror' has both strengthened Muslim resistance and fuelled Islamophobia, and each of these has boosted the other. Divisions have been widened by the radical Islamist groups looked at in Chapter 8, as well as by the far right and by conservative and xenophobic elements in the mainstream parties.

As a result of all this emphasis on faith and ethnicity, as well as the numerical growth of the Bengali community, Tower Hamlets has seen the emergence of a new populism that chases the votes of the new Bengali Muslim majority, as Chapter 9 demonstrated.

Faith schools are public institutions that have come from a much earlier politics, but they too have had a major impact on segregation. There are, as yet, no state-funded Islamic schools in Tower Hamlets, however, there are church schools – both Church of England and Roman Catholic – and these have enabled segregation to be greater among school children than among the general population. There is no significant Christian revival, but church schools can use religious affiliation as a basis for selection and many white parents who are concerned about bringing up their children in an increasingly Bengali-dominated milieu work hard to boost their church-going credentials.[4]

In recent decades, the nature of segregation has changed with the changing economic profile of the East End. Neoliberal governments have promoted gentrification, including subsidising large-scale 'regeneration'. They have promoted commercial development and home ownership, and privatised and demolished social housing. This has brought in a new professional class and displaced older residents. However, the Bengali community has continued to expand and occupies a large part of the cheaper housing that remains. And, while Bengalis are still disproportionately in low-income households, a minority have had commercial success and been able to benefit from these developments. Old rhetoric lingers on, and there is a confusing tendency to simplify the pressures of gentrification as 'white' incomers competing with the now-established 'Bengali community'. However it is clear that the biggest divisions in the East End today are often not those of ethnicity, but of class.

Does segregation matter?

At the beginning of the new century, just when liberal multiculturalism and the celebration of difference seemed to have become the litmus test of progressive thought and political correctness, politicians of all hues began to compete to declare multiculturalism in crisis. 9/11 has come to be seen as a watershed for multiculturalism, but fears of Islamic radicalism had already been growing through the 1990s, and in the summer of 2001 – a few months before the planes hit the twin towers – 'race riots', involving young Muslims in the northern English towns of Oldham, Burnley and Bradford, had already produced calls for a new integrationism. The UK government responded to the riots with the establishment of a Community Cohesion Review Team that raised concerns about different ethnic groups leading 'parallel lives' and called for the development of 'shared principles of citizenship'.[5] The growing concern (bordering on panic) over separatism was summed up for many commentators by the public warning from Trevor Phillips, Chair of the Commission for Racial Equality, that 'we are sleepwalking our way to segregation'.[6] By the time Phillips gave that warning, in September 2005, Al Qaeda had become a household name, British troops had gone into Afghanistan and Iraq, and bombs on London's public transport system had demonstrated the destructive potential of 'home-grown' terrorists.

Politicians are concerned about segregation because of its potential to alienate people from British society, leaving them open to 'extremist' ideologies, and because it can breed division and unrest in the competition for limited resources and no one wants the destructive violence of 'race riots'. But, as discussed in the previous section, many politicians also want to avoid deep-rooted socio-economic change and they may welcome a bit of competition between ethnic groups as a useful counter to much more challenging class-based unrest. Better, they might argue that different groups should compete for a small share of the cake, than that they should combine and demand a larger share. Divide-and-rule politics is a dangerous balancing act.

Media coverage of segregation is often driven by a populist, right-wing xenophobia, and politicians are often criticised for riding the populist horse. Meanwhile, many liberal commentators have preferred to focus on the resulting victimisation of minority ethnic groups,[7] and the increasingly xenophobic turn against multiculturalism that is taking place in mainstream politics has encouraged many on the left to spring to its defence. In *Defending Multiculturalism: A Guide for the Movement*, published ten years after 9/11, a range of writers, from academics to politicians and activists, set out their case.[8] However, the book exhibits a general failure to distinguish between the defence of difference (and of immigration *per se*, which is another issue again) and the defence of multiculturalism as a political programme. With defence of the 'Other' elided with multiculturalism, no space is allowed for a left critique of the impacts of multiculturalism or of other identity politics. Tariq Modood does make a useful distinction between 'multiculturalism', where 'the public sphere must accommodate the presence of new group identities and norms',[9] and what he labels 'cosmopolitanism', which 'emerges by accepting the concept of difference while critiquing or dissolving the concept of groups',[10] but he continues to assert that for Muslims it is the multicultural route that is appropriate. This is based not on analytical argument but on the empirical observation that '[p]erceptions of Muslims as groups, by themselves and non-Muslim majorities, are hardening'. Xenophobic attitudes are also hardening,[11] but while we need to analyse these developments, we do not have to accept them as either inevitable or desirable. The book makes the important claim that immigrant groups are being used as scapegoats for the failures of neoliberal economics so as to cut across resistance to the imposition of austerity politics and welfare cuts, but it does not address the argument that the practice of multiculturalism makes it easier for different groups to blame each other and harder for them to unite together to fight the cuts and austerity policies.

Exponents of multiculturalism have continued to focus on attempts to resolve the inevitable conflicts that result from extending the Rights of Man as an individual to cover the rights of different cultural groups, and of what to do when western liberal concepts of difference-blind equality run up against the mores of other traditions.[12] Bhikhu Parekh's *Rethinking Multiculturalism*, published in 2000, set the tone for an approach that, rather than question fundamental concepts, becomes absorbed in the practical details and difficulties of interpreting hegemonic liberal values so as to accommodate cultural, ethnic and religious distinctions and conflicts.[13]

Some writers have contrasted segregation with ideas of citizenship, building on the growing involvement of Muslims in civil society. This approach can be set against simplistic attempts by various politicians to define an elusive shared Britishness, but remains little more than another name for the same communitarian forms that we have at present. So, for example, John Rex has attempted to develop multicultural theory by using the concept of citizenship to promote a culturally sensitive form of integration.[14] He 'draw[s] upon the sociology of Emile Durkheim ... who had argued for the necessity under conditions of organic solidarity for there to be some group standing between the family and the state within which individuals could feel at home', and suggests that this function could be fulfilled through the 'concept of separate communal structures and immigrant group organisation'.[15] In a similar vein, Justin Gest, whose field work included a study of young Bengali men in Tower Hamlets, discusses countering alienation through schemes for promoting the acceptance of Muslims as citizens, but ignores the need for wider socio-economic change.[16]

The Institute of Race Relations' journal, *Race and Class*, has proved a bastion of multiculturalism, or at least of separate organisation. Its recent editor, Arun Kundnani, has supplied a cogent criticism of the turn towards a new intolerant assimilationism and its imposition in the form of a government-sponsored monolithic British nationalism, and also of the conservative impact of institutionalised multiculturalism.[17] However, his alternative prescription relies on a vague plea for universal human rights and a return to the anti-racist movements that came out of the fights for Black Power and against colonialism; and he sees possibilities for a new political engagement in progressive British politics mediated through a Muslim identity. He welcomes the opportunity for a 'revival of the left-wing critique of multiculturalism'[18] begun by *Race and Class* two decades ago, but this was a critique that itself rejected materialist analysis and class unity in favour of the dead-end of organisation based around identity. Also in *Race and Class*, Anandi Ramamurthy's study of the Asian youth movements looks back approvingly at their 'broad-based black unity' – which she contrasts with the later splintering into cultural and religious identities – but doesn't look at what this focus of organisation might mean for relations with the white working class and for wider class unity.[19]

Meanwhile, Will Kymlicka has presented a teleological view of the evolution of liberal democracies in which forty years of multiculturalism 'has often helped deepen democratic citizenship and created more just and free societies'.[20] Although there have been big changes in inter-ethnic relations, this seems rather too complacent as a description of a period for almost three-quarters of which the gap between rich and poor has been widening. Indeed, this period has led us into a global economic crisis where, in the absence of a significant left alternative, social frustrations will increasingly turn towards scapegoat politics and intolerance of all kinds.

Criticisms of multiculturalism are often associated with conservative and xenophobic understandings, however there have been a few dissident voices from within the liberal tradition. Brian Barry's *Culture and Equality* is very different in tone from Amartya Sen's *Identity and Violence* and Kenan Malik's many writings, but all three authors argue against the prioritising of cultural difference as political process – which, as Malik points out, has to be distinguished from 'diversity as lived experience'. 'I am critical of multiculturalism', he writes, 'precisely because I want to defend diversity.'[21] Barry's central concerns are for a fundamental equality of individual treatment and the application of universal human rights, including the right for people to exit a group at minimal 'cost'. He criticises a wide range of multicultural theories and practices for their impact on these basic liberal concepts. Sen argues that those who regard humanity as a federation of different cultures or religions, and ignore the plurality of cross-cutting identities, help to prepare the ground for confrontation. The emphasis given to cultural group can reinforce prejudices, restrict understanding and feed into sectarianism, with its potential for brutal violence. For Malik, multicultur-alism represents a fundamental attack on Enlightenment values of secular ration-alism, equal rights, and – the main subject of his book *From Fatwa to Jihad* – of freedom of expression.[22] Both Sen and Malik argue that multiculturalism not only restricts individual freedoms, but also strengthens religious authorities and cultural conservatism at the expense of progressive secular movements and organisations and of cultural evolution. Both Sen and Barry compare the way that politics is increasingly being mediated through community leaders with the approach taken by colonial rulers.[23] And all three regard the emphasis on group difference as an impediment to greater economic equality. Sen is especially concerned with multiculturalism's impact on global politics, where discontent at inequality, instead of being focussed on improving economic policies, is diverted into ethnic-based vengeance. Barry, who concentrates on domestic policies, argues that multiculturalism directs attention away from other inequalities, makes it harder for people from different groups to work together in pursuit of common interests and can result in destructive intergroup competition:

> Not only does [identity politics] do nothing to change the structure of unequal opportunities and outcomes, it actually entrenches them by embroiling those in the lower reaches of the distribution in internecine warfare.[24]

These arguments primarily look at multiculturalism as government policy, but could also be applied to the politics of resistance.

Malik acknowledges that 'the collapse of the left [and] the demise of class politics ... helped pave the way for multicultural policies',[25] but his own far-left politics are in the past and his interest now is not in putting forward an alternative political strategy, but in defending the Enlightenment project. The bitter rejection that this line of argument can elicit is evidenced by Kundnani's review of *From Fatwa to Jihad* on the Institute of Race Relations' website. Although it may be reasonable to accuse Malik of unrealistic optimism in his assessments of current racism, it is unhelpful to say the least simply to dismiss his relevance by branding him in the heading as an 'ex-anti-racist', and also quite inaccurate to compare his approach with the forced secularism of the French state. But it probably would not have mattered what arguments Malik had used, since Kundnani believes that 'Liberal anti-multiculturalism now serves, by default if not intent, to reinforce the ideological underpinnings of today's racism and imperialism'.[26]

While both Barry and Sen are concerned about addressing economic inequality, they are very far from advocating that this be done through an alternative emphasis on economic structures and class-based politics. For Sen, class is just one factor in a person's multiple identity. He quotes Marx's own refutation of the simplistic view that sees 'workers "only" as workers',[27] but does not engage with the argument that this does not preclude class from being the major organising factor in the fight for greater equality. Instead, Sen is left to rely for improvement on the powers of democratic reasoning. Barry begins his book by declaring Marxism dead and jumping on its grave.[28]

It seems to have become acceptable to dismiss the whole cannon of Marxist thought without having to resort to an argument. The contention of this book is that not only is this poor academic practice, it also denies us access to crucial ideological tools with which to attack inequality and – the focus of my study – to construct approaches for campaigning for greater equality in a diverse environment. It is not enough to dismiss Marx, as Barry does, on the grounds that his 'contemptuous attitude to standard liberal rights provided an ideological underpinning for the monstrous abuses of the legal system perpetrated by the regimes' run by 'Lenin, Stalin and Mao'.[29] Even putting aside the important differences between these regimes, this ignores the debates within Marxism over interpretations of Marx's views and actions with respect to rights, and also (which is a different issue) over the role of rights within Marxist thought more broadly. Some Marxists are, indeed, wary of the concept of rights, but others are not. Many, including Marx himself, have been at the forefront of campaigns for civil and political liberties, and this is quite compatible with a distrust of 'universal rights' talk for its potential to be used to mask 'bourgeois interests'. These arguments are clearly addressed in Amy Bartholomew's article, 'Should a Marxist believe in Marx on rights?', which also contrasts Marx's firm rejection

of egoistic individualism with 'his persistent attention to individual self-develop-
ment ... within the community'.[30]

A left alternative

Marxism has a long history of engagement with ethnically diverse societies, both
theoretically and in political practice. This has allowed the development of a
distinct critical perspective on political multiculturalism and related ideologies
and has provided the basis for alternative forms of political organisation. Within
most recent scholarship these ideas and experiences are simply off the radar, but
in this history I have attempted to re-engage with them both through theoretical criticism and through the use of comparative historical examples.

Multiculturalism's liberal critics have exposed its inherent dangers, but they
have failed to provide an alternative route to a fairer and less prejudiced society.
Marxism argues that racism and ethnic discrimination are derived ultimately
from socio-economic structures, and the struggle against discrimination and
prejudice must be incorporated in the struggle to change those structures – it
must be primarily a socio-economic struggle. Divisions that cut across and
hinder that socio-economic struggle also hinder the struggle against racism and
discrimination.

Although multicultural politics is generally associated with post-colonial
immigration, the issues it attempts to address are much older. In searching for the
evolution of Marxist ideas about such issues, it is helpful to look at the responses
of the early Marxist theorists to the juxtaposition of different national and ethnic
groups within European nations and within the Russian and Austro-Hungarian
empires. Of particular interest is the discussion of the 'Jewish Question', because
this could have no territorial resolution (at least within the countries
concerned); and also because this question and the theories surrounding it were
brought to London's East End by the Russian Jewish immigrants of the late
nineteenth and early twentieth centuries.

Marx's own, much discussed, relationship to Judaism might best be described
as dismissive. To him, both religion and racial distinctions were regressive forces
that he did not wish to promote. If these forces were removed then, he argued,
Jews would be distinguished only by their place in the economic structures of
society, structures that he hoped to see demolished. Jewishness would then cease
to be, as Jews would be simply part of wider humanity.[31] The stark language of
his writing on the 'Jewish Question' has discouraged more sympathetic Marxists
from referring to it,[32] and Marx himself demonstrated no particular interest in
the plight of the Jewish worker. However, Engels engaged with the Jewish socialists in London and encouraged others to work with the East End Jews,[33] and
Marx's daughter Eleanor, who was active in the East End labour movement,
taught herself Yiddish and was glad to refer to her own Jewish roots.[34]

While active opposition to anti-Semitism and racism would today be considered fundamental to Marxist practice, many nineteenth-century socialists were not convinced of its importance.[35] The central figure in developing and promoting a Marxist understanding of the predicament of the Jewish worker was Karl Kautsky, who was largely based in Austria and Germany but also spent some time with Engels in London. For Kautsky the problem was anti-Semitism and the ultimate solution assimilation, though this could not and should not be forced. Kautsky recognised that anti-Semitism was not just a problem for the Jews. He understood its reactionary force in deflecting anger from the real causes of exploitation, and in an article published in 1885, he described anti-Semitism as socialism's 'most dangerous opponent'.[36] The article also argued that Jewish 'racial characteristics' were products of history rather than nature, themes he was later to develop much more fully.[37] Kautsky was consistently supportive of Jewish socialist movements, such as the General Union of Jewish Workers in Lithuania, Poland and Russia, or Bund, but he also insisted on the importance of avoiding isolation, and saw the Jewish movements as a transitional step towards a time when separate Jewish socialist institutions would be redundant.

During the last century, similar arguments were taken up by Marxists of all ethnic backgrounds and especially those fighting colonial or racial oppression. However, as in the Bengali examples in this history, many of these theorists and activists were persuaded to postpone the economic struggle and class unity for a later stage that never came.

Perhaps the best-known recent exponent of these ideas is Robert Miles. Miles argued that 'race' is a human idea commonly used to explain and excuse unequal societies generated by the historical processes of capitalist development and the formation of the nation state and make them appear 'natural'.[38] The effects of racism are thus not the result of a thing called 'race' but of processes of racialisation that emerge through the material conditions of capitalist development. Today, minority groups are more often identified by their 'ethnicity' than their 'race', and the choice of this term (which is deemed non-essentialist) gives an implied acknowledgment that this refers to a social construct; but that does not mean that society will refrain from giving that construct negative connotations.

Miles (as noted in the introduction) saw immigrant workers and their children as forming a racialised class fraction within the broader working class. He made it clear that the working class should never be regarded as a homogenous group, as it is always fractured by different and sometimes overlapping interests (such as those based on gender or work skills).[39] He explained:

the construction of 'race' occurs within the context of class boundaries ... [O]ne must always recognise that a racialised class fraction is simultaneously (and dialectically) a fraction of a class which has an antagonistic relation to other classes. An important consequence of the latter point is that divisions within the working class should not be assumed to be absolute and universal.[40]

In the case of most post-war immigrants from the New Commonwealth, the work they found was poorly paid and unattractive, often in the decaying manufacturing sector. Their class position was determined by the historical and material conditions of the post-war labour shortage, and then on top of that by the processes of racialisation used to justify and encourage the discriminatory practices that put them and kept them in some of the worst jobs and housing. This fractionalisation was reproduced in the second generation under the deeper racism generated by the competitive material conditions of growing unemployment.

Although Miles gives most attention to racisms that have their roots in colonial relations, this was just one aspect of capitalist development. In *Racism After 'Race Relations'*, he traced the generic roots of racism to the 'ideology of the civilising mission'. He argued that in each different historical instance, 'the civilisation project has been initiated by a class, or a fraction of a class, in order to establish and to legitimate a social hierarchy, and therefore a set of relations of domination'.[41] He showed that this is a process that has occurred within nations, across national boundaries and as part of colonisation, and also that these are the same 'civilising' processes and to some extent the same terminology that have been employed to control the lower classes.[42]

Miles demonstrates that, far from ignoring racism as is often claimed, Marxism provides a coherent explanation for its development. Consequently it also provides the basis for undermining it:

> We do not need to articulate the struggle against these exclusions as a 'race struggle' when we can express them as specific instances of a wider and longer struggle for a universal citizenship.[43]

In contrast, those who prioritise 'racial' difference, even as a form of radical resistance to discrimination, serve to generate confusion. They reinforce the racialisation of society while ignoring, and drawing attention away from, the socio-economic structures that created racialised distinctions and that continue to thrive through dividing potential working-class resistance. Though they would see themselves as progressive, the result of their actions is reactionary.

Miles' analysis concentrates on racialised divisions, but similar arguments can be extended to include divisions based on faith. As we saw in Chapter 9, Marxism also understands religion as a social construct that often acts to preserve social hierarchies and that can similarly be used to obscure understanding of economic structures and disrupt working-class unity.

As this history has shown, developments in progressive left politics ensured that the political mobilisation of the East End Bengalis was never primarily based on socio-economic lines, and this has contributed to physical and social segregation and hampered the fight against endemic social inequalities. But there are examples of Marxist organisation from the East End, as well as elsewhere, that demonstrate the possibilities – and also the problems – of putting Marxist ideas into practice.

Chapter 5 looked at how the East End's early Jewish immigrants attempted to use trade-unionism to build working-class solidarity across the ethnic divide, while organising separately for practical reasons. Aaron Lieberman, who established the East End's first Jewish socialist organisation, the Hebrew Socialist Union, in 1876, had previously broken new ground in organising Jewish workers in Vilna (modern Vilnius). His socialism was tinged with a romantic love of his Jewish heritage, but he was a professed internationalist and he set the pattern for the combination of internationalist principles with pragmatic Jewish organisation.[44]

Almost eight years after this prologue to London Jewish socialism, Morris Winchevsky, who had been inspired by Lieberman's writing back in Russia, launched Britain's first socialist paper aimed at an immigrant readership. The *Poylisher Yidl* claimed to 'treat the Jew ... as a man, as a Jew, and as a worker'.[45] It listed four kinds of Jew:

> The 'indifferent' care only about themselves: 'assimilationists' consider Jewish separateness to be the root of Jewish troubles; 'nationalists' blame the Jews' homelessness for their sufferings; 'socialists' consider the Jewish problem to be part of the general social problem, not one apart'.[46]

Winchevsky followed Lieberman's lead in combining internationalism with community organisation. Although he was clearly at home in a Jewish cultural milieu, the fate of that culture was not what was important to him, or to others at that time. The Jewish socialist, he argued, considers the Jewish problem to be part of the general social problem, not one apart. And anti-Semitism was the result not of cultural difference but of economic conditions, with Jewish capitalists being used as scapegoats.[47]

For Bill Fishman, Winchevsky's writings, with their Yiddish satire and religious parody, exemplified 'the paradox of the outcast Jew in the diaspora', because 'he intellectualised revolution as the weapon to end all anachronisms, yet remained a hemische Yidl ("a homely Jew") emotionally committed, in language and life, to his own Jewish poor'.[48] But Winchevsky demonstrated a strong understanding of the internationalist solution to that paradox by preserving the essential ideological core of his socialism while adapting his method to suit those among whom he lived and worked. Looking back at his earlier activities from the perspective of the 1920s, Winchevsky did, however, criticise the emphasis given to a strident atheism. 'For me – and I was not alone in this – disbelief and hatred towards all faiths reached a high pitch of fanaticism', he wrote.[49] Jewish socialists and anarchists did not abandon their atheism, but they came to believe that provocative anti-religious propaganda could be counter-productive and damage their wider cause.[50]

The ability of these early socialists to instigate concrete changes was limited, and not helped by what Winchevsky described as a 'civil war' between social democrats and anarchists.[51] They faced widespread antagonism from British workers, who were fearful of competition for their jobs and susceptible to racist rhetoric. The Yiddish paper, *Arbayter Fraynd* (Workers' Friend), showed unwarranted optimism when it announced to its readers after the 1889 tailors' strike, 'You will now cease to feel strangers in a foreign land, and the great English working-class mass will accept you as brothers in their midst'.[52] However, without Jewish attempts at forging internationalist links and building trade unions, and especially the great tailors' strikes of 1889 and 1912 (described in Chapter 5), relations could have been worse.

Back in Russia, the Bund was turning separate Jewish organisation from a tactical position to a point of principle. But their insistence on their exclusive right to speak in the name of the Russian Social Democratic and Labour Party (RSDLP) on all Jewish affairs was overwhelmingly defeated at the party's second congress, held in London in 1903. Julius Martov told delegates:

> we cannot allow that any section of the party can represent the group, trade, or national interests of any sections of the proletariat. National differences play a subordinate role in relation to common class interests. What sort of organisation would we have if, for instance, in one and the same workshop, workers of different nationalities thought first and foremost of the representation of their national interest?[53]

Lenin had argued against the Bund's call for federation on the grounds that this institutionalised 'obligatory partitions'.[54] In the RSDLP journal, *Iskra*, he pointed out the 'bitter mockery' of the Bund's call for a joint struggle to avoid a repeat of the pogrom at Kishinev, which was made at the same time as they put forward rules to keep the Jewish workers separate,[55] and he complained of the Bund misinterpreting the RSDLP's actions towards itself as specifically anti-Jewish, and so stirring distrust among Jewish workers.[56] (Those who have found themselves branded as racists for arguing against multiculturalist positions may find a parallel here.)

Lenin's many attacks on the Bund pulled no punches. Although his argument, in essence, was similar to that put by Kautsky, he drew the line at what constituted dangerous separatism in a different place, and he saw the Bundist position as a threat to the unity and strength of the movement in Russia. 'There is a borderline here,' he wrote, 'which is often very slight, and which the Bundists … completely lose sight of. Combat all national oppression? Yes, of course! Fight for any kind of national development, for "national culture" in general? – Of course not.'[57]

Lenin's response to cultural difference was pragmatic. A Marxist, he explained, should oppose the slogan of national culture 'by advocating, in all languages, the slogan of workers' internationalism while "adapting" himself to all local and national features'.[58] The orientation remains Marxist, and this Marxism is articulated through different cultures for practical and not dogmatic reasons.

This could describe the approach adopted by Winchevsky almost thirty years earlier.

Bolshevik ideas were forged in a crucible of international modernism, and Trotsky explained (in his criticism of the idea of 'cultural autonomy') that 'the thought of artificially preserving national idiosyncrasies was profoundly alien to Bolshevism'.[59] Lenin's response to this issue, and to the key question of the segregation of schools, shows a careful placing of his tactical borderline. He argued that segregation would be reactionary but that, under 'real democracy', which 'can be achieved only when the workers of all nationalities are united', 'it is quite possible to ensure instruction in the native language, in native history, and so forth, without splitting up the schools according to nationality'.[60] Children of all nationalities should be mixed and equal rights and peace would be achieved through solidarity.

The Bolsheviks' attitude to religion was discussed in the previous chapter. Their line was uncompromising but, theoretically at least, they aimed at a tactical sensitivity. This sensitivity was one of the many things that disappeared under Stalin. Like so much else in the Bolsheviks' original programme, these approaches to religious and ethnic minority groups never got the chance to be put properly into practice in the country at large,[61] but they did guide policy and tactics within the party in the early years, and the debates are still relevant today.

Chapter 6 described how, in the East End of the 1930s, the Communist Party used the campaigns against fascism and for better housing to bring everyone together, Jew and gentile, to fight the bigger battle for fundamental economic and social change. This was an exemplary demonstration of co-ordinated campaigning, but it cannot pass without criticism. As is well known, Communist Party members found that any questioning of positions dictated by Moscow and by the party hierarchy was not tolerated.[62] In addition, the universalist outlook of party politics was not always matched by integration in political organisation or daily life. The Workers' Circle, where so much of this political activity was planned and discussed, was a Jewish organisation, and this not only reflected the still-continuing Jewish separateness but also helped to perpetuate it. Despite this, the Communist Party could claim real achievements in bringing together Jews and Gentiles and in containing the fascist threat, as well as in forcing improvements to rents and housing conditions for tenants of all backgrounds. Their activities were cut across by the Second World War, and by the cautious approach to British politics that the Party adopted in its wake.

The 1930s was the last time that the East End's main immigrant struggles were fought through class-based politics, though there have been attempts by left organisations to reintroduce a class line. Chapter 6 described how East London Workers Against Racism tried to involve the white working class in the fight against racism and so resist the need for Bengalis to be restricted to separate safe areas. Chapter 7 recorded that Militant Tendency resisted the idea of separate Labour Party black sections. (In contrast, Chapter 9 showed that, although Respect claimed a socialist pedigree, its tactics were compromised from the start.)

These practical examples can only give an indication of what might be achieved if multi-ethnic campaigns that focused on socio-economic issues were adopted consistently over a long period – and, of course, really fundamental change would require such politics to extend well beyond the confines of the East End. However, even this limited history demonstrates possibilities for a return to a class-based politics that could bring about real improvements in people's living conditions and opportunities across all ethnicities. At the same time, it highlights the importance of striking the correct balance between the pragmatic demands arising from working with ethnic minority groups and the dangers of separatism.

The political and socio-economic integration implied by this approach does not require the homogenisation of cultural differences, and it still allows room for the continually evolving intermingling of different cultures that Paul Gilroy has labelled 'ordinary multiculture'.[63] We can still enjoy – and spend public money on – Bengali cultural events.[64] However, if we continue to nurture a political focus on culture and identity – be it through multiculturalism or faith-groups, reactionary nationalism or even identity-based anti-racist organisation – this can distract attention from fundamental socio-economic divisions and hold back progress towards greater equality. When, in consequence, society polarises and rifts widen, the frustrations of those at the bottom can turn against ethnic minorities, and everyone suffers.

In a fair society, resources should be allotted according to need – rather than to each according to his (or her) ethnicity. If one ethnic group is generally more deprived than others, it would still benefit – or at least those members would who actually needed more help. Today, the Bengali community, like many other former immigrant groups, has come of age, and Bengalis have taken their place within local structures at all levels. This does not mean that there is not institutionalised racism or growing levels of Islamophobia, or that ethnic minorities (or anyone else) can relax their vigilance in the fight against prejudice of all kinds; and it also does not mean that there is not huge social deprivation in the Bengali community and beyond. What it does mean is that community-based organisation is not enough. In fact, as this history shows, identity politics can even be counter-productive. There are deep and fundamental inequalities that cut across all ethnicities and communities, and these can only be addressed by a united working class. As in the past, effective political action needs to combine international socialist principles with pragmatic – and also sensitive – work within and between different communities, being careful not to cross the invisible line into dangerous separation.

Notes

1 John Solomos, *Race and Racism in Britain* (Basingstoke: Macmillan, 1993), pp. 63–70.
2 S.J. Smith, *The Politics of 'Race' and Residence: Citizenship, Segregation and White Supremacy in Britain* (Cambridge: Polity Press, 1989), p. 50.
3 It is important, here, to distinguish between celebrating cultural diversity and *prioritising* cultural identity in the organisation of civil society.
4 Geoff Dench, Kate Gavron and Michael Young, *The New East End: Kinship, Race and Conflict* (London: Profile, 2006), pp.145–6.
5 Home Office, *The Cantle Report - Community Cohesion: A Report of the Independent Review Team* (2001) pp. 9 and 11, http://resources.cohesioninstitute.org.uk/Publications/Documents/Document/DownloadDocumentsFile.aspx?recordId=96&file=PDFversion, accessed 21 November 2012.
6 Speech given in Manchester Town Hall, 22 September 2005, http://83.137.212.42/sitearchive/cre/Default.aspx.LocID-0hgnew07r.RefLocID-0hg00900c001001.Lang-EN.htm, accessed 12 December 2008.
7 See, for example, Deborah Phillips, 'Parallel Lives? Challenging Discourses of British Muslim Self-segregation', *Environment and Planning D*, 24:1 (2006), 25–40.
8 Hassan Mahamdallie (ed.), *Defending Multiculturalism: A Guide for the Movement* (London: Bookmarks, 2011).
9 Tariq Modood, 'Multiculturalism and Integration: Struggling with Confusions', in Mahamdallie, *Defending Multiculturalism*, 61–76, p. 68. A slightly longer version of Modood's chapter was published as part of the British Academy's 'New Paradigms in Public Policy' project in February 2012, see Tariq Modood, *Post-immigration 'Difference' and Integration: The Case of Muslims in Western Europe* (London: British Academy, 2012).
10 Modood, 'Multiculturalism and Integration', p. 67.
11 *Ibid.*, p. 76.
12 Charles Taylor, *Multiculturalism and 'The Politics of Recognition'* (Princeton: Princeton University Press, 1992), p. 43.
13 Bhiku Parekh, *Rethinking Multiculturalism: Cultural Diversity and Political Theory* (Basingstoke: Palgrave, 2000). See also Paul Kelly (ed.), *Multiculturalism Reconsidered: Culture and Equality and its Critics* (Cambridge: Polity Press, 2002), written in response to Brian Barry's *Culture and Equality: An Egalitarian Critique of Multiculturalism* (Cambridge: Polity Press, 2001).
14 In line with Roy Jenkins' groundbreaking speech at the Commonwealth Institute, given as Home Secretary in May 1966, where he defined integration 'not as a flattening process of assimilation but as equal opportunity accompanied by cultural diversity, in an atmosphere of mutual tolerance'. Quoted in A. Sivanandan, *Communities of Resistance: Writings on Black Struggles for Socialism* (London: Verso, 1990), p. 80.
15 John Rex, 'An Afterword on the Situation of British Muslims in a World Context' in Tahir Abbas, *Muslim Britain: Communities Under Pressure* (London and New York: Zed Books, 2005), 235–43, p. 241.
16 Justin Gest, *Apart: Alienated and Engaged Muslims in the West* (London: Hurst and Company, 2010).
17 Arun Kundnani, 'The Death of Multiculturalism', *Race and Class*, 43:4 (2002), 67–72; Arun Kundnani, 'Integrationism: The Politics of Anti-Muslim Racism', *Race and Class*, 48:4 (2007), 24–44; Arun Kundnani, 'Islamism and the Roots of Liberal Rage', *Race and Class*, 50: 2 (2008), 40–68, p. 58.
18 Kundnani, 'The Death of Multiculturalism', p. 72.

19 Anandi Ramamurthy, 'The Politics of Britain's Asian Youth Movements', *Race and Class*, 48:2 (2006), 38–60, p. 58.

20 W. Kymlicka, 'Reply to Review Symposium on *Multicultural Odysseys*', *Ethnicities*. 8 (2008), p. 280.

21 Kenan Malik, 'What is Wrong with Multiculturalism?', Milton K. Wong Lecture given to the Laurier Institute, University of British Colombia and broadcast on CBC on 22 June 2012, http://kenanmalik.wordpress.com/2012/06/04/what-is-wrong-with-multiculturalism-part-1/, accessed July 2012.

22 Kenan Malik, *From Fatwa to Jihad: The Rushdie Affair and its Legacy* (London: Atlantic Books, 2009).

23 Brian Barry, 'Second Thoughts – and Some First Thoughts Revised', in Paul Kelly (ed.) *Multiculturalism Reconsidered:* Culture and Equality *and its Critics* (Cambridge: Polity Press, 2002), 204–38, p. 228. For another colonial parallel see Monica Ali in Chapter 7, footnote 104.

24 Barry, *Culture and Equality,* p. 326.

25 Malik, 'What is Wrong with Multiculturalism?' He also cites 'the narrowing of the political sphere' and 'the erosion of more universalist visions of social change'.

26 Arun Kundnani, 'Kenan Malik: Journey of an Ex-anti-racist', Institute of Race Relations website (2011), www.irr.org.uk/news/kenan-malik-journey-of-an-ex-anti-racist, accessed July 2012 .

27 Amartya Sen, *Identity and Violence: The Illusion of Destiny* (London: Penguin, 2007), pp. 24–5.

28 Barry, *Culture and Equality*, p. 3.

29 *Ibid.*, p. 14.

30 Amy Bartholomew, 'Should a Marxist believe in Marx on Rights?', *The Socialist Register* (1990), 244–64, p. 254.

31 Karl Marx, *On The Jewish Question* (1844), www.marxists.org/archive/marx/works/1844/jewish-question, accessed 21 November 2012 .

32 Such as Karl Kautsky, see Jack Jacobs, *On Socialists and 'the Jewish Question' after Marx* (New York: New York University Press, 1992), p. 9.

33 *Ibid.*, p. 29.

34 Yvonne Kapp, *Eleanor Marx: Volume II, The Crowded Years (1884–1898)* (London: Lawrence and Wishart, 1976), p. 521; letter from Eleanor Marx Aveling, October 1890 (now in the Wess Archive, Modern Records Centre, Warwick) in which she is glad to accept an invitation to speak at a public meeting condemning persecution of the Jews in Russia, adding 'the more glad, that my father was a Jew'.

35 Nora Levin, *Jewish Socialist Movements, 1871–1917: While Messiah Tarried* (London: Routledge and Kegan Paul, 1978), pp. 100–12.

36 Jacobs, *On Socialists and 'the Jewish Question' after Marx*, p. 12.

37 Karl Kautsky, *Are the Jews a Race* (1926) www.marxists.org/archive/kautsky/1914/jewsrace/index.htm, accessed 21 November 2012.

38 See Robert Miles, *Racism after 'Race Relations'* (London: Routledge, 1993), pp. 27–52.

39 See Robert Miles, *Racism and Migrant Labour* (London: Routledge and Kegan Paul, 1982), pp. 151–88. Stuart Hall and Paul Gilroy also talked about class fractions, but their meaning was very different. Their fractions were not part of the heterogeneous and changing groups that make up the working class, but – potentially at least – a class in themselves.

40 Miles, *Racism and Migrant Labour*, p. 187.

41 Miles, *Racism after 'Race Relations'*, pp. 89–90.

42 *Ibid.*, p. 103. This is still a Eurocentric history and needs to be extended to include non-European racism, but this can be done without contradiction. Miles' argument

is supported by the attitudes shown at the end of the nineteenth century towards 'Outcast London', the less respectable residents of the East End, as described by Gareth Stedman Jones in *Outcast London: A Study in the Relationship between Classes in Victorian Society* (Harmondsworth: Penguin, 1984), especially pp. 11 and 14.

43 Miles, *Racism after 'Race Relations'*, p. 23.

44 William J. Fishman, *East End Jewish Radicals 1875–1914* (London: Duckworth, 1975), pp. 97–134; Levin, *Jewish Socialist Movements*, pp. 40–6.

45 Quoted in Lloyd P. Gartner, *The Jewish Immigrant in England, 1870–1914* (London: George Allen and Unwin, 1960), p. 107. Although the language is masculine, consistent with the time in which it was written, Winchevsky was also concerned with the rights of women.

46 Paraphrased in Gartner, *The Jewish Immigrant in England*, p. 107.

47 Gartner, *The Jewish Immigrant in England*, pp. 107–8.

48 Fishman, *East End Jewish Radicals*, pp. 151–2.

49 Morris Winchevsky, *Gezamlte Verk Vol IX* (New York, 1927), p. 155, quoted in Elias Tcherikower (trans. Aaron Antonvosky), *The Early Jewish Labor Movement in the United States* (New York: Yivo Institute for Jewish Research, 1961) p. 248.

50 Tcherikower, *The Early Jewish Labor Movement in the United States*, pp. 266–71; Fishman, *East End Jewish Radicals*, p. 169.

51 Levin, *Jewish Socialist Movements*, p. 132.

52 Quoted in Fishman, *East End Jewish Radicals*, p. 178. The biblical reference is typical of Yiddish writing, even by non-religious socialists. ('I have been a stranger in a strange land' – *Exodus* 2.22).

53 Congress Minutes, quoted in Alan Woods, *Bolshevism: The Road to Revolution* (London: Wellred, 1999), p. 139. Eight years earlier, in a historic speech to Jewish socialists in Vilna, Martov had himself put forward the aim of building 'a special Jewish labor organisation'; however, this was for the purely practical reason that the mobilisation of the Jewish workers had been so successful while the general Russian movement was still weak. 'A working class that is content with the lot of an inferior nation will not rise up against the lot of an inferior class', he had told his listeners, but he warned them that 'the growth of national consciousness must go hand in hand with the growth of class consciousness'. He was clear that 'We must remain steadfast in our ties with the Russian and Polish movements … If their struggle fails, we will not be able to achieve much.' – quoted in Levin, *Jewish Socialist Movements*, p. 247.

54 V.I. Lenin, *Collected Works* (Moscow: Progress Publishers, 1961–5), Vol. 6, p. 485.

55 *Ibid.*, Vol. 6, p. 519.

56 *Ibid.*, Vol. 7, pp. 101–2.

57 V.I. Lenin, *Critical Remarks on the National Question* (Progress Publishers: Moscow, 1951), pp. 24–5.

58 Lenin, *Collected Works*, Vol. 20, p. 25.

59 Trotsky in *Stalin*, published 1940, quoted in Peter Buch's introduction to *Leon Trotsky, On the Jewish Question* (New York: Pathfinder, 1970), p. 11. Theories of cultural-national autonomy (or extra-territorial national autonomy) were developed by the Austrian Socialist Party and adopted by the Jewish Bund.

60 Lenin, *Collected Works*, Vol. 19, p. 533.

61 Stalin promoted both anti-Semitism and separate organisation. Pragmatic use of Yiddish crossed the line into active segregation and he even established an Autonomous Territory designated for Jewish colonisation in Birobidzhan in the inhospitable Soviet Far East. See Robert Weinberg, *Stalin's Forgotten Zion: Birobidzhan and the Making of a Soviet Jewish Homeland* (Berkeley: University of California Press, 1998).

62 A detailed account of what this meant for one East End activist, who was eventually excluded from the party, is given in Joe Jacob's autobiography: Joe Jacobs, *Out of the Ghetto: My Youth in the East End. Communism and Fascism 1913–1939* (London: Janet Simon, 1978).

63 Paul Gilroy, 'Melancholia and multiculture', *Open Democracy* (2004), www.opendemocracy.net/arts-multiculturalism/article_2035.jsp, accessed July 2012.

64 Though this approach would question the desirability of promoting organisations such as specifically Bengali youth clubs and football teams.

Bibliography

'A Voice from the Aliens', pamphlet produced by Jewish trade unionists (1895).

Abbas, Ali Mohammed, autobiographical memoir (manuscript, n.d., shown to the author by his brother, Ali Mohammed Azhar).

Abbas, Tahir (ed.), *Muslim Britain: Communities Under Pressure* (London and New York: Zed Books, 2005).

Adams, Caroline, '*They Sell Cheaper and They Live Very Odd*' (London: Community and Race Relations Unit of the British Council of Churches, 1976).

Adams, Caroline, *Across Seven Seas and Thirteen Rivers* (London: THAP Books, 1994).

Adams, Caroline, 'The Bangladesh Welfare Association in Great Britain' (manuscript notes in the Tower Hamlets Local History Library, 1982).

Ahmed, Faruque, *Bengali Journals and Journalism in the UK (1916–2007)* (London: The Ethnic Minorities Original History and Research Centre, 2008).

Ahmed, Faruque, *Bengal Politics in Britain: Logic, Dynamics and Disharmony* (North Carolina: Lulu, 2010) .

Ahmed, Tasadduq (edited by Faruque Ahmed), *Jeeban Khatar Kurano Pata* (London: The Ethnic Minorities Original History and Research Centre, 2002).

Akhtar, Muhammad Yousuf, 'Ali Muhammad Abbas Bar-at-Law: "A Great Son of Pakistan"', pamphlet published for the installation of a plaque in memory of Abbas on his home at 33 Tavistock Square (1987).

Alam, Fazlul, *Salience of Homeland: Societal Polarization within the Bangladeshi Population in Britain* (Coventry: Centre for Research in Ethnic Relations, University of Warwick, 1988).

Alderman, Geoffrey, *The Jewish Community in British Politics* (Oxford: Clarendon Press, 1983).

Alexander, Claire, '(Dis)Entangling the 'Asian Gang': Ethnicity, Identity, Masculinity', in Barnor Hesse (ed.), *Un/Settled Multiculturalisms: Diasporas, Entanglements, 'Transruptions'* (London: Zed Books, 2000).

Ali, Monica, *Brick Lane* (London: Doubleday, 2003).

Ali, Rushanara, 'Let Power Reflect the People', *Guardian*, 20 February 2008.

Allen, Chris, *Housing Market Renewal and Social Class* (London and New York: Routledge, 2008).

Ambrose, Peter, *A Drop in the Ocean: The Health Gain from the Central Stepney SRB in the Context of National Health Inequalities* (Brighton: Health and Social Policy Research Centre, 2000).

Ambrose, Peter and Dee MacDonald, *For Richer For Poorer? Counting the Costs of Regeneration in Stepney* (Brighton: Health and Social Policy Research Centre, 2001).

Ansari, Khizar Humayun, *The Emergence of Socialist Thought Among North Indian Muslims (1917–1947)* (Lahore: Book Traders, 1990).

Ansari, Humayun, *'The Infidel Within': Muslims in Britain Since 1800* (London: Hurst and Company, 2004).

Anthias, Floya, 'Race and Class Revisited – Conceptualising Race and Racisms', *The Sociological Review*, 38:2 (1990).

Anthias, Floya, 'New Hybridities, Old Concepts: The Limits of "Culture"', *Ethnic and Racial Studies*, 24:4 (2001).

Anwar, Muhammad, *Between Cultures: Continuity and Change in the Lives of Young Asians* (London: Routledge, 1998) .

Asghar, Mohammad Ali, *Bangladeshi Community Organisations in East London* (London: Bangla Heritage Ltd, 1996).

Ashe, Stephen D. and Brendan F. McGeever, 'Marxism, Racism and the Construction of "Race" as a Social and Political Relation: An Interview with Professor Robert Miles', *Ethnic and Racial Studies*, 34:12 (2011), 2009–26.

Asian Drug Project, '"Substance Use": An Assessment of the Young Asian Community in Tower Hamlets and a Summary of the Development Work of the Asian Drug Project', Report commissioned by East London and City Health Authority (1995).

Azhar, Ali Mohammed, 'Introduction' to Ali Mohammed Abbas, autobiographical memoir (manuscript, n.d.).

Back, Les, Michael Keith, Azra Khan, Kalbir Shukra and John Solomos, 'Islam and the New Political Landscape: Faith Communities, Political Participation and Social Change', *Theory, Culture & Society*, 26 (2009), 1–23.

Bailey, Ron, *The Squatters* (Harmondsworth: Penguin, 1973).

Ballard, Roger (ed.), *Desh Pardesh: The South Asian Presence in Britain* (London: C. Hurst, 1994).

Banton, Michael, *The Coloured Quarter: Negro Immigrants in an English City* (London: Jonathan Cape, 1955).

Barry, Brian, *Culture and Equality: An Egalitarian Critique of Multiculturalism* (Cambridge: Polity Press, 2001).

Barry, Brian, 'Second Thoughts – and Some First Thoughts Revised', in Paul Kelly (ed.) *Multiculturalism Reconsidered: Culture and Equality and its Critics* (Cambridge: Polity Press, 2002), 204–38.

Bartholomew, Amy, 'Should a Marxist Believe in Marx on Rights?', *The Socialist Register* (1990), 244–64.

Barton, Stephen, *The Bengali Muslims of Bradford: A Study of their Observance of Islam with Special Reference to the Function of the Mosque and the Work of the Imam* (Leeds: Department of Theology and Religious Studies, University of Leeds, 1986).

Begum, Halima and John Eade, 'All Quiet on the Eastern Front? Bangladeshi Reactions in Tower Hamlets', in Tahir Abbas (ed.), *Muslim Britain: Communities Under Pressure* (London and New York: Zed Books, 2005), 179–93.

Begum, Julie, *The Bengali Language Movement* (London: Nirmul Committee, 1996).

Bergman, David (director and researcher), *War Crimes File* (television documentary) Twenty Twenty Television, Channel 4 *Dispatches*, 3 May 1995.

Bergman, David, 'My Response to Tahmina Anam's Article on "Shahbag", 1971 War Crimes Trials in Bangladesh, and Demands for Hangings', *Bangladesh Chronicle*, 15 February 2013, www.bangladeshchronicle.net/index.php/2013/02/my-response-to-tahmina-anams-article-on-shahbag-1971-war-crimes-trials-in-bangladesh-and-demands-for-hangings, accessed 12 November 2013.

Bethnal Green and Stepney Trades Council, 'Blood on the Streets: A Report by Bethnal Green and Stepney Trades Council on Racial Attacks in East London' (1978).

Bethnal Green and Stepney Trades Council, The Joint Docklands Action Group, Tower Hamlets Branch Workers' Educational Association, and Tower Hamlets Co-op, 'Tower Hamlets: The Fight for Jobs - Tower Hamlets Unemployment Crisis Report' (1975).

Birnbaum, Ben, John Eversley, Tony Clouting, Dick Allard, John Hall, Cheryl Morgan, Kevin Woods, Roger Allen and Richard Tully, 'The Clothing Industry in Tower Hamlets: An Investigation into its Structure and Problems 1979/80 and Beyond' (manuscript, 1981, Tower Hamlets Local History Library).

Blackaby Bob, and Raj Patel, 'Black and Minority Ethnic Housing Associations: The Shape of the Future of the Sector, Chartered Institute of Housing Case Study Report' (London: CIH, 2003).

Blumenfeld, Simon, *Enough of All This! A Rent Strike Play* (London: Left Book Club Theatre Guild, 1939?). There is a copy of the play in the Unity Theatre collection in Merseyside Maritime Museum.

Booth, Charles, *Life and Labour of the People of London, 1st Series Vol. 4* (London: Macmillan, 1902).

Bornstein, Sam and Al Richardson, *Two Steps Back: Communists and the Wider Labour Movement, 1935–1945* (Ilford: Socialist Platform, 1982).

Borochov, Ber, *Essays on Nationalism, Class Struggle and the Jewish People* (London: Marxist Zionists – Young Mapan, 1971).

Boyle, J.W., book review of *The Life and Times of James Connolly* by Desmond Greaves, *Labor History*, 14:1 (1973).

Branson, Noreen and Margot Heinemann, *Britain in the Nineteen Thirties* (London: Weidenfeld and Nicolson, 1971).

Brill, Kenneth, 'The World is his Parish', in Kenneth Brill (ed.), *John Groser: East London Priest* (London: Mowbrays, 1971).

Brubaker, Rogers, 'The Return of Assimilation? Changing Perspectives on Immigration and its Sequels in France, Germany, and the United States', *Ethnic and Racial Studies*, 24:4 (2001), 531–48.

Burney, Elizabeth, *Housing on Trial: A Study of Immigrants and Local Government* (Oxford: Oxford University Press, 1967).

Bynon, Huw, 'Chaos in Tower Hamlets Respect', *Weekly Worker*, 6 July 2006.

Carey, Sean and Abdus Shukur, 'A Profile of the Bangladeshi Community in East London' *New Community*, 12:3 (1985).

Carter, Trevor, *Shattering Illusions: West Indians in British Politics* (London: Lawrence and Wishart, 1986).

Centre for Bangladeshi Studies, *Routes and Beyond: Voices of Educationally Successful Bengalis in Tower Hamlets* (London: Centre for Bangladeshi Studies, 1997).

Chandravarkar, Rajnarayan (2003) *The Origins of Industrial Capitalism in India: Business Strategies and the Working Classes in Bombay, 1900–1940* (Cambridge: Cambridge University Press, 2003).

Choudhury, T., 'The Role of Muslim Identity Politics in Radicalisation', paper commissioned by the Department for Communities and Local Government, London (2007).

Choudhury, Yousuf, *The Roots and Tales of the Bangladeshi Settlers* (Birmingham: Sylhet Local History Group, 1993).

Choudhury, Yousuf, *Sons of the Empire: Oral History from the Bangladeshi Seamen who Served on British Ships During the 1939–45 War* (Birmingham: Sylheti Social History Group, 1995).

Choudhury, Yousuf, *The Roots of Indian Sub-Continental Catering in Britain* (Sylhet: Rina Publishers, 2002).

Commission for Racial Equality, 'Homelessness and Discrimination: Report of a Formal Investigation into the London Borough of Tower Hamlets' (London: CRE, 1988).

Commission for Racial Equality, 'Statuary Code of Practice on Racial Equality in Housing (England): Consultation Draft' (London: CRE, 2006).

Connolly, James, 'The New Evangel', *Workers' Republic*, 17 June 1899, www.marxists.org/archive/connolly/1901/evangel/socrel.htm, accessed 21 November 2012 .

Connolly, James, 'Workshop Talks' (1909), www.marxists.org/archive/connolly/1909/talks/shoptlks.htm, accessed October 2012.

Cox, Anthony, *Empire, Industry and Class: The Imperial Nexus of Jute, 1840–1940* (London and New York: Routledge, 2013).

Dame Colet House, *Tenants Tackle Racism: An Account of a Series of Experimental Workshops held in Stepney – 1984/5* (London: Dame Colet House, 1986).

Daniel, Susie and Pete McGuire (eds), *The Paint House: Words from an East End Gang* (Harmondsworth: Penguin, 1972).

Dench, Geoff, Kate Gavron and Michael Young, *The New East End: Kinship, Race and Conflict* (London: Profile Books, 2006).

Department for Communities and Local Government, 'The English Indices of Deprivation 2010' (London: DCLG, 2011).

Dhondy, Farrukh, 'The Black Explosion in Schools', *Race Today* (February 1974).

Dhondy, Farrukh, *East End at Your Feet* (Basingstoke: Macmillan Education, 1976).

Dhondy, Farrukh, *Come to Mecca* (London: Collins, 1978).

Dhondy, Farrukh, *King of the Ghetto* (4-part drama for Channel 4, shown May 1986). This can be viewed at the British Film Institute.

Dixon, Conrad, 'Lascars, the Forgotten Seamen', in R. Ommer and G. Panting (eds), *Working Men Who Got Wet – Proceedings of the Fourth Conference of the Atlantic Shipping Project* (St Johns: University of Newfoundland, 1980).

Drewes, Sabine, 'Ethnic Representation and Racist Resentment in Local Politics: The Bangladeshi Community and Tower Hamlets Liberal Council 1986–93' (manuscript, 1994, Centre for Research on Nationalism, Ethnicity and Multiculturalism, University of Surrey).

Dromey, Jack and Graham Taylor, *Grunwick: The Workers' Story* (London: Lawrence and Wishart, 1978).

Duffy, Patrick, 'The Employment & Training Needs of the Bengali Community in Tower Hamlets' (summary report for the Commission for Racial Equality and the Manpower Services Commission, 1979).

Dwyer, Claire, 'Contradictions of Community: Questions of Identity for Young British Muslim Women', *Environment and Planning A*, 31 (1999), 53–68.

Eade, John, *The Politics of Community: The Bangladeshi Community in East London* (Aldershot: Avebury, 1989).

Eade, John, 'Nationalism and the Quest for Authenticity: The Bangladeshis in Tower Hamlets', *New Community*, 16:4 (1990), 493–503.

Eade, John, 'The Political Construction of Class and Community: Bangladeshi Political Leadership in Tower Hamlets, East London', in Pnina Werbner and Muhammad Anwar (eds), *Black and Ethnic Leaderships in Britain: The Cultural Dimensions of Political Action* (London: Routledge, 1991).

Eade, John, 'Identity, Nation and Religion: Educated Young Bangladeshi Muslims in London's "East End"', *International Sociology*, 9:3 (1994), 377–94.

Eade, John, 'The Political Articulation of Community and the Islamisation of Space in London', in Rohit Barot (ed.), *Religion and Ethnicity: Minorities and Social Change in the Metropolis* (Kampen (NL): Pharos, 1994).

Eade, John, 'Roots and Routes: Bangladeshis in Britain and Narratives of "Home"', in S. Weil (ed.), *Ethnicity and Migration in Global Perspective* (Jerusalem: Hebrew University Magnes Press, 1997).

Eade, John, 'Reconstructing Places: Changing Images of Locality in Docklands and Spitalfields', in John Eade (ed.), *Living the Global City* (London: Routledge, 1997).

Eade, John, Isabelle Fremeaux and David Garbin, 'The Political Construction of Diasporic Communities in the Global City', in P. Gilbert (ed.), *Imagined London* (Albany: SUNY Press, 2001).

Eade, John and David Garbin, 'Changing Narratives of Violence, Struggle and Resistance: Bangladeshis and the Competition for Resources in the Global City', *Oxford Development Studies*, 30:2 (2002), 137–49.

Eade, John, Ansar Ahmed Ullah, Jamil Iqbal and Marissa Hey (eds), *Tales of Three Generations of Bengalis in Britain* (London: Nirmul Committee and Centre for Research on Nationalism, Ethnicity and Multiculturalism, 2006).

Elliott, James and Sharifur Rahman, *Waiting for Change: Restaurant workers and the informal economy in Brick Lane* (London: Toynbee Hall and Community Links, 2009).

Feldman, David, *Englishmen and Jews: Social Relations and Political Culture 1840–1914* (New Haven and London: Yale, 1994).

Feffer, John, 'Interview with Arun Kundnani', *Foreign Policy in Focus* (25 February 2011), http://fpif.org/interview_with_arun_kundnani, accessed 20 November 2013.

Fishman, William J., *East End Jewish Radicals 1875–1914* (London: Duckworth, 1975).

Fishman, William J. (with photographs by Nicholas Breach), *The Streets of East London* (London: Duckworth, 1979).

Forman, Charlie, *Spitalfields: A Battle for Land* (London: Hilary Shipman, 1989).

Foster, Janet, '"Island Homes for Island People": Competition Conflict and Racism in the Battle over Public Housing on the Isle of Dogs', in Colin Samson and Nigel South (eds), *The Social Construction of Social Policy: Methodologies, Racism, Citizenship and the Environment* (Basingstoke: Macmillan, 1996).

Franda, Marcus, *Bangladesh, the First Decade* (New Delhi: South Asian Publishers, 1982).

Fuller, Crispian and Mike Geddes, 'Urban Governance Under Neoliberalism: New Labour and the Restructuring of State-space', *Antipode*, 40:2 (2008), 252–82.

Galloway, George, *I'm Not the Only One* (London: Penguin, 2004).

Garbin, David, 'Immigration, Territoires et Identités: Enquête dans un quartier de l'East End de Londres' (DEA Dissertation, University of Tours and University of East London, 1999).

Garbin, David, 'Migration, territoires diasporiques et politique identitaires: Bengalis musulmans entre "Banglatown" (Londres) et Sylhet (Bangladesh)' (PhD dissertation, University of Tours, 2004).

Gardner, Katy, *Global Migrants, Local Lives: Travel and Transformation in Rural Bangladesh* (Oxford: Clarendon Press, 1995).

Gardner, Katy, *Songs at the River's Edge* (London: Pluto Press, 1997).

Gardner, Katy, *Age, Narrative and Migration: The Life Course and Life Histories of Bengali Elders in London* (Oxford and New York: Berg, 2002).

Gardner, Katy and Abdus Shukur '"I'm Bengali, I'm Asian and I'm Living Here": The Changing Identity of British Bengalis', in Roger Ballard (ed.) *Desh Pardesh: South Asian Presence in Britain* (London: Hurst, 1994).

Garrard, John A., *The English and Immigration: A Comparative Study of the Jewish Influx 1880–1910* (Oxford: Oxford University Press, 1971).

Gartner, Lloyd P., *The Jewish Immigrant in England, 1870–1914* (London: George Allen and Unwin, 1960).

Geaves, Ron, *Sectarian Influences Within Islam in Britain – With Reference to the Concepts of 'Ummah' and 'Community'* (Leeds: Department of Theology and Religious Studies University of Leeds, 1996).

Geddes, Mike, 'Partnership and the Limits to Local Governance in England: Institutionalist Analysis and Neoliberalism', *International Journal of Urban and Regional Research*, 30:1 (2006), 76–97.

Gest, Justin, *Apart: Alienated and Engaged Muslims in the West* (London: Hurst, 2010).

Gilligan, Andrew, *Dispatches: Britain's Islamic Republic* (television programme), Channel 4, 1 March 2010.

Gilligan, Andrew, blogs.telegraph.co.uk/news/author/andrewgilligan.

Gilroy, P., 'Steppin' Out of Babylon – Race, Class and Autonomy', in Centre for Contemporary Cultural Studies, *The Empire Strikes Back: Race and Racism in 70s Britain* (London: Hutchinson, 1982).

Gilroy, Paul, *There Ain't no Black in the Union Jack* (London, Routledge,1991).

Gilroy, Paul, 'Melancholia and Multiculture', *Open Democracy* (2004), www.opendemocracy.net/arts-multiculturalism/article_2035.jsp, accessed July 2012.

Girouard, Mark, Dan Cruickshank, Raphael Samuel *et al.*, *The Saving of Spitalfields* (London: The Spitalfields Historic Buildings Trust, 1989).

Glynn, Sarah (ed.), *The Way We Worked: An Oral History by Members of St Hilda's East Community Centre and Stepney Jewish Community Centre* (London: St Hilda's East Community Centre, 1999).

Glynn, Sarah, 'Bengali Muslims: The New East End Radicals?', *Ethnic and Racial Studies*, 25:6 (2002) 969–88.

Glynn, Sarah, 'East End Immigrants and the Battle for Housing: A Comparative Study of Political Mobilisation in the Jewish and Bengali Communities', *Journal of Historical Geography*, 31 (2005), 528–45.

Glynn, Sarah, 'The Spirit of '71 - How the Bangladeshi War of Independence has Haunted Tower Hamlets', *Socialist History Journal*, 29 (2006), 56–75.

Glynn, Sarah, 'East End Bengalis and the Labour Party – The End of a Long Relationship?', in Claire Dwyer and Caroline Bressey (eds), *New Geographies of Race and Racism* (Aldershot: Ashgate, 2008), 67–82 .

Glynn, Sarah, 'Liberalising Islam: Creating Brits of the Islamic Persuasion', in Richard Phillips (ed.), *Muslim Spaces of Hope: Geographies of Possibility in Britain and the West* (London: Zed Books, 2009), 179–97.

Glynn, Sarah, 'Marxism and Multiculturalism', *Human Geography*, 3:1 (2010), 108–27.

Glynn, Sarah, 'Playing the Ethnic Card – Politics and Segregation in London's East End', *Urban Studies*, 47:5 (2010), 991–1013.

Glynn, Sarah, 'Book Review: The Invisible Empire: White Discourse, Tolerance and Belonging', *Urban Studies*, 48:8 (2011), 1755–7.

Glynn, Sarah, 'Muslims and the Left: An English case study', *Ethnicities*, 12:5 (2012), 581–602.

Godley, Andrew, *Jewish Immigrant Entrepreneurship in New York and London 1880–1914: Enterprise and Culture* (Basingstoke: Palgrave, 2001).

Gough, Jamie, Aram Eisenschitz and Andrew McCulloch, *Spaces of Social Exclusion* (Abingdon: Routledge, 2006).

Graves, Bob, *Quinn Square Tenants' Rent Strike Victory* (London: London District of the Communist Party, 1938).

Groser, Father St John B., *Politics and Persons* (London: SCM Press, 1949).

Hackworth, Jason and Neil Smith, 'The Changing State of Gentrification', *Tijdschrift voor Economische en Sociale Geografie*, 92:4 (2001), 464–77.

HM Government, 'The Prevent Strategy: A Guide for Local Partners in England' (London: HMSO, 2008).

Hakim, Mansoor Abul (trans. Rafiq Abdur Rahman), *Women who Deserve to go to Hell* (Karachi: Darul Ishaat, 2004).

Hall, Stuart, 'New Ethnicities', in James Donald and Ali Rattansi (eds), *'Race', Culture and Difference* (London: Sage, 1992).

Hall, Stuart, Chas Critcher, Tony Jefferson, John Clarke and Brian Roberts, *Policing the Crisis: Mugging, the State, and Law and Order* (Macmillan, Basingstoke, 1978).

Hall, Tarquin, *Salaam Brick Lane: A Year in the New East End* (London: John Murray, 2005).

Hardy, P., *The Muslims of British India* (Cambridge: Cambridge University Press, 1972).

Hizb ut-Tahrir, *Hizb ut-Tahrir* (London: Al-Khilafah Publications, 2000).

Hizb ut-Tahrir, *The Inevitability of the Clash of Civilisations* (London: Al-Khilafah Publications, 2002).

Hizb ut-Tahrir 'Jihad in Islam' (2008), www.english.hizbuttahrir.org/images/pdfs/JihadinIslam2.pdf, accessed October 2012 .

Home Affairs Committee, *Bangladeshis in Britain* (London: HMSO, 1986).

Home Office, *Working Together: Co-operation between Government and Faith Communities* (London: HMSO, 2004).

Home Office, *The Cantle Report – Community Cohesion: A Report of the Independent Review Team* (2001) pp. 9 and 11, http://resources.cohesioninstitute.org.uk/Publications/Documents/Document/DownloadDocumentsFile.aspx?recordId=96&file=PDFversion, accessed 21 November 2012.

Hoodbhoy, Pervez, 'Jinnah and the Islamic State: Setting the Record Straight', *Economic and Political Weekly*, 42:32 (2007), 3300–03.

Hossain, Ashfaque, 'Historical Globalization and its Effects: A Study of Sylhet and its People, 1874–1971' (PhD dissertation, University of Nottingham, 2009).

Howe, Darcus, 'Fighting Back: West Indian Youth and the Police in Notting Hill', *Race Today*, 5:11 (1973), 333–6.

Howe, Irving, *The Immigrant Jews of New York: 1881 to the Present* (London and Boston: Routledge and Kegan Paul, 1976).

Human Rights Watch, 'Bangladesh: Stop Harassment of Defense at War Tribunal', 2 November 2011, www.hrw.org/news/2011/11/02/bangladesh-stop-harassment-defense-war-tribunal, accessed 19 October 2013.

Human Rights Watch, 'Blood on the Streets: the use of excessive force during Bangladesh protests', August 2013, www.hrw.org/reports/2013/08/01/blood-streets, accessed 4 March 2014.

Human Rights Watch, 'Bangladesh: Azam Conviction Based on Flawed Proceedings', 16 August 2013, www.hrw.org/news/2013/08/16/bangladesh-azam-conviction-based-flawed-proceedings, accessed 19 October 2013.

Hunter, Kathleen, *History of Pakistanis in Britain* (privately published, 1962).

Husain, Ed, *The Islamist: Why I Joined Radical Islam in Britain, What I Saw Inside and Why I Left* (London: Penguin, 2007).

Interfaith Network for the United Kingdom, *20 Years: Milestones on the Journey Together Towards Greater Inter Faith Understanding and Cooperation* (London: The Interfaith Network for the UK, 2007).

Iqbal, Jamil, *Indian Independence (Part 3) – Role of the Communist Party of India During Partition* (2007), www.marxist.com/indian-independence-role-communist-party.htm, accessed 16 November 2013.

Iqbal, Muhammad, *The Reconstruction of Religious Thought in Islam* (1930), www.yespakistan.com/iqbal/reconstruction, accessed 21 November 2012.

IQra media, *Muslims & Politics*, DVD written and presented by Wakil Ahmed, directed and edited by Shofiquez Zaman (London, 2005).

Islam, Nurul, *Probashir Kotha* [The Tale of the Emigrants] (Sylhet: Probashi Publications, 1989).

Jacobs, Jack, *On Socialists and 'the Jewish Question' After Marx* (New York: New York University Press, 1992).

Jacobs, Jane M, *Edge of Empire: Postcolonialism and the City* (London: Routledge, 1996).

Jacobs, Joe, 'The Police and the Fascists: East London 1932–36', *Race Today*, 5:11, (December 1973).

Jacobs, Joe, *Out of the Ghetto: My Youth in the East End. Communism and Fascism 1913–1939* (London: Janet Simon, 1978).

Jacobs, Stephen 'Sylhet Partnership Summary Evaluation Report: January – 2003' (London: SDP Regeneration Services, 2003).

James, Selma, 'Sex, Race and Working Class Power', *Race Today* (January 1974), 12–15.

Jamoul, Lina and Jane Wills, 'Faith in Politics', *Urban Studies*, 45:10 (2008), 2035–56.

Jones, Owen, *Chavs: The Demonization of the Working Class* (London and New York: Verso, 2012).

Kabeer, Naila, 'The Structure of "Revealed" Preference: Race, Community and Female Labour Supply in the London Clothing Industry', *Development and Change*, 25:2 (1994) 307–31.

Kabeer, Naila and Peroline Ainsworth, 'Life Chances, Life Choices: Exploring Patterns of Work and Worklessness Among Bangladeshi and Somali Women in Tower Hamlets' (Report for Tower Hamlets Council, 2011).

Kadish, Sharman, *Bolsheviks and British Jews: The Anglo-Jewish Community, Britain and the Russian Revolution* (London: Frank Cass, 1992).

Kamran, Tahir (2009) 'Early Phase of Electoral Politics in Pakistan: 1950s', *South Asian Studies,* 24:2 (2009), 257–82.

Kapp, Yvonne, *Eleanor Marx: Volume II, The Crowded Years (1884–1898)* (London: Lawrence and Wishart, 1976).

Katznelson, Ira, 'Working-Class Formation: Constructing Cases and Comparisons', in Ira Katznelson and Aristide R. Zolberg (eds), *Working-Class Formation: Nineteenth-Century Patterns in Western Europe and the United States* (Princeton: Princeton University Press, 1986).

Kautsky, Karl, 'On the Problems of the Jewish Proletariat in England', *Justice*, 23 April 1904, www.marxists.org/archive/kautsky/1904/04/jewish.htm, accessed 18 November 2013.

Kautsky, Karl, Are the Jews a Race (1926), www.marxists.org/archive/kautsky/1914/jewsrace/index.htm, accessed 21 November 2012.

Keith, Michael, 'Ethnic Entrepreneurs and Street Rebels: Looking Inside the Inner City' in Steve Pile and Nigel Thrift (eds), *Mapping the Subject: Geographies of Cultural Transformation* (London: Routledge, 1995).

Keith, Michael, 'Making the Street Visible: Placing Racial Violence in Context', *New Community*, 21:4 (1995), 551–65.

Kelly, Paul (ed.), *Multiculturalism Reconsidered:* Culture and Equality *and its Critics* (Cambridge: Polity Press, 2002).

Kempson, Elaine, *Overcrowding in Bangladeshi Households: A Case Study of Tower Hamlets* (London: Policy Studies Institute, 1999).

Kenning, S.W. 'Decline, Paranoia and Discontent', *Weekly Worker*, 2 December 2004.

Kershen, Anne J., *Uniting the Tailors: Trade Unionism Amongst the Tailors of London and Leeds, 1870–1939* (Ilford: Frank Cass, 1995).

Kershen, Anne J., *Strangers, Aliens and Asians: Huguenots, Jews and Bangladeshis in Spitalfields 1660–2000* (Abingdon: Routledge, 2005).

Khalidi, Toufique Imrose, 'Behind the rise of Bangladesh's Hifazat', *Al Jazeera*, 9 May 2013, www.aljazeera.com/indepth/features/2013/05/201356134629980318.html, accessed 19 October 2013.

Kibria, Nazli, *Muslims in Motion: Islam and National Identity in the Bangladeshi Diaspora* (New Brunswick, New Jersey and London: Rutgers University Press, 2011).

Kundnani, Arun, 'The Death of Multiculturalism', *Race and Class*, 43:4 (2002), 67–72.

Kundnani, Arun, 'Integrationism: the politics of anti-Muslim racism', *Race and Class*, 48:4 (2007), 24–44.

Kundnani, Arun, 'Islamism and the Roots of Liberal Rage', *Race and Class*, 50:2 (2008), 40–68.

Kundnani, Arun, 'Kenan Malik: Journey of an Ex-anti-racist', Institute of Race Relations website (2011), www.irr.org.uk/news/kenan-malik-journey-of-an-ex-anti-racist, accessed July 2012.

Kushner, Tony and Nadia Valman (eds), *Remembering Cable Street: Fascism and Anti-Fascism in British Society* (London: Vallentine Mitchell, 2000).

Kymlicka, W., 'Reply to Review Symposium on *Multicultural Odysseys*', *Ethnicities*, 8 (2008), 277–83.

Le Lohé, M.J., 'Participation in Elections by Asians in Bradford', in Ivor Crewe (ed.), *The Politics of Race (Vol 2 British Sociology Yearbook)* (London: Croom Helm, 1975).

Leech, Kenneth, *Brick Lane 1978: The Events and their Significance* (London: Stepney Books Publications, 1994).

Lenin V.I., *Draft Programme of the R.C.P.(B.)*, 'Section Of The Programme Dealing With Religion' (1919), www.marxists.org/archive/lenin/works/1919/mar/x02.htm, accessed 11 January 2012.

Lenin, V.I., *Critical Remarks on the National Question* (Progress Publishers: Moscow, 1951).

Lenin, V.I., *Collected Works* (Moscow: Progress Publishers, 1961–65).

Levin, Nora, *Jewish Socialist Movements, 1871–1917: While Messiah Tarried* (London: Routledge and Kegan Paul, 1978).

Lewis, David, 'The Paradoxes of Bangladesh's Shahbag Protests', 21 March 2013, http://blogs.lse.ac.uk/indiaatlse/2013/03/21/the-paradoxes-of-bangladeshs-shahbag-protests, accessed 19 October 2013.

Lewis, Philip, *Islamic Britain: Religion, Politics and Identity Among British Muslims* (London: IB Tauris, 1994 and 2002).

Lewis, Philip, *Young, British and Muslim* (London: Continuum, 2007).

Liberal Democrats, 'Political Speech and Race Relations in a Liberal Democracy: Report of an Inquiry into the Conduct of the Tower Hamlets Liberal Democrats in Publishing Allegedly Racist Election Literature Between 1990 and 1993' (Liberal Democrats Tower Hamlets Inquiry, 1993).

Liebman, Arthur, *Jews and the Left* (New York: John Wiley and Sons, 1979).

Lifschultz, Lawrence, *Bangladesh: The Unfinished Revolution* (London: Zed Press, 1979).

Lipman, Vivian, *Social History of the Jews in England 1850–1950* (London: Watts and Co., 1954).

Lipman, Vivian, *A Century of Social Service* (London: Routledge and Kegan Paul, 1959).

London, Louise 'The East End of London: Paki Bashing in 1970', *Race Today*, 5:11 (December 1973).

Mahamdallie, Hassan (ed.), *Defending Multiculturalism: A Guide for the Movement* (London: Bookmarks, 2011).

Making Britain Database, www.open.ac.uk/researchprojects/makingbritain.

Malik, Kenan, *The Meaning of Race: Race, History and Culture in Western Society* (Basingstoke: Macmillan, 1996).

Malik, Kenan, *From Fatwa to Jihad: The Rushdie Affair and its Legacy* (London: Atlantic Books, 2009).

Malik, Kenan, 'What is Wrong with Multiculturalism?', Milton K Wong Lecture given to the Laurier Institute, University of British Colombia and broadcast on CBC on 22 June 2012, http://kenanmalik.wordpress.com/2012/06/04/what-is-wrong-with-multiculturalism-part-1/, accessed July 2012.

Maniruzzaman, Talukder , 'Radical Politics and the Emergence of Bangladesh', in Paul R. Brass and Marcus F. Franda (eds), *Radical Politics in South Asia* (Cambridge, Mass: MIT, 1973).

Manson, Peter, 'Gerrymandering, Exclusions and the Farce of Three-minute Democracy', *Weekly Worker*, 4 November 2004.

Manson, Peter, 'It's Not What You Know But Who You Know', *Weekly Worker*, 8 February 2007.

Manson, Peter, 'Respect – the Party for Everyone', *Weekly Worker*, 2 August 2007.

Manson, Peter, 'Fighting Over the Corpse', *Weekly Worker*, 1 November 2007.

Manson, Peter, 'No Respect for Socialist Principle', *Weekly Worker*, 31 January 2008.

Manson, Peter, 'Choosing Between Opportunists', *Weekly Worker*, 24 April 2008.

Marx, Karl (1844) *Introduction to A Contribution to the Critique of Hegel's Philosophy of Right* (1844), www.marxists.org/archive/marx/works/1843/critique-hpr/intro.htm, accessed 21 November 2012.

Marx, Karl, *On The Jewish Question* (1844), www.marxists.org/archive/marx/works/1844/jewish-question, accessed 21 November 2012 .

Marx, Karl, *1845 Theses On Feuerbach* (1845), www.marxists.org/archive/marx/works/1845/theses/index.htm, accessed 21 November 2012.

Mascarenhas, Anthony, *Bangladesh: A Legacy of Blood* (London: Hodder and Stoughton, 1986).

Mawdudi, Abul A'la (1981) *Towards Understanding Islam* (Leicester: The Islamic Foundation, 1981).

Mawdudi, Abul A'la, *Capitalism, Socialism and Islam* (Kuwait: Islamic Book Publishers, 1995).

Mayhew Harper Associates Ltd, 'Counting the Population of Tower Hamlets: A London Borough in Transition' (Report for Tower Hamlets Council, 2010).

Mendelsohn, Ezra, *Class Struggle in the Pale: The Formative Years of the Jewish Workers' Movement in Tsarist Russia* (Cambridge: Cambridge University Press, 1970).

Messina, Anthony M., 'Ethnic Minorities and the British Party System in the 1990s and Beyond', in Shamit Saggar (ed.), *Race and British Electoral Politics* (London: UCL, 1998), 47–69 .

Miles, Robert, *Racism and Migrant Labour* (London: Routledge and Kegan Paul, 1982).

Miles, Robert, *Racism After 'Race Relations'* (London: Routledge, 1993).

Miles Robert, and Annie Phizacklea (eds), *Racism and Political Action in Britain* (London: Routledge and Kegan Paul, 1979) .

Miles, Robert and Annie Phizacklea, *Labour and Racism* (London: Routledge and Kegan Paul, 1980).

Miles, Robert and Annie Phizacklea, *White Man's Country: Racism in British Politics* (London: Pluto Press, 1984).

Mitchell, Richard, *The Society of the Muslim Brothers* (Oxford: Oxford University Press, 1993).

Mitter, Swasti, 'Industrial restructuring and manufacturing homework: immigrant women in the UK clothing industry', *Capital and Class,* 27 (1986). 37–80.

Modood, Tariq, '"Black" Racial Equality and Asian Identity', *New Community*, 14:3 (1988), 397–404.

Modood, Tariq, 'British Asian Muslims and the Rushdie Affair', in James Donald and Ali Rattansi (eds), *'Race', Culture and Difference* (London: Sage, 1992).

Modood, Tariq, *Multiculturalism: A Civic Idea* (Cambridge: Polity, 2007).

Modood, Tariq, 'Multiculturalism and Integration: Struggling with Confusions', in Hassan Mahamdallie, *Defending Multiculturalism: A Guide for the Movement* (London: Bookmarks, 2011), 61–76.

Modood, Tariq, *Post-immigration 'Difference' and Integration: The Case of Muslims in Western Europe* (London: British Academy, 2012).

Mohsin, Amena A., 'Religion, Politics and Security: The Case of Bangladesh', in Satu P. Limaye, Mohan Malik and Robert G. Wirsing (eds), *Religious Radicalism and Security in South Asia* (Honolulu: Asia-Pacific Centre for Security Studies, 2004).

Neveu, Catherine, 'The Waves of Surma have Created Storms in the Depths of the Thames – Electoral Representation of an Ethnic Minority: A Case Study of Bangladeshis in the East End of London', paper given to APSA 85th Annual meeting, Atlanta Georgia, 1989 (manuscript in Centre for Bangladeshi Studies, Roehampton).

Nicholson, John, 'SWP in denial', *Weekly Worker*, 4 November 2004.

Norris, Pippa, 'Anatomy of a Labour Landslide', www.hks.harvard.edu/fs/pnorris/Acrobat/landslide.pdf, accessed 20 November 2012.

Open University/BBC2, *The Secret History of Our Streets: Arnold Circus* (television programme), BBC, 11 July 2012.

O'Toole, Therese and Richard Gale, 'Contemporary Grammars of Political Action Among Ethnic Minority Young Activists', *Ethnic and Racial Studies*, 33:1 (2010) 126–43.

Parekh, Bhiku, *Rethinking Multiculturalism: Cultural Diversity and Political Theory* (Basingstoke: Palgrave, 2000).

Peace, T., 'All I'm Asking, Is For a Little Respect: Assessing the Performance of Britain's Most Successful Radical Left Party', *Parliamentary Affairs*, 66:2 (2013) 405–24.

Peach, Ceri, 'Estimating the Growth of the Bangladeshi Population of Great Britain', *New Community*, 16:4 (1990), 481–91.

Però, Davide and John Solomos, 'Migrant Politics and Mobilization: Exclusion, Engagements, Incorporation', *Ethnic and Racial Studies*, 33:1 (2010), 1–18.

Phillips, Deborah, 'What Price Equality? A Report on the Allocation of GLC Housing in Tower Hamlets', *GLC Housing Research & Policy Report No. 9* (London: GLC, 1986).

Phillips, Deborah, 'Parallel Lives? Challenging Discourses of British Muslim Self-segregation', *Environment and Planning D*, 24:1 (2006), 25–40.

Phillips, Mark, *Homelessness and Tenants' Control: Struggles for Council Housing in Tower Hamlets 1974–1976* (London: Dame Colet House, 1977).

Phillips, Richard, 'Standing Together: The Muslim Association of Britain and the Anti-war Movement', *Race and Class*, 50:2 (2008), 101–13.

Phillips, Richard (ed.), *Muslim Spaces of Hope: Geographies of Possibility in Britain and the West* (London: Zed Books, 2009).

Phillipson, Chris, Nilufar Ahmed and Joanna Latimer, *Women in Transition: A Study of the Experiences of Bangladeshi Women Living in Tower Hamlets* (Bristol: Policy Press, 2003).

Pierre, Hugo 'Stopping the BNP in Tower Hamlets' (Youth Against Racism in Europe website, undated), www.yre.org.uk/towerhamlets.html, accessed 9 October 2012.

Piratin, Phil, *Our Flag Stays Red* (London: Lawrence and Wishart, 1978, first edition 1948).

Poulsen, Michael and Ron Johnston, 'Commentary', *Environment and Planning A*, 38 (2006), 2195–9.

Powell, Enoch, speech given 1968, www.telegraph.co.uk/comment/3643823/Enoch-Powells-Rivers-of-Blood-speech.html, accessed 20 November 2012.

Purbashuri (drafted by Kabiruddin Ahmed), 'Unhappy East Pakistan' (n.d., available from the London School of Economics Library).

Qutb, Sayyid, *Milestones* (1964), www.youngmuslims.ca/online_library, accessed 24 March 2005.

Race Today Collective, *The Struggle of Asian Workers in Britain* (London: Race Today Publications, 1983).

Rahnema, Ali, *An Islamic Utopian: A Political Biography of Ali Shari'ati* (London: IB Tauris, 2000).

Ramadan, Tariq, *Western Muslims and the Future of Islam* (Oxford: Oxford University Press, 2004).

Ramamurthy, Anandi, 'The Politics of Britain's Asian Youth Movements', *Race and Class*, 48:2 (2006), 38–60.

Ramdin, Ron, *The Making of the Black Working Class in Britain* (Aldershot: Gower, 1987).

Rennap, I. (pseudonym for Issie Panner), *Anti-Semitism and the Jewish Question* (London: Lawrence and Wishart, 1942).

Rex, John, 'Black Militancy and Class Conflict', in Robert Miles and Annie Phizacklea (eds), *Racism and Political Action in Britain* (London: Routledge and Kegan Paul, 1979) 72–92.

Rex, John, *Ethnic Minorities in the Modern Nation State: Working Papers in the Theory of MultiCulturalism and Political Integration* (Basingstoke: Macmillan, 1996).

Rex, John, 'An Afterword on the Situation of British Muslims in a World Context', in Tahir Abbas, *Muslim Britain: Communities Under Pressure* (London and New York: Zed Books, 2005), 235–43.

Riaz, Ali, *Islam and Identity Politics Among British-Bangladeshis: A Leap of Faith* (Manchester: Manchester University Press, 2013).

Robinson, Francis, 'Varieties of South Asian Islam', *CRER Research Paper*, no. 8 (Warwick: CRER, 1988).

Rocker, Rudolf (trans. Joseph Leftwich), *The London Years* (London: Robert Anscombe and Co Ltd, 1956).

Ronson, Jon, *Tottenham Ayatollah* (television documentary), Channel 4, shown 8 April 1997, and re-shown 5 September 2005 under the title *Tottenham Ayatollah Revisited*.

Russell, C. and H. S. Lewis, *The Jew in London* (London: T. Fisher Unwin, 1900).

Ruthven, Malise, *Islam in the World* (Harmondsworth: Penguin, 1984).

Ryan, Nick, 'Children of the Abyss', *Telegraph* (2005), www.nickryan.net/articles/abyss.html, accessed 28 July 2011.

Ryan, Nick, 'In the Shadow of the City', *Observer* (2006), www.nickryan.net/articles/city.html, accessed 28 July 2011.

Ryan, Nick, 'Soldiers of God', *Esquire* (2009), www.nickryan.net/aticles/soldiersofgod.html, accessed 28 July 2011.

Saggar, Shamit, 'Analyzing Race and Elections in British Politics: Some Conceptual and Theoretical Concerns', in Shamit Saggar (ed.), *Race and British Electoral Politics* (London: UCL Press, 1998), 11–46.

Salway, Sarah (2008) 'Labour Market Experiences of Young UK Bangladeshi Men: Identity, Inclusion and Exclusion in Inner-city London', *Ethnic and Racial Studies*, 31:6 (2008), 1126–52.

Samad, Yunas, 'Book Burning and Race Relations: Political Mobilisation of Bradford Muslims', *New Community*, 18:4 (1992), 507–19.

Samad, Yunas, 'The Politics of Islamic Identity Among Bangladeshis and Pakistanis in Britain', in Terence Ranger, Yunas Samad and Ossie Stuart (eds), *Culture, Identity and Politics: Ethnic Minorities in Britain* (Aldershot: Avebury, 1996), 90–8.

Sayyid, S (2000) 'Beyond Westphalia: Nations and Diasporas – the Case of the Muslim

Umma', in Barnor Hesse (ed.), *Un/Settled Multiculturalisms: Diasporas, Entanglements, 'Transruptions'* (London: Zed Books, 2000), 33–50.

Sen, Amartya, *The Argumentative Indian* (London: Allen Lane, 2005).

Sen, Amartya, *Identity and Violence: The Illusion of Destiny* (London: Penguin, 2007).

Shaikh, Asima, 'Industrial Restructuring, Informalisation and Casual Labour in the "East End" Clothing Industry', *UCL Development Planning Unit Working Paper no. 69* (London: Development Planning Unit, 1995).

Shari'ati, Ali, *Marxism and Other Western Fallacies: An Islamic Critique* (Berkley: Mizan Press, 1980).

Shari'ati, Ali, *What Is To Be Done: The Enlightened Thinkers and an Islamic Renaissance* (Houston: The Institute for Research and Islamic Studies, 1986).

Shari'ati, Ali, *Red Shi'ism (the Religion of Martyrdom) vs. Black Shi'ism (the Religion of Mourning)* (n.d.), www.iranchamber.com/personalities/ashariati/works/red_black_shiism.php, accessed 11 January 2012.

Shawcroft, Christine, 'Report of the NEC meeting held on 21 September 2010. Emergency Item: The Tower Hamlets Mayoral selection', http://trialbyjeory.wordpress.com/2010/09/22/an-nec-members-account/, accessed 21 November 2012.

Sherwood, Marika, 'Lascars' Struggles Against Discrimination in Britain 1923–45: The work of N.J. Upadhyana and Surat Alley', *The Mariner's Mirror*, 90:4 (2004), 438–55.

Shukra, Kalbir, *The Changing Pattern of Black Politics in Britain* (London: Pluto Press, 1998).

Shukra, Kalbir, 'New Labour Debates and Dilemas', in Shamit Saggar (ed.), *Race and British Electoral Politics* (London: UCL, 1998), 117–44.

Silver Jubilee Commemorative Volume of Bangladesh Independence (London: Silver Jubilee Celebration Committee, 1997).

Simpson Ludi, 'Statistics of Racial Segregation: Measures, Evidence and Policy', *Urban Studies*, 41:3 (2004), 661–81.

Sivanandan, A., 'Race, Class and the State: The Black Experience in Britain', *Race and Class*, 17:4 (1976), 347–68.

Sivanandan, A., 'The Liberation of the Black Intellectual', *Race and Class*, 18:4 (1977, first written for a symposium on 'immigrant intellectuals' in 1972), 329–43.

Sivanandan, A., *Communities of Resistance: Writings on Black Struggles for Socialism* (London: Verso, 1990).

Smith, S. J., *The Politics of 'Race' and Residence: Citizenship, Segregation and White Supremacy in Britain* (Cambridge: Polity Press, 1989).

Soage, Ana Belén, 'Shaykh Yusuf al-Qaradawi: Portrait of Leading Islamic Cleric', *Middle East Review of International Affairs*, 12:1 (2008), 51–68.

Socialist Workers Party, 'An Appeal to Respect Members' 24 October 2007, www.swp.org.uk/respect_appeal.php, accessed 25 October 2007.

Solomos, John, *Race and Racism in Britain* (Basingstoke: Macmillan, 1993).

Solomos, John and Les Back, *Race, Politics and Social Change* (London: Routledge, 1995).

Srebrnik, Henry Felix, *London Jews and British Communism, 1935–1945* (Ilford: Vallentine Mitchell, 1995).

Stedman Jones, Gareth, *Outcast London: A Study in the Relationship Between Classes in Victorian Society* (Harmondsworth: Penguin, 1984).

Swadhinata Trust and University of Surrey Centre for Research on Nationalism, Ethnicity and Multiculturalism, 'Oral History Project' (2005–6), www.swadhinata.org.uk/index.php?option=com_content&view=article&id=48&Itemid=52, accessed October 2012 .

Taylor, Charles, *Multiculturalism and 'The Politics of Recognition'* (Princeton: Princeton University Press, 1992).

Taylor, William, *This Bright Field: A Travel Book in One Place* (London: Methuen, 2000).

Tcherikower, Elias (trans. Aaron Antonvosky), *The Early Jewish Labor Movement in the United States* (New York: Yivo Institute for Jewish Research, 1961).

The Koran (trans. N.J. Dawood) (London: Penguin, 1999).

Tompson, Keith, *Under Siege: Racism and Violence in Britain Today* (London: Penguin, 1988).

Tower Hamlets Trades Council, *No More Blood on the Streets: How to Fight Facism and Racism* (London: Tower Hamlets Trades Council, 1994).

Tower Hamlets Borough Council and NHS Tower Hamlets, 'Health and Wellbeing in Tower Hamlets: Joint Strategic Needs Assessment' (2009).

Traverso, Enzo (trans Bernard, Gibbons) *The Marxists and the Jewish Question* (New Jersey: Humanities Press, 1994) .

Trotsky, Leon (edited and introduced by Peter Buch), *On the Jewish Question* (New York: Pathfinder, 1970) .

Uddin, Pola, 'Once, Muslims and Labour were Natural Allies. Not Now', *Guardian*, 19 June 2004.

Ullah, Ansar Ahmed, John Eversley et al., *Bengalis in London's East End* (London: Swadhinata Trust, 2010).

Visram, Rosina, Ayahs, *Lascars and Princes: The Story of Indians in Britain 1700–1947* (London: Pluto, 1986).

Visram, Rosina, *Asians in Britain: 400 Years of History* (London: Pluto Press, 2002).

Weinberg, Robert, *Stalin's Forgotten Zion: Birobidzhan and the Making of a Soviet Jewish Homeland* (Berkeley: University of California Press, 1998).

Wemyss, Georgie, *The Invisible Empire: White Discourse, Tolerance and Belonging* (Farnham: Ashgate, 2009).

Williams, Rowan, 'Civil and Religious Law in England: a Religious Perspective', lecture at the Royal Courts of Justice, 7 February 2008, www.archbishopofcanterbury.org/1575, accessed March 2008.

Woods, Alan, *Bolshevism: The Road to Revolution* (London: Wellred, 1999).

Woods, Alan and Ted Grant, *Marxism and the National Question* (2000), www.marxist.com/marxism-national-question250200.htm, accessed 20 November 2013 .

Wrench, John and Tarek Qureshi, *Higher Horizons: A Qualitative Study of Young Men of Bangladeshi Origin* (London: HMSO, 1996).

Wright, Tessa and Anna Pollert, *The Experience of Ethnic Minority Workers in the Hotel and Catering Industry: Routes to Support and Advice on Workplace Problems* (London: ACAS, 2006).

Young, Phyllis, 'Report on Investigation into Conditions of the Coloured Population in the Stepney Area' (manuscript, 1944, in Tower Hamlets Local History Library).

Yuval-Davis, Nira, 'Fundamentalism, Multiculturalism and Women in Britain', in James Donald and Ali Rattansi (eds), *'Race', Culture and Difference* (London: Sage, 1992), 278-291.

Zirling, Lawrence, *Bangladesh − From Mujib to Ershad: An Interpretative Study* (Karachi: Oxford University Press, 1992).

Index

EU authorised representative for GPSR:
Easy Access System Europe, Mustamäe tee 50,
10621 Tallinn, Estonia
gpsr.requests@easproject.com

www.ingramcontent.com/pod-product-compliance
Lightning Source LLC
Chambersburg PA
CBHW051953270326
41929CB00015B/2640